Joseph H. Lyman

CORRESPONDENCE ON CHURCH AND RELIGION OF WILLIAM EWART GLADSTONE

THE MACMILLAN COMPANY
NEW YORK · BOSTON · CHICAGO
ATLANTA · SAN FRANCISCO

MACMILLAN & CO., LIMITED
LONDON · BOMBAY · CALCUTTA
MELBOURNE

THE MACMILLAN CO. OF CANADA, LTD.
TORONTO

1-52

The Right Hon. William Ewart Gladstone
From a portrait by John Mc Lure Hamilton
painted in 1895

CORRESPONDENCE ON

CHURCH AND RELIGION

OF WILLIAM EWART GLADSTONE

SELECTED AND ARRANGED
BY D. C. LATHBURY

WITH PORTRAITS AND ILLUSTRATIONS

IN TWO VOLUMES
VOL. II.

NEW YORK
THE MACMILLAN COMPANY
1910

COPYRIGHT, 1910,
By THE MACMILLAN COMPANY.

Set up and electrotyped. Published July, 1910.

Norwood Press
J. S. Cushing Co. — Berwick & Smith Co.
Norwood, Mass., U.S.A.

CONTENTS OF VOL. II.

CHAPTER	PAGE
I. OXFORD ELECTIONS	1
II. THE CONTROVERSY WITH ROME	23
III. THE CONTROVERSY WITH UNBELIEF	75
IV. EDUCATION	125
V. LETTERS OF MR. GLADSTONE TO HIS CHILDREN	149
VI. PERSONAL	197
APPENDIX:	
I. CHURCH AND STATE	343
II. THE OXFORD MOVEMENT	364
III. OXFORD ELECTIONS	373
IV. CONTROVERSY WITH ROME	383
V. CONTROVERSY WITH UNBELIEF	403
VI. CHILDREN	411
VII. PERSONAL	421
VIII. ST. DEINIOL'S LIBRARY	451
INDEX	455

LIST OF ILLUSTRATIONS TO VOL. II.

FACING PAGE

MR. GLADSTONE AT WORK IN THE 'TEMPLE OF PEACE'
(*photogravure*) - - - *Frontispiece*
From a picture by John M'Lure Hamilton.

THE 'TEMPLE OF PEACE,' HAWARDEN CASTLE - - 190

INTERIOR OF ORIGINAL LIBRARY IN WHICH THE BOOKS WERE PLACED BY MR. GLADSTONE'S OWN HANDS - 220

MR. GLADSTONE, 1897 - - - - - 254
From a photograph.

MR. AND MRS. GLADSTONE, CHÂTEAU THORENC, CANNES, FEBRUARY, 1898 - - - - - 300

LYING-IN-STATE, WESTMINSTER HALL, MAY 26–28, 1898 - 341

FUNERAL PROCESSION FROM WESTMINSTER HALL TO THE ABBEY, MAY 28, 1898 - - - - 365

MEMORIAL TOMB AND CHAPEL IN HAWARDEN CHURCH - 421

ST. DEINIOL'S LIBRARY AND RESIDENCE, AND PARISH CHURCH, HAWARDEN - - - - 451

THE ECCLESIASTICAL AND RELIGIOUS CORRESPONDENCE OF WILLIAM EWART GLADSTONE

CHAPTER I

OXFORD ELECTIONS

1847–1865

THE letters relating to the Oxford Elections show the exceptional character of Mr. Gladstone's tenure of the seat. Not for him was reserved the unbroken series of uncontested returns which is commonly associated with University representation. Between him and many of his constituents ecclesiastical differences at first, and political differences later, opened a chasm not to be bridged by any considerations of University etiquette. To be Member for Oxford was, in his case, little more than a barren honour. More than once it embarrassed his relations with the party he was in the end to lead, while it never secured him against the prospect of an electoral contest. One condition, indeed, which Mr. Gladstone laid down from the first was always satisfied. 'In my mind,' he wrote to Phillimore in 1847, 'the whole question of the propriety of my being a candidate has turned upon the prior question whether I was to be made such, and to be returned, if returned at all, by a party only, or by a more general and legitimate expression of the feeling of the constituency. . . . I have constantly thought and said that the evils of my being returned to Parliament in the former sense were so manifest and great that success could afford no compensation for them.' Upon this point he was never left in doubt. In every contest—in 1865 as much as in 1847—he had supporters in both camps. That Liberals should vote for the man who was more and more marked out as their future leader was only natural. But there were always Conservatives who saw in his Church policy the one hope of reconciling the just claim of the Church to freedom of speech and action in spiritual things with the equally just claim of the State—so long as the Church is established —to control that freedom in temporal things. In each successive contest, indeed, there were defections. Men who at first had followed him hesitatingly, or with no clear understanding of the end to which he was guiding them, fell away when they realized that, in certain not inconceivable circumstances, they might be asked to vote for Disestablishment. The kind of piety which would rather see the Church poor and free than rich and in chains did not appeal to them. They had been accustomed all their lives to identify 'Church Defence' with an obstinate fight for every incident of Establishment. They were now warned that their commander might one day call upon them to make a willing surrender of one civil privilege after another in order to make the spiritual society more secure against State interference. For many of them the appeal proved too severe. Sorrowfully or cheerfully, one elector after another sought a representative whose demands on his confidence were less exacting.

The success of 1847 was in part a victory of the

Masters of Arts over the Hebdomadal Board. Sixteen Heads of Houses voted for his opponent; only four voted for Mr. Gladstone. In part it marked the failure of the last effort of a party which rightly saw in Mr. Gladstone their most irreconcilable foe. His own estimate of this party is given in a letter to his father, written on the eve of the poll:

'I have many sympathies with men in the Low Church party, while I desire a more firm, a more comprehensive, and a more vigorous and elevated system than theirs, which I find in the laws and institutions of the Church as a whole. But there is one kind of religion, one kind of Protestantism, with which I have no sympathy whatever, and which constitutes no small part of the force arrayed against me. It is the Protestantism which grew into fashion during the last century, and has not yet quite grown out of it: that hated everything in religion which lived and moved; which lowered and almost paganized doctrine, loosened and destroyed discipline, and much defaced, in contempt of law, the decent and beautiful order of the Church; which neglected learning, coolly tolerated vice, and, as it has been said, was never enthusiastic except against enthusiasm; which heaped up abuses mountain high in the shape of plurality, non-residence, simony, and others more than I can tell, drove millions into dissent, suffered millions more to grow up in virtual heathenism, and made the Church of England — I say it with deliberate sorrow — instead of being the glory, in many respects the shame of Christendom. This kind of Protestantism has always been the plague spot of Oxford, which, like every other human institution, must have its weaknesses and faults: it is this false and hollow system of religion, hating all who have disturbed its leaden slumbers, which now unites itself with an honest and vehement fanaticism to raise a cry "No Popery," and under that cry denounces the genuine spirit of the Church of England.'

The opposition to Mr. Gladstone in 1847 was based in the main on his votes — in Parliament on the

Dissenters' Chapels Bill and the Maynooth question; in the Oxford convocation on Mr. Ward's case. The opposition candidate was a Mr. Round, a gentleman whose best title to fame is that sixteen heads of colleges thought him good enough to run against Mr. Gladstone. His committee sent a circular to the electors directly challenging Mr. Gladstone's action on all these points, and Mr. Gladstone's committee saw in this step — 'very unusual in a University contest — a sufficient occasion for submitting the circular to the candidate himself. As the material parts of his reply to the three charges are given in the appendix,* there is no need to say more of it here. As regards Maynooth, indeed, the case is put even better in a single sentence of a letter to a constituent in doubt about his vote. 'I have been one of those who clung the longest and the latest to the exclusive policy in questions of Church and State, but, having been driven from it as a whole, I cannot be any party to its partial and one-sided application.' A difference going even deeper appears in a letter written to Hope by Charles Wordsworth, the first Warden of Glenalmond, — the college of which Mr. Gladstone had been one of the founders — and afterwards Bishop of St. Andrews.* For many years Wordsworth had looked upon Gladstone as a man who had a mission from God to save the nation 'upon the principles of the Constitution in Church and State.' Fascinated by Sir Robert Peel, his hero had abandoned the only foundation on which the union of the three kingdoms can be built — uniformity in religion. In view of this fall, Wordsworth could only vote for him on condition that he became once more 'the wise philosopher and

* See Appendix.

devout divine' he formerly was. A candidate and a voter divided by such a chasm as is here indicated were plainly destined to remain apart. Wordsworth was left in the fortress raised by his own imagination, secure, had he but known it, in the fact that it would never again be thought worthy of a serious attack.

In the election of 1852 the opposition had firmer ground to go upon. Since his return in 1847 Mr. Gladstone had dissociated himself from the convocation of the University upon two grave questions — the admission of Jews into Parliament, and the assumption of territorial titles by the Roman Bishops. On neither of these was there any room for compromise. The vote in favour of the Jews lost him the support of Pusey. The vote against the Ecclesiastical Titles Bill was held to dispose of his claim to represent a Protestant University. Upon the former issue he had, however, the full support of James Hope, Tory and High Churchman though he was. 'On the Jewish question,' he writes to Gladstone, 'my bigotry makes me Liberal. To symbolize the Christianity of the House of Commons in its present form is to substitute a new Church and Creed for the old Catholic one, and as this is a delusion, I would do nothing to countenance it. Better have the Legislature declared what it really is — not professedly Christian — and then let the Church claim those rights and that independence which nothing but the pretence of Christianity can entitle the Legislature to withhold from it. In this view the emancipation of the Jews must tend to that of the Church.' Mr. Gladstone's attitude towards the Ecclesiastical Titles Act stood in less need of defence. The course which the agitation in favour of that measure had taken had, by this time, disillusioned its more reasonable supporters, and the reaction which, six months later, was to place the leading opponent of the Act in office was nearly complete.

The nature of the difference between Mr. Gladstone and a section of his early friends had been made plain by his pamphlet on 'The functions of Laymen in the Church.' In 1851 he had already made his own the conclusions which were to govern his whole ecclesiastical career. He had recognized the danger which awaited the Church from 'the exercise of State influence and of State power, not only by way of due check and control over her movements, but by way of assuming the privilege or function of ultimately deciding both her doctrine and her discipline.' He had welcomed full religious freedom in the interests alike of common justice, of religious peace, and of Divine truth. He had rejected for ever 'the servile doctrine' that religion cannot live but by the aid of Parliament. That aid might be a greater or lesser good according to circumstances, but under certain supposable conditions it might be the greatest of evils. A doctrine such as this naturally came as a shock to men who had accepted the conclusions of 'The State in its Relations with the Church' without taking in the arguments on which those conclusions were founded or realizing that in the modern world 'all systems, whether religious or political, which rest on a principle of absolutism, must of necessity be, not indeed tyrannical, but feeble and ineffective systems.' When in 1865 defeat at length came, Mr. Gladstone's regret was more for the Church than for himself. 'Do not conceal from yourself,' he writes to Bishop Wilberforce, 'that my hands are much weakened. It was only representing Oxford that a man whose opinions are disliked and suspected could expect, or could have a title, to be heard.' But the change affected nothing but his opportunities. 'As far as my will, my time, my thoughts, are concerned, they are where they were.'

223. *To R. J. Phillimore.*

HAGLEY,
February 15, 1847.

MY DEAR PHILLIMORE,

. . . I fear that my reply to your letter of the 13th may be the means of tearing out of your breast a cherished thought; perhaps some special purpose, unseen to us, has led you forward even beyond your wonted speed to feel the way for me towards the representation of our loved Oxford, in order that I might know that the thought of years is ripe, and might without though not against my will put it into words.

I think that recent changes have made resistless an argument, a practical argument, which was previously strong; and that it is now impossible to regulate the connection between Church and State in this country by reference to an abstract principle. I have stood for that abstract principle as long as I could, and longer, *i.e.*, later, than (I believe) any other man in Parliament: but when the principle as such is gone I will be no party to applying it occasionally, by dint of the aid of circumstances, against particular bodies — I mean especially against the Roman Catholics of Ireland.

I still think, as firmly as ever, that the connection between Church and State is worth maintaining, and that it both can and should be maintained; but I cannot pledge myself to uphold, under all circumstances, all the civil and proprietary claims of the Church, and this for two reasons, both weighty: the one, that I think some of them may require to be qualified in deference to the spirit and recognized principles of our modern legislation; the other, that I have too plainly seen them, with my own eyes, hampering and obtruding the fair demands of the Church upon the State for her own more essential purposes.

I do not think that any of these civil and proprietary claims are likely to be brought into serious question at a very early period; but I think the University, and therefore her members, have a right to know from those whom they are invited to choose, all that they can see, or believe they see, in the political future, and as I am deeply and painfully sensible of the moral evils attending any even apparent breach of pledge, or any disappointment of fairly conceived and dearly prized expectations, I am resolved, with the help of God, not to expose myself to the danger of producing them.

I have no difficulty in stating the principle on which I shall judge any public question of religion: but it is far less easy to say aye or no to such a question itself, especially if not yet before us. I have never seen my way, as it is called, to the payment of the Irish Roman Catholic clergy out of the revenues of the Church, even in part. But I am not sure that it is for the true interests of the Church (or that it is compatible, after all we have done, with social justice), for the Church to insist, say for the remainder of our natural lives, upon the possession of the whole of those revenues; therefore I will give no pledge which might have the effect of preventing my assent to what I might conscientiously believe advantageous to her and to the country. I say I can conceive such a case, while I must own that I have never seen it in form, and cannot presume to say how it is to take form. But I think either that will come or what is worse.

We live in times which are especially times of change, which lead, and sometimes even compel, both those who are to give confidence to limit it, and those who are to receive confidence to enlarge their demand for it. But it is especially an object of high price in my sight that the constituent should neither be deceived nor, otherwise than by his own fault, misled. The way to secure this is clear. It is, to speak boldly and fearlessly, to risk all mistaken and exaggerated constructions, all anticipations of possibility into fact: and with cheerfulness to accept the consequence, which in this case is clear enough. Only part with a desired object for me as manfully as I am sure you would do it for yourself, and your mind will be soon at rest. Oxford has plenty of choice among her sons, and she can with character and with comfort select the shade of political opinion nearest to her own. But you would hurt your own character if you were to allow private considerations to bias you in a matter of this kind, and you might hurt public interests too.

I hope it is not necessary for me, in addressing you, to say that the sentiments I entertain have no relation to any sort of change in religious convictions, such as those which we have seen in sorrowful abundance. After the storms and trials of the last few years, I find my mind, as to everything substantial, upon the ground where it was before them, so that in this one essential condition I humbly hope I might not have misrepresented the University.

I have written as freely as if my reply was for your own breast alone; but I observe the purpose for which it was sought, and I cannot possibly ask you to limit the use you may make of it.

Believe me, with the warmest sense of your kindness and friendship,
Your sincerely attached
W. E. GLADSTONE.

224. *To R. J. Phillimore.*

HAGLEY,
February 26, 1847.

MY DEAR PHILLIMORE,
. . . I not only see multitudes of objections to any disappropriation of the possessions of the Church in Ireland, but multitudes also of practical obstacles in the way of it. But I am unwilling to lay down any principle at the present time with respect to which I can in my own mind entertain so much as a suspicion that I may some years hence be forced to abandon it. And as I think we are no longer in a condition to occupy high and secure ground in arguing for the integrity of the Irish Church temporalities, as I think we shall find it difficult at once to vindicate our own acts and to furnish grounds for a permanent adherence to the present state of things, I feel that to hold the high language with these sentiments and other presentiments about me would be to march into the

Caudine forks, from which there is no escape with honour.

Of two things I feel pretty certain — We shall *not* see a simple redistribution of the Irish Church property among those who hold it on the present conditions. We shall *not* see a simple payment of the Roman Catholic priesthood out of the Consolidated Fund. Again, I *fear* that we may do as we have done before — *i.e.*, fritter away the ecclesiastical property of Ireland, with scarcely a disguise, in order to enable ourselves to blink the question by arguing that there is no surplus. . . .

        Believe me always,
          Your attached friend,
            W. E. GLADSTONE.

225. *To the Right Hon. J. S. Wortley.*

13, CARLTON HOUSE TERRACE,
June 17, 1847.

MY DEAR WORTLEY,

My wife tells me that you had more or less entertained the idea of writing to me on the subject of my relation to parties in the Church, and had refrained from it for fear of causing me embarrassment or compromising me with some of those who will support me in the Oxford Election. I have, however, no fear of any such embarrassment, and while I am most thankful for the delicacy which made you hesitate, I consider the subject one on which there ought to be no reserve, I do not say only from yourself, but from any member of Convocation — and I hope my language upon it has been uniform: I am sure it has not been intentionally varied.

I distinguish between holding opinions and belonging to a party. Some opinions every man must hold, but it seems to me the duty of every Christian to disclaim in word, and to avoid to the best of his power in act, party connections, which imply something quite distinct from even identity, much more from qualified resemblance of opinion. They imply, I imagine, combination and concert in the pursuit of ends which are peculiar and do not fully harmonize with the spirit and laws of the Church: and they even imply, as in politics, more or less of the compromise of opinion for the sake of such concert. They imply the effort to think and act in common with some persons who are regarded as leaders, instead of individually or with friends according to the tenor of private and personal intercourse. In all these and all kindred senses I think the recognition of party blamable on the part of any man, but decidedly and by far most blamable on the part of those who endeavour to realize to themselves the idea of the Church as a living authority or guide.

I may perhaps be regarded as a party man either on the ground of public acts in which I have shared, and in which I have been accompanied for the most part by persons who are so regarded, and, indeed, who avow the fact, or else on the ground of my published opinions. With respect to the former, such as the vote on Ward, all I can say is that I have not done any act of the kind without the belief (how far owing to bias I am of course unable to judge) that it was required by a principle of general justice as distinct from any tie of party, and to this exclusively, as I afterwards explained. As to my published opinions, they have been variously viewed. I should be very sorry to propose to anyone that he should make himself acquainted with them. There, however, they are, and in a religious sense I stand by them, and I cannot object *in limine* to any judgment founded upon them. Moreover it is now, for the present purpose, too late to argue upon or explain them.

So much for what I am in myself. I could not dispense with the topic, however ungrateful, because it is absurd to suppose there is no relation between a man's private views and the character he proposes to fill in Parliament. But though there is a connection between them there is also a distinction. Some things, which we may hold and even cherish dearly for ourselves, we may yet feel ought to stand apart from our representative capacity. What the representative of Oxford ought in these times to be, I do not doubt in so far at least as this, that if he enters the House of Commons possessed with any other idea than that of representing *her*—such as she is in her members and in her institutions taken at large and as a whole—he can only sit there to her damage and dishonour. Even had I been in the habit of recognizing in myself a party character, which is the very reverse of the fact, I should still have felt and said, what I have felt and said all along during the present contest, that I could neither sit as the representative of a party nor stand as its candidate, and consequently that, if the complexion of my leading supporters and the course of events was such as to stamp that character upon me, I would at all hazards and disadvantages withdraw. These would be dangerous words for an advertisement, but you will readily understand the sense in which I employ them.

I have troubled you with this letter, dismissing any scruple on your account, because it requires no answer —its only object is to give such information as the case admits of—and I shall be glad to hear from you only if you desire more, and more which it may be in my power to render.

226. To R. J. Phillimore.

13, CARLTON HOUSE TERRACE,
June 24, 1847.

MY DEAR PHILLIMORE,
I did not mean to go beyond a suggestion. Even in my own mind it had not yet expanded into an argument. It is an idea which I wish to separate altogether from my own position, and to consider on its own merits, not by comparison.

The members for the Universities are in an imperfect sense, but still a true one, representatives of the Church in the House of Commons, and though but partially, yet they are exclusively her representatives.

This applies to the members for Oxford even in a higher degree than to those for Cambridge.

We have come upon a time when a merely or mainly obstructive policy will be fatal to the Church. It means these three things: that she will lose all she has; that she will be kept, and will keep the whole country, in a fever, or even a fury, while she is fighting to retain it; and that when it is gone she will find herself left with nothing to replace it.

She is now in a condition in which her children may and must desire that she should keep her national position and her civil and proprietary rights, and that she should by degrees obtain the means of extending and of strengthening herself, not only by covering a greater space, but by a more vigorous organization. Her attaining to this state of higher health depends in no small degree upon progressive adaptations of her state and her laws to her ever enlarging exigencies; these depend upon the humour of the State, and the State cannot and will not be in good humour with her, if she insists on its being in bad humour with all other communions.

It seems to me, therefore, that while in substance we should all strive to sustain her in her national position, we shall do well on her behalf to follow these rules: to part earlier, and more freely and cordially, than heretofore with such of her privileges, here and there, as may be more obnoxious than really valuable — and some such she has — and further, not to presume too much to give directions to the State as to its policy with respect to other religious bodies.

Whatever good can be done for her in Parliament must be done by influence and moral strength. If she is content with a mere numerical representation, with the votes of the members for the Universities, there they are, 6 out of 656, enough to make divisions contemptible enough, but *ad infinitum* in number. And with what issue? Incessant quarrels, continual bad blood, certain defeat: and not only this, but to adopt a merely negative and obstructive policy is the abandonment of her function, which requires her indeed to check and control, but also to teach and guide the country, to join herself, for the better pursuit of her spiritual work, with the course of external events, and so direct it as to obtain from it the greatest good.

This is not political expediency as opposed to religious principle. Nothing did so much damage to religion as the obstinate adherence to this negative, repressive, and coercive course. For a century and more from the Revolution it brought us nothing but outwardly animosities and inwardly lethargy. The revival of a livelier sense of duty and of God is now beginning to tell in the altered *policy* of the Church. Hence the Bishops, who in 1836 would not have a new bishopric because it would, they thought, be without a seat in the House of Lords, are now happy to take one on those terms. Hence they take grants for education, which are avowedly given on principles of religious equality and impartiality, or indifference, whichever it may be called. Thus then, as her sense of her spiritual work rises, she is becoming less eager to assert her exclusive claim, leaving that to the State as a matter for itself to decide; and she also begins to forego more readily, but cautiously, some of her external prerogatives.

This by her Bishops: but I do not think that a claim which founds itself upon having opposed Maynooth, opposed the Dissenters' Chapels Bill, opposed Mr. Watson, opposed (right or wrong) everything which went to qualify a single civil privilege of the Church, or confer a single civil privilege on any other body, will adequately support in the Commons that rule upon which the Bishops begin to act in the Lords. If it be replied that privileges shall be freely given to all except Roman Catholics and Unitarians, the answer is, that does not save truth, while it more grievously violates social justice; besides which, such a system cannot and will not stand. And the University, as the organ of the Church in the Commons, should not exhibit itself as always grasping, always resisting, always trying to rule by strength and not through good-will, and always failing in it.

This is a sad scrawl, and can be but of very little use — but I thought it better than further delay.

Your attached friend,
W. E. GLADSTONE.

227. *To the Rev. J. W. Warter.*

13, CARLTON HOUSE TERRACE,
July 21, 1847.

MY DEAR SIR,
If you are content to abandon all hope of obtaining through the medium of Parliament real advantages for the Church in the improvement of her law and organization, to continue to fight the miserable battle (for under such circumstances it will be miserable) of civil privileges under the now seductive

flag of 'No surrender,' with constant irritation for your present reward, and certain defeat for the final issue — *then* continue also to be governed in your choice of representatives in Parliament mainly by a regard to simple aye or no upon the question (to me or any other) 'Are you prepared to resist under all circumstances any and every further concession to Roman Catholics?' But if you still think the State has a work of whatever kind to do *for* the Church — as I do — then beware how you allow a question affecting the conduct of the State to other communions to become the governing question for you. I tell you plainly there is ruin in that course. If Churchmen, and the clergy in particular, direct their energies, too feeble for their own work, not to the doing of their own work, but towards binding the State to a negative and repressive policy as respects other bodies, they will not succeed. But that is little in comparison with what remains — they will feel the first, and full, and by far the worst, pressure of that policy themselves.

Forgive me if I say that those who have sat many years in Parliament, and have given their mind and time to their task, and have under heavy responsibilities shared in working the laws, institutions, and policy, of this great Empire at the fountain-head, have not undergone that slavery (for such it may too truly be called) absolutely for nothing, nor without acquiring some opportunities of view into the political future. Many things indeed are dark in it, but some are clear. What I have now told you stands, believe me, in the latter class. I tell you, however it may seem to you, not what I think, but what I know, as well as I know that the next Parliament will not convert our limited and free monarchy into a despotism. If Oxford elects me, she elects a man under very deep and fixed convictions with regard to these matters — let me say under hitherto unvarying convictions, for with whatever tacks I am always making for the same point. If *she* is to raise in the House of Commons what was known twenty years ago, in very different times, as the No Popery cry, I say fearlessly she may spare herself the trouble of looking for other qualifications in her members, and of ascertaining whether they have any positive views of serving the Church or not, for it will make little difference. She will have her $\frac{1}{318}$ share of the representation, and she will have little more; she will be a drag-chain more or less on a descending wheel, but she will be as powerless as any drag-chain ever known for progress in the direction in which she desires and pants for it. The stern adherence to an exclusive policy — the stern and inconsistent adherence to it, for consistent *now* such adherence is not in any single case, and scarcely *can* be — is, I say, utterly fatal to any further beneficial use of the principles of connection between the Church and the State.

I give you full credit 'for having read arguments *pro and con*,' but permit me to say that something more is necessary. My firm belief is that, had you seen and felt and lived what I have seen and felt and lived, you would now be uttering these words, or the same sentiments in better words, to me. I have spoken of the contingency of my being elected. But if I am rejected, to my latest hour it will be a consolation to me that, so far as my position would permit, I have not kept back from men like you such truths as I have gathered from experience, at the hour when it was yet time (as we hope) to speak them.

I have spoken and written thus throughout the controversy. The debates and votes on the Manchester Bishopric Bill greatly confirm and very little surprise me. Can any man read those debates, estimate them with all the circumstances, and fail to see that the Church has to deal with other work, and nearer home, than the endowment of Maynooth, and that she cannot do her own work and other people's too? . . .

I am much indebted to you for the kind tone of your letter, and I fervently trust I have said nothing inconsistent with a warm regard and a true respect for you. . . .

     Sincerely yours,
      W. E. GLADSTONE.

228. *To the Rev. A. W. Haddan.*

6, CARLTON GARDENS,
May 18, 1852.

MY DEAR MR. HADDAN,
 . . . I can feel no surprise at your repugnance to my vote on the Jew Bill. Assuming myself, as I

must do, to be right, still, I can hardly expect others from a different standing-point to take the same view. All I ask of you or them is to believe that it is with me a part, and believed by me to be a necessary part, of a system of action, to which I came slowly and with struggles, but have now long adhered, and of the necessity of which, taken generally, I am glad indeed to find that your conviction is as strong as my own. Speaking to Churchmen, I would say I am quite willing that system of action should be tried by them on the single issue, not of its usefulness merely, but of its necessity to the Church — setting aside every other public interest and social principle.

I cannot affect to stand on the ground that this general idea and course of action is merely permissible, however thankful I may feel to those who are willing to go so far while they have no convictions to carry them farther. But with me it is not so. I see too vividly in the working of our institutions, and in the daily experience of my Parliamentary life, the sickening extent and miserable effects of that worship of idols and deification of impostures which still forms so large a part of statecraft as regards its ecclesiastical relations. It is not difficult, at least to me, to bear with any such forms and symbols as, having been venerable or useful, are now simply neutral and without use; but when I see them set up against the substance, thrusting it out and trampling it under foot, I cannot be indifferent any longer. All this is too much in the form of abstraction, but I could readily supply the application — as, for instance, from the history of to-day, in which I have received from the Colonial Secretary an intimation that he will oppose the second reading of my Colonial Church Bill, after I had received repeated assurances on the part of the Government that they would support it. Imagine the order of ideas which leads them to this conclusion, and then you have the true and really dangerous enemies of the Church, nestling, alas! nowadays in the bosoms of its 'friends.'

Hook agrees to serve on my Committee again. I mention this only because I think that from him it is an act of singular generosity. . . .
Most truly yours,
W. E. GLADSTONE.

229. *To the Rev. C. Marriott.*

6, CARLTON GARDENS,
May 31, 1852.

MY DEAR MR. MARRIOTT,

. . . Though I had no right to presume on Dr. Pusey's support, yet I thought it possible that prudential motives might have kept his name back, as you inform me is the case. But I could not reckon on him, for I knew the extreme strength of his feeling about the admission of the Jews to Parliament. Only this morning Phillimore (for one) had a positive refusal from the Bishop of Glasgow on that ground. He adds that he voted against me in 1847, because he saw that I should, on the principles I then laid down, necessarily vote for their admission.

On the subject of change my conscience is sound. Not that I can say or wish I am in every point and particular what I was in 1847: to say that would be to plead guilty to having learned in five busy years absolutely nothing. But as to principles, civil, religious, or mixed, I feel conscious that I am what I was, as to everything of ground and substance: and this being so, I also feel that *therefore* the struggle now going on is the affair of the University in the first place, and mine in the second. But I am not the less gratified at, and grateful for, the very energetic support which is now given me.

I remain,
Most sincerely yours,
W. E. GLADSTONE.

230. *To the Rev R. Greswell.*

DOWNING STREET,
January 11, 1853.

MY DEAR MR. GRESWELL,

I thank you for your letter, and will reply to the last part of it, which alone requires an answer.

I presume that the issue of the present contest is no longer doubtful, and that the University will again place the trust of representing her, or rather the moiety of it, in my hands.

I am convinced that the spirit which is abroad towards me, which raised the contest at the poll last July, after the sense of the University had been made clear to demonstration, and which has now not scrupled at the most disgraceful falsehoods in order to gain its end — I speak no doubt only of the dregs of my present opponents, but I observe that from these men the rest of them do not feel it necessary to dissociate themselves — can never be appeased, and will always proceed to punish me when I exercise an independent judgment in opposition to what the party think right.

But of the punishment so inflicted, a great part, the main part, falls upon my friends.

If wounded and hurt by the opposition offered me, by its quality much more than its quantity, on the other hand the support, confidence, and sympathy, exhibited towards me are as remarkable and signal.

I think the University *ought*, for its own honour, in some manner to declare its sense of the falsehoods — I shall never use a weaker word — of Dr. Lempriere and certain as yet invisible coadjutors. But that is a matter of opinion, and I cannot say I will not serve the University now or hereafter because she does not adopt my views on that subject.

The upshot of the whole is this: my own inclination is to adopt your conclusion — to say, when the trust now given me shall have been discharged, I shall not ask its renewal; for I feel that, even if it were in my power to render any services to the University I love so much, they would be purchased far too dearly by these incessant and bitter contests, by the pain, anxiety, toil, and charge, which they entail, above all by their ruinous effect on the dignity and value that have hitherto belonged to the representation of Oxford.

But I cannot settle this matter for myself. The part so bravely taken by my friends gives them an absolute claim upon me. If they, upon calm and full consideration, think fit to release me, I will gladly go. If they say, 'No, you must remain, then, please God, I will unhesitatingly remain, and will shrink from no part of that share of the burden which falls upon me so long as the power of bearing it is continued to me. I hope, therefore, that they will feel that the whole decision rests with them, and that its importance to

Oxford, whichever way it be, is not to be measured by the insignificance of the individual whom it seems primarily to affect.

For the moment I have no doubt you will use this letter with reserve. Sir S. Northcote knows me so well that, whoever else sees it, he should.

With renewed and warm thanks,
I remain, etc.,
W. E. GLADSTONE.

231. *To Sir R. Phillimore.*

HAWARDEN,
July 17, 1865.

MY DEAR PHILLIMORE,
I received your telegram, or 'The Chairman's,' to-night soon after nine, and I now enclose my farewell address.* Please to publish it immediately after the close of the poll, and after consulting Bernard and any others, and unless it is disapproved by you and them. But I do not propose to be bound by the mere etiquette of the case. . . .

But these wise men have taken a weapon out of my hands in a sense they little dream of. These last words to yourself.

Affectionately yours,
W. E. GLADSTONE.

232. *To Sir William Heathcote, Bart.*

HAWARDEN,
July 21, 1865.

MY DEAR HEATHCOTE,
I did not doubt of your feelings in this crisis, but the expression of them is very pleasant to me, and most thankful to you I am. As to my own, I can hardly yet tell what they are. I know a vital cord is snapped, I know nothing else, except it be that to the indictment under which I have been condemned I plead not guilty. Beyond the region of knowledge I have enough of gloomy surmises. It is a question between gold and faith: and the gold always carries it against the faith. Hence the present disasters and present

* See Appendix.

perils of the Church of England, and from the same source, I fear, those of the future are to flow. It is absolutely necessary that some people should be ready to be (from their point of view) sacrificed in the endeavour to open minds and eyes which will not read the signs of the times.

This will all appear to you strange and one-sided, but you see that both Keble and Pusey write very much in the same sense; and as for you, were I more vigorous and more free, I should never rest in the endeavour to gain so priceless a proselyte. I *know* I have a friend, I would almost say a witness, in your breast. I know that, like me, you mournfully compare the efforts which are made so gallantly to win a triumph like that of Tuesday, with the manner in which questions are fought when nothing is imperilled, nothing put in issue, but only the Christian Faith.

Do not, however, my dear friend, ever let either of us recognize that we are one inch more distant from each other on account of my defeat at Oxford. You know I have always held that we were much nearer than you would allow — that is, than you could bring yourself to believe. I still hold by the same cheerful text, and will do, please God, to the end of the chapter.

I rejoice that you are able to begin, with bettered prospects of health, another series of sessions. And it is, you well know, from no ill-nature to Mr. Hardy if I close with saying, I wish it could have been Northcote. . . .

W. E. GLADSTONE.

233. To Sir S. Northcote, Bart.

HAWARDEN,
July 21, 1865.

MY DEAR NORTHCOTE,

I cannot withhold myself from writing a line to assure you it is not my fault, but my misfortune, that you are not my successor at Oxford.

My desire or impulse has for a good while, not unnaturally, been to escape from the Oxford seat; not because I grudged the anxieties of it, but because I found the load, added to other loads, too great. Could I have seen my way to this proceeding, had the advice or had the conduct of my friends warranted it, you would have had such notice of it as effectually to preclude your being anticipated. I mean no disrespect to Mr. Hardy, but it has been a great pain to me to see in all the circulars a name different from the name that should have stood there, and that would have stood there, but for your personal feelings.

I am aware that nothing is more flat and lame in these matters than the potential mood, and dwelling on contingencies that have not taken effect, but, so far as I am concerned, they have not, only because they could not. My regret with respect to you is enhanced by what is in other respects a compensation, namely, that Mr. Hardy is not likely to be disturbed, and the seat for the University has a prospect of regaining through permanence its primitive and peculiar, and by no means unimportant, kind of value, which it lost in the time of its late ill-starred member.

Pray bear in mind that this letter expects no reply.
W. E. GLADSTONE.

234. *To Lord Richard Cavendish.*

CARLTON HOUSE TERRACE,
July 27, 1865.

MY DEAR CAVENDISH,
Your warm friendship prompts the language in which you describe the late contest at Oxford, and it is a painful business. But the incidental consolations in every kind of expression of feeling have been great, and I believe there is a purpose in it which will work for good. In myself, I have many titles to the mistrust of the Liberal party, at present the governing party of this country. But these wise gentlemen at Oxford seemed determined to force me into possession of its confidence, and have done their very best for that end. All this, please God, we may talk over hereafter. . . .

W. E. GLADSTONE.

CHAPTER II

THE CONTROVERSY WITH ROME

1850–1891

THE unending controversy between the Roman and Anglican Churches appealed to Mr. Gladstone under three aspects. First of all, there was the effect it had on the minds of many of his friends. How were they to be made to share the undoubting conviction with which he argued the Anglican case that to them seemed so full of uncertainty? Following upon this comes the long correspondence with Manning which grew out of the relations between the Papacy and the new Italian Kingdom. This in its turn gives place to the pamphlet warfare which followed upon the Vatican Council. The reader of this part of the letters will do well to bear in mind a fact which has already been mentioned. The very strength of Mr. Gladstone's confidence in the Anglican position made him an ineffective defender of it to some minds. The book which had done most to fix his own convictions was Palmer's 'History of the Church,' and throughout his life he went on advising everybody to read it. But to some of those who were disturbed by the absence of a living authority in the Church of England, Palmer's reasoning seemed better fitted for the pupils of a conveyancing counsel than for men and women living in the world. His demonstration that the laws of a local church provide all the guidance that her children can require did not meet the complaint that the Church of England had ceased to make laws. This was not a circumstance that greatly troubled Mr. Gladstone. He did not deny that for the time the Church of England was unable to speak with the authority he would have liked her to exercise; he only pleaded that the changes actually in progress would in the end give her back the power she had for the time lost.

The two arguments on which he most relied when trying to prevent secessions were in themselves unanswerable. The question to which Church a man ought to belong was not to be treated as a matter of personal taste. No one could be justified in abandoning the Church of England because he preferred Roman services, or thought that he 'got more good' from Roman teaching. This was merely a variant of the reasoning which Nonconformists had found so successful in parishes where the clergy were careless or inefficient. Nor, whatever his ultimate decision might be, had a man any right to leave the Church of England until he had studied the arguments on both sides with at least equal care. In many cases, Mr. Gladstone thought, this condition had not been satisfied. The seceder had listened to the case put forward on behalf of the Roman Catholic Church, but he had never inquired whether the case on the Anglican side was not as strong or stronger. There were instances, however, to which neither of these criticisms applied — instances in which there had been no question of anything but fundamental principles, and the doubter of to-day had himself perhaps furnished the most convincing statement of the Anglican claims — and here Mr. Gladstone's controversial success was not equal to his strength of conviction. His reliance on Palmer led him to rest his argument too exclusively on the local identity of the Church of England before and after the Reformation. He did not appreciate the force of the retort that, though the body might remain, the spirit had fled. Palmer's contention gives the modern reader a feeling that he has proved almost too much. The Anglican argument, as he presents it, is over-conclusive for a world in which men have constantly to put up with demonstrations that stop short of completeness because they have learnt that the alternatives offered them are in this respect quite as defective. There was another feature in Mr. Gladstone's method of carrying on the controversy, which, though admirable in itself, may sometimes have helped to defeat his purpose. Down to 1870, at all events, the strong words which he used in reference to particular Roman doctrines, his passionate descriptions of the impassable gulf which a friend's secession had opened between them, did not hinder him from saying — sometimes in the same letter — that the differences between Rome and England did not touch a single essential point. The people to whom he was writing may sometimes have asked themselves how, if on every vital issue there was so complete an identity between the two Churches, the act of leaving one for the other in obedience to what the seceder held to be a call of conscience could make so tremendous a change. Mr. Gladstone would have been a worse theologian and a worse Christian if he had treated Rome as an heretical communion; but he might at times have proved a better controversialist. It is to be feared that the Roman apologist who magnified every difference between the two Churches occasionally found that, though his treatment of the subject might have less charity, it had more success.

235. *To Archdeacon Manning.*

6, CARLTON GARDENS,
June 1, 1850.

MY DEAR MANNING,

. . . If I were obliged to make an answer to a person putting to me what appears to be the essential point in this letter — that the Church of England must be understood really to deny that the Church of Rome is a true Church, because they differ 'on essential points,' I should answer that I know of no such points. On the point of Transubstantiation, accepting from and with the Church of England the truth and reality of the visible elements in the Holy Eucharist, I have not the misery of thinking that the Church of Rome, in her denial of that reality, within the limits to which she has confined it, constitutes a difference on an essential point. We have with us, I fear, those who do not believe that 'whole and entire Christ' is received in that sacred ordinance by the faithful; and they have those, I likewise fear, who pay worship to that which they see, and who, if judged severely in the abstract (as God will not judge them), do evacuate and destroy the realness of a sacrament. But I do not think it lawful to hold either the one or the other [Church] fully responsible for error that has crept into and kept a place within its borders: and I have always remembered with much comfort a passage quoted by Newman, in his former self, from Bishop Van Mildert, setting forth the outlines of that one faith which always has been and now is professed by the Church. Much less am I aware that as to Penance any essential difference, upon matter of faith, is alleged, much less can be proved, to exist between the Churches.

The rejection from the fellowship of the Christian covenant of all who do not receive the authority of the See of Rome is to me an awful innovation on the faith, and a dark sign of the future for the large part of Christendom which is in communion with that see, and with which we have so deep a common interest in the maintenance of the Faith.

I will not refer to any other point; the details to some of which she refers are details upon which you doubtless will give this lady to understand that the matter does not and cannot turn.

But, independently of my own inability duly to handle those details, I must own there never was a time when I should have felt so much disposed to strive earnestly to draw off a disturbed and unsettled mind from their contemplation, and to fix it on the great and noble work which God has now given to the children of the Church in England amid trouble, suspense, and it may be agony, to perform. I do not believe that a more arduous, a more exalted, or a more exalting task ever was committed to men. They are called and charged to do battle for the Faith in the very point now plainly selected for the great battlefield of modern infidelity, and with the consolation of being sustained by declarations of the local Church, not sufficient only, but redundant, and not clear only, but of overpowering clearness. I hope you will induce this interesting pupil to take her part in this battle and her share of the prize. . . .

Your affectionate friend,
W. E. GLADSTONE.

236. *To the Hon. Maud Stanley.*

HAWARDEN,
November 27, 1855.

MY DEAR MISS STANLEY,

. . . When we met upon this subject last year, it struck me that your mind was in a different state from that of others whom I had seen when they were meditating a similar course — that in general the arguments, on the strength of which it is designed so to act, are sufficient to warrant the conclusion, if only they were true, but that your arguments, even if they were true, yet did not warrant your conclusion.

And it is remarkable that I find the very same character in the letter you have now addressed to me, where you say that you have heard no argument to shake your 'increasing belief that the Roman Catholic Church in point of unity and holiness comes nearest to the Scriptural definition of the Church of Christ.'

I confess it seems to me that this is a question which neither of us is very competent to decide. My fixed conviction has long been that the Roman Church remarkably unites within itself the opposite extremes — that it has much of the very best, and a great deal of the very worst, of Christianity. But I feel that this is a matter of private and personal opinion, and that for me to make the little shreds and fragments of experience, which I can gather within my own atomic sphere, the ground of my hold upon the Faith, and titles to the reality of membership in Christ, is a sad error both in itself and in its consequences to me.

If it was the ordinance of God that each Christian was to institute a search, and to discover for himself, which of the various Christian communities came nearest in unity and holiness to the Scriptural representation of the Body of Christ, it seems to me that the whole design of the historical, visible, and traditive character of the Church is overthrown.

Where has God promised that in all parts of the Apostles' fellowship the light should burn with equal purity and brightness? Even at the first, the Church of Sardis was not equal in 'unity and holiness' to the Church of Ephesus, nor the Church of Ephesus to the Church of Smyrna. But St. John did not command the Christians of Sardis to join the communion of Ephesus, nor both to leave their own and go into that of Smyrna; he bid them through their rulers to amend their ways and become more like their Lord.

I avoid and eschew that question which Church is most holy — alas! it is too sadly easy to make a case against all — but I earnestly assure you, from the evidence your letter gives me, that you are bound in duty to seek to have a sound mind as well as an upright heart, and that, upright as I am certain your heart is, your mind is not upon the line which leads to true conclusions and indicates the path of just and safe action.

Believe me, I neither doubt nor make light of your sufferings; I trust they may be lightened, but especially that, when they are lightened, they may be lightened once for all, and that you will find the true solution of your present dilemma in a more just and searching examination of the whole grounds on which such a question should be handled.

I will not apologize for the manner in which I write, but I trust to your indulgence, and I remain,
                    Always most sincerely yours,
                              W. E. GLADSTONE.

237. To the Hon. Maud Stanley.

4, CARLTON HOUSE TERRACE,
January 27, 1856.

MY DEAR MISS STANLEY,
    It will be quite as much as I can write, or as you can read with patience, if I explain upon *one sentence* of your last letter, in which you say that 'you understood me to bring forward the Arian heresy as a proof that open questions existed in the Primitive Church of equal importance with those which have been the pride of the Church of England since the Reformation.' You did not mean to impute to me this language, but how *my* language could be such as to lead you into such a statement I am at a loss to conjecture. It makes me a calumniator of the Primitive Church, and you the utterer of (in my opinion) a precipitate and untrue charge against the Church of England.

You think that I said the Arian hypothesis was an open question because I said it remained long and struggled long in the Church before the final victory of the truth.

What I have said (I speak from memory only) amounts, I believe, to this: Place yourself as an orthodox believer in the Church of the Fourth Century, and I will show you that there were times when, even as regarded the vital doctrine of the Godhead, the voice of authority was liable to the charge of a doubtful utterance, so far that the private Christian might not unreasonably doubt in what path it bid him walk.

You seem to me (forgive me) not to have considered the nature of the Church, but rather in regard to it, as it exists in England, to have rested in a creed or scheme of opinion that in other respects you have repudiated; you likewise seem to me not to have examined into the nature of the provision made by Almighty God in the

Church for the establishment of the truth, and when I refer to a great case in which the horizon was long clouded, and for a time it seemed doubtful which creed would gain the mastery, you think I say it was an open question.

An open question I take to be a question which the authority ruling the Church has either by speech or general and long-continued silence, or by its falling plainly within some general rule, declared to be open — *i.e.*, indifferent. Two men wrestle for a prize; till one wins, the question is contested. Two men agree not to wrestle for it at all, the question is open. Have I made myself clear?

Bishop Butler is not controversial; but his works are more fruitful in sound principles applicable to the mode of Providential government in the Church as well as in the world than almost any others.

Now for the Church of England. A glance at her history, in my opinion, shows the injustice of your charge and (I cannot but add) its precipitancy. The legal settlement of the Church of England dates from 1662. *She* has never retraced, never qualified any part of that settlement. Was that settlement founded on the notion of open questions? Why then did 2,000 ministers quit their benefices? The principle on which that settlement was founded was, it seems to me, the Divine Constitution of the Church; at any rate, plainly enough, it was founded upon a principle in dogma and in polity, as were the decrees of Trent. Both left open questions, but both closed some questions — the questions which they thought to be essential.

What you have to show in order to make good your charge is that the Church has left open any question which involves matter of faith properly so called. This you will find very difficult. As respects the case of Baptism which you quoted, I ask in what sense is it open? You will hardly say the language of the formularies is not clear. You will perhaps say Mr. A. and Mr. B. who deny it are unpunished. I answer Pope Liberius was unpunished when he had renounced the orthodox communion, Pope Honorius remained unpunished until after his death. If a Pope, then why not any man lesser than a Pope? I hope the day will come when you will regard these questions in their true light as trials of your faith.

I must not let my letter go without referring to your words, 'my first questions, to which I have received no definite answer.' I ask you plainly whether I was not justified — nay, bound — to interpose my preliminary condition? What can be the use of my answering questions until I get you to admit the principle on which we are to proceed, and the responsibility under which you have placed yourself by desiring me to enter on these subjects; for I need not say we are [as] responsible for using the light of a farthing candle when we have called for it, as we should be were it the sun.

My position is this: you are bound by duty and allegiance to the Church of England. If you have doubts in regard to her authority, you are bound (as one in the Church of Rome would be bound in the converse case) to *bring those doubts to a fair trial.* To do this you ought to state them, and to say: These and these questions being answered properly (of course without prejudice to future *lights*), my mind will be satisfied. But question after question, charge after charge, without any specification to yourself or me of the whole of what you want, is just the course which a person would take whose wounded feelings had made him determined *not* to be satisfied; it is a course into which you may unknowingly be entrapped, but into which I shall not by my conduct help to entrap you.

Some day I may ask you to let me look at these letters again. You, I know, forgive their haste, and will not make me an offender for a word.

Most sincerely yours,
W. E. Gladstone.

In the letters written while the Kingdom of Italy was being built up Mr. Gladstone is seen to greater advantage. The Pope, he argued, had no moral right to treat the interests of the Roman people as a matter of infinite unimportance by the side of the interests of the Roman Church. The two belonged to different regions. The one was temporal, the other was spiritual; and to sacrifice either to the other was to confound things that had nothing in common. Upon one point Mr. Gladstone felt as strongly as Manning himself. In spiritual things the Pope's action must not be controlled by the Italian or any other Government. This was a matter which concerned in varying degrees every State that had Roman Catholic subjects. Where Manning and he parted company was on the means by which this independence could be secured. Manning would hear but of one — the maintenance of the Temporal Power. Mr. Gladstone would have conceded even this, if the Pope had been strong enough to defend his throne without foreign aid. But when this condition was flagrantly unsatisfied, when the 'Pope King' had ceased to have any authority in his own capital except what he derived from its occupation by French troops, the Temporal Power had become valueless for the very purpose for which Manning was insisting on its retention. When Mr. Gladstone was asked what better means he could suggest, he had a plan of his own ready. Unlike most of the opponents of the Temporal Power, he saw that the end which must be kept in view was beyond the reach of the Italian Government acting alone. No matter how satisfactory the conditions might be to the Pope at starting, what was to prevent a change of mind on the part of the Parliament which had agreed to them? The best-drawn statute can have no greater permanence than the purpose of the legislature which has voted it. What was wanted to secure the Pope in the enjoyment of his spiritual freedom was the sanction of a European guarantee. Mr. Gladstone seems to have thought that if this plan had been seriously put forward by the Roman Curia, it would have been accepted by the Italian Government. Whether he was right in thus thinking is not a matter of much interest, because there never was a moment in which the Curia were disposed to make advances of this kind. To the Pope and his advisers the Temporal Power seemed the one thing that was worth fighting for, and so long as they felt this the Roman question admitted of no compromise. Till 1870, what was left of the Pontifical States remained French — for what other term can be applied to a territory in which public order is only maintained by the presence of French soldiers? Then it became Italian, with the singular result that the Pope's independence as a spiritual ruler has been as absolute since the loss of the Temporal Power as at any period in ecclesiastical history. Under no concordat with the Italian Government, by no arrangement between the European Powers, could this end have been so well secured as by the extraordinary series of events which has made the 'Prisoner of the Vatican' the most active spiritual force in Christendom.

238. *To Dr. Döllinger.*

11, Carlton House Terrace,
June 22, 1862.

My dear Dr. Döllinger,

. . . I come to that which, though the smaller, is the more vital part of [your work]: namely, the later part, in which you discuss the nature and conditions of the Papal Government. I cannot but regard this as highly important and highly beneficial. In a calm, clear, and truthful narrative, you have exhibited the gradual departure of the Government in the States of the Church from all those conditions which made it tolerable to the sense and reason of mankind, and have, I think, completely justified, in principle if not in all the facts, the conduct of those who have determined to do away with it.

In the autumn of 1859, I think the British Cabinet would have been very glad to use any influence it possessed for the purpose of securing to the Pope the *Suzerainty* of all his States, with competent revenue, and European guarantees for his independence, and with the King of Italy exercising, as his permanent and hereditary vicegerent, the ordinary functions of Government. But it is now, I apprehend, too late for such a measure.

We have in this country, as, I suppose, in all Protestant and indeed in almost all European countries, a number of people who may be called enemies of the Roman Church — who wish to see her, not improved (as we may all with much reason wish for ourselves), but destroyed, and the Papal Supremacy, not reformed, but rejected. All these are in a state of great delight at what is going on. For them it has been a great triumph, and a source of exulting hope, to see the Roman See and Court deliberately take its stand upon the propositions that the civil rights of the Roman people must be held secondary to the interests of the Church, and that without a temporal Sovereignty for its support the spiritual power of the Pope cannot be maintained. Yet more must they be delighted when they find the astonishing licence of vituperation and foul language which has marked the recent proceedings taken at Rome under cover of the canonization of the Japanese martyrs.

I confess that I view such things very differently, and that I deeply lament the scandal and real damage to religion which must result from these proceedings. On behalf of every Christian communion without exception, I wish heartily that all its best tendencies may be fully developed, and all its worse ones neutralized; most of all must I cherish this desire in regard to the greatest of them all, and one which must clearly have in the counsels of Providence its own special work to perform.

The persevering annexation of unlawful to lawful claims must at some time, in the loss of the former, entail heavy detriment upon the latter.

I am far from presuming to identify your view with

my own, but I confess I think that, notwithstanding all the qualifications you interpose, they are substantially akin to one another; and in any case I am desirous to show that it is in no spirit of religious controversy that I for one fervently desire the extinction of the temporal power properly so called. In truth, as to religious controversy, my appetite for it has never been keen, and I am more and more convinced, with the lengthening of life, that, except for those who are sentinels at posts of special dangers, the wise course is to endeavour, each in his sphere, however humble, to strengthen the foundations of belief, to ascertain and widen all real grounds of concord, and to revere and make the most of the elements of Divine truth whatever they may be found. . . .

Sincerely and respectfully yours,
W. E. GLADSTONE.

239. *To the Very Rev. H. E. Manning, D.D.*

WORSLEY HALL,
October 15, 1864.

MY DEAR MANNING,

. . . You will smile when I tell you that, in my sincere and sad conviction, it is you, and not I, who are helping on the 'Anticatholic' movement in Italy. I told General Garibaldi that if the Italian people lost the Christian Faith it would be a misfortune admitting of no compensation, to which declaration he seemed to assent. And in speaking of the Christian Faith, I mean the Christian Faith even with its accompaniments of a religious kind such as they now are. It is with no Protestant, no Anglican eye, that I look upon the present condition of Italy. I profoundly desire that that people may be kept in the position of Christian believers; and I am as profoundly convinced that the exercise of the Temporal Power in its present conditions is working powerfully to thrust them out of that position: from this point of view, my hostility to it is, I hope, intelligible, provided you give me credit (no small credit, I admit, in these times) for knowing what I mean and meaning what I say. I much dread the effect of the provocation and encouragement which, as

I think, you are giving (most involuntarily) to the unbelieving power in Italy and elsewhere. Some years ago I earnestly desired, in common, I think, with my colleagues, that the question of the Temporal Power could have been settled by placing it on the basis of a Suzerainty over the whole States of the Church. Perhaps, on a more restricted basis, if some such plan could be devised, it might be for the permanent interest of all parties to accept it. But Time is fighting against you, and he is a mighty foe.

To those proceedings of English religionists in Italy which you mention I have never given, and could not give, the smallest encouragement.

240. *To the Very Rev. H. E. Manning, D.D.*

Hawarden,
December 26, 1864.

My dear Manning,

. . . Now about the Italian question one word. In speech and letter I have tried to offer you suggestions in the hope of being useful, but forgive me if I say I have had nothing from you except in negatives — or in generals. But really neither of them help in the least. It is wholly vain to attempt to work out an understanding with those who will not contribute. What *will* do? That is the question.

My position is that Rome is inhabited by human beings, and that these human beings ought not to be taken out of the ordinary categories of human right to serve the theories of ecclesiastical power. But they are taken out of those categories, established by the Almighty, if, while other peoples are parties entitled to have something to say in the choice of their Governors, they are to be permanently held down in the basest of all servitudes, that imposed by foreign arms.

I have never said, and do not say, the Italian kingdom is entitled to put down the Papal Sovereignty: and I am well content with this treaty because it will open a clearer and more indisputable way to learning their real sentiments than there has yet been.

If on the one hand you are determined to fight in the name of religion against natural right and justice, you will not only set your teeth upon a file, but vitally hurt that which you dream of upholding. If on the other hand what you think necessary for the Head of your Church is security and dignity, defined by yourselves, depend upon it there are more effectual modes of securing them than clinging to the present state of things, which in truth not only gives neither, but brings the one into question, and I will make bold to say totally destroys the other.

241. *To Archbishop Manning.*

WILTON HOUSE,
September, 1866.

MY DEAR ARCHBISHOP,

. . . I wish to revert to the position of the Roman See with reference to its temporal power. No one who has to do in any capacity with the course of affairs in Europe *or* in Christendom can exclude such a subject from his mind. I have no mission in regard to it. It seems to be imagined that I am to repeat in Rome the step I took at Naples; I have no such intention, and I think the circumstances are wholly different. What stirred me in that case was a state of illegality armed with supreme power. The present question involves nothing of the kind, but offers to view a problem at once the most arduous and the most delicate. It has, however, probably been forgotten what my proceeding in the Neapolitan case really was. It was an appeal to the Neapolitan Government through the Court of Vienna and Lord Aberdeen. I resorted to the Press only on the failure of that appeal. In the Roman question I made certain assumptions which I presume are common to us both. That the Italian Government has not, as such, a title to the possession of Rome; that an ample provision, under the best guarantees which the European Order can afford, for the dignity, safety, independence, and becoming sustentation, of the Papal Court is an indispensable condition of any plan which ought to be entertained for averting any future or removing any present difficulties (in my view of such a plan it should contemplate the Pope's residence in Rome — nothing could be wholly satisfactory which should impair his freedom of choice in that respect); that the present political position of the Sovereign of Rome is such as to make it not less suitable for friends than adversaries to entertain the subject, and even to take the initiative if need were (in this proposition I refer especially to finance, which involves the independence and still more the dignity of the Roman See); that this political position is likely in one way or other to present aggravated difficulties after the withdrawal of the French force.

To these propositions I should add one of considerable breadth, in which, I fear, you would not give me countenance. I mean this, that it cannot be for the interests of religion to contravene the established principles of civil right by forcing a Government on the inhabitants of the Roman States through the employment, actual or impending and expected, of foreign arms. This I should call, in the Political Order, a *peccatum contra naturam*. I import this last proposition into the case because, in my opinion, if the Roman people are content to submit to civil government by a clergy, no one else has a title to interfere. But some think they will not be content, and others, who assert their contentedness, assert also that by smart practices they will be made to act as if discontented, so that on the whole, I suppose, there is ground enough common to us both for inquiring without impertinence whether any plan can be suggested which should at once place in the hands of the population, or of a Government accepted by them, the management *de facto* of civil affairs, and yet satisfy the conditions above laid down with regard to the dignity, safety, independence, and becoming sustentation, of the Pope and of the Roman Court. I look, then, for an answer to this question: and will seek it on either of two suppositions — the first, that of a local autonomy; the second, that of a transfer of the civil government to the hands of the King of Italy. A gift or delegation by the Pope himself, like a lease made perpetual if only the covenant be performed, guaranteed by the Powers of Europe and clothed in either of these two forms, might evidently be made effective for satisfying the popular and civil claims of justice, as I should like to call it, or the political and prudential exigency of the case, as it might be termed by others (whose language, I may add, would suffice for the purpose of my argument).

As between these two forms I rather suppose that the transfer to the King of Italy would be the better one for the interests of the Roman See. For not only could an ample source of revenue then be provided, but the gift or delegation might extend to the whole of the provinces recently subject to the sceptre of the Pope; and, what is more, a body so small as would be formed of the Pope's present subjects would have little sense of security, and foreign interference in the concerns of such a body might not only be used in the interest of the Church, but as a covert means of interference with the independence of the Supreme Pontiff.

Now, in looking over the four conditions, it seems to me as though there could be no difficulty in securing, under such an arrangement with such guarantees, the dignity, safety, and opulence, of the Pope and his Court. But the knot of the question lies in independence. What is demanded is that the free exercise of the spiritual power shall not be liable to be controlled by the action of the civil power in the country where the Pope resides. It was on this great subject that our conversation mainly turned. It is evidently difficult, but I cannot see that it is hopeless — provided, however, that each party will only ask what is *required for its avowed aim and purpose*. In this sense I shall try to treat of the points that were raised between us. I shall honestly endeavour to do as I would be done by, and to look at these points from your point of view at least as much as from my own. And what I understand you to mean is this: 'Not that the exercise of some temporal power is *per se* necessary for the Popedom, since then, indeed, "My kingdom *is* of this world," but that *in ordine ad spiritualia* it is necessary, if a perfect freedom and immunity in her exercise of the spiritual office cannot be maintained without it.'

Now, the first point you raised was that, if the temporal power were abandoned, the ecclesiastical corporations could not be maintained under the present law of Italy.

On this point I would submit that it is plainly *not* a question which would justify rupture on either side. To abolish the legal character of these corporations, even to confiscate their property, is different (as I apprehend) from the suppression of a religious Order, and is a matter of civil concern. It has been done in other countries compatibly with retaining communion with the Roman See; and consequently it might be done in the Roman State without essentially inverting any prerogative inherent in the Church. But on the other hand I cannot suppose that, if it were part of a great settlement otherwise satisfactory, the Italian Government would hesitate to recognize and maintain these corporations within the present Roman States just as the British Government recognize and maintain them in Canada.

The second point raised by you was, I think, the double one of civil marriage and divorce.

As regards the first I see no difficulty. Civil marriage, prevailing already in other countries of the Roman obedience, might prevail throughout Italy without raising any new question of difficulty. The Church ought, of course, to be allowed to take its own course in refusing to recognize such marriages as sufficient for religious purposes. With regard to divorce, I was not aware that it had received the sanction of the Italian Legislature. But if it has, it seems to fall under the same observations as the topic of civil marriage. It is not essential to the office of the Church that the State should prohibit divorce, though it is a violation of liberty and conscience if the State undertakes to give orders respecting the religious position of divorced persons. The independence of the Roman See is not impaired by the permission of remarriage in other countries where Roman Catholics dwell and exercise their religion: neither would it be so if the case (which, for one, I do not wish to see) should arise in Italy and in the States of the Church.

The third head mentioned by you as a difficulty was, I thought, of a more critical character. You stated that the Pope must have an absolute uncontrolled freedom of utterance on all matters appertaining to his office. I replied that I presumed his personal immunity would be a first condition of any arrangement, and that there could be no difficulty in guaranteeing freedom of utterance, if we reserve the right of the civil magistrate to maintain public tranquillity. To this you rejoined, Who is to be the judge whether any particular utterance of the Pope is dangerous to public tranquillity or not? The Pope, you urged, must have some one spot of ground where he shall be sovereignly free to prophesy as he may think meet, and where he shall not be gagged by any superior or rival authority. We referred to the case of France; and you contended that the inhibition recently issued by the Emperor with respect to a document proceeding from St. Peter's Chair was only tolerable in France *because* there was another place where no such inhibition could take effect, *videlicet*, the Roman territory, thus illustrating what was said, I believe, by Montalembert, that Church and State were capable of being separated everywhere else *by virtue* of their being identified in Rome.

In this one point of the case I admit that the claims on either side are such as may be viewed by the respective advocates in a manner that makes them difficult to bring together. Nevertheless I am convinced that neither is this a case in which rupture would be warranted. *Against* you I should argue as follows. The Civil Government, responsible for life [and?] property, cannot allow things to be done under the name of religion which assail public order. Words, not only of treason, but of sedition, must be repressed, by whomsoever they may be said. On the other hand, you need have no fear that the Pope will be unable to convey to the world whatever he may desire to make known to it. To what did Louis Napoleon's inhibition amount? Simply to a protest. It did not and could not limit the absolute publicity of any declaration which either the Pope or persons of infinitely less influence or consequence might desire to utter. It resembled a course often taken by our Government when we refuse to produce to Parliament some document which has already been in all the newspapers; because we do not wish to be made parties to the publication. Free utterance is essential, but it would not be in the least impaired by the retention of the right of the civil magistrate to put down whatever menaces the public peace. And a further practical answer is that it is not to be supposed, and never would happen, that the Pope would utter words of such a character. But if those whose main purpose it is to secure Papal independence were dissatisfied with the argument on that side, I should then turn to the other, and say that, however exceptionable it may be in the abstract for the civil power to abridge any of its essential prerogatives, this is a case in which an exception might be made. In delegating the power of Civil Government, and retaining only suzerainty or supremacy of dignity, of course any special reservation might be introduced. The right and power of the Pope might be kept entire to publish within the limits, say, of the city of Rome whatever he should think fit, without any limitation as to its political tendency. This would be his ποῦστῶ from whence by moral leverage to move the world: this the Delos where Latona might find refuge for the coming childbirth. Of course there must be a multitude of questions arising at the meeting-points of the secular and the spiritual spheres, which would have to be dealt with in detail. But all these, as far as I can yet imagine, are of the same character as have formed, from time to time, the subject-matter of *Concordats* between the See of Rome and the various States of Europe. And they would be dealt with for the local territory now under the Papal sway with no difficulty in kind different from those which have already in so many instances been encountered and overcome by the skill of negotiators like Gonsator.

The character of this letter is defensive. I have only noticed the points as to which it may *primâ facie* be contended that the surrender of the powers of Civil Government would apparently tend to weaken or disparage the Roman See. It would perhaps be impertinent in me were I to open the other side of the question, and consider the points in which such a change would go to secure and to enlarge the freedom and independence of the spiritual power. But I cannot do less than express my own conviction — entertained ever since, at the time I translated Farini, I began to think much and earnestly on this great subject

— that even at the very worst, even without the special guarantees which I fully admit should, at the instance of the Holy See, be given with every circumstance of solemnity, the general effect of the change would be to untie the hands of the Pope, and to leave him much more free to exercise his great and real powers than he is now, or than he can be while he remains in the ordinary and secular meaning of the term a Prince: and as a Prince subject to be dealt with as other Princes.

My feeling has ever been that those who are not in communion with the Latin Church, but who might be called upon from other causes to take any part, great or small, in this question, should not, and without gross breach of duty could not, even if they were polemically keen enemies of the Papacy, seek to destroy or diminish its spiritual powers under false pretences of civil right or justice. Nor, on the other hand, if they see that the civil change we have now in view would contribute to fortify the spiritual power of the Holy See, would they be justified on such a ground in forbearing to promote that change. In principle I feel myself entirely precluded from allowing any calculation of the effects of the change on the vast spiritual influence and power of the Roman See to govern my wishes or opinion respecting the change itself. But, in fact, I came to the conclusion that an increase rather than a diminution of such influence and power is to be expected as its result. To me the day when this necessary and beneficial mutation should be by consent accomplished would recall that verse of the psalm: 'Mercy and Truth are met together; Righteousness and Peace have kissed each other.'

It would be like a solemn reconciliation between the kingdoms of Providence and of Grace, between the two systems of kindred laws — the one which governs the structure of society, the other that which provides in so great a part of Christendom for the discipline of the soul.

I will only add one word. I think that provision of the treaty of September which prevents Rome from becoming, against the Pope's will, the seat of the Italian Government was a very wise and useful provision. And now I have done, forbearing to weary you with apologies which would make yet longer what is too long already.

    Believe me,
      Affectionately yours,
        W. E. GLADSTONE.

Mr. Gladstone's estimate of the importance of the Vatican Council was not exaggerated. When the Pope was declared infallible, the conciliar system, under which the Church had — in theory at all events — been governed since the third century, came to an end. The Latin Episcopate had cast their mitres at the feet of Pius IX. It would be a mere idle ceremony to call them together again when all that an Œcumenical Council had ever claimed to do could be done in future by the Pope in the exercise of his personal infallibility. The last trace of constitutionalism in ecclesiastical government had disappeared. From being an aristocracy the Roman Church had become an absolute monarchy. The letters that follow show how eagerly Mr. Gladstone watched for any opportunity of pressing upon the Curia the consequences of the step they were contemplating. It was hard, however, for a Protestant Power to take action when the Catholic Powers sat still, and the difficulty was the greater because England was unrepresented at the Vatican. But this unlucky circumstance only compelled her to 'fall into the rear'; it did not necessitate her remaining silent. It was specially important that we should not discourage other more happily-placed governments who might be meditating some combined action. One mode of such action might, he writes to Lord Clarendon in May, 1869, be to press the Curia to submit to the governments of Christendom a statement of such of the subjects intended to be brought before the Council as bore upon civil rights or the relations of Church and State. 'Such a representation would be reasonable, might act as a salutary check, and is such as even we in case of need might join in or support.' In this way we might help 'to do what the Reformation in many things did to save the Pope and the Roman Church from themselves.' In another letter he describes the Council as 'a pure piece of ultra-sacerdotalism. The pretence for the exclusion of the lay element is a piece of effrontery. There never was a Council which dealt so much with matter mixed as between religious and temporal interests.' Somewhat later he tells Mr. Odo Russell that 'the child yet unborn will rue the calling of this Council. For even if the best result arrive in the triumph of the Fallibilitarians, will not even this be a considerable shock to the credit and working efficiency of the Papal system?'

This last sentence is a testimony to Mr. Gladstone's genuine desire to see the Roman Catholic religion retain its influence in Europe, provided that this influence could be exercised on the old lines and through the old methods. Non-Latin, as well as Latin, powers were affected by these 'insane proceedings,' and he explains this view, as regards England, by his fear that the action of the Council may present 'augmented obstacles to political and social justice' in the English Parliament, even if it does not lead to 'a repetition of the fury of 1850-51.' In a letter to Döllinger he laments the existence of a feeling very widely spread and in strong contrast with his own. 'It is the feeling which first identifies the whole Latin Church with the Court of Rome and the Pope (and for this identification or solidarity present proceedings afford but too strong a plea), and then, treating this body as a sort of Incarnation of an evil principle, assumes that the worse it behaves, the greater will be the reaction and recoil of mankind, which reaction and recoil they treat as so much of accession on the side of good and truth. The whole of this theory, I need not say, I regard as radically false, but it prevails, and widely.' A very few days after this letter was written he had practical proof that his fears were well founded. On April 3, 1870, he writes to Mr. Odo Russell: 'We maturely considered in Cabinet yesterday whether we should try to reverse or alter the vote on Conventual Institutions. [Mr. Newdigate's motion for the inspection of convents, which had been carried against the Government.] We decided that we could not attempt it. . . . On Friday, Mr. Fawcett proposed a motion respecting Trinity College, Dublin, the real *effect* of which would have been to prevent anyone educated in a Roman Catholic College from proceeding to any Irish University Degree. It was only by making this question a question of confidence outright (and the use of such a weapon must needs be very rare) that we were enabled to defeat it.'

It is to be regretted that the Vatican Council coincided with the most engrossing period of Mr. Gladstone's political life. But for this, 'The Vatican Decrees in their Bearing on Civil Allegiance: a Political Expostulation' would have been written in 1870. As it was, the appearance of the pamphlet was delayed until four years after the Council had pronounced the memorable decree which declared it to be 'a dogma divinely revealed that when the Roman Pontiff speaks *ex cathedra* — that is, when in discharge of the office of Pastor and Teacher of all Christians, by virtue of his supreme Apostolic authority he defines that a doctrine regarding faith or morals is to be held by the Universal Church, he enjoys, by the Divine assistance promised to him in blessed Peter, that infallibility with which the Divine Redeemer willed His Church to be endowed in defining a doctrine regarding faith or morals; and that therefore such definitions of the Roman Pontiff are irreformable of themselves, and not from the consent of the Church.' But by 1874, when the 'Expostulation' appeared, the question had in a great measure passed out of men's minds. The material changes effected by the Franco-German War, though in reality of far less importance than the changes in the region of thought and opinion which can be traced to the Council, had for the time driven it into the background. The Old Catholics were already preparing a haven for those for whom submission was an impossibility, while those who were better versed in the art of reducing definitions put forth by a supreme authority to their smallest significance were already finding relief in the rarity of the occasions on which the Papal pronouncements satisfied all the conditions set out in the Vatican Constitution. On the appearance of Mr. Gladstone's pamphlet, the storm broke out with far greater violence than at first. In 1870 its publication might have served the cause he had most at heart; in 1874 it was more likely to injure it. In 1870 it might have encouraged moderate Roman Catholics who accepted the decree to minimize a dogma which had furnished occasion for so tremendous an indictment; in 1874 it only gave the Roman authorities an excuse for associating all who sought to reconcile the conclusions of the Council with history in a common condemnation with Mr. Gladstone. To attach the worst possible meaning to the decree would have seemed only natural at the moment when it first startled the world. To do it after a four years' interval seemed like ignoring the obvious fact that English Roman Catholics, at all events, had not the smallest intention of placing their 'civil loyalty and duty at the mercy of another,' even if that other were the Pope. At all times and in all countries the Roman Catholic laity have found ways of ignoring the Pope's commands when they go against their civil convictions. The proclamation of infallibility had not called forth a single effective remonstrance against the new order of things in Italy. To make his own spiritual subjects consistent in their acceptance of the new dogma, where politics came in, was as much beyond the power of Pius IX. after 1870 as it had been before that date. Not many years afterwards Mr. Gladstone was himself to discover this when, in the country in which above all others the Pope is revered, not a particle of attention was paid to the Pontifical condemnation of the Plan of Campaign.

Mr. Gladstone does not seem to have foreseen — perhaps no one in 1874 could have foreseen — the effects of the Vatican Council in another direction. The civil danger was imaginary; the spiritual danger was real — though how real was not to be fully understood until the temper and purpose of the Vatican Decree were revealed in Part III. of the Encyclical *Pascendi Gregis*. It is impossible not to wish that Mr. Gladstone's thoughts had turned in this direction rather than in that which they actually took. No man would have been better fitted to essay the tremendous task of reconciling the conflicting claims of authority and freedom. He saw the need of both. He saw that a revealed religion implies authority somewhere; he saw also that in these days the acceptance of authority must come from a convinced reason, not merely from a recognition that resistance is useless. There are things in Modernism that Mr. Gladstone would have disliked as heartily as Pius X. But he would equally have disliked the steps by which Pius X. has laboured to make his hostility effectual. 'A Theological Expostulation' founded on such a forecast as this would have been a permanent contribution to a controversy of which, in its present form, Mr. Gladstone was to see only the beginning.

242. *To Lord Acton.*

HAWARDEN,
December 1, 1869.

MY DEAR LORD ACTON,
I thank you for your most interesting letter. It is a very sad one. I feel as deep and real an interest in the affairs of other Christian communions as in my own, and most of all in the case of the most famous of them all, and the one within which the largest number of Christian souls find their spiritual food.

I habitually attach very great weight to information received from you. On this account I cannot wholly put aside, though I cannot fully accept, your belief that my opinion may be cited and turned to account in Rome. Therefore, from the great interest attaching to the subject, I have at once requested Lord Clarendon to telegraph to Mr. Odo Russell in cipher to-morrow as follows:

'Please tell Lord Acton he may use the strongest language he thinks fit respecting my opinion on the subject about which he desires it should be known. I will write by the earliest opportunity.'

That subject I take to be the effect in this country of 'Ultramontane' doctrines and proceedings upon legislation, policy, and feeling, with respect to Ireland,

and to the Roman Catholic subjects of the Crown generally.

That effect is, in my opinion, most unfavourable. Comparing this moment with thirty or forty years back, the number of Roman Catholics in England is increased, persons of extraordinary talent and piety have joined the Latin Church; but the bulk of thinking, conscientious, and religious people are, so far as I can judge, much farther removed from, or at any rate very much more actively and sharply adverse to, the Church of Rome than they were at the former period.

There is one question of first-rate national importance coming on, with respect to which I regret that this effect of Ultramontanism will be conspicuously exhibited: it is the question of popular education in the three countries. Indeed, we have already had a taste of it in the powerful opposition which was raised against the very moderate measure of justice which we attempted to carry in 1866 with respect to the Irish colleges and the Roman Catholic University, and the storm will rise again when we come back, as we must before long, to the subject of the higher education in Ireland.

The specific form of the influence will be this — it will promote the advancement of secularism. Ultramontanism and secularism are enemies in theory and intention, but the result of the former will be to increase the force and better the chances of the latter. Notwithstanding my general faith in any anticipation of yours, I cannot think it possible that Archbishop Manning will represent my opinions at Rome in any light different from this, and for the simple reason that he is a man of honour. He is, from our old friendship, thoroughly aware of my general leanings on these matters, and he has had particular reason to know them with reference to the present function. For recently he wrote to me about an interview, and in replying (it was to be just before his departure) I used expressions which I would cite textually if I had them at hand. But the purport was this: 'How sad it is for us both, considering our personal relations, that we should now be in this predicament, that the things which the one looks to as the salvation of Faith and Church, the other regards as their destruction!'

There has since been a very amicable correspondence between us, in which this idea has been canvassed and developed, but not in any measure qualified. Of course the terms used would have admitted of qualifications, had I not been desirous that my words should be strong and definite with respect to the present crisis, and plain speaking is our invariable rule. I shall send this letter to the Foreign Office, to go by the earliest safe opportunity for Rome. And much as I should like to have you here, I am glad you are there. It is also a great pleasure to me to address you by your new title, not as a mere decoration, which you would want less than any other man, but because I trust it opens to you a sphere of influence and action. We are in the thickest of the difficulties of Irish land tenures.

W. E. G.

243. *To Lord Acton.*

HAWARDEN,
January 8, 1870.

MY DEAR LORD ACTON,
I take the opportunity of a messenger from the Foreign Office to write a few lines.

My answer to your appeal was written on the instant, and I stated that which first occurred to me — namely, the additional difficulties which the rampancy of Ultramontanism would put in the way of our passing measures of public education which should be equitable, and not otherwise than favourable to religion.

But in truth this was only a specimen. There is the Land Bill to be settled, and there are the wings of the Church Bill: one the measure relating to loans for building, the other having reference to the Ecclesiastical Titles Act. Even the first will be further poisoned, and either or both of the two last may become the subject of fierce and distracting controversy, so as to impede our winding up the great chapter of account between the State and — not the Roman Church or Priesthood — but the people of Ireland.

The truth is that Ultramontanism is an antisocial power, and never has it more undisguisedly assumed that character than in the Syllabus.

Of all the prelates at Rome, none have a finer opportunity, to none is a more crucial test now applied than to those of the United States. For if there, where there is nothing of covenant, of restraint, or of equivalents between the Church and the State, the propositions of the Syllabus are still to have the countenance of the Episcopate, it becomes really a little difficult to maintain in argument the civil right of such persons to toleration, however conclusive be the argument of policy in favour of granting it.

I can hardly bring myself to speculate or care on what particular day the foregone conclusion is to be finally adopted. My grief is sincere and deep, but it is at the whole thing, so ruinous in its consequences as they concern faith.

In my view, the size of the minority, though important, is not nearly so important as the question whether there will be a minority at all. Whatever its numbers, if formed of good men, it will be a nucleus for the future, and will have an immense moral force even at the present moment — a moral force sufficient, perhaps, to avert much of the mischief which the acts of the majority would naturally entail. For this I shall watch with intense interest.

Believe me,
Most sincerely yours,
W. E. GLADSTONE.

244. *To Archbishop Manning.*

HAWARDEN,
April 16, 1870.

MY DEAR ARCHBISHOP MANNING,

Your letter of the 7th has only reached me to-day. In answering it I must draw a clear distinction between my personal opinions and the action of the Government, which represents, and ought to represent, something much weightier. *My* feelings and convictions are, as you well know, decidedly with your 'opposition,' which I believe to be contending for the religious and civil interests of mankind against influences highly disastrous and menacing to both. But the prevailing opinion is that it is better to let those influences take their course, and work out the damage which they will naturally and surely entail upon the See of Rome and upon what is bound to it. Consequently there has been here a great indisposition to forward even that kind of interference which alone could have been dreamt of — namely, a warning, in terms of due kindness and respect, as to the ulterior consequence likely to follow upon the interference of the Pope and Council in the affairs of the civil sphere. If asked, we cannot withhold, perhaps, the expression of our conviction, but we have not been promoters: nor do I consider that any undue weight would be given even to the most reasonable warnings by the authorities at Rome.

But there is a more limited aspect of these affairs in which I have spoken to you and to others, and that without the smallest idea of anything that can be called interference. From the commencement of the Council I have feared the consequences of (what we consider) extreme proceedings upon the progress of just legislation here. My anticipations have been, I regret to say, much more than realized. An attempt was made to force our hands on the subject of the higher education in Ireland, and practically to bind the House of Commons to an absolute negation of the principle which we laid down in 1865 and 1866. This attempt, premature, I think, even from the point of view held by its friends, we were only able to defeat by staking our existence as a Government upon the issue. Then came Newdegate's motion on inspection of religious establishments. Not only was this carried entirely against our expectations, but the definitive reports since made to me of the state of feeling in the House are to the effect that it cannot be reversed, even by the exercise of the whole influence of the Government. These facts are striking enough. But I seem to myself to trace the influence of the same bitter aversion to the Roman policy in a matter, to me at least, of the most profound and absorbing interest — I mean the Irish Land Bill. Perhaps Bishop Furlong's extraordinary letter, and the manner in which it seems to exhibit his ideas of the mode of discriminating between things secular and things spiritual, have helped to establish in the minds of men an association they might not otherwise have conceived. Be that as it may, the tone and atmosphere of Parliament have changed about the Land Bill: again for the second time within a fortnight I have been obliged to resort to something like menace, the strain thus far has been extreme, and I regret to say it is not yet over. I apprehend that these ill effects will be felt in other matters which impend, in two especially which are close at hand — ecclesiastical titles and national education. What I have described is no matter of speculation: I know it by actual and daily touch. I am glad you have moved me to state it in some detail. It is to me matter of profound grief, especially as regards land in Ireland. For I feel as if the happiness of some millions of God's creatures were immediately committed to us, so far as the things of this life (and their influence on the other) are concerned, and until it is disposed of, it seems to engross and swallow up my whole personal existence. *When* it is settled I shall begin to detach my hopes and interests, if I may, from the political future. Quite apart from what I have said, the question of national education is passing, I fear, into great complications; and crude opinion of all kinds is working blindly about like hot and cold, moist and dry, in Ovid's Chaos. . . .

245. To Dr. Guthrie.

December 11, 1870.

Excited, as it appears, by part of my letter to Mr. Dease which was recently published, and in which I state, on the part of the Government, that they consider what relates to the dignified support, freedom, and independence of the Pope to be legitimate matter for their notice, Mr. Matheson states that we 'do not charge ourselves with any responsibility in regard to the spiritual functions of the Moderator of the free Church or any other Dissenting body.' On this allegation of fact I join issue, and I say distinctly that we do charge ourselves with responsibility in the same sense as that in which I have said the Pope's condition is matter for our notice, and to a much greater extent. In the case of the Moderator of the Free Church we take care by law to maintain his independence, and to prevent its being interfered with. This independence, in the case of the Pope, we 'notice'; that is, we think it a fit subject for friendly representations against civil interference, in case of need, and so long as the Pope confines himself to spiritual functions. It is true we also speak of due support [for] the Pope. Now consider. He is a Sovereign, who was in lawful possession of large revenues, and who had charged himself with the support of a body of Cardinals, Ministers, Nuncios, servants, and guards, out of those revenues. He has been dispossessed, not for any fault of his own, but because clerical dominion was deemed intolerable. In the maintenance of the Pope and his Court followers and agents, six millions of our fellow-subjects, or thereabouts, are deeply interested; and they are making demands upon us which we are forced to decline. But I should, for one, be ashamed to deny that there are the strongest equitable claims upon the Italian Government growing out of the past state of things; that in these equitable claims the six millions I speak of have a real interest and share: and as the matter is international, and they have no *locus standi* with the Italian Government, it is our part so far to plead their cause if need be. I hope Mr. Matheson will consider what has been the state of things in Rome from 1849 to 1870. If he desires to prevent its return, I think the best way of estopping the unreasonable claims of the Roman Catholics and the Pope is freely to recognize those which are reasonable. . . .

246. *To Lord Acton.*

HAWARDEN,
August 22, 1872.

. . . I am struck with what seems to me something like an essentially false position in the case of the Italian Government. From the formation of the Italian Kingdom, or at any rate for a good many years, the Italian Government has refused to take any cognizance of the state of parties in the Roman Church. 'Tros Tyriusque mihi nullo discrimine habetur.' There is a party there which is at war with liberty and civilization. There is another party which holds principles favourable to both. The first party is strong, the other weak. The Italian Government has done nothing to uphold the weak and nothing to discountenance the strong, and now, with the Papal election in view, it desires to find means of averting the mischiefs which are too likely to follow from an election conducted by the dominant or Papal party. Its arguments, overtures, and wishes, seem to me to be in hopeless contradiction with its own conduct. Were it indeed possible to treat the question as purely religious, their attitude might be justified by logic. They might say Governments do not interfere in theological questions. We want our Ultramontanes to be good citizens, and such they may be however extravagant their merely ecclesiastical or theological opinions. Do they, then, hope to convert and pacify Ultramontanism in the civil sphere by letting it alone in the religious sphere? That may be possible, although I do not think it free from doubt, in England. But it is utterly and evidently impossible in Italy until the idea of restoring the temporal power shall have been utterly abandoned. Meantime temporal means, the powerful engine of starvation, are freely used by the ecclesiastical power against any priest who makes peace with the Kingdom of Italy. And nothing (as I believe) is done to sustain such priests in their unequal conflict. If this is so, how can the Italian Government wonder that its deadly and irreconcilable enemies should act towards it in conformity with the policy which it allows them to enforce against its own loyal subjects? The German Governments (I do not speak of the law against the Jesuits, on which I am ill able to give an opinion) are surely far nearer the mark, for they give some kind of support and countenance to what may be called the rational party in the Church. I feel deeply the reasonableness of the views of the Italian Government about the new election, but I also feel that it lies with itself to take the first step towards causing such views to prevail by giving countenance within its own sphere to loyal and right-minded priests. . . .

247. *To Dr. Döllinger.*

COLOGNE,
September 23-24, 1874.

MY DEAR DR. DÖLLINGER,
I will not leave Cologne for London and Hawarden (Chester, England) without writing to you a few lines on the subject which we last mentioned at Munich. But first I will mention the article agreed on at Bonn with regard to the Immaculate Conception: for I see that even the better newspapers in England, like the *Spectator*, are in a state of puzzle as to the scope of the propositions. The *Spectator* says every man who believes in the Immaculate Conception is to be shut out of the Bonn Concordia. This I take to be an error. You have not, if I am right, been fixing terms of communion among lay Christians, but considering of the terms on which theological controversy may be adjusted or narrowed in accordance with Scripture and Christian history. The measures of the two things are, I apprehend, totally distinct, and until corrected I shall rest with confidence in my own construction of the remarkable meeting at Bonn....

There is another subject on which I have been reflecting since I saw you, and on which I should be very glad to know your judgment. It concerns the position of those members of the Roman community who are resolved not to submit to the doctrine of Infallibility. I speak, of course, only of such as have a call and opportunity to inform themselves fully on the subject. Now, I do not see how such persons can be justified in point of consistency. They acknowledge the authority of the Pope by remaining in his communion, and yet they claim the title to repudiate what he, now backed by his Episcopate with scarcely an exception, declares to be an article of the Christian faith. It strikes me that it is in principle far less anarchical to seek for Christian ordinances at the hand of a provisional but orthodox organization such as the *alt-Catholische* than to claim the title at once to be within the pale and privileges of a certain communion, and to exercise the power of annulling by private judgment its solemn and formal ordinances of faith. I do not speak of any case except that in which faith is involved, and in which there can be no doubt or question that the living voice of the particular Church has actually spoken. Nor do I speak of the duty of to-day or to-morrow, but of the deliberate adoption of this or that position after sufficient time; for I suppose there can be no matter of greater difficulty, none in which conduct ought to be judged with more indulgence, than the decision by each individual on the precise *time* at which he is to move for his own defence and welfare, at a period when the scheme and system, under which he has lived, is itself shifting around him, and vitally altering its own character.

These considerations, again, can only apply, if I am right, to the case in which the false steps taken by authority are not only in subject-matter vital, but also in their character and expression final, so that no place or hope remains of the retrieval of the error through the normal action of the body.

Now I pass to my third and, I think, last subject (except the personal one). I understood distinctly that the work of theological conciliation begun at Bonn is to be continued in the future. I venture to ask whether it would not be well if each of those who co-operated in the late Conference were, in the interval before another one, to employ such opportunities as he may possess in obtaining the adhesions of weighty and competent men within his own circle to what has been done? I am led to offer this suggestion from the belief that in England, at least, much might be effected in this way. My idea would be the submission of the propositions to those likely to agree (on the very same principle as that of the Bonn Conference itself), not to those likely to differ, as the time for wide and general discussion cannot have arrived until further progress has been made. Of course this is not as a substitute for, but as an addition to, your design of preparing further adjustments on the points which have not yet been dealt with. . . .

W. E. GLADSTONE.

248. *To Dr. Döllinger.*

HAWARDEN,
November 1, 1874.

MY DEAR DR. DÖLLINGER,
This paper on Ritualism has attracted an attention that I did not expect from the general public. . . . Independently of its general aspect, it contains a sharp passage against the actual Roman Church. This passage has excited great wrath in the *klerikale partei.* There has been plenty of private remonstrance, and from the Papal Press some public indignation. A sentence in which I say that a convert joining the Roman Church 'places his civil loyalty and duty at the mercy of another' has told most. Now, in respect to this passage I hold that *they* are the aggressors. I feel it necessary to make good my words, and I have accordingly written, and am sending to press, a tract which will be entitled 'The Vatican Decrees in their Bearing on Civil Allegiance: a Political Expostulation.'

In this pamphlet I offer a friendly challenge to my Roman Catholic fellow-countrymen, inviting them to exculpate the decrees, or, if they cannot do that, to renounce and repudiate the civil consequences.

Had the facts been before me when I was in Munich, I should have desired to consult you largely. As it is, I feel the step to be one of some importance, and I have not taken it without anxious deliberation, and a great hope and desire to do my *duty.* I have to beg of you that you will read it as soon as you conveniently can: for it has an undoubted, though indirect, bearing on your position. I do not ask criticisms on the proof, nor shall I wait for them; but I much wish to know what you may think of it in its European aspect, if I may say without presumption that it has one. I can only add that, if you think its translation desirable, I hope you will either at once let me know, or even order it to be done. The sheets as struck off will be sent you, but I have been over them so many times that they can hardly differ much from the proofs.

All this may be a ludicrous over-estimate of the affair. But even the little passage has already been designated in a Romish periodical 'Mr. G.'s Durham letter,' and it is necessary or well to be prepared for all alternatives. . . .

Respectfully and affectionately yours,
W. E. GLADSTONE.

249. *To Dr. Döllinger.*

HAWARDEN,
December 8, 1874.

MY DEAR DR. DÖLLINGER,

. . . If [in his advertised reply] Manning goes back to his favourite thesis — that the Papal Church only asserts an independence which other communions also demand — I think it not difficult to answer him. The differences, I think, are these: 1. The *foreign* headship. 2. The Infallible Executive. 3. The claim to the *absolute* obedience of members. 4. The Roman Church alone, not content with liberty of judgment as a mental operation, claims it as a judicial power. (Thus the Pope declares to be *null* and *void*, not merely culpable, laws which he disapproves. I dare say you could give me instances where he has done this *outside* the States of the Church.) 5. In the case of the Roman Church these claims must be read in the light of her peculiar history.

An old antagonist of mine declares that, in my pamphlet, I do not show myself to be a Protestant (which he says I am not). This is true, and the nature of my book required that I should not attack the admitted religion of those to whom I was making what I declared to be a friendly appeal. For this, and for other reasons, I shall endeavour to hold this ground, and be deaf to whatever people may say on a subject which is really irrelevant.

Bishop Clifford has replied in the tone of a gentleman and a Christian. I think his argument fails entirely. . . .

250. *To Professor Mayor.*

HAWARDEN,
December 9, 1874.

I agree, I can hardly say how strongly, with all the leading propositions of the letter of Bishop Reinkens.

Between 1788 and 1829 the English Roman Catholics had slid all the way from rejection of Papal Infallibility to alleging merely that they were not bound to believe it. Between 1829 and 1874 the large majority of their laity have gone over, I fear, to what was in 1829 mainly a clerical belief among them. Unless some action is taken on behalf of conscience, another half-century will reduce the whole to a dead level of Manningism.

And what else? At the present day the Papal Communion in England is strong with a strength wholly factitious and unnatural, the imported strength of a most remarkable body of seceders. The strength of these men conceals the hollowness of the system, and keeps it in a certain amount of relation to human thought and culture, though from the purely national life it is totally estranged. But it will be impossible for these men to rear up within the present Anglo-Roman Communion successors equal to themselves. Ultramontane as they are, they are essentially hybrid, and there can be no propagation, so that in the next generation, according to all likelihood, not only will all be Ultramontanes, but the intellectual level of English Ultramontanism itself will have sunk enormously. As to a renewal of strength by immigration, that is beyond all reasonable likelihood. It supposes the repetition of Dr. Newman's genius and Dr. Newman's eccentric movement, due probably to a character not equal in force to his genius. And those who wish to anticipate the future in this respect may be aided by considering that some twenty years (or thereabouts) have now elapsed since any man of mental strength, in the theological sphere, surrendered himself from without to the Church of Rome.

For myself I lament all this deeply. It is impossible not to feel, objectively and historically, a strong interest in the *old* Anglo-Roman body. Suffering from proscription, and in close contact everywhere with an antagonistic system, it refused all extremes, and remained loyal in its adhesion, devout in religious duty, moderate and rational in its theological colour. All this is gone, and replaced by what Tennyson might call its 'loathsome opposite.'

I should be quite ready to join in any well-digested plan for making *Altkatholicismus* better known in

England through the medium of its recognized publications.

But when I look to the final appeal of Bishop Reinkens, my mind replies at once, 'Yes, it ought to be done,' but also I certainly am not the man to do it. Bishop Reinkens perceives that the political discussion has opened the way for the great theological and perhaps yet greater moral question. But were I at present even to open the second argument, I should simply with my own hand bar the access for the first to the mind of every Roman Catholic. To have a hope of getting a part, I must forbear to ask the whole.

251. *To Dr. Döllinger.*

HAWARDEN,
August 29, 1875.

MY DEAR DR. DÖLLINGER,
I have read with the best attention I could give the reports in the *Guardian* of your meeting at Bonn — and a half-sheet kindly sent me by Mr. MacColl, in which your whole result, as I understand it, on the great subject of the *Filioque* is presented.

I write under the impression that the four propositions drafted by you, and the six in which the doctrine of St. John Damascene is expressed, have not received a formal, but a moral assent, that they will be submitted shortly to the judgment of the Eastern Churches, that the Orientals of the Conference look confidently to an approval (query, whether any scruple may arise on the 6th?), that, if so approved, they would come before you at Bonn again next year, for a formal acceptance.

If that acceptance is obtained, a great practical question then seems to arise, Will the Eastern Church *thereupon* be prepared to join in the consecration of an Old Catholic Bishop, supposing another such Bishop to be needed? Or what further steps, if any, will be required before this joint consecration can take place, which would, I apprehend, be a full consummation of ecclesiastical communion?

This question, which interest in the subject prompts me to raise, is perhaps premature. I will therefore turn from it to two or three remarks which you will take as made by an outside spectator.

1. You have happily found a basis which recognizes the Oriental form, and yet saves the Western one from condemnation on the merits. Do not suppose I am suggesting any further concession in this respect when I say the impression left on my mind is that the Easterns have proceeded in that spirit of love which the Swiss pastor so awkwardly reçommended, and have admitted all they could. Does not this charge seem to lie against the *Filioque, on the showing of both parties:* viz., that the word *proceed* must, in order to obtain a warranty, be construed in two different senses, one as to the Procession from the Father, the other as to the Procession from the Son? Can this be denied? If it cannot, then can there be imagined a graver fault, short of heresy and theological falsehood, than to introduce into the great symbol of faith an equivocal term, which is made at the same time and in the same proposition, to assist two things in different senses? Is there any other example of such a thing in the Creeds? I remember being startled by an inscription on a tombstone in Rome, which commended somebody for *Religio in Deum et in Sanctos*. To justify this, the term *Religio* must be split into two senses: but then this was not in a *Creed*. Forgive me for presenting this to your mind.

2. It seems to me that your Conference has gone far towards the attainment of a purpose never (so far as I see) named in the debates, but yet of the utmost importance to your general design: viz., that of establishing the voice of the undivided Church as the legitimate traditional authority. . . .

252. *To Archbishop Lycurgus of Syra and Tenos.*

HAWARDEN,
October, 1875.

MOST REVEREND AND DEAR ARCHBISHOP,
The great pleasure which I derived from your Grace's letter of September 3 is almost lost in my sense of its weight and importance. Together with the other accounts I have received of the Conference

of 1875 at Bonn, it fully satisfies me of the reality of the progress that has been made; for I do not doubt that I may take your own language and spirit, and the proceedings of the Orientals at Bonn, as trustworthy indications of the general sense of the Eastern Churches. I look at the great question of the *Filioque* with none of the pretensions of a theologian or of a widely instructed historical student, but yet I am a layman whose habit it has been through life to observe, so far as he was able, the course of questions of this kind, and to gather in an irregular way all he could in respect to them. So regarding it, I have ever felt strongly the claims of the Eastern position, upon such grounds as these: that, when the Creed had once been (both) formulated and fully accepted by the Church, no addition could be made to it except by the fullest and most unequivocal force of authority that the constitution of the Church supplies; that the principle of authority was most deeply wounded in this case by an addition, which came into conflict with an injunction not to add; that in so high a matter, where the human understanding and language entirely fail, the simplest expressions, and those closest to Holy Scripture, are the best; that it was difficult to plead for this new definition the usual and valid reason that it was needed in order to exclude some new and threatening error; that rather, on the contrary, the Western form, though free from heretical or false intention, was not without danger of misleading the uninstructed; and, finally, I see not how to deny that the word 'proceed,' in the Western formula, is equivocal, since it means one thing in reference to procession from the Father, and another in reference to procession from the Son. Alike, then, as an individual, and on large and general grounds, do I rejoice to think that by efforts, to which your Grace has so importantly contributed, a solid ground of concord, scanned in a spirit of love and caution by most acute and instructed minds, has been reached, and measured out in theological language.

This, then, seems to be in your Grace's view a foundation laid, and the next question at once arises, What is to be built upon it? Now I have supposed, I hope not wrongly, that the proceedings at Bonn will be laid before the ruling authorities of the Eastern

Churches, and means taken in due time to ascertain whether those proceedings are approved. If they be approved, then we seem at once to find ourselves at the door of *action;* for will not the next question be, In what way can the Old Catholics of Germany obtain, upon the basis already defined, the participation of duly delegated Eastern prelates in the consecration of their Bishops? When a satisfactory answer to *that* question shall have been attained, what an enormous progress will have been made! A great controversy, obstinate for 1,000 years, will have found its practical solution. An exceedingly important dogmatic act will have been performed, which will excite very wide sympathies in the West, even among those not, perhaps, immediately included in its effects — I mean among all believing Protestants, not to speak of Anglicans, or of moderate men in the Roman Church — and that opposition to Curialism, of which the Old Catholics of Germany are the foremost representatives, will have hardened into a form such as immensely to strengthen its promise both of durability and of influence. It will also have sealed, by a formal act, the *principle* on which it has necessarily fallen back, namely, adhesion in all matters *de fide* to the rule of the undivided Church. For myself as a mere unit, or I might say atom, in the Christian world, I can only say that I regard the promotion of a work such as I have here faintly sketched, in the light of the Crusades of history, but which escapes what in them there was of danger, and utterly shuts out that vein of ambition and self-seeking which, I fear, had much to do at times with the Papal action in regard to them.

At a period when the extraneous action of the Eastern Churches has been so beneficial to Christendom, I naturally feel an enhanced interest in their inward state and reciprocal relations. I trust that the Bulgarian Schism may have been less mischievous than seemed probable, and that means may speedily be found of healing it. With regard to the great ethnical division of Sclavonic and Hellenic Christians, only misconduct or political scheming on one side or both can make it dangerous, because the principle of local circumscription, faithfully maintained by the Eastern Churches against the overreaching supremacy asserted by Rome, will provide for each country and people according to its own rights, duties, and necessities.

I should much rejoice to hear that the outrageous invasion by the Papal See of the rights [of] the Americans was likely to bring about their union with the Eastern Church.

And now I turn to matters nearer home. I read with very great interest and pleasure your Grace's report of your visit to England, which of itself constitutes no inconsiderable event in ecclesiastical history. I pass by your little-merited notice of me with my cordial thanks only, for I am coming to what is more important, namely, your description of the Thirty-nine Articles of the Church of England as its * . Your Grace will not be sorry if, by a perfectly impartial statement, I can satisfy you that this description is not historically accurate. A confession of faith is, I apprehend, in the strictest sense binding upon all members of a Church. But the Thirty-nine Articles are in no sense binding upon the laity of the Church of England: they touch only the clergy. For more than 200 years they were subscribed by lay members of the University of Oxford, but this was by an obligation not ecclesiastical, it was purely exceptional, and it has ceased to exist.

There is a law which forbids a layman to 'deprave,' which I suppose means violently to assail or deny what is in the Book of Common Prayer; but even this law, I believe, does not touch the Articles. But neither as respects the clergy can it be said that the Articles have a greater binding force than the Prayer-Book. They do not profess to be a confession of faith, and they contain some things which have nothing to do with faith. They are prefaced by a title quite distinct from that of a Creed, and the Church of England at the Reformation added nothing whatever to these Creeds accepted by the West. The clergy are bound to the Articles in the same manner and terms as to the Book of Common Prayer. In legal authority they are conjoined together. But in practice there is this

* Blank in original.

difference, that the Book of Common Prayer supplies the subject-matter of religious worship, and this most vitally enters into the spiritual food of the people, and, in fact, gives them in a very high degree their specific religious tone.

In a practical point of view, the Prayer-Book represents the Catholic and historic aspect of the Church of England, the Articles the particular phase brought out by the events of the sixteenth century. I speak of both in the main: for some of the most Catholic declarations are in the Articles, and one or two of the most Protestant are in the Prayer-Book. Lord Chatham said the Liturgy, or Prayer-Book, was Popish, the Articles Calvinistic. No doubt their colour is distinct, but I do not think that, rationally and comprehensively understood, they are in contradiction. Our divines would say generally that they integrate one another, but would assign the greater moral weight in importance to the Prayer-Book. Much depends upon a careful consideration of the date of the Articles, and of their precise language. In some important points, when the Council of Trent has been moderate and guarded in its statements — for instance, the doctrine of Purgatory — the Articles preceded the Council, and what they condemn is the current or popular doctrine, of which there was so terrible a specimen in Tetzel. With rubrics the Articles have no concern. Their vague definition of the Church determines little or nothing, and bears the stamp of accommodation to the difficulties of the times out of which they grew. When Queen Elizabeth came to the throne, all the parochial clergy except less than a hundred conformed, and it was necessary to have some rule or standard of preaching, but the Queen did not then allow the Articles to become a law of the land; and this she only acceded to when the violence of Pope Pius V. led him to excommunicate and depose her, and she was compelled to consolidate her means of resistance. Excuse this long explanation, for the matter is of some consequence.

Allow me to subscribe myself, with profound respect,
   Your most faithful and humble servant,
        W. E. GLADSTONE.

253. *To the Rev. T. G. Law.*

HAWARDEN,
October 24, 1880.

. . . I will answer your question by relating a conversation which took place between Dr. Döllinger and myself when I first knew (and greatly admired) him in the year 1845.

I opened this question, and said I understood that it had not been proved that anyone was put to death in the reign of Elizabeth who was willing to abjure the deposing doctrine.

He rejoined that he believed this was so, but observed that they were required to abjure it *inter alia* as heretical, and that this was a technical term with a special definition, under which the deposing doctrine did not fall.

I was struck with the answer, and reserved it for reflection. When I reflected on it, I thought the reply after all insufficient, because it did not appear that the refusal to abjure had ever turned upon this rather nice though not unreal point; nor does anyone, so far as I know, suppose that the Government sought to catch people in a trap like this.

I understand by persecution proceedings taken for opinions in religion which do not involve consequences dangerous to the existing order. . . .

254. *To the Rev. R. R. Suffield.*

HAWARDEN,
December 31, 1882.

. . . I pray you to join in the representation which I have more than once pressed upon Mr. Law, that he, a highly qualified person, would in the interest of historic truth deal thoroughly and once for all with the really important question *whether and how far* religious persecution, properly so called, was used by the Government of Queen Elizabeth against the Papal party: a question which as yet I do not believe to have found its public solution. His knowledge makes him formidable, but I am sure he would not execute the work in the spirit of a partisan. . . .

255. *To Lord Acton.*

ST. LEONARDS,
March 26, 1891.

. . . Your account of Dr. Döllinger is intensely interesting. With my inferior faculty and means of observation, I have long adopted your main proposition. His attitude of mind was more historical than theological. When I first knew him in 1845, and he honoured me with very long and interesting conversations, they turned very much upon theology, and I derived from him what I thought very valuable and steadying knowledge. Again in 1874, during a long walk, when we spoke of the shocks and agitation of our time, he told me how the Vatican decrees had required him to reperuse and retry the whole circle of his thought. He did not make known to me any general result, but he had by that time found himself wholly detached from the Council of Trent, which was indeed a logical necessity from his preceding action. The Bonn Conference appeared to show him nearly at the standing-point of Anglican theology.

I thought him more liberal as a theologian than as a politician. On the point of Church Establishment he was as impenetrable as if he had been a Newdigate. He would not see that there were two sides to the question.

I long earnestly to know what progress he had made at the last towards redeeming the pledge given in one of his letters to me, that the evening of his life was to be devoted to a great theological construction.

I once proposed to him the idea of republishing in series the works of (so to call them) the Henotic writers. He entered into it warmly. I then propounded it to Dr. Mozley, the Regius Professor, who did the like. I wanted it done by the Oxford Faculty. But Dr. Bright took some sideways objection which blocked it, and Mozley's life was unhappily soon cut off. . . .

I should have called Dr. Döllinger an anti-Jesuit, but in no other sense, that is in no sense, a Jansenist. I never saw the least sign of leaning in that direction. . . .

He was surely built upon quite other lines. Jansenism was too narrow for such a profound and comprehensive historic mind.

256. *To the Lord Chancellor (Herschell).*

LONDON,
November 9, 1892.

Is it quite certain that the following points have been fully considered (*re* Princess Marie's descendants):

1. Is there a general definition in law of a Protestant?
2. Or in usage?
3. If it be said a Protestant is a Western Christian who disagrees with, and is separated *de facto* from, the Church of Rome, this definition would cover (1) the Old Catholics, (2) the Church of Utrecht, neither of which would, I believe, accept the name of Protestant. What, then, is the true legal definition?
4. It seems to me as an outside ignoramus that the two Acts of 1 William and Mary — (1) for establishing the coronation oath; (2) for settling the succession to the Crown — are oddly but substantially related. This Act of Settlement is wholly penal, negative, and anti-Roman. It enacts that the Sovereign shall be Protestant, but, without defining the word, it ascertains the fact by the stringent declaration from 30 Charles II. Is that declaration still imposed upon the Sovereign at coronation? If it is, it is amply and directly sufficient of itself to exclude not only Roman but Orthodox (this, not by its condemning Transubstantiation, but by its condemning invocation). In this case *cadit quæstio.*
5. Besides this [the] Act for maintaining, the coronation oath requires the Sovereign to maintain the Protestant reformed Religion established by law, but it points to no Protestantism other than that of the Established Church, and even of this it does not require the profession.

So that thus far, the intention manifestly being to have a Protestant throne, Protestantism had only a negative definition by renunciation.

6. But when we come to 12 and 13 William III. we find a more complete arrangement. Nothing is

done to derogate from the affirmative provision already established for the succession, but a new affirmative provision appears. The Sovereign must join in communion with the Church. May it not be said that, for the purposes of the Act, this provides a statutory definition of Protestantism? and that it attempts no other? and that it might be hard to exclude a person complying with this condition *by virtue* of the enactment that the Sovereign is to be Protestant? What right would there be to interpret the law penally against a person fulfilling its only defined positive condition, by virtue of a form to which the legislature has not thought fit to annex any other definition?

7. It being borne in mind that if dissent from the Pope be the popular idea of Protestantism, the Orthodox dissent from him rather more strongly than we do — *i.e.*, on the Nicene Creed itself.

A curious question arises whether a Stundist could succeed. They believe rather less than a Quaker; so that if limitation of belief (which is far from the historical and original meaning) were the condition they might qualify; but then they are Easterns.

All this, which may be quite worthless, tends to the conclusion that there is no absolute barrier to exclude an Eastern from the throne (if willing to communicate and take the coronation oath), unless it be in the declaration of 30 Charles II. . . .

257. To the Bishop of Tenos.

HAWARDEN,
January 4, 1895.

TRÈS RÉVÉREND ET VÉNÉRABLE ÉVÊQUE,

Un dérangement de mes yeux m'a empêché de répondre plus promptement à la lettre, également pieuse et condescendante, que votre Grandeur a bien voulu m'adresser.

Très, vieux au seuil même de la mort, je suis bien sensible du besoin de m'attacher à la foi de N.S. Jésus-Christ, et à l'Église qu'Il a bâtie sur la terre avec la promesse de perpétuité indéfectible.

Baptisé peu de jours après ma naissance, je n'ai rien

fait sciemment pour me séparer de cette Église, et je crois fermement que, bien que tout-à-fait indigne, j'y appartiens.

J'aime toujours me reposer sur le doux souvenir de l'Homme-Dieu, et sur le fait que toutes les parties du monde Chrétien le confessent, plutôt que d'entrer sur la voie des controverses épineuses qui divisent les Chrétiens, et qui se sont beaucoup aggravées depuis que l'action et le nouveau dogme de 1870 ont expulsé du sein de l'Église latine mon cher ami Dr. Döllinger et une foule de personnes les plus dévouées et les plus instruites de cette Eglise.

A l'île de Tinos, votre Grandeur se trouve à côté de cent million Chrétiens orientaux qui n'ont pas changé leur foi, et qui croient que le Pape, qui doit être le premier de tous les Evêques, est malheureusement le plus ancien des Dissidents, qui a débité des nouveautés, et coupé l'Eglise de Jésus-Christ en deux parties.

Vers l'Occident, je trouve près de cent cinquante million de Chrétiens de maintes parties du monde, qui, comme les Orientaux, ne peuvent pas souscrire à l'infaillibilité du Pape, et qui savent, comme moi je sais :

1. Que, parmi les Papes, il y a eu au moins trois hérétiques, viz., Liberius, Vigilius, et Honorius.

2. Que, pendant 40 ans, il y avaient deux Papes et deux églises latines ; l'une à Rome et l'autre à Avignon. Y avaient-il donc deux Saints Pierres ?

3. Que, selon le Concile œcuménique de Constance, c'était à un pareil Concile, le cas échéant, de se faire juge du Pape.

Depuis l'année 1845, j'ai connu, révéré, aimé Dr. Döllinger ; il était même à cette époque, très bienveillant pour moi, et m'a enseigné maintes choses. R.I.P. Pour lui, avec son instruction énorme, l'infaillibilité du Pape était un mensonge. Ce serait pour moi la même chose, et la profession d'un mensonge frayerait donc pour moi le chemin de l'enfer.

J'ai connu pendant une demie-siècle les Cardinaux Newman et Manning, et le Marquis de Ripon, et je suis solidement conviancu qu'ils joueront à l'autre monde, tous les trois, de la Vision béatifique de Dieu. Continuez donc, je vous prie, vos bons offices pour moi, et suppliquez que la miséricorde de Dieu et le Sang précieux de Jésus-Christ me donnent leur aide efficace, et à la fin admettent à la porte du Paradis *me principem peccatorum.*

En remerciant chaudement votre Grandeur de votre charité paternelle, j'ai l'honneur de me souscrire de votre Grandeur le fils et serviteur très dévoué et très humble,

W. E. GLADSTONE,
Ancien Ministre.

258. *To the Rev. T. A. Lacey.*

HAWARDEN,
July 3, 1896.

MY DEAR SIR,
  I thank you for your tracts, and I think we are all indebted to you and Father Puller for undertaking so bravely an arduous work, which I do not suppose could have been better performed.

I have read the Encyclical, and have not enough knowledge to see in it all that Mgr. Gasparri describes: but I see nothing at variance with his view, nor anything which ought to inspire dark anticipations as to the Pope's eventual utterance on the subject of Anglican Orders. I do not allow myself to be very sanguine about that utterance: but I read the Encyclical, with its strong self-assertion of the Papacy, as intended to clear the ground for whatever he may have to say, and to let his flock know that, whatever it may be, they have nothing to do but to obey it

The Pope has sent through Cardinal Rampolla to the Abate Tosti for transmission to me a very kind and gracious message.

We were much pleased with the Abbé Duchesne, whom Lord Acton conceives to be the most learned man in France.

The 'Life of Manning' and the Duchesne movement are enough to make this a considerable year in the history of the Church.

  I remain, my dear sir,
    Faithfully yours,
      W. E. GLADSTONE.

259. *To Sir Walter Phillimore, Bart.*

Penmaenmawr,
November 2, 1896.

My dear Phillimore,

You have laboured most unsparingly and kindly, and clearly seem to be at the end of your tether. It is a pity that Halifax has no information to give: absolute zero. I think that everyone concerned was generously unwilling to disturb what seemed to be a generous proceeding, and you seem to have been the only person who knew how to affix any meaning to the restrictions intimated.

The only object of my questions was to obtain additional security against falling into injustice towards anyone, if and when I come to write anything which I feel still that I probably ought to do.

The whole affair gives me the lowest possible idea of the Pope's statesmanship, but I do not think we can make a case against him in point of fairness and truth.

I have obtained from Tosti the letter I wanted to see, and have written to him again to wind up the matter and say a word for the Church of Henry VIII.

If I write, depend upon my eschewing all that could implicate others.

Ever yours sincerely,
W. E. Gladstone.

CHAPTER III

THE CONTROVERSY WITH UNBELIEF

1864–1894

At first sight the letters in this chapter have a strangely antiquated air. There is nothing in them about the authorship of the Fourth Gospel, or the alleged symbolical character of the incidents recorded in it, or the conflict between the Christology of St. Paul and that of the Synoptic Gospels, hardly anything about Evolution, and very little about the date of the Hexateuch. But the two themes which recur so often in the following letters — the mystery of sin and the limitations of human knowledge — hold as large a place in the controversies of to-day as in those of a generation ago.

In two letters written earlier than any here printed, Mr. Gladstone applies to Miss Martineau's 'Deerbrook' very much the same treatment that he afterwards applied to Mrs. Humphry Ward's 'Robert Elsmere.' Good fiction had always a serious attraction for him. Of 'Deerbrook' he says that, while 'there is much in it that is good,' and 'the latter part is very interesting,' the religious system on which the book is founded deserves only condemnation. 'It is fatal.' It recognizes 'some of the ends which Christianity proposes to effect upon the human character,' but it puts aside the Divine provision which can alone bring those ends about. Modern Unitarianism he characteristically compares to 'a tall tree scientifically prepared for the saw by the preliminary process, well known to woodcutters, of clearing away with the axe all projecting roots, which as long as they remained rendered the final operation impossible. This first process leaves the tree standing in a very trim condition, much more mathematical in form, as it is more near a cylinder, than in its native state. The business of the saw, when the horse and the man arrive, is soon accomplished.' His handling of 'Robert Elsmere' is on the same lines. The aim of the writer is to preserve the moral elements in Christianity while rejecting the supernatural elements. Had Mr. Gladstone lived a little longer, he would have seen the impossibility of this attempt demonstrated by its abandonment — not, indeed, by Mrs. Ward, but by almost every other Agnostic teacher. There is no longer the professed acceptance of the moral precepts of Christ that there was in the eighties. Science claims to have shown that in some of its features the morality of the Sermon on the Mount is the morality of an ascetic or a mystic, not that of a man or woman living in a world the conditions of which were unknown to the Preacher. The newest attack on Christianity is an attack directed, not against this or that article of the Christian creed, but against the whole Christian system. That system is as bad morally as it is intellectually or theologically. It is Mr. Gladstone's chief merit as an apologist that he recognized the inevitableness of this development long before it had been reached. 'I am always inclined,' he says, speaking of 'Robert Elsmere' (Letter 282), 'to consider this Theism as among the least defensible of the positions alternative to Christianity.' To-day there is hardly anyone left to defend it. Over the whole field of the relations of the sexes, for example, the restraints of Christianity are less and less accepted as binding. They are openly challenged or quietly ignored alike in our novels and in our plays, and when he who seeks to maintain their permanent character is no longer allowed to plead the precepts of Christ, he may easily find it impossible to make good his case.

In some of these letters we meet the same method as that on which Mr. Gladstone so much relied in the Roman controversy. The doubter is blamed, not because he cannot believe, but because he does not really wish to believe. Difficulties have been first played with out of curiosity, and then welcomed without any real effort to get the better of them, or any adequate knowledge of the other side of the argument. Here comes in his devotion to Butler. An opponent maintains that the orthodox conclusions are not certain. 'Granted that they are not,' Mr. Gladstone replies, 'are the conclusions you seek to substitute for them any more certain? Upon other matters we are constantly compelled to accept probable conclusions as the best we can get, and we do in fact act upon them as though they were certain. Religion is not exempt from this universal law. The exceptional thing about it is that the honest and practical acceptance of its teaching generates a moral conviction different alike in kind and in force from that which is felt in other matters. 'For Doubt,' says Mr. Gladstone, 'I have a sincere respect, but Doubt and Scepticism are different things. I contend that the sceptic is of all men on earth the most inconsistent and irrational. He uses a plea against religion which he never uses against anything he wants to do or any idea he wants to embrace — viz., the want of demonstrative evidence. Every day and all day long he is acting on evidence not demonstrative: he eats the dish he likes without certainty that it is not poisoned; he rides the horse he likes without certainty that the animal will not break his neck; he sends out of the house a servant he suspects without demonstration of guilt; he marries the woman he likes with no absolute knowledge that she loves him; he embraces the political opinion that he likes, perhaps without any study at all, certainly without demonstrative evidence of its truth. But when he comes to religion he is seized with a great intellectual scrupulosity, and demands as a pre-condition of homage to God what everywhere else he dispenses with, and then ends with thinking himself more rational than other people.' In another letter there is a passage much to the same effect: 'What does a little surprise me is, the facility with which many men persuade themselves that by the adoption of certain negative processes they can cut these difficulties away. This I find to be far beyond my power; and it is my conviction, so far as my thought and experience have carried me, that departures from what is called Orthodox Christianity in its main points, while they remove or lessen certain difficulties of a minor class, greatly aggravate the more serious parts of the problem.'

For the last thirty years of his life Mr. Gladstone gave much thought to the question of Future Punishment. There is among his papers a packet of manuscripts on this subject, with the date of 1879 on them, and the note: 'From this I was called away to write on Bulgaria.' A pretty complete statement of his views on the question will be found in the letter to his daughter-in-law,

Mrs. W. H. Gladstone (Letter 289). His attitude towards the theory of Natural Immortality may have changed somewhat during the last years of his life, but his sense of our ignorance of everything connected with the future life, beyond the certainty that judgment awaits us, and that it will be the judgment of an absolutely just God, Who knows our actions and our motives, and will weigh everything that either mitigates or adds to our responsibility in regard to them, never varied. It follows from this that, while all dogmatizing on the subject is out of place, it is especially so in the case of the heathen. To them applies the description of the last judgment given in St. Matthew's Gospel, where the final sentence turns wholly on the natural virtues, while the principle on which Christians will be judged is rather to be looked for in the Parable of the Talents.* The certainty of future retribution is not a greater mystery than the existence of evil (Letter 287). Why should those who have to accept the one, because they see it all around them, find the other a stumbling-block? What does man know of the ways of God beyond that small fraction of them which is revealed to him for his personal guidance? This is the question which Mr. Gladstone asks again and again, and what is there to be added to the 'Nothing' which was his constant answer? The difficulties honestly felt about future retribution seem to derive their main force from a lurking doubt of Divine justice or of Divine omniscience. 'There is no one,' says Mr. Gladstone (Letter 280), 'whose ultimate judgment would carry more weight with me' than Dean Church, and in view of this I will

* This illuminating distinction may be generally drawn by theologians, but I am indebted for it to some 'Notes on the Gospels,' by the present Bishop of Salisbury.

venture to quote from his letters a passage which seems to me to express Mr. Gladstone's conclusion even better than anything of his own writing: 'Of the publicans and sinners I do not doubt that many will see and know Him *there* who did not know Him *here*. But I cannot tell who they are. I only know that now, as far as I can see, they are going against His will. I do not know, for He has not said a word to tell me, what He will do with them. Man's destiny stops not with the grave. There may be discipline for character and will beyond it. But I cannot speak of it, for I know nothing of it. I only know the discipline which goes on here, and which we are told is so eventful. I have, on the one hand, all the hopes which spring out of God's infinite perfection. I have, to check the speculations of anxious human sympathy, the certainty of my own ignorance — ignorance the depth of which I cannot measure or comprehend; and, further, the very awful fact of the difficulty with which character and will undergo a change when once they are fixed and confirmed.'*

For the Book of Genesis Mr. Gladstone had an affection akin to that which he felt for the 'Iliad.' He held that the account of the Creation in the first chapter had not been invalidated by the discoveries of geologists, and he accepted this without the modifications which he found no difficulty in admitting as regards other parts of the narrative. Speaking for himself, he would not reject the historical sense of the book, but he thought that 'the aim and sense of Scripture' might 'stand with the parabolical.' Whether there was an earlier man than Adamic man seemed to him an open question, and apparently he saw no difficulty in the

* 'Life and Letters of Dean Church,' p. 264.

evolution of man from the anthropoid apes. The 'dust of the earth' out of which Adam was created may have been dust that had already passed through many forms. His opinion of the controversy about the dates and authorship of the Old Testament books will be found in a letter to Lord Acton (Letter 288). But it is in the letter to Sir Thomas Acland (Letter 291) that we shall find, I think, the best expression of Mr. Gladstone's permanent attitude towards unbelief. Inconclusive as he thought its reasoning, disastrous as he believed its influence to be upon human conduct and human happiness, he was under no illusions as to the steadiness of its advance. The only force that could offer any successful resistance to its progress was the Church, 'the appointed instrument of the world's recovery.' But the Church seemed no longer equal to the work. Where spiritual gains and losses were concerned, Mr. Gladstone had no faith in statistics. Lists of new churches, of additional services, of young men's clubs, of mothers' associations, of all the nominally religious machinery which makes so fair a show on paper, left him unmoved by the side of the fact that the incoming tide was steadily covering fresh ground.

260. *To the Bishop of Salisbury (Hamilton).*

February 8, 1864.

MY DEAR BISHOP OF SALISBURY,
  I did not like to speak to you about the coming judgment of to-day, which has, I fear, weighed upon you by anticipation, and which I have just heard nearly the whole of. You will not, I hope, allow it to depress you overmuch. You have done to the best of your judgment what seemed to be your duty. The result did not lie with you. What that result is in its ulterior meanings and consequences is a question, I

suppose, much too vast for us. This new and grave occurrence appertains to a transition state through which the Christian faith is passing. The ship is at sea, far from the shore she left, far from the shore she is making for. This or that deflection from her course, from this or that wind of heaven, we cannot tell what it is, or whether favourable or adverse to her true work and destination, unless we know all the stages of the experience through which she has yet to pass. It seems to me that these judgments are most important in their character as illustrations of a system, or, I should rather say, of the failure of a system, parts of a vast scheme of forces and events in the midst of which we stand, which seem to govern us, but which in reality are themselves governed by a hand above. It may be that this rude shock to the mere Scripturism which has too much prevailed is intended to be the instrument of restoring a greater harmony of belief, and of the agencies for maintaining belief. But, be that as it may, the valiant soldier who has fought manfully should be, and I hope will be, of good cheer.

261. *To the Bishop of London (Tait).*

11, Carlton House Terrace,
April 26, 1864.

My dear Lord Bishop,
You have been so obliging as to send me a copy of the sermons you have recently preached on the Word of God and the ground of Faith. I had been fortunate enough to hear one or more of them, and have read with cordial admiration the powerful arguments and exhortations contained in others. But I think it is the preface which I am to regard as having been specially in your lordship's view when you sent me the book; and it would be an ill return for your uniform kindness, were I to receive such an appeal in silence, and keep back from your lordship my sentiments, unimportant to everyone besides myself as they are, on the subject to which it refers.
I heard the judgment delivered in the cases of Dr. Williams and Mr. Wilson. It was impossible to

avoid being struck first with its ability, and next with its reserve; and I restrained myself from passing any hasty judgment upon its character and tendencies, for I could not but admit its importance, though I do not understand that either history, religion, or the Constitution, permit me to regard the Court as 'the highest authority in Church and State,' or as being an authority in the Church at all, though it may be one which is in a certain and an important sense over the Church.

The result of as much reflection as I have been able to bestow upon the subject during the weeks that have followed up to the present time has been growingly and extremely painful.

It appears to me that the spirit of this judgment has but to be consistently and cautiously followed up in order to establish, as far as the Court can establish it, a complete indifference between the Christian Faith and the denial of it.

I do not believe it is in the power of human language to bind the understanding and conscience of man with any theological obligations, which the mode of argument used and the principles assumed would not effectually unloose.

The same processes which have now been applied to the inspiration of Holy Scripture and to the doctrine of future punishment will, in my opinion, when the time arrives, be found equally effectual in their application to the doctrines (for example) of Original Sin, of the Atonement, and of the Divinity of our Lord; and I can only thank God for the sake of my children and my country, that the Primates of the Church have given their voices in the sense which refuses all concurrence in the responsibility of the proceeding, and leads to the hope that belief is still to be vigilantly guarded and maintained among us.

I freely admit that nothing can be more innocent in itself than a declaration that we may, without contradicting the doctrine of the Church, freely question matter which is found in the text of the Holy Scriptures, but which is 'unconnected with religious faith or moral duties.' But this affords me little comfort when I reflect that the issue raised in these cases was not at all about a liberty to be exercised in matter 'unconnected with religious faith or moral duties,' but, on the contrary, about the exercise of such liberty in regard to the declarations of Scripture which directly belong to its office as the Word of God.

With respect therefore to the real meaning of the judgment, it seems to me that this must be found in the scope and character of the inculpated matter which it has acquitted, and which it has mulcted the Bishop of Salisbury and Mr. Fendall in costs for questioning. I confess it appears to me that a person deriving his knowledge of this portion of the case from your lordship's preface would be entirely misled as to the nature of the transaction that has taken place.

With respect to the mode in which the judgment has dealt with the question of punishment hereafter, it is a mode which seems to me, under the notion of judicial construction, to destroy the force of words, and to encourage men to tamper with their own consciences and sense of truth by accepting from a Court that absolution for breach of engagement which they would justly and indignantly reject if tendered to them from a different quarter.

I hope the day is distant when the work of the Church of England as a national establishment must cease: yet it would be better that that day should arrive than that she should consent even to a silent and gradual obliteration of the lines which mark off belief from its opposite.

It is needless to pursue farther this painful subject, and I will conclude with assuring your lordship that I remain, with cordial respect for your pastoral zeal and labours and much sense of your kindness,

Most faithfully yours,
W. E. GLADSTONE.

I ought in this letter to have stated my full acceptance of the rule that all documents imposed by way of theological test ought to be continued in a favourable sense; but this, I apprehend, means a favourable sense subject to the limits fixed by the time and natural meaning of the words employed, and is perfectly consistent with the definitions and integrity of the Faith.

262. *To Lord Radstock.*

11, Carlton House Terrace,
June 24, 1865.

My dear Lord Radstock,
   Since my note of yesterday I have considered the passage which you kindly sent me, and which I understand to be extracted from a recent work of Mr. Mill.

When I expressed, and allowed to be published, my opinion of Mr. Mill's claims to represent Westminster, I was not aware that exception had been taken, on religious grounds, to any passage in his works. But had I seen the passage now before me, it would not, with the view I take of it until better advised, have altered my course of proceeding.

I will say nothing on the form or language of this extract, or on the necessity or propriety of the hypothesis on which it turns; for, after all, I could not properly judge of these matters without a knowledge of the context, which I do not possess.

But the substance of the passage seems to me to be just and sound, and not only not to involve unbelief, but to be based on what is really the fundamental principle of all belief. The nature of man is the work of God, and it is not that nature, but only the evil in it, which is not His work. What can be more seemly, to say the least, than the proposition that, when the great Physician and Restorer of that nature comes, He should be known, not merely by exhibitions of power, but by the radical correspondence of what He does and teaches with all that is recognized, by the great and never-failing, though often obscured, tradition of humanity, as good in that nature which we bear?

But what I have above called seemly I might more justly call inevitable and binding. On what foundations can the Almighty be expected by us to build, other than those which He Himself has laid? What was the blessed working of our Lord's habitual daily life, except an appeal to those principles of love, truth, justice, and the like, which abode in man, not strong enough to govern, but yet strong enough to witness? Why does St. Paul find fault with the heathen for not acknowledging the goodness of God in His works, if they had not within them what ought to have taught and led them to acknowledge it? The whole Bible, all the first ideas of Revelation, imply that there is in man a moral standard by means of which its divinity can be recognized. It is not this principle, but the opposite of this principle, which destroys belief. For belief is essentially founded in reason, not in the narrow, arrogant, and perverted thing that some men mean when they talk of reason, but in reason as that faculty which attaches us to the truth, as conscience attaches us to the right. Apart from defects of expression, I am at a loss to know how these things can be questioned, or what counter-proposition can be set up. God is [in] my mind nothing else than a name for Good attached to Personality, and invested with the perfection of every other attribute. But good is the essence; and the interpretation of good must, if it is to govern us, have the sanction and attestation of all that remains of good either in the speculative or in the active being of man — of all that in us which in our best hours we recognize as alone entitled to govern. For truths esteemed to be of such breadth, it may seem superfluous to quote individual witnesses. But I am sure that, if I owe to any one man more than another the clear and strong perception of these in my mind, it is to one who is justly called the great evangelical doctor — I mean to St. Augustine.

I have reserved, and I wish to reserve, all questions, except the one of the substance. But even on the form, though it startles, and though I do not think I should be ready to adopt it, yet I am slow to condemn. Not only because a person of so powerful and dispassionate mind as the Bishop of St. David's is stated, I see, to withhold his condemnation, but because I know nowhere any more startling expression to be found than that which comes from one of the deepest human hearts and souls, from the greatest of all Gospel teachers not Divine, from the inspired Apostle, when he wrote those transcendent words:

'I have great heaviness and continued sorrow in my heart; for I could wish that myself were accursed from Christ for my brethren, my kinsmen according to the flesh. . . .'

      I remain,
        Sincerely yours,
          W. E. G.

263. *To the Duke of Argyll.*

HAWARDEN,
July 14, 1865.

MY DEAR ARGYLL,

. . . The question which you put me . . . is of the deepest interest, and well deserves being answered, not in a word but in a volume. Still, the affirmative answer which you anticipate may be given with general truth. The idea of conversion requires and depends upon the idea of sin. I doubt if this latter idea can properly be said to exist even in Homer, whose age, as represented in him, had a far higher moral standard than that of classical Greece. Of the East beyond Judea, I must not speak, for I have none of the requisite knowledge. But speaking of the race of man from the Valley of the Jordan westwards, I think it is perhaps the greatest peculiarity of the Hebrew race, and, if so, the strongest proof of a Divine Revelation among them, that they alone preserved, during so many centuries, the true moral conception of sin and of that personal and individual relation between each man and his God on which the idea of sin depends.

Among the heathen, I mean in what we call Paganism, there remains a standard of right and wrong, but this standard is neither derived from, nor intelligibly related to, the Divine will or character. Singularly enough, some idea of national or collective sin seems to have remained even when it had been lost for the individual. I would I were free to travel on these roads farther and *sine fine*, but that cannot be yet. . . .

264. *To Macmillan and Co.*

HAWARDEN,
December 25, 1865.

DEAR SIRS,

I have sometimes had tokens of your kind remembrance, in the receipt of new publications, when I have felt ashamed to send you a mere formal acknowledgment; and now, when my acknowledgment must be more than formal, I still feel ashamed: because it will be wholly insufficient. It is very rare with me, under the pressure of office, to read a book of the nature of the 'Ecce Homo,' which you lately sent me. But, from the moment when I opened that volume, I felt the touch of a powerful hand drawing me on. The author of it is a man who evidently would not look for an undiscriminating eulogium or concurrence, and, indeed, as the book is avowedly but half the work, and as what remains is not less vital than what has been accomplished, the time even for competent judges to pronounce upon it is not yet come. With regard, however, to the portion of it as yet unborn, I please myself with thinking that the seed of it is to be found in the last half-line.

I will not attempt to draw out the long catalogue of its praises; but I will venture to say I know of, or recollect, no production of equal force that recent years can boast of, and that it is with infinite relief as well as pleasure that, in the present day, I hail the entrance into the world of a strong constructive book on the Christian system. And I venture to add, I hope not impertinently, the opinion that the author of such a work, on such a subject, ought to give the world the benefit also of his name. It *must* be some name that would powerfully help to draw to it the attention it deserves, and the more present responsibility of open authorship would be useful, as I believe, even to this most remarkable writer, and would make worthier still what I cannot but call this noble book.

W. E. GLADSTONE.

265. *To Dr. Newman.*

CARLTON HOUSE TERRACE,
February 18, 1866.

MY DEAR DR. NEWMAN,

To those who have once known you or your writings, any work from your pen must be a matter of interest, and to receive the letter you have just published from yourself, with words of kindness upon it, has been to me that and something more. It lets in a rush of memories of what was, and of what might have been; but with these it stirs up sentiments of admiration and of thankfulness, on which it is more seemly and more suitable to dwell. Your style, as you must well know, loses none of its clearness with the gathering in of years, but what I have a better right to thank you for is the frank, kindly, and tender spirit which possesses you, and which breathes in every line. I am sure that this is widely felt and appreciated, and that in that recognition you will think you have your reward.

I hope you will allow me to claim a common interest with you in works such as this and that which preceded it. The internal condition of the great and ancient Church, which has for its own one half of Christendom, cannot be matter of indifference to Christians beyond its borders. Ignorantly, perhaps, I contemplate with pain and alarm what appears to be the ruling course of influences and events within them. It seems hardly too much to say that we see before us an ever-growing actual necessity, in the world of thought, for a new reconciliation of Christianity and mankind. Any who have the feeling that these words very coarsely and crudely express must earnestly wish God-speed to those distinguished persons in the Roman Church who, like yourself or like Dr. Döllinger, seem to labour in the great and sacred cause.

Forgive my having said so much, in reliance on your generous indulgence, and in the haste to which I am a slave. May I hope — let me rather say *I will* hope — to see you if you come to town.

Believe me, etc.,
W. E. G.

266. *To Archbishop Manning.*

August 26, 1872.

. . . I am sorry to say that in one matter, which lies at the root of all, I am hardly less a follower of Cassandra than you, for I think there is a more powerful combination of influences now at work in the world which have atheism for their legitimate upshot, than at any former period known to me. They are alike hostile to God the Creator, God the Ruler, and God the Judge; and the only deities they have are the gods of Epicurus.

267. *To the Duke of Argyll.*

December 28, 1872.

. . . I return your very interesting letter on the fossil man in the Mentone Cave. I do not perceive that there are cogent reasons for assuming in this case a very great lapse of time, but I am not qualified to judge whether the circumstances warrant that inference or not. If, however, the lapse of time is very great, the identity of type in the skeleton is the more remarkable. I have been touching upon deep and dangerous subjects at Liverpool. Whether I went beyond my province many may doubt. But of the extent of the mischief I do not doubt more than of its virulence. All I hear from day to day convinces me of the extent of this strange epidemic, for it is not, considering how it comes, worthy of being a rational or scientific process. Be it, however, what it may, we politicians are children playing with toys in comparison to that great work of and for mankind which has to be done and will yet be done in restoring belief. . . .

268. *To R. B. Morier.*

April 12, 1873.

. . . The arrival of Strauss and so many others at materialism as the result of their toil and of the light and researches of the age is, I do believe, one of the strangest and most pitiable phenomena upon record in the history of the human mind. Though Strauss's book did not seem to me to indicate any general decay of vigour, yet there really were some particular arguments, such as that connecting the immortality of the soul with the plurality of worlds, which appear nothing less than puerile. So also that upon Schopenhauer's pessimism as destroying the weight of his authority. I do not think that Strauss's book has attained to any great celebrity or notoriety in England, but I grieve to say we have many of native growth which, for every practical purpose, are just as deplorable, and some of which in opinion go even farther. . . .

269. *To the Provost of Oriel (Hawkins).*

July 27, 1873.

... I turn to the Athanasian Creed. First, with respect to the Creed itself, I have no doubts or difficulties. It is not by ideas as such, but by conduct in its largest sense and including the use of all our powers, that I presume we shall be judged. Further, I think that one main source of difficulty in the matter arises from importing the popular sense of terms such as 'saved' into theology, and another from assumptions in the region of philosophy that we know more about eternity than we really do know. Were I compelled to decide the question, and for myself alone, I should be for adopting the rubric of 1689, or the earlier part of it. But as it is not to be decided for myself alone, I should not be the man to preclude any other form of change that I believed to be practicable, and that might fairly be held to tend to health and peace. I think, however, you are scarcely aware how very limited are my means of action in this class of subjects. Though Mr. Miall is probably as yet very far from the attainment of his favourite objects, yet undoubtedly the power of legislating through the medium of Parliament with safety or steadiness on the higher matters of Church and religion is brought down to a very low ebb. An immense amount of out-of-doors consent is requisite to enable any Government to undertake with prudence such an enterprise. The two Bills of which I have had the care, on the New Lectionary and the Shortened Services, had every possible advantage of consent and authority, but it taxed me very hard indeed to steer them without admitting changes by pure Parliamentary initiative, which would have formed most dangerous precedents for the future. I am bound to add my opinion that the Archbishop of Canterbury has done much to embroil and entangle this difficult matter by the premature and therefore rash adoption of ground which he has been unable to hold, though possibly, now that Bishop Wilberforce is dead, he may be tempted to resume it. Be that as it may, anything like initiative or personal activity on my part in any of these matters is really out of the question. There is only a certain stage of ripeness at which I, or even the Government, could with any advantage interpose. I had no personal desire for shortened services or a new lectionary: but I gladly lent myself to promoting changes which were supported by general though not universal consent: and which tended to edification. So I should do again, if Atropos do not cut the thread of my Ministerial life before an occasion arise. One thing I can do without waiting for it, and that is promise to read with interest and pleasure all that you may write or send me on the subject of the Athanasian Symbol. I do not know if you have read Dr. Brewer's writings; they are on the other side: but he is a very able man, and he seems to beat Newman in his knowledge of the ecclesiastical phraseology of the fourth century, which I always supposed to be Newman's stronghold. . . .

270. *To the Earl of Pembroke*

HAWARDEN,
September 29, 1873.

MY DEAR GEORGE,
I have never accused you of being either misty or uncandid, and I am sorry that my practice of speaking out so freely my whole meaning against you, whatever it may be, should give you the pain of always or often believing that I have more to say which I keep back. However, my expression about your using the vagueness of your language as a kind of defence was an unhappy one; as it did not bring out my meaning clearly, I will try again, but I write from memory. I found in the same book a denunciation of belief and a recommendation of belief. My hope was that between these two contradictions you would adhere to the one last named, and would thus find in your own mind the antidote to what I thought the bane. But I had besides this the opinion that the inconsistency thus indicated in your language, going as it did to the root of the whole matter, would, together with other evidence, serve to illustrate and support my main proposition, which is that you have undertaken a tremendous task without being properly prepared for it by reflection and comprehensive study, and that you are a teacher where

you ought to be a learner. I certainly was struck with the quiet way in which you gave up your affirmative proposition, or deprived it of its vitality as a mere affair of verbal explanation without any misgiving suggested to you by the necessity of such an operation; and I am afraid that in giving this fuller statement of my meaning I charge you with a heavier intellectual offence that in my former less-developed words. You will, however, see that I did not attack either of your propositions in themselves, but that what you have said on this head is said under misapprehension. My argument all along was an *argumentum ad hominem*, a denial of your *locus standi* in controversies of this kind, until you should have fulfilled certain conditions. But this was, in other words, simply an appeal to you against yourself; and admitting in my last letter that it had failed, I still thought I would hazard a trial of one of your arguments on its own merits, not by a proper counter-argument, which, unhappily, I am not in a condition to make as it ought to be made, but by one or two questions, which were in effect counter-propositions. In like manner, with respect to the Book of Genesis, I had sought to convey to your mind that you had made a remark as unwarrantable as it was contumelious, not by supplying positive proofs as to that invaluable book, but by putting a question, which I hoped would suggest to you that, whatever be the true state of the question, you had not legitimately earned a right to pass a judgment upon it. But in this also I grossly failed, but I quit that ground.

Let us therefore try if we can make anything, in the way of argument, of your dogma of the unknowableness of God. When I spoke of this subject, I referred to your words in the letter before me: 'the belief in the unknowableness of God by our finite intelligences.' Do not let me offend you by imputing to you a dogma. I mean your assertion; and I certainly affirm that a negative assertion, 'We can know nothing about the moon' may be as dogmatic as the positive one, 'We may know something about the moon' — an illustration, I think, much closer to the point than yours. But as to your assertion or dogma, whichever it may be, I take some comfort for the time from the fact that I am really at a loss to understand what is your actual meaning. Whether my concessions, or Bishop Butler's, rather, are suicidal we may see more clearly hereafter. I will only observe that I have never said there is no absolute knowledge of God possible to man. That is a question for separate and very careful inquiry; nor is it even necessary now to define the terms. It is quite enough for me to point out (and here I am glad we are agreed) that (at most) of very few things have we absolute or even certain knowledge. And yet we form judgments upon a multitude of things, and act upon those judgments, and should be regarded as idiots if we did not form and act upon them. Probable knowledge, or, to speak more accurately, probable evidence, may entail the obligation of action, the obligation of belief, as truly as knowledge which is demonstrative, and this probable knowledge is the 'guide of life' — it is that upon which, as rational beings, we commonly and chiefly act. Now, here it is that I am at a loss to discover what your position really is. Do you deny the proposition that probable evidence entails the obligation of belief and action in correspondence with it? or do you deny that we have probable evidence of the existence and character of God? If both these are admitted, a foundation is laid: but I am not yet able to make out whether you admit them or not.

You say in your letter of the 20th that you do not assume that we are incapable of 'true points of contact with an infinite God.' But you say also: (1) The existence of any such points of contact has to be proved. (2) You question the ability of man to decide what these points of contact are 'without any prior knowledge of God to guide him.' I am afraid we are here again at issue upon words. My points of contact were contradistinguished from the absolute knowledge which you appeared to me to consider as the sole condition which could entail the obligations of religion. My proposition is that partial knowledge may be true knowledge. I am afraid you attach some other meaning to my words, as if I had said a stone might have true points of contact with the infinite God; which would have been wholly unmeaning though true. Otherwise you could not have made 'prior knowledge' a condition of any knowledge. Please then to observe that against your general doctrine, that to finite man the infinite God is unknowable, I reply that this is either untrue or irrelevant to the question of religious obligation: untrue if it means that because finite we can have no knowledge of God, irrelevant if it only means that our knowledge of God does not correspond with His infinity. Just as, if you were to say the light of the sun cannot be taken in by the human eye, that would be untrue if it meant that none of it could be so taken in, irrelevant to the inquiry whether this light could guide us, if it only meant that the organ was not equal to taking in the whole of the sun's light. But, again, you contend against any right to assert the truth of dogmas which are beyond verification. I do not recollect your having previously employed this favourite phrase of our modern philosophers. I should be glad to know what meaning you attach to it. And to let you see my meaning I will illustrate. The child of A. falls into habits of lying. A. punishes him. Because, says A., there is a law of right and wrong; and *lying is wrong.* Here is a dogma about lying. I want to know whether this dogma is 'beyond verification.' If it is, then I am afraid we have no right to say lying is wrong; and A. has transgressed in punishing his child, if he has acted on such a principle. If it is not, if the principle that lying is wrong can be 'verified,' I deny that the being of God is beyond verification. There is much of your letter that I pass by, because it would entail such lengthened verbal questioning. My desire is to get to close quarters upon some one point. So that, having failed in my personal impeachment, I confront your assertion that God is unknowable because we are finite, by saying that our finiteness in no way prevents our having true though imperfect knowledge; just as (to use a feeble illustration) a dog has true though imperfect knowledge of a man, and a child of an adult; and that this true though imperfect knowledge, if it exist, entails obligations of belief and action; and that these obligations cannot be laughed down as theological, for they are in their ground rational, and they simply apply reason to the subject-matter of theology, as the baker applies reason to the business of baking. And now at all events we meet in the open plain, and you have the opportunity of striking me where and how you please.

271. *To the Rev. J. B. Mozley, D.D.*

October 16, 1873.

. . . It appears to me that a large portion of the 'thinkers' have gone mad about Socrates. After failing in London, I have obtained from Oxford Mr. Highton's tract, 'Dean Stanley and St. Socrates.' It appears to me to display many of the qualities necessary for the effective handling of this profoundly interesting and very important question. But the issue is raised far too narrowly as between him and Stanley, from whose name and picturesque intervention I should like to see the subject detached. It *is* very important, for the name of Socrates is an integral part of the leverage now set to work for oversetting Christianity. The Socrates of Grote would form, without any personalities, an excellent basis for a careful discussion. Do you not think it important that there should be such a discussion? Can you promote it? Do you know anything of Mr. Highton; or could you learn about him whether he is fit? I was very near writing to him, when I bethought me I had better write to you. I should not mind proposing the subject to the Dean of St. Paul's — should that seem the best course to take. . . .

272. *To the Rev. J. B. Mozley, D.D.*

October 22, 1873.

. . . I am glad you enter into the importance of the present controversy about Socrates. And I quite agree as to the one-sidedness of Mr. Highton's pamphlet, which has been evidently written to strike a blow at Stanley, and which succeeds in striking it. At present the extravagant doctrines held about Socrates are a part of the *   brought to bear against

---

* Blank in original.

Christianity and all belief. In reducing him to his own proportions as a sage, it is not necessary to exaggerate. My own impression is that he practised what he acquiesced in, but that such things as he so practised were not vices at all, according to the standard of the age. In making a true statement of the case, the most important lights would be thrown upon the character of that age itself, and the havoc that, with all its culture, it had wrought upon the moral laws in this great department. And this is, again, of immense importance with regard to the great controversy of belief — that the real state of Athens at its climax, that is, of human nature at its climax, should be understood. It appears that Aristophanes, in the 'Clouds,' assails Socrates for his theology or atheology, but not in respect of the prevailing vices. If I understand the matter rightly, the case of Aristophanes himself was in some important points analogous to that of Socrates: he was a great political and moral reformer, and (I take it) honestly sought to throw back his countrymen upon the less scandalous age of the *Marathonomachoi*. But the character of his *Dikaiopolis* in the 'Acharnians' distinctly shows that vice, and even foul vice, was admitted into, if not incorporated in, his idea of the happy and virtuous life.

273. *To T. Scott.*

November 16, 1873.

... The autobiography of Mr. J. S. Mill shows, had there been a doubt before, how deeply the question of eternal punishment enters into the modern controversy of belief, with very serious and earnest minds. And I always find this satisfaction in Mr. Mill, that he is thorough and does not put up with makeshifts. Were it in my power to write on the subject in a manner worthy of it, I would gladly do so; but I neither have the time for research and thought, nor have I seen the question exhaustively stated on the side of objectors. I find most of what I see on the subject defective even in the first condition — the definition of the terms used. What is eternity? There appears to be a tacit assumption that it is an endless prolongation of time. What is the authority for this assumption? Then there appears to be a notion that by some doctrine of final restoration all difficulties, or the main difficulties, are removed. On which I would ask, What are the philosophical grounds for predicating this final restoration? And is it really agreeable to all we know from observation and experience (not religion) of the laws of human nature? And, lastly, does it remove the difficulties? You will see, therefore, that I have large demands to make before answering any demands.

274. *To Herbert Spencer.*

HAWARDEN,
January 12, 1874.

. . . To characterize Science as having gone to war with Providence would be, for a man with my convictions, both altogether irrational and very nearly blasphemous. There is, indeed, a practice which seems to me to be widely spread among many persons in the present day, of first unduly narrowing the definition of Science, and then as unduly extending it to all the opinions which those persons think fit to hold, and all the theories they erect on the subjects they term scientific. With this there is an appropriation to themselves of the phrase 'scientific men,' which appears to the rest of the world unreasonable and unwarranted. Under the provocation thus given, ill-advised things may sometimes be spoken of Science itself. I have striven to avoid saying such things. I shall ever feel grateful to those who, by enlarging the field of knowledge, enrich the patrimony of mankind. But I hold that they are themselves bound by the laws of reason. To treat a man as the enemy of Science is to treat him as the enemy of Truth. For those who revere Truth, and who, above all things, desire to follow it, this is simply charging them with the breach of a most sacred duty. And perhaps some anxiety, if not sensitiveness, on this subject may be intelligible in a man, much (many and weighty persons think too much) of whose life and strength has been spent in the endeavour to deliver himself, for the sake of Truth, from the sway of preconceived opinions. . . .

275. *To Sir A. Panizzi.*

February 8, 1874.

MY DEAR PANIZZI,

I give you in a note the substance of the memorandum which I ought to have brought. The question was, What has religion done for man? The answer relates to Christianity: (1) Because the term Religion is so vague, and includes even things monstrous; (2) because its results are so very diverse, and in some cases doubtful or bad; (3) because Christianity alone is the religion with which we have to do. I say, then, choosing points of the most definitive character, that Christianity *abolished* — (1) Gladiatorial shows, and other spectacles of horrid cruelty to man; (2) human sacrifices; (3) polygamy; (4) exposure of children; (5) slavery (in its old form, and has nearly accomplished the work in its new); (6) cannibalism. Next, Christianity drove into the shade all unnatural lusts, and, indeed, all irregular passions. But the former it effectually stamped as infamous. Next, Christianity *established* — (1) Generally speaking, the moral and social equality of women; (2) the duty of relieving the poor, the sick, the afflicted; (3) peace, instead of war, as the ordinary, normal, presumptive relation between nations. Here is a goodly list. I speak not of what it *taught*. It taught the law of mutual love. It proscribed all manner of sin. But the preceding particulars refer to what, besides saying, it did, besides trying, it accomplished. And in every one of these instances, except that of cannibalism, the exhibition of what it did is in glaring contrast, not with barbarous, but with the most highly civilized life, such as it was exhibited by the Greeks or Romans of the most famous ages, or both. Now, I think this is a fair statement not easily shaken. I admit that many of these results are negative. And as to those of them which are positive, there are other and higher results in the excellence and perfection of the human soul individually; but I have taken such as are palpable, and I think undeniable.

Ever warmly yours,
W. E. G.

276. *To Professor Stanley Jevons.*

HAWARDEN,
May 10, 1874.

I have this day in a quiet hour read with attention the closing chapter of your book, and I cannot resist paying you the very indifferent compliment of saying how greatly I am impressed and pleased with it. I am not, indeed, altogether an impartial witness, for in several points of great importance it indicates or asserts what have very long been favourite points with me, amidst those speculative disturbances of the present age which have reached me even in the sphere of politics:

That there is gross ambiguity and latent fallacy in much that we hear about 'uniformity of laws';

That we are not warranted in predicating, of time and space themselves, that they are necessarily conditions of all existence;

That there is real insoluble mystery in some of the formulæ of mathematics;

That we are in danger from the precipitancy and intellectual tyranny of speculation;

That the limits of our real *knowledge* are (if I may use the word), infinitely narrow;

That we are not rationally justified in passing over our inward perceptions of things inward, and confining the sphere of knowledge to things outward —

[These] are my old convictions, which I live in the hope of doing something, before I die, to sustain and illustrate; and they are, I think, all, nearly in these terms, supported by your authority.

But I hope I have a better reason for admiring this chapter. I find it in the true and high philosophic spirit in which it seems to me to be conceived. I hope you will not be shocked if I designate it by an epithet which to my mind conveys the highest commendation: it seems to me eminently *Butlerian*.

With respect to Evolution and to Darwinism I had never formed any opinion, when Mr. Spencer criticised me, except that the results assigned to them were unwarrantable. Since that time I have a little examined them, not as propositions of natural philosophy, but in their moral and speculative aspects. Having done this, I entirely subscribe to what you say of them. Indeed, I must say that the doctrine of Evolution, if it be true, enhances in my judgment the proper idea of the greatness of God, for it makes every stage of creation a legible prophecy of all those which are to follow it.

What you said of your own theology inspired me with great respect, although I am myself much addicted to what I may call historical Christianity, and profoundly disbelieve the notion of some, and of some able and eminent, men that it is to be overthrown in its old historic form, and to revive and flourish in a new form, simplified as they say, but as I think attenuated. . . .

277. To C. A. Hardy.

HAWARDEN,
January 4, 1876.

. . . My first anxiety is that you should feel to how great and arduous a work you commit yourself in retrying the foundations of religion. If you can truly, humbly, and manfully give yourself to it, I hope all will end well.

Perhaps you have not quite understood me about Religion and Arts. If I say to a person, 'You could not jump this brook, how then could you jump that river?' I do not assert that the river is a brook.

Even the reading of Butler is a serious matter. He has a meaning everywhere, and (to be of use) it implies knowing and weighing this meaning. Two much stronger men than the one we mentioned were James Mill and John Mill. Both said no one, from the Deist's point of view, could answer Butler: any such, any beginning with belief in God, he compels to be a Christian.

With respect to Authority, there is *great* value in the early chapters of a book just now republished, Sir George Lewis on the influence of Authority in matters of opinion.

It is true he says his argument does not embrace morals or religion. In that I think him wrong. But at any rate his argument is well worth reading, and will supply light to many on the subject of Authority, such as they do not expect.

If our law of acquiring knowledge, as to its starting-point, is to be that of a dog's litter, our condition will soon be worse than theirs: for we have not the same degree of aid from mere instinct. Why do you on trust eat your meat dressed, or your corn ground and baked, instead of taking them as Nature sent them and the first man had them?

In the Christian view, the attitude of Jesus Christ with respect to Authority, He being inspired and Divine, does not supply *ipso facto* a measure for us. But for what did He attack Authority, except for abandoning the Scriptures — its highest law?

Acceptance of the collective evidence is not what Rome demands; she demands acceptance of the voice of her own episcopal majority from hour to hour, or, worse still, of the Pope alone.

I am not aware of any ancient book or ancient tradition carrying the notes, or anything like the notes, of the Bible and the Christian system, which have led the highest intellect of mankind for the last 1,500 years, and have created modern society. It is where humanity has reached its highest and its best developments that I must look for the means of future energy, stability, and advancement, not in the systems of less nobleness and strength. . . .

W. E. GLADSTONE.

278. *To the Rev. C. Voysey.*

73, HARLEY STREET,
July 2, 1876.

Nothing can be more kind than the tone and spirit, as towards myself, of your discourses.

They afford me, as might be expected, additional evidence that, in dealing so succinctly with so vast a subject, I could not give my readers all the helps which they might reasonably expect or desire for the avoidance of misapprehension.

A very little more such aid I may now try to give:

1. You have yourself perceived that I recognize the

distinction between a system and the sentiments of men who embrace it.

I am a good deal acquainted with the writings of theists, including the three you name.

The writings of Parker have much in them that moves sympathy and admiration. But your citation appears to me much more emotional than philosophical, and all durable religion must in my view be in relation to a true basis of philosophy.

I ought, perhaps, to have explained distinctly that I spoke of 'the system' in its relation to our nature as it is.

2. I hope you have understood that my reference to the sense of relief afforded by Universalism is meant for those who may be led to it by predisposition rather than by reasoning. Such I conceive there are.

3. On this subject at large I will only observe that you substitute, to a great extent, the aggressive method for the defensive one which I had suggested; that Universalism implies a knowledge of the nature of Eternity wider and clearer than any that I at least possess; that I doubt not there are works setting forth fully its philosophy, but I have never yet been able to find them.

That the proposition 'His unrest must work its cure' is one of those which seems to me most to require to be fully developed and searchingly tested by analogy.

That, in my opinion, the whole scheme is too much open to the charge of resting on the basis of *a priori* assumptions untested by experimental evidence.

But these are only isolated remarks. Only much time and thought, and perhaps not these, could embolden me to think of dealing with the great demands of the subject. . . .

W. E. GLADSTONE.

279. *Incomplete. Probably to Lord Blachford, about* 1876.

Your standing ground is this: that however, as viewed at a given moment, the future suffering of the wicked be proportioned to the amount and nature of this wickedness, this proportion is destroyed by the simple fact of perpetual duration.

I do not as yet feel myself constrained to assent to his proposition. I think it implies more knowledge of the meaning of its terms than we possess.

It may be that a present amount is aggravated by anticipation of the future, and by recollection of the past.

But how can I assert that, by natural—*i.e.* Divine—laws, amount is not so adjusted as with the inclusion of these elements to compare to proportion?

It would surely be an unwarrantable daring to hold that any amount of punishment, however reduced, must by including the element of perpetuity pass out of proportion to the sin.

Is not this carrying arithmetic and quantitative laws farther into the unseen world than is philosophically just?

But again: what if consciousness in the future state of the wicked be so adjusted as that the anticipation of the future and the recollection of the past shall stand differently related to it, or even shall be cut off from it? That is to say, that the elements of aggravation, on which stress is placed, shall disappear.

It may be said that this is not a human consciousness. It is more like the consciousness of animals, who know when they suffer and when they enjoy, but apparently without recollection or anticipation like ours.

This is true, but the champions of natural immortality might hesitate to travel so far on their chosen line as to deny all limiting modifications in the future state. *All* modifications whatever they hardly can deny. Take, for example, that biological sum which makes the automatic functions of life, the normal current of it, so to speak, pleasurable. It seems, therefore, that natural immortality need not absolutely include limitation of the present functions of consciousness.

Much less is there here a difficulty for those who contend against natural immortality; who hold that immortality is or may be an endowment not inherent in our original constitution, and one of which the conditions may be variously adjusted in various cases according to their respective ends.

Yet again: those who think that in the idea of

eternity there may or must be included perpetual duration may yet think that eternity is, as it were, a perpetual present without succession of ideas. If this be so, it may be too bold to predicate in what form or in what degree recollection and anticipation are applicable to such a state.

On the whole, I still propound that amount and conditions of suffering may in the future world be so proportioned to sin that we cannot rightly assert that the proportion cannot subsist should perpetuity be found to be included among the elements of the case. It may indeed be alleged —

1. That the considerations I have urged in bar of judgment are such as could hardly be made intelligible to the common perceptions of man.

2. That the idea of the wicked as thus always defacing the creation of God is derogatory to His dignity.

On these observations I will remark that I have been dealing only with a charge against the Divine Justice regarded as requiring (which I admit) an adjustment between offence and penalty in each individual sufferer: an adjustment which cannot rightly be disturbed by any advantages intended or obtained through the effect of the exhibition upon others.

280. *To the Rev. G. W. Potter.*

WOBURN ABBEY,
October 22, 1878.

DEAR SIR,
The very first touch of the subject [of Future Punishment] opens such a number of points that I dare not even dream of giving you any sort of satisfaction within the compass of a brief letter. If you think there could be any advantage in your conversing with me when I come to town (probably for a day or two in the end of November), I should be happy to see you.

In the meantime I will only note certain isolated points:

1. Our cause of difficulty in the matter, which seems also to be a reason for much patience, is the want of what may be called standard and exhaustive works on the subject, whether in the positive or the negative sense. At least I myself have felt this difficulty, and

can only get at fragmentary, and therefore unsatisfactory, statements.

2. It is surely a cause for thankfulness that the Church has been able to abstain from dogmatizing upon this subject, and thrusting it upon her members. I refer to the Apostles' and Nicene Creeds, and the Athanasian only recites the words of our Lord.

3. The dogmatism of individuals on the small number of those to be saved need hardly trouble us. Our Lord's words on the strait gate, standing in isolation, may have been *relative* rather than absolute, and can hardly without violence be held to lay down a rule for all mankind. They may be of the place, the hour, the people.

4. I do not know where we find our supposed right to say that the *nature* of eternity, of the *beyond*, has been revealed to us. Of the illegitimate mixture of metaphysics with religion we have a significant instance in the adoption by the Lateran Council of the *phrase* 'Transubstantiation' to express the Real Presence.

5. My own inquiries into this subject have been intercepted by other urgent duties: but I have always thought that there were, in the field to be traversed, some guiding lines — for example:

(*a*) That this dispensation of life, in which we are placed, is assuredly special; and not one of an undefined series, but probationary.

(*b*) That the essence of this probation may lie in the planting of germs, as Bishop Butler appears to think, which germs may be invisible to us, but yet effectual.

(*c*) That the constitution of our nature, through the law of habits, tends in a marked manner to fixity of state.

(*d*) That (in my opinion) the arguments for a doctrine of universal restoration are weak and futile as far as they purport to be Scriptural: and they fail to satisfy that ideal of the character of God which prompts men to devise them.

(*e*) It is a grave matter to overset or reconstruct the faith of ages in aiming at an ideal, and then to find that it remains logically unattained.

(*f*) Much of what is urged about future punishment really runs up into the old mystery of the origin of evil; the question is, how much, and possibly even whether *all*.

(*g*) The absolute faith in the justice of God, and in the adaptation of enjoyment and suffering to the laws of right and wrong, must, it would seem, embrace and override all particular beliefs, and constitute a lawful and needful reserve under which they ought to be held. In Paley there is a crude sentence to the following effect: 'If you say that the shades of good and bad in character are severed by an invisible line, I answer that there may be just as little difference between the conditions of the worst man in heaven and the best man in hell.' But, jarring as this may be, there may be in it the indication of a truth lying at the foundation of all.

Dean Church is indeed eminently, as you say, wise and tender. There is no one whose ultimate judgment would carry more weight with me. From what I have said, you will see that I am very jealous for the great moral truths enfolded in the popular doctrine, but I do not now see that — *talis qualis* — it is enforced by the Church upon her members, or even upon her clergy. And as to your second query, I hope I have also in a measure indicated such means, for I think what is called the ordinary doctrine bears the marks of popular exaggeration.

Oxford of to-day is indeed very far from the Oxford of my day. In some respects it is better, and much better. In others it is such that one is tempted to cry, 'The wild boar out of the forest doth root it up, and the wild beast of the field doth devour it.' But yet I trust that her inner vitality will fight through it all.

I am, dear sir,
Your very faithful servant,
W. E. GLADSTONE.

281. *To Sir Richard Owen.*

HAWARDEN,
October 23, 1885.

MY DEAR SIR R. OWEN,

I am extremely obliged to you for your interesting letter, although concerned to have given you so much trouble. There is nothing in it inconsistent with what I have intended to convey. But I am very familiar with the tendency of the more negative and destructive writers to stretch affirmations beyond their proper scope; therefore, availing myself of the light you afford, I have added to my list of the limitations, under which I affirm a revelation in the Book of Genesis, as accordant with what is now known, by inserting the following passage in p. 10 (which I return in its original shape; I do not want it):

A. 'There is here no question of the chronology or of the date of man, or of knowledge or ignorance in the primitive man; or whether the element of parable enters into any portion of the narrative; or whether every statement of fact contained in the text of the book can now be made good. It is enough for my present purpose to point to the cosmogony and the fourfold succession of the living organisms as entirely harmonizing, according to present knowledge, with belief in a revelation, and as presenting to the rejecter of that belief a problem which demands solution at his hands, and which he has not yet been able to solve.'

With the other contents of the Book of Genesis in their bearing on this question, it would take volumes, perhaps, to deal. As to the Deluge, may it not be a question whether the word 'earth' is used like the οἰκουμένη of the New Testament for the known or local world? The genealogies of chapter x. on the division of the earth among races are, according to Renan, a marvellous proof of genius. This to me sounds very like nonsense pure and simple. They convey a knowledge nowhere else, I believe, to be had; but whether they are accurate in *every* point I dare not say, and they seem to prove great antiquity rather than revelation. Of the patriarchal ages some solutions have been offered, but whether satisfactory or not I do not know. The first person who pointed out to me that there were *some* errors of fact in the Gospels was Dr. Pusey; it was nearly sixty years back. It may not be agreeable to find that error of fact can be found at all in the Scriptures; but what would exclude them short of a miraculous conservation of the text? And would it not be wild and irrational to say *therefore* they could contain no revelation?

I cannot here find when Cuvier died, but I will notice the fact of his comparative remoteness. Herschel and Whewell (if not Cuvier) must have been cognizant of the geological man, but I never heard their views. The declaration obtained by Dr. Reusch from Herschel was in 1864. Whewell died in 1866.

The assertion of 'absolute ignorance' is Réville's, not mine. On human longevity, I do not know if you ever came on a curious passage, in Wilkinson's 'Dalmatia,' about seven generations found living in one Montenegrin house.

A more curious subject still there is, which you may or may not have considered. Are there any traditions existing which *seem* to show communication between what I may roughly call the Adamic, or Noachic, and the pre-Adamite man? Is the tradition of *Atlantis* one bearing this character? Another, I think, may be found. The text of Homer testifies unequivocally to a belief, existing or known in his time, that the great central and northern plain of Europe was under water, and that there was an open waterway eastward from the Adriatic. Can this belief be a like indication to the other?

With renewed thanks for your great kindness,
I remain, etc.,
W. E. GLADSTONE.

282. *To Lord Acton.*

ASTON CLINTON, TRING,
Easter Day, April 1, 1888.

MY DEAR ACTON,
. . . You perhaps have not heard of 'Robert Elsmere,' for I find, without surprise, that it makes its way slowly into public notice. It is not far from twice the length of an ordinary novel; and the labour and effort of reading it are, I should say, sixfold, while one could no more stop in it than in reading Thucydides.

The idea of the book — perhaps of the writer — appears to be a movement of retreat from Christianity upon Theism — a Theism with a Christ glorified, always in the human sense, but beyond the ordinary measure. It is worked out through the medium of a being — one ought to say a character, but I withhold the word, for there is not sufficient *substratum* of character to uphold the qualities — gifted with much intellectual subtlety and readiness, and with almost every conceivable moral excellence. He finds vent in an energetic attempt to carry his new Gospel among the skilled artisans of London, whom the writer apparently considers as supplying the norm for all right human judgment. He has extraordinary success, establishes a new Church under the name of 'The New Christian Brotherhood,' kills himself with overwork, but leaves his project flourishing in a certain 'Elgood Street.' It is, in fact (like the Salvation Army), a new Kirche der Zukunft.

I am always inclined to consider this Theism as among the least defensible of the positions alternative to Christianity. Robert Elsmere, who has been a parish clergyman, is upset entirely, as it appears, by the difficulty of accepting miracles, and by the suggestion that the existing Christianity grew up in an age specially predisposed to them.

I want, as usual, to betray you into helping the lame dog over the stile: and I should like to know whether you would think me violently wrong in holding that the period of the Advent was a period when the appetite for, or disposition to, the supernatural was declining and decaying; that in the region of human thought speculation was strong and scepticism advancing; that if our Lord were a mere man, armed only with human means, His whereabout was in this and many other ways misplaced by Providence; that the Gospels and the New Testament must have much else besides miracle torn out of them in order to get us down to the *caput mortuum* of Elgood Street. This very remarkable work is in effect identical with the poor, thin, ineffectual production published with some arrogance by the Duke of Somerset, which found a quack remedy for difficulties in what he considered the impregnable citadel of belief in God.

Knowles has brought this book before me, and, being as strong as it is strange, it cannot perish stillborn. I am tossed about with doubt as to writing upon it. . . .

Ever yours,
W. E. GLADSTONE.

283. *To Lord Acton.*

OXFORD,
April 8, 1888.

MY DEAR ACTON,
 I have neither space nor capacity at command for the adequate discussion of the questions which shattered the faith of Robert Elsmere; whether miracles can happen, and whether an universal preconception 'in their favour at the birth of Christianity, governing the work of all men of all schools,' adequately accounts for the fact that, notwithstanding their impossibility, they are alleged in the New Testament as available proofs of the Divine mission of our Lord. But I must, in passing, at least demur to the authority of the Squire, and even of Mr. Grey. As to miracles, I cannot regard the doctrine of impossibility as either philosophical or scientific until its advocates have shown that they have ascertained some limit beyond which the extraneous force of will (the most familiar of all experiences) cannot act upon matter in derogation of laws merely physical. For it seems that the old basis of 'impossibility' — namely, I mean, want of support from experience — is now out of fashion, and that what is demanded, and legitimately demanded, for every alleged effect is adequacy of cause to produce it. And as to the period, let it be granted for argument's sake that, if Christianity had been a religion for the Jews, they at least were open to the charge of a blinding appetite for signs and wonders. But how came this religion at once to spread among Greeks and Romans? These Gentiles, who detested and despised the Jews, had no disposition to receive a religion at their hands or upon their authority. Were they, then, during the century which followed our Lord's birth, swayed by this devouring thirst for the supernatural? The recent and prevailing schools of philosophy were not theistic schools, and the contemporary Academy itself might be described as a receptacle of universal doubt. A deluge of profligacy had gone far to destroy at Rome even the external habit of public worship; Horace, himself an indifferentist, denounces the neglect and emptiness of

the temples; farther on we have the stern and emphatic testimony of Juvenal:

> 'Esse aliquid manes, et subterranea regna,
> Et contum, et Stygio ranas in gurgite nigras
> Nec pueri credunt, nisi qui nondum ære lavantur.'

Recent research has indeed shown that the advance of the Gospel faith was greatly slower than had once been supposed. Still, it took root, and spread steadily by its innate strength, in face of the acute and subtle speculations of the Eastern mind, and of the highly organized political and aristocratic religion, which in Rome regarded it from the first, and with reason, as a deadly foe. Might it not be said, and with some show of reason, that in the capital of the Empire portent was the property and the tool of the established and intensely national hierarchy; and that a system which bristled with rival portent, and aimed directly at the overthrow of the older institutions, would concentrate upon itself every prejudice, and that in fact it invited, as no other religion did invite, the use of every available means for its suppression? Had the new faith been invented and launched in reliance on the universal preconception, it was surely so far an anachronism that the venture ought to have been made in an earlier, simpler, and purer time? But I must not expect to win the reader by dealing with the Squire almost as summarily as he deals with the Gospel.

284. *To Lord Acton.*

DOLLIS HILL,
May 13, 1888.

MY DEAR ACTON,

. . . I am not so much impressed as you appear to be with the notion that great difficulties have been imported by the researches of scientists into the religious and theological argument. As respects cosmogony and *geogony*, the Scripture has, I think, taken much benefit from them. Whatever be the date of the early books, Pentateuch or Hexateuch in their present *edition*, the Assyriological investigations seem to me to have fortified and accredited their substance by producing similar traditions in variant forms inferior to the Mosaic forms, and tending to throw these back to a higher antiquity — a fountain-head nearer the source. Then there is the great chapter of the Dispersal, which Renan (I think) treats as exhibiting the marvellous genius (!) of the Jews. As to unbroken sequences in the physical order, they do not trouble me, because we have to do, not with the natural, but the moral order; and over this science, or as I call it natural science, does not wave her sceptre. It is no small matter again (if so it be, as I suppose) that, after warring for a century against miracle as unsustained by experience, the assailants should now have to abandon that ground, stand only upon sequence, and controvert the great facts of the New Testament only by raising to an extravagant and unnatural height the demands made under the law of testimony in order to a rational belief. One admission has to be made, that death did not come into the world by sin — namely, the sin of Adam — and this sits inconveniently by the declaration of St. Paul. . . .

Ever yours,
W. E. GLADSTONE.

285. *To S. Laing.*

HAWARDEN,
September 9, 1888.

DEAR MR. LAING,
. . . The question of belief has immense attractions for me and a great authority over me. But it is only indirectly and slowly, and on particular points, that I can approach it. I know, in some degree, what I am dealing with on the positive side; and am desirous of some guidance, if not from authority, at least from correct and accepted opinion, on the negative side. My pace and yours are very different. It is little to say I am a canal boat, and you an express train. You, without electricity, put a girdle round the earth in twenty minutes. I am amazed at the multitude of solutions included in your paper: were my life now clear and at my disposal, I should be too glad to think I could deal in the time remaining to me with one-tenth part of the field of debate which you open. It is not

altogether in the spirit of controversy that I look at these matters: for I do not think, so far as I know my own mind, that I could satisfy any school or party: certainly not the Ultramontane, which I commonly find to be the only one admitted to a relative respectability by negative writers, and complimented with a logical consistency which, in my opinion, it is as far as possible from exhibiting. But while I have probably on that side 'more kicks than halfpence' to expect; from you and from the sceptical movement, I am at a terrible distance. With an unbounded acceptance of the facts of science, I am amazed at the uses made of them, and in vain try to comprehend how it is that very clever men, whom in their own department I go as near as possible to taking on trust, can be so utterly outside the spirit (as I conceive it) of philosophy. Perhaps I ought just to state that I am a Butlerian, by which I mean, not so much the champion of any particular argument, as the follower of the Butlerian method.

You give me credit which I do not deserve, for probably agreeing with you in thinking 'every fair-minded man must admit that the "evidence for a revelation" ought to be extremely strong, and almost irresistible.' Now, I do not want consciously to forfeit the claim to be a fair-minded man, and this broad and profoundly important proposition is one on which I should not arrive at a final conclusion without much more consideration than I have been able to give it. But, as at present minded, I cannot accept the doctrine, and, indeed, I am surprised at your deeming it a thing almost to be taken for granted. I ask myself two things *in limine*. First, how am I enabled to know that a creature like man is well qualified to judge of the degree (or kind) of evidence which ought to accompany a revelation? Secondly, from whatever source this claim is to be made good, I do not think it is from the experience of life and the rules recognized as those of common sense in conducting it. As a patient I do not ask from my doctor, in a mortal strait, evidence almost irresistible about his medicine. Nor, if tidings is brought me that my house is on fire, do I remain inactive until it is demonstrated. Nor, when men hear, I will not say of new goldfields, for gold acts abnormally on the imagination, but of new enterprises with the promise of great profit, does each wait until he has evidence almost irresistible that he will make his fortune? These hasty illustrations throw their light from different points of view.

Again, I do not feel at all sure of your ground against the atheist, whom you dispose of as summarily as if he were the first chapter of Genesis. There is (in my opinion) evidence against the being of GOD, real, but outweighed by vastly preponderating evidence in favour of that belief. If, however, the Agnostic parts with the whole, or by far the larger share, of the affirmative evidence, I am not sure of his easily persuading the atheist to admit, 'charm he never so wisely,' that there is after all a curtain — the curtain of death — and behind the curtain a lottery. *He* sees before him creation 'red with ravin'; he will make much of the sight, and when his contention is that the grounds for an ethical judgment on the whole matter are palpable, I should not as an Agnostic exactly know how to get out of view what Aristotle would call the πίστεις in his favour. He will not understand the Agnostic very well when he is told that the pain, sin, waste, and misery, in the world are known, but nothing can be known of them beyond what is phenomenal; and he may have some sympathy from the theist when he refuses to arrest at such a point as this the exercise of his faculties, and close the book.

When I am told that GOD is unknowable, I ask the meaning of the word. If it is that He cannot be perfectly known, I agree: here, I think, comes in Tennyson's 'behind the veil' (do you think that Agnosticism could have produced 'Guinevere'?), in consonance with St. Paul, 'we see through a glass darkly.' And then I ask, how many things are there which we know in the sense of perfect knowledge? Perhaps, even, are there any? But we live and work with imperfect knowledge. It is real, available, and valuable, especially if we know its limitations. To my mind, to say that we cannot have partial but real knowledge of GOD is, I will not say irreligious — for we are simply testing in the region of fact — but in the highest degree irrational, and most of all irrational, as I think, in relation to that evidence of the being and acting of GOD which not only the exterior course of the world, but the interior daily experience of mind and soul, afford. I will add to this fragmentary and desultory letter one word on the mode now so fashionable of handling the Scriptures. In a book intended to convey special knowledge to mankind, I expect above all things to find the modes of speech which will make it most intelligible. In this view, the use of figure and parable, which both believers and non-believers are apt to treat as weakening the Bible, may be among the most solid proofs, in the end, of its august origin. And again, on a lower ground, I entirely contest your statement of fact that in the early chapters of Genesis this practice of explanation has only of late begun to be adopted. It had broad ground in the early Christian literature. And I think you have mistaken a literalism, which grew incidentally out of the circumstances of the Protestant Reformation, for the true Christian tradition. . . .

Most faithfully yours,
W. E. GLADSTONE.

286. *To Lord Acton.*

NAPLES,
January 23, 1889.

MY DEAR ACTON,

. . . Most of my reading here has been about the Jews and the Old Testament. I have not looked at the books you kindly sent me, except a little before leaving Hawarden: but I want to get a hold on the broader side of the Mosaic dispensation and the Jewish history. The great historic features seem to me in a large degree independent of the critical questions which have been raised about the *redaction* of the Mosaic books. Setting aside Genesis and the Exodus proper, it seems difficult to understand how either Moses or anyone else could have advisedly published them in their present form, and most of all difficult to believe that men going to work deliberately after the Captivity would not have managed a more orderly execution. My thoughts are always running back to the parallel question about Homer. In that case, those who hold that Peisistratos or someone of his date was the compiler have at least this to say, that the poems in their present form are such as a compiler, having liberty of action, might have aimed at putting out from his workshop. Can that be said of the Mosaic books? Again, are we not to believe in the second and Third Temples as centres of worship because there was a temple at Leontopolis, as we are told? . . .

       Ever yours,
        W. E. GLADSTONE.

287. *To B. M. Malabari (of Bombay).*

July 20, 1889.

. . . I do not mean to undervalue the gravity of the tremendous problem which confronts and besets all theists alike — I mean the existence of evil in its relation to the power and goodness of God. I sometimes feel astonished at the thinness and poverty of the material with which men sometimes think they can construct solutions of it. It is demonstrated that infinite series cannot be closed, and that the circle cannot be squared. It is not demonstrated that there can be no solution of this problem, but I suppose it clear that none has yet been found. I take refuge, with Bishop Butler, in believing that, from the very limited nature of our faculties, our failure to solve a problem does not lead, by any rational process, to the conclusion that it is insoluble. At the same time I am thankful for all alleviations or mitigations of the difficulty which stares us in the face. The idea is attractive to me, that it may be in the nature of all moral evil to wear itself out of existence. But, even if such an idea proved to be true, it does not afford an answer to the problem, to the question how and why it came into existence. Neither is such an answer furnished by another conception which suggests itself to me both as a theist and as a Christian, and which, as I think, finds countenance in the Scriptures. It is this, that, perhaps or probably, this world of ours (which I cannot help believing to be a very wonderful world, even among the mighty and countless works of God) serves the purpose of a great object-lesson, as it is termed, to the denizens of other worlds, and serves for them very high purposes of instruction and edification.

There is another mode of looking at this question, which I will venture to sketch. As an individual human being, I am placed here, primarily and mainly, not to construct a theory of the universe; not, in the words of Milton, to 'justify the ways of God to man'; but to do my own duty and work out my own destiny. In this task I am largely affected by the presence of evil within and without, and I may succumb to it. But I cannot honestly say that I am conscious of being obliged to succumb to it; while I am constantly impressed with the belief that resistance to it is a wonderfully fruitful and efficacious instrument of progress in good. So that it does not at once appear what title I have to complain of my Maker on this score. But pray observe that I do not put this forward as a solution of the general question, or as an answer to many other questions, such as those growing out of the terrific inequality of human destinies or allotments of state and circumstances. The questions relating to physical evil are, or seem to me to be, of a less formidable order.

I am concerned to learn from you that, among Indians, the sense of responsibility is widely on the decline. If this be so, what can improve, or what that improves can be appreciably worth having? There is, I think, in Christian communities at the present time something painfully analogous to your allegation — namely, a decline in the sense of sin, which, instead of being, as under the Christian system it ought to be, piercing and profound, is passing with very many into a shallow, feeble, and vague abstraction; and which does not hold the place in religious teaching, so far as my observation goes, to which it is entitled. I do not know whether you have paid much attention to this part of the Christian system; but I dare say you may be aware that our Saviour, in the Gospel of St. John, predicts the giving of the Holy Spirit as the instrument for establishing His doctrine, and says that the Holy Spirit, when He is come, shall convince the world *of sin*, of righteousness, and of judgment; thus succinctly setting out what may be termed a code of moral regeneration for mankind, and setting the great fact of sin, often in Christian theology termed 'the fall,' at the threshold.

You will see that I sympathize much with your aspirations after an ending for the evil that is amongst and in us, and feel that this is a kind of half-refuge to which the speculative mind naturally has recourse. . . .

288. *To Lord Acton.* (*No date, but probably sometime in* 1889.)

My dear Acton,

. . . On the old subject of the Old Testament books and the Mosaic legislation, on which I have been so much pressed to write something with a special view to the working class. Now, I think that the most important parts of the argument have in a great degree a solid standing ground apart from the destructive criticism on dates and on the text: and I am sufficiently aware of my own rawness and ignorance in the matter not to allow myself to judge definitively, or condemn. I feel also that I have a prepossession derived from the criticisms in the case of Homer. Of them I have a very bad opinion, not only in themselves, but as to the levity, precipitancy, and shallowness of mind, which they display; and here I do venture to speak, because I believe myself to have done a great deal more than any of the destructives in the examination of the text, which is the true source of the materials of judgment. They are a soulless lot; but there was a time when they had possession of the public ear as much, I suppose, as the Old Testament destructives now have, within their own precinct. It is only the constructive part of their work on which I feel tempted to judge; and I must own that it seems to me sadly wanting in the elements of rational probability. But outside of all this lies the question how far we may go past the destructives and their pickaxes and shovels, and deal with the great phenomenon of the Old Testament according to its contents, however put together, and its results actually achieved. . . .

To a rationally destructive book such as Bentley on Phalaris I can yield my admiring homage.

Ever yours,
W. E. Gladstone.

289. *To the Hon. Mrs. W. H. Gladstone.*

DALMENY PARK,
July 10, 1892.

One of the special griefs of the present day is the shallow treatment of great subjects. On the subject of future or eternal punishment, in particular, every quack and every stripling tries his hand. Yet they do not know — and who does know? — what eternity is. Some argue, plausibly at least, that it is time with a limit. Some think of it as time indefinitely prolonged — I believe without sufficient authority. The Church at large has been very cautious, and has not, I think, endeavoured to explain eternity: and it seems as if the Almighty had purposely left a veil upon this great subject.

But I *believe* that Dr. Farrar, when Dr. Pusey had written on the doctrine, accepted such an eternal punishment as he had maintained. The proposition, I think, is something like this. Punishment may be considered as a judgment from without, but it is also a natural growth from within, and is the consequence, in the way of natural growth, which sin deliberately persisted in of itself brings about.

Philosophy seems to teach that character is formed mainly by customary action, which forms mental habit, and by long continuance hardens, so as finally to become unchangeable. In cases where evil runs this full course, it is difficult to see where lies the escape from that state which our Saviour describes by the worm that dieth not, *here* using the figure, not of an infliction from without, but of a self-growth from within.

Persons think they honour God by imagining (apparently) some higher form of redeeming process in a future state than the present Christian one. For this, however, there is no warrant in Scripture, the tradition of the Christian Church, or reason, if I estimate reason rightly. It is very dangerous for us to set about well-meant vindications of God which He Himself has not revealed to us, and of which no one that I have read at all solves the admitted difficulties of the subject.

There are those who say sin is a disease, and a mortal disease, and it must, like other mortal diseases, when it has taken final possession of a being, destroy that being: and when our Saviour says, 'whose worm dieth not,' these would hold His meaning to be, the worm in these unhappy creatures, being inseparably annexed to the life, eats it out, destroys it, and is only itself destroyed in it. I do not rely on this, the subject is too far beyond me: I am not able altogether to put this plea wholly aside.

The upshot of the whole matter thus far seems to be that over-bold and rather flimsy speculations have become so much the fashion that, as a matter of fact, clergymen are intimidated from preaching about the future punishment of sin at all, and I really believe this is one cause which at present helps to enfeeble the 'arm of the Lord' used in preaching.

W. E. GLADSTONE.

290. *To the Rev. H. Mackeson.*

BLACKCRAIG,
September 13, 1893.

No book is fuller than the Scripture (especially, I think, the New Testament) of verbal contradictions. If a teacher rides off upon one of the statements, arbitrarily choosing to take it as the supreme, entire, exclusive truth, he makes great havoc of the Holy Book, and perhaps of his own title to be considered as a man of sense. It is a cruel return for the wise and tender consideration which adopted, in condescension to our narrowness and weakness, this mode of exhibiting the various sides of truth and the comprehensiveness of its nature.

It is indeed a daring and a narrow proposition that God has no foreknowledge. A knowledge of the future is necessarily foreknowledge. He who denies this is guilty of a contradiction in terms.

When God created Time, He created what may be termed futurition. If we say all things are present to Him, we use a figure of speech which is only true in the sense of saying that this accuracy and precision of foresight are such as to make them be as if they were present.

Can anything be clearer than the separability of predestination and foreknowledge? The man who uses Babbage's machine foreknows with certainty his results, but in no way predestines them.

When the Apostle speaks of predestination, he means, I suppose, to illustrate the fixity of things future. He adds nothing to the Divine foreknowledge, but he adds much to our sense of it, and helps us towards an adequate conception of what without this trait would would have been an abstraction. I hope your ex-parishioner will escape from the labyrinth in which he is entangled.

291. *To Sir Thomas Acland, Bart.*

London,
December 3, 1893.

... I am rather more painfully impressed with the apprehension that the seen world is gaining upon the unseen. The vast expansion of its apparatus seems to have nothing to balance it. The Church, which was the appointed instrument of the world's recovery, seems, taking all its branches together, rather unequal to its work. I doubt, however, whether any effectual and permanent efforts can be made except within its precincts (largely viewed) and under its laws.

I venture to hope that, when you pronounce judgment on the undue predominance of logic in positive dogma and in the negative scepticism, you will not regard these two as standing upon quite the same level in regard to claim upon our respect and deference. It seems to me that the singular mode in which the dogma of the Church was matured in centuries 3–5, and the obstinate durability it has shown, constitute a great marvel of Providential government. I do not mean that my poor private judgment follows sympathetically *all* the dogmatic procedure of that great period. Were I to take my stand on it, I should say the case of Nestorius was a hard one, and the Nestorianism of to-day hardly seems to carry all the marks of heresy.

But in judging of those conclusions, accepted by the great body of the people of God from that day to this, I feel that I do not approach them upon the level, but have to look a little upwards. As to the present scepticism, I have no such sentiment, and think that the common Christian is entitled to deal with it very freely on its merits. The large family of *isms*, huddled together under its name, present to my view not much either of duty or of strength. They have had a factitious advantage in this, that the work of clearing orthodoxy of its factitious encumbrances has seemed to be, perhaps has been, more or less their work.

I am driven back more and more upon the question, 'When the Son of Man cometh, shall He find faith upon the earth?' which cannot be frivolous or unmeaning, since it was put by our Saviour. . . .

292. *To the Rev. S. E. Gladstone.*

BIARRITZ,
February 3, 1896.

. . . I can only give you very summary indications of the contents of my paper, which will touch, I think, 100 pages.

1. My impressions about 'Eternal Hope' are much like yours.

2. What is much more grave in my view is that 'the terrors of the Lord' are fading and dying out of orthodox preaching. A bad sign of the times was Mivart's 'Happiness in Hell.'

3. With them will fade and dwindle the idea of sin.

4. I am profoundly struck on finding that Butler declines to *commit* himself to 'natural immortality,' or avoids it.

5. Next, I find it is nowhere in Scripture or the Creeds, and am not inclined to allow it to be an article of religion.

6. I suppose it to be a philosophical opinion which gradually, from *about* the time of St. Augustine, found its way into the popular tradition: but has never been affirmed by the Church at large.

7. What I find in Scripture is, a flood of light upon the blessed future of the righteous, but much reserve,

beyond a certain line or precinct, on that of the wicked.

8. That line thus defined, they are described generally as passing into misery; a veil falls on them there, and is never lifted; no more than this misery is revealed.

9. I do not embrace or recommend the opinion of annihilation, which never, so far as I know, until now has found any wide [acceptance?].

10. What I am led to desire is *reserve* beyond the precinct, free and bold teaching within it.

11. My opinions on the disputed points are *subject to correction*.

12. But I see plainly that it is natural immortality, considered as an article of religion, that has forced on the question of 'eternal punishment,' and that from that question religion is suffering fearful disadvantage. Those who deny are bold and rash against it; those who believe hardly dare say so, and practically it is on the way to becoming obsolete.

13. I am printing in America, where I hope to gain the benefit of *criticism without stir or excitement*. Presently I shall consider whether to reprint in my Butler Essays. But I expect to see proofs of the important parts before publication in America.

14. General upshot — I am moved to meddle by the sense of a very threatening danger: and I wish to be very cautious as to means for checking it.

15. I may add that I was on this subject twenty years ago, and was torn away from it by the Eastern Question (1879). . . .

CHAPTER IV

EDUCATION

1843-1894

IN 1843 Sir Robert Peel's Government, of which Mr. Gladstone was a subordinate member, made the first serious attempt at dealing with elementary education. Lord Ashley had called the attention of the House of Commons to the vicious condition of the manufacturing population, and Sir James Graham at once gave notice of a Factory Bill which should provide some moral training for the children in these districts. Morality and religion were not then supposed to be separable, and Graham's proposals amounted to an endowment of religious instruction under the superintendence of the clergy of the Established Church. New schools were to be set up partly by local exertion and partly by a Government grant. The managers were to be the incumbent and churchwardens of each parish and certain elected trustees. The teachers must be approved by the Bishop of the diocese, and the books used were to be the Authorized Version of the Scriptures and certain portions of the Prayer-Book. By the time that the Bill came up for the second reading, the impossibility of carrying these clauses had become plain even to their author. The whole Nonconformist community was in arms against them. Dissenters, it was said, would be excluded from the management of the schools by the composition of the trust, and the Bible, being taught by Church teachers, would be interpreted in a Church sense. In vain did Graham promise that any teacher misusing his opportunities in this way should be removed by the Committee of Council, and make provision for Nonconformist children being taught the religion of their parents on one day in the week. Petitions against the education clauses poured in from all quarters, and on the 19th of June the Government withdrew them. Mr. Gladstone saw clearly the force of the Nonconformist objection, and the difficulty of meeting them except by the surrender of the very points which made the clauses valuable to Churchmen. But his position 'in office, yet not one of the Cabinet who are parties to such a measure,' necessarily kept him silent. 'Anything that I might say,' he writes to a clergyman, 'could hardly fail to bear in the eyes of the public an official character, whereas in point of fact I have no authority whatever to express in whole or in part the views of the Government. If I made a strong and warm speech, it would inflame the opposition of the Dissenters; if a feeble and indecisive one, it would dishearten Churchmen and arouse their suspicions — and in neither case could they avoid drawing inferences, though in neither case would there be any foundation for them.'

In 1870 these same questions presented themselves in a more urgent form, and Mr. Gladstone's share in the Education Act of that year has often been made the foundation of a charge of inconsistency. It cannot be denied that his position towards that Act was very unlike that in which a Prime Minister ordinarily stands to one of the chief measures of an eventful session. It was reserved for Mr. Gladstone to denounce with remarkable persistence a law passed by his own Government, and defended by himself under a total misapprehension of its actual results. The undenominational teaching which was created by his own Education Act became the 'moral monster' of his closing years. It is worth while to inquire what Mr. Gladstone expected from this measure as finally shaped, and why his anticipations were so signally disappointed.

The undenominational principle which for years past has been attacked and defended with equal vigour had no place in the original Education Bill. As it left the Parliamentary draftsman's hands, it put it in the power of each School Board to decide for itself what the character of the religious teaching in its schools should be. This was the plan 'chosen deliberately by the Government,' and the plan which Mr. Gladstone thought in itself the best (Letter 304). Judging by the subsequent action of the School Boards, it is probable that, even if this liberty had been left to them, the great majority of them would have used it to establish a kind of religious teaching substantially identical with that actually adopted under the Cowper-Temple clause. But no one, unless it were W. E. Forster, thought this at the time. The strength of the undenominational feeling in the country had not been tested, and Mr. Gladstone was probably of opinion that the religious teaching given in Board Schools would be Anglican in the many districts where the Church was strong, and limited to 'Christian instruction *minus* Catechism, Church, clergy, and Sacraments,' only in the few districts where the Nonconformists were strong. This was also the opinion of Dale of Birmingham. There was nothing, he said, in the Bill as it stood at first to prevent the Board Schools from being, what in his opinion many of them would be, purely denominational institutions. The Nonconformist objection to this provision proved too strong to be resisted, the use of any 'catechism or religious formulary distinctive of any particular denomination' was forbidden in Board Schools, and the very teaching which Mr. Gladstone so hated was set up, as the event proved, in every rate-provided school.

Why, then, was he a party to so radical a change in the Government Bill? Simply because he did not foresee in what sense the words 'catechism or religious formulary' would be read by the authorities which had to interpret them. He had no love for the clause which was forced upon him. He held the original form of the Bill to be the best, and, when the retention of this proved impossible, he would have preferred that the State should pay for nothing but secular teaching, and leave religious teaching to be provided by the voluntary efforts of the several denominations. But in the Cowper-Temple compromise he saw, as he thought, a last refuge for the denominational principle. All that was forbidden was the use of distinctive formularies. Not a word was said against the teaching of distinctive doctrines. 'Under the new clause,' said Forster to a friend, 'you may teach Transubstantiation in every Board School in England, so long as you don't teach it out of the Penny Catechism.' 'The amendment,' said Dale, 'excluded the Church Catechism, but left the Board absolutely free to teach every one of its characteristic doctrines. . . . The formulary was forbidden, but the dogma of the formulary was permitted.' In this way, Mr. Gladstone thought, the 'popular imposture of undenominational instruction' would be killed by the very words by which Mr. Cowper-Temple proposed to give it life. Probably it seemed to him almost unconceivable that every School Board in the kingdom should deliberately choose a kind of teaching of which he had so low an opinion, or that any considerable number of teachers would make the Bible a mere peg on which to hang their religious speculations by way of comment. Had he been able to bring the Cabinet to his own point of view, he would probably have carried out the complete separation of religious and secular instruction which he had suggested to Lord Ripon in the previous autumn; and at that time this simple way out of the difficulty would have had a better chance of being accepted than it has ever had since. It would have been supported by Dale and his friends — then the most influential section of Nonconformists — and it would have averted the Nonconformist revolt which was so important a factor in the Liberal defeat of 1874. Unfortunately, this solution encountered, and gave way to, the rooted hostility of Forster. He thought that to leave religious instruction to be given and paid for by those who believed in it was to make religion 'a thing of no account,' and when this strange misconception had once taken possession of him, nothing could dislodge it. Possibly, had the Cabinet foreseen the injury which the religious strife engendered by the Cowper-Temple clause was to inflict on elementary education, Forster's resignation would have been accepted and Mr. Gladstone's plan adopted. But its author saw no farther into the future than anyone else. He knew, of course, that dogma would be taught most naturally and most safely by the aid of formularies, but he also knew that it could be taught quite as effectually by a teacher with only a Bible in his hand. Consequently, as the Bill promised to pass more easily if the latter method were alone permitted, he was willing to accept Mr. Cowper-Temple's proposal. We, who are wise after the event, can see that he underrated the strength of the English dislike of dogma, and forgot that, when School Boards found themselves forbidden to use denominational formularies, they would interpret this as a prohibition to teach the doctrines which gave these formularies their importance.

293. *To Lord Lyttelton.*

13, CARLTON HOUSE TERRACE,
March 24, 1843.

. . . With respect to my speaking on the Bill [Factory Bill — Education Clauses], I am not, to my knowledge, under any implied engagement to confine myself to the subjects which belong to my department, but it naturally happened that, as they were new, numerous, and pressing, they drew me off from other matters. What I feel, however, is this: If I am prepared to support the measures of Government, I may properly speak on them off-hand; if I am not, I think it my duty to lay my objections *first* before them, and not before Parliament.

On a question of this kind, however, it requires some time and digestion to get one's thoughts into just and fixed forms, and then to apply them to a series of provisions in a Bill. I am not sure that I can do so in time to be able to speak upon the second reading, even if it be postponed from to-night. But I quite agree with you that, without inquiring whether it is of the least importance in its results upon others, I am bound, by my character, not by my conduct to utter no uncertain sound upon any controverted Church question, but to be decisive and intelligible.

My general positions as yet are these:

1. I am not prepared to agree to *limit* the teaching of the Church in the exposition of Scripture in schools,

and I consider myself to know that no idea is entertained of any such partial exposition.

2. I should think it a strange plan to allow the reading of Scripture without exposition. But if Dissenting parents choose to send their children to the reading, and keep them from the exposition, I should not refuse them the legal right so to do.

3. If Dissenting parents think fit to say they will not send their children to either the reading or the exposition, but claim to send them to other parts of the instruction, I am not prepared to say it should be refused. The position of a State and of a society to which such a system is adapted is indeed far from enviable: but I think that, while we have to keep the Church inviolate, our business with respect to the State is to bolster up its practice as well as we can.

4. As to trusteeship, I think we ought cheerfully to encounter *inconveniences*, taking, however, adequate security against the invasion of the religious system under any circumstances. . . .

294. To Sir James Graham, Bart.

13, CARLTON HOUSE TERRACE,
March 25, 1843.

MY DEAR SIR JAMES GRAHAM,

I am very anxious to avoid troubling you with any crude or premature expression of opinion upon the matters involved in the Education Clauses of the Factory Bill; but one practical difficulty occurs to me with respect to a particular point, which I think it best to state at once.

I understood you to say last night that the schoolmaster is to teach from the Holy Scriptures by explaining the meaning of the text, but so as to avoid matter of controversy. By matter of controversy I understand tenets contested between the Church of England and the general body of Protestant Dissenters, and I exclude those on which she is at issue with the Church of Rome.

The difficulty that occurs to me is this: There are many texts of Scripture of which the meaning would be stated *bona fide* in one sense by the Church, and in another by the Protestant Dissenters. Take, for instance, such a passage as the discourse of our Saviour with Nicodemus. According to the Office of Baptism and the Catechism, the *meaning* of this passage is to be found by a reference to that Sacrament, whereas according to Dissenters it is to be sought in a separate and wholly unseen operation. So that by giving an interpretation to the language of Scripture the school-master, as it seems to me, takes a side *pro tanto* in the controversy.

In *this* case his exposition would not be objected to on its own merits by Roman Catholic parents; but I am afraid you will find Lord Arundel last night represented himself rather than the religious body to which he belongs, and that they would take an objection to the child's receiving even orthodox doctrine at the hands of a teacher supposed by them schismatical.

I have contemplated the two alternatives of the teacher's giving one or the other exposition of this text. There is a third: he may avoid giving any — but then he does not convey to his pupils the meaning of the Scripture.

I believe it to be quite true, and a gratifying circumstance, that in practice, by a man of tact and ability, there need be no offence given in such a case as I have supposed. But difficulties which may be, and often are, smoothed away in practice will be objected to your plan in their most rigid argumentative forms, and you will be expected to find a solution for them beforehand. And, further, that kind of remedy to which I have referred is evidently a discretionary one — one not capable, I apprehend, of being reduced to rule and provided for by legal enactment: and if so, is it of a sort to which parties can be called upon to trust? Will the Church agree to the deliberate and systematic exclusion of the *bona-fide* meaning of portions of the text from that part of the instruction which is declared to be instruction in Holy Scripture? Or will the Dissenters agree to compulsory attendance upon lessons of which the criterion is to be their representing the meaning of Scripture according to the sense of the Church? Or will the Roman Catholics as a body agree to receiving religious instruction *at all* from a teacher belonging to the communion of the Church of England? . . .

295. *To the Rev. W. F. Hook, D.D.*

London,
March 30, 1843.

My dear Dr. Hook,

It was without my knowledge that Miss Georgiana Harcourt did me a kindness and gave you trouble by requesting you to state your views of the Education Clauses in the Factory Bill, and I have read your letter with the greatest interest. The establishment of any school system by public rate is so new, and opens such a width of possible results, that it almost makes a man start at his own shadow, and mistrust conclusions apparently the most just, merely from the impression that there are no adequate means as yet of estimating their consequences. Subject only to this general description of misgiving, I am very glad to find that you approve of the clauses of the Bill as to their main scope and outlines. I am not yet able to believe, however, that the country will bear a good measure, and we had far better have none than a bad one. Almost from year to year those difficulties seem to increase which hinder the proper action of the State in the high province of religion. We must hope to see them mitigated or removed, but this hope is slender, and we are poor indeed if it constituted the sole object of our reliance. But all experience inclines my mind to look more and more to another quarter — namely, the development of the intrinsic resources of the Church, both spiritual and secular. And in the latter branch, not according to the noble sentiments which you express, by taxation of the Bishops and clergy, which is no matter for my consideration (and it must also be said for the body that, if it be far in the rear of your standard of charity and self-denial, it is as far in advance of the general practice of the day), but by better husbandry of those immense means which her landed possessions, though the mere wreck of what they once were, still present, and likewise by the regular organization of a system of Christian offerings in their proper place as an accompaniment of the administration of Christian ordinances. There is another question which some day or other it may be right to entertain — namely, that of public rating, with exceptions in favour of those who declare themselves dissidents. I know great objections are laid against any plan of this nature: I admit there is force in them, and I do not say that the time for raising the question has come, or necessarily will come, but merely that there are conditions under which it might be the least undesirable alternative of those open to choice. It would be a very great relief to the Church if all those who are *deliberately* Dissenters would declare themselves so, and assume that legal standing. But I suspect one of the great difficulties of the Church in this generation will be to gain a point apparently so simple, and in point of right so incontrovertible.

W. E. GLADSTONE.

296. *To the Bishop of Salisbury (Denison).*

DOWNING STREET,
August 5, 1853.

MY DEAR BISHOP,
I have no doubt you are right in your view of the private leaning of Lord John Russell's mind with respect to education. It is obvious that, if England were a 'nose of wax' in his hands, he would have something in the nature of a comprehensive or united system. But I must grant to him what I should require to claim for myself on many public questions — namely this, to be judged, not by [merely] crude personal instincts, but by the complex result at which the judgment deliberately arrives, and of which those instincts are, after all, but one element. Now, when thus tried, I think Lord John will, with reference to education in England, stand the trial. From all I have seen, I believe that he acquiesces *bona fide* in what he sees to be, on the whole, the sense of the country, and that he acts consistently upon that acquiescence.

I am not friendly to the idea of constraining by law either the total or the partial suppression of conscientious differences in religion with a view to fusion of different sects, whether in church or school. I believe that the free development of conviction is, upon the whole, the system most in favour both of truth and of charity. Consequently, you may well believe that I contemplate with satisfaction the state of feeling that prevails in England, and that has led all Governments to adopt the system of separate and independent subsidies to the various religious denominations. And I should be the last man to concur in any measure that tended to alter that state of things. I think the late Minute of the Government tends powerfully to maintain it. I do not think the Education Bill hostile to it. If in any way it is thus hostile, it is, I think, through the medium of the rating principle. It is hard to foresee in what precise manner this principle, so new among us in regard to education, will work. But in its first aspect it tends to decentralize the system, and place it under the control of local opinion, which opinion is generally favourable to the separate system. The clause which prevents giving religious instruction objected to by parents or guardians, is *primâ facie* a relaxation of the separate system, but I confess I think it is one of those reasonable and guarded relaxations which gives increased security to the substance of the very system which it relaxes. You are aware that the Government entirely repudiate the construction which some have been inclined to put upon the clause — namely, this, that parties having the charge of schools would be obliged to admit children of all religious creeds, as well as that, having admitted them, they would be put under control as to the instruction to be given. I do not myself see that there is any ground or colour for such a construction: and, at any rate, in what I say of the Bill, I entirely put it out of view.

W. E. GLADSTONE.

297. *To the Rev. J. Woolley (University College, Sydney, N.S.W.).*

GLENQUOICH, N.B.,
August 22, 1853.

REVEREND SIR,

. . . In the year 1845 I gave an earnest support, as an independent Member of Parliament, to Sir Robert Peel when he introduced a Bill for founding colleges in Ireland not subject to any religious test, nor invested with any distinctively religious character. I did this deliberately, not from any preference for such a scheme of education, but because I was convinced that it was framed in a spirit friendly to religion as well as to liberty of conscience, that it was the best of which the case admitted, and that, mainly because of the animus of the plan as evinced by its subsidiary provisions, it would in its operation tend not to sap, but rather to consolidate, the foundations of belief in Ireland.

I trouble you with this recital because, from the circumstances which you are good enough to detail, I would hope that the case of Sydney may in its essentials be a parallel case, and because in any parallel case I should undoubtedly pursue the course — so far as I might be concerned with the subject-matter — which I took with reference to the Queen's Colleges in Ireland.

You have no cause, therefore, to believe that I could read your letter or your remarks on the late admirable Bishop Broughton with adverse and disparaging prepossessions. It would indeed be presumption in me were I to affect, with my imperfect knowledge, to have an opinion upon a question so grave as the question what line of conduct the clergy ought to have pursued or to pursue with regard to the Sydney University. But I would not only assent to, I would ever and strongly assert, the principle that it is in this day their especial duty to take to heart the lessons which the time is teaching, and to inquire in what way they can best use for the fulfilment of the essential and perpetual mission of the Church those new instruments, and those altered and still altering opportunities, which this critical period of human destiny affords them. Like other men combined into a profession, they contract more or less of peculiarities not requisite for the fulfilment of its work: nay, more, beyond other men, as being especially charged with a Divine unchangeable deposit, they are bound to be jealous for its security, and circumspect in committing it to the action of novelty and vicissitude. But their paramount obligation must still be, like that of other men, to judge for the best by the light of prudence within the lines laid down for them; and this conception of their duty is, I think, making at any rate perceptible progress, at least in this country, from year to year among them.

W. E. GLADSTONE.

298. *To the Archdeacon of Nottingham.*

11, Carlton House Terrace,
July 16, 1867.

My dear Archdeacon,
I used words in the debate on Mr. Bruce's Bill corresponding in substance with those which you quote, and they are the expression of a conviction to which I have sought for nearly thirty years to give effect. That conviction has become, not more clear, but more urgent, with the increased urgency of circumstances. If anything is to be done to save denominational education, it should be done with speed. The time is short, and the final issue drawing near.

The Conscience Clause has been regarded by the Church with an evil eye; it is, in my view, the last plank. By it I understand free teaching on the one side for the body in connection with which the school is founded; free withdrawal for children of other bodies.

I do not think we can claim as a right on the part of the State that the Church should take the Conscience Clause. It is a matter of free compact. I would urge it, not in the name of the State, but in the name of the true interests of the Church itself.

Your plan would admit the Conscience Clause within certain limits into all State-aided schools. Would not those limits be difficult to observe in practice wherever the clause operated extensively? Would those who object to the clause not object to your compromise?

I hail with pleasure any plan which, like yours, lets in the principle of the Conscience Clause. But it is fair to say, I think the clause would follow bodily in its entire and unrestricted application.

I hope the clergy will, before it is too late, decline to commit themselves finally in another battle which can only end in a crushing defeat.

W. E. Gladstone.

299. *To Earl De Grey.*

November 4, 1869.

My dear De Grey,
I have read Forster's able paper, and I follow it very generally. On one point I cannot very well

follow it: the proposal to found the rate schools on the system of the British and Foreign Society would, I think, hardly do. Why not adopt frankly the principle that the State or the local community should provide the secular teaching, and either leave the option to the ratepayers to go beyond this *sine qua non* if they think fit, within the limits of the Conscience Clause, or else simply leave the parties themselves to find Bible and other religious education from voluntary sources? I suppose you have got exact information as to the mode in which (so we are told) religious education is reconciled with nationality and universality in Prussia? . . .

W. E. GLADSTONE.

300. *To Earl Russell.*

March 24, 1870.

. . . The Education Bill itself is the one critical measure. It involves principles of vast sweep and much novelty, the questions of universality, compulsion, local rating, gratuitous teaching, and along with these, of course, comes up again our old friend the religious difficulty, with the rival claims of all the different modes of eluding or arranging it. A state of clear, firm, and well-balanced opinion is the best help we can have in working through such a mass of complication, but such is not the actual state of opinion. Men are decided, not between two courses, or even three, but four or five: secularism, Bible-reading, Bible-reading with unsectarian teaching (to be limited and defined on appeal by a new sort of Pope in the Council Office), Bible-reading with unlimited exposition, or, lastly, this plus Catechism and formularies, each of these alternatives viewed more or less in the light of private interests and partial affections, and these complications recomplicated with the competition between local and central authority. All this shows a state of things in which it will be very difficult to maintain the equilibrium of the measure, and in which mere resolute resistance, or even untoward help, might be attended with very awkward results. Still, there are favouring circumstances. Forster's position is excellent. Great admissions are made. The Dissenters and the Church are both represented by many reasonable men. Lastly, all except pure secularists or very bitter men seem to feel that great embarrassment would ensue upon the loss of the Bill for the year. Such is the map of the situation—not very legible. For my own part, I think the sum of my desires is that, with a measure on all the other points worked up to the point of real efficacy, we should leave religion free, and not discountenanced or disparaged, protect conscience effectually, and keep the State out of all responsibility for, or concern in, religious differences. . . .

301. *To Henry Richard.*

March 28, 1870.

. . . I have, however, read with much interest the memorial you have sent me. And I should be much obliged if, in the course of the next three or four weeks, you were able to give me an answer to the following question: whether in the view of the memorialists generally the unsectarian education in the rate schools, for which they ask, would (setting aside the question of pædobaptism) admit of a pretty complete religious instruction in those schools, according to the use and within the limits of the ordinary teaching of the Nonconformist pulpits? I would also submit one other point of inquiry.

Supposing that, in unsectarian schools such as are intended by the memorial, a schoolmaster is charged with expounding the Holy Scriptures in the sense of the sacramental doctrines of the Church Catechism, *who* is in this, and in any series of like questions, to have fixed authority to decide the case, and thus to draw the line between sectarian and unsectarian education? This seems to be a matter of great difficulty, but it lies at the root of the proposal. I am very thankful for the kind terms in which you write; and I sincerely trust that a spirit of intelligent equity towards all parties will enable us to dispose of the controverted matters in the Education Bill, which many appear to find so perplexing. . . .

302. *To Archbishop Manning.*

June 22, 1870.

... You ask what we will do for the Roman Catholic University in Dublin. Nothing could be less desirable than that there should be any correspondence between you and me on that subject at present. Already the shadow of the question of Irish education is cast darkly over the English Bill. Upon that Bill we have striven as far as we could to serve the interests of the Roman Catholic body, in and by serving the interests of general justice. I must say in honesty that, in the general proposals and manifestations throughout the country, while no very enlightened view is taken of justice to the Church of England, justice to the Roman Catholics appears, except by a very few, to be wholly forgotten. It is coolly proposed by a large section that, while undenominational education shall be made to reign in schools founded by the rate, the Privy Council grants shall remain provisionally until the schools which they aid can be gradually swallowed up in the so-called national system. Communications with those who represented your communion seemed to show that their views with reference to the Bill were summed up in seeking adequate provision for the voluntary schools, and that there were no terms which could be proposed for rate schools of a nature to be accepted by them. Mr. Allies told me, if they could make sure of one moiety of the school charges from the State, he thought they could perhaps perform their work; and this moiety will, I apprehend, now be secured for efficient schools by the proposals of the Government. While the Roman Catholic interest is most concerned of all, I feel sure we have served the general and comprehensive interests of justice by the new provision. But the business is a very heavy one. Time is against us, so is much prejudice. On the other hand, there is a lack of firmly organized opinion, and possibly the weight of the Government may in this state of things suffice to carry the Bill. ...

303. *To W. E. Forster.*

October 17, 1870.

... I have thought over the question which you put to me about the three Creeds, and have looked a little into the case of their character and reception. It appears to me that it is quite open to you at once to dispose of the Nicene and Athanasian Creeds, and to decline inquiring whether they are distinctive, upon the ground that they are not documents employed in the instruction of young children; and to this refusal it would seem quite safe to adhere until proof to the contrary can be alleged. Obviously, no one has a right to call on you to define the distinctive character of a formulary such as the Thirty-nine Articles, or of any but such as are employed in schools. With respect to the Apostles' Creed, it appears to me not to be a distinctive formulary in the sense of the Act. Besides the fact that it is acknowledged by the great bulk of all Christendom, it is denied or rejected by no portion of the Christian community; and, further, it is not controversial in its form, but sets forth in the simplest form a series of the leading facts on which Christianity, the least abstract of all religions, is based. ...

W. E. G.

304. *To Lord Lyttelton.*

11, Carlton House Terrace, S.W.,
October 25, 1870.

... I have read your letter with much interest, and with every disposition to concur in what you say of the Cowper-Temple clause. I should much like to talk the matter over with you at large. Meantime I will only say that it was in no sense my choice, or that of the Government. Our first proposition was by far the best. But it received no active support, even from the Church, the National Society, or the Opposition; while divers Bishops, large bodies of clergy, the Education Union, and—earliest of all, I think—Roundell Palmer in the House of Commons, threw overboard the Catechism. We might then have fallen back upon the plan of confining the application of the rate to secular subjects, but this was opposed by the Church, the Opposition, most of the Dissenters, and most of our own friends. As it was, I assure you, the very utmost that could be done was to arrange the matter as it now stands, where the exclusion is limited to the formulary, and to get rid of the popular imposture of undenominational instruction. . . .

305. *To John Bright.*

HAWARDEN,
November 25, 1871.

. . . The state of things as to the Education Bill is singular and threatening. The subject lay deep in my mind and motives when I saw you, but I did not dwell on it very largely, as it is hardly ripe for its crisis. At least not ripe in the view of the Government; but there is so much jealousy, suspicion, and irritation, that it may ripen or explode without our agency. It seems more likely than any other matter to be the death of this Government in connection with some one of the three countries.

As to me, I know not whether the Nonconformists and I shall always be able to 'put up our horses' together; but they have behaved honourably and handsomely to me, and I desire to reciprocate in fair and straightforward conduct. I should wish to retire from public life, rather than at this advanced hour of my little day go into sharp and vital conflict with them.

I feel also that some reserve in speech, and much careful reflection, are the present duty of the Government with regard to the question of English education in its present stage. It may be interesting to you that I should state what took place in the Cabinet to bring the provision as to rate schools and the religious instruction in them to its present form.

I enclose a memo containing five methods of dealing with this point, all of which had advocates.*

* This has not been found.

No. 1 was that chosen deliberately by the Government (I rather think before you left it, but as to my present purpose this is immaterial); and I for one think, as I believe we generally think, that, if the country would have taken it, this is the *best*. But it was, or was deemed, untenable in Parliament.

This being so, my own view was, and still is, that there was no other solid and stable ground to be taken except that of No. 5.

But this was not the view of —

1. The Cabinet. I may add that I doubt whether anything would have induced Forster to acquiesce in it.

2. The Church, which without doubt much preferred No. 1: but yet the body in general acquiesced in No. 2, and a not unimportant fraction of the clergy recommended it. A fraction of this fraction would have taken No. 3.

3. The Dissenters. This I know well, because my own preference of No. 5 was too decided to allow me to be blind to any indications in its favour. I satisfied myself by separate and detailed conversations with many deputations, and with such men as Miall, Richard, and Winterbotham, that they were, in vast majority, determined on having No. 2 if they could not get No. 3, which the Church would not have tolerated, and which would only have laid the foundation of fresh controversies. Some went as far as No. 4, but a decided minority.

Nonconforming opinion is now altered, and altering; and part of the blame they award to Forster is because he was then and now of the opinion which they held then, but not now.

I think what I have said will show (of course to you in great secrecy, as to the Cabinet) how we were led to our conclusion. I think I can say it was the only form in which the Bill could have passed, and that it should pass was what all demanded.

I hope that a little time will bring the Dissenters to clear and decided views, not only on Clause 25 (for the matter cannot be dealt with piecemeal), but on the whole subject, so that we may know with what materials we have to deal.

Upon the whole matter I do not despair; I am

rather inclined to despond, but I wish not to hurry.

An election fought upon this battle at the present time would certainly, I apprehend, throw the Liberal party into a minority, as the whole party has not adopted, nor, indeed, has the whole Protestant part of it adopted, the creed of the dissatisfied as it stands.

I do not even feel that I yet understand the whole argument. As far as I do understand it, I am not surprised that the Dissenters should run restive.

Finally, I have read with care Mr. Dale's most able and striking speech — a speech quite sufficient of itself to make a man; I only make on its matter this one observation: it contains no answer whatever to the question, 'What right have you on your own principles to compel the ratepayer to pay for what you are pleased to term unsectarian religious instruction in rate schools, when he chooses to object to it?' The more so as this unsectarian instruction is to a great extent Dissenting instruction—the instruction which a Nonconformist would spontaneously give in a school of his own: being, in brief, Christian instruction *minus* Catechism, Church, clergy, and Sacraments. It seems hardly too much to say that the speech blinks the question.

306. *To the President of Maynooth* (*Dr. Russell*).

January 2, 1873.

. . . We are approaching a third great and critical question, and the redemption of our last specific Irish *pledge*, though not the fulfilment of our last duty, for duty can never cease. If we fail, I think it will not be from an inadequate sense of the character of our engagement, nor from want of pains, nor from what is called the fear of man. From the nature of the case in part, but more from the temper of men's minds on this particular question, no plan can be proposed which will not attract much criticism; but I think, if upon the whole we are met in the same spirit as in 1869 and 1870, we may, please God, accomplish this step also towards the improvement of Ireland. . . .

307. *To Archbishop Manning.*

11, CARLTON HOUSE TERRACE,
March 8, 1873.

MY DEAR ARCHBISHOP MANNING,
The violent outburst (as I think it) from the Irish Roman Catholic Bishops has been exaggerated, but, strange to say, the exaggeration marks the views taken by those who follow as much as by those who repudiate them. They as lords and masters (which I suppose them to be) of the Roman Catholic College refuse the place offered it in the Bill. This is a blow to the Bill, but it could be borne. They have expressed a desire that the Bill should not pass in its present form, and the consequence is that I am saluted by their followers with an announcement that they must vote against the second reading, and so prevent the House of Commons from modifying or altering the Bill in Committee. This is a grave matter: for it comes to a question of votes. *Your* (*my*) demands are easily dealt with: I should be ashamed to offer a measure that did not concede them. I shall fight to the last against all comers, but much against my inclination, which is marvellously attracted by the vision of my liberty dawning like a sunrise from beyond the hills. For when this offer has been made, and every effort of patience employed to render it a reality, my contract with the country is fulfilled, and I am free to take my course.

I remain,
Affectionately yours,
W. E. G.

308. *To John Bright.*

January 27, 1874.

. . . The Dissenters will, in my opinion, greatly damage their own cause, not generally alone, but in connection with the specific matter of the Education Act, if they ask from our candidates a positive pledge to go against the present denominational grants to the Roman Catholics.

The fact is, it seems to me, that the Nonconformists

have not yet as a body made up their minds whether they want unsectarian religion, or whether they want simple secular teaching, so far as the application of the rate is concerned. I have never been strong against the latter of these two, which seems to me impartial, and not, if fairly worked, of necessity in any degree unfriendly to religion. The former is, in my opinion, glaringly partial, and I shall never be a party to it. But there is a good deal of leaning to it in the Liberal party. Any attempt to obtain definitive pledges now will give power to the enemies of both plans of proceeding. We have no rational course as a party but one, which [is] to adjourn for a while the solution of the grave parts of the Education problem, and this I know to be in substance your opinion. . . .

309. *To Dr. Döllinger.*

April 28, 1873.

My dear Dr. Döllinger,
    Mr. Meyrick has kindly allowed me to peruse a most interesting letter which he has recently received from you. It shows me what I should hardly have ventured to hope, that you had been able amidst all the pressing, and even harrowing, interests of your own position to give attention to our late debates and transactions on the Irish Universities Bill, and it emboldens me to send you copies of two speeches delivered by me in regard to that Bill. I cannot wonder that much which it contained, and many also of its omissions, should stand ill when measured by a German standard, as they do even when tried by an English one. But I am sorry to say that almost all, if not all, its defects were virtues in relation to the lamentable state of the University question and of the higher education in Ireland. And nothing struck or pleased me more than the great favour which was won by the Bill among our highest and most practical academic men, particularly at Oxford. Goldwin Smith, a real leader among academic reformers, thought it worth while to send his eulogy from America, which he has made his home. If you should see Pattison's 'Suggestions on Academical Organizations' (he is the head of a college at Oxford), you would find in it a most

trenchant exposition of the case of Oxford, and very daring proposals of change. It was a disappointment to me when, six weeks ago, the Leader of the Opposition flinched from facing the consequences of his own operations, and left us no choice but to retain our offices: for without at all complaining of the conditions of public life, I feel that it ought to be subject to a measure of time and quantity; and if a choice is permitted, I do not mean to exhaust the decline of life in such excess of strain and in such an atmosphere of incessant contention.

Believe me, with warm respect and regard,
Your attached friend,
W. E. G.

310. *To the Rev. S. E. Gladstone.*

HAWARDEN,
November 26, 1877.

Before learning that the question of compulsion for this school district was to be raised next week, I had made appointments in London which will compel me to be absent.

It is however, I think, a question which should be decided according to the conscientious and informed judgment of the ratepayers.

In arriving at that judgment, they ought, I think, to fortify themselves by full and authentic information on a variety of points, such as —

1. The known or probable feelings of those who will not take an active part at the time, but who may hereafter judge, and censure freely, those who do take such a part.

2. The numbers of children not now attending school, and particularly the increase or decrease of this neglected class.

3. The particular circumstances of the cases of neglect, especially how far it is wilful and obstinate.

I have not the close and minute acquaintance with the state of the case which is needed for useful advice to the ratepayers.

But I may say there are *two* suppositions upon either of which I should regret the adoption of the proposal for compulsion at once:

1. *If* the voluntary attendance is growing in such a way as to promise becoming in a short time nearly universal.

2. *If* the ratepayers generally are not thoroughly apprised of what is being done in their name.

I presume you will do all in your power to inform your parishioners, without, perhaps, taking in other respects a very active part.

311. *To the Rev. Septimus Buss.*

HAWARDEN,
September 13, 1894.

. . . I have not followed the particulars of the controversy in the London School Board. Nor do I intend to do so; for, after a contentious life of sixty-two years, I am naturally anxious to spend the remainder of my days in freedom from controversy.

I will not undertake to say what precise scheme as to religious instruction was in the contemplation of the Act of 1870. I always thought, however, that the Act for Scotland, which soon followed it, was more wisely framed.

I believe that the piety, prudence and kindness of a teacher may do a great deal in conveying the cardinal truths of our Divine religion to the minds of pupils without stumbling, or causing them to stumble, on what are termed denominational difficulties. But the contentions so called form part of the religious convictions of those who advance them, and they are entitled to respect, and ought not to be rudely overridden.

In my opinion (which I have endeavoured recently to set forth in the pages of the *Nineteenth Century*) an undenominational system of religion, framed by or under the authority of the State, is a moral monster. The State has no charter from Heaven such as may belong to the Church or to the individual conscience. It would, as I think, be better for the State to limit itself to giving secular instruction (which, of course, is no complete education) than rashly to adventure upon such a system.

Whether the Act of 1870 requires or permits anything of the kind, I cannot say; but if it did, its provisions would involve a gross error. . . .

CHAPTER V

LETTERS OF MR. GLADSTONE TO HIS CHILDREN

1847-1893

In this chapter I have included a few letters which have no direct reference to religion. Mr. Gladstone's interest in his children knew no limits; it extended to everything in which they took part. Their prayers; their work, whether at home or at school; their expenditure, alike of time and of money; the questions he thought likely to arise in the course of their reading; the special difficulties presented by their characters, their health, or their careers — all find a place in his letters, and I have not attempted to make any separation between them. There was no need, indeed, to do anything of the kind, since, whatever may be the subject on which he is writing, the reference to religion as the universal and immutable standard of thought and action is always implied.

312. *To W. H. Gladstone.*

Fasque,
Sunday, August 29, 1847.

My beloved Willy,
You are now a little more than seven years old, and are more able to think on what you are, and on what you do, than when you were a very little child. You must therefore try to render a more strict account to God; must pray for more and more of His grace;

and must try harder to be like the Lord Jesus Christ, and to love Him with all your heart.

To help you so far as I may in this, I wish to see you from henceforth every Sunday morning (at the time at which on other mornings you come for lessons), that you may then look back upon the past week, consider whether you have advanced in goodness during its course, and whether you have committed sins of which you have not before that time repented; and try to know, to confess and to repent them, and pray for pardon.

In this, and in all things may your Father in heaven bless you and make you more and more His beloved and loving child. Amen.

313. *To W. H. Gladstone.*

HAWARDEN,
September 24, 1852.

... I hope you recollect having seen and shaken hands with so great a man as the Duke [of Wellington], for it is a circumstance worth remembering, especially because the remembrance may assist you in learning some of the lessons which we *all* may learn from his character. Observe that many men have been more brilliant than the Duke of Wellington, and have had greater natural gifts, but it was the *use* he made of his powers which rendered him so remarkable. His steadiness and fixedness of purpose, his solidity of judgment, his vigorous good sense, his deep sense of *duty*, his determination, when he knew a thing was right, to do it, and not to swerve from it — these, possessed by him in so extraordinary a degree, were properties that we all may imitate and profit very greatly by imitating, each according to our measure and capacity. ...

314. *To W. H. Gladstone.*

HAWARDEN,
October 18, 1853.

... I gather from what Mr. Coleridge says that you do not take the same pains with your Latin prose as with your verses.

The art of writing really good Latin prose is a very difficult one, and possessed by few persons, you can only advance towards it by slow degrees; but it is a most valuable accomplishment, and helps much in making up the character of a scholar and a gentleman by its refining effect upon taste and judgment in expression. It is an admirable preparation for writing good English.

I dare say you do not find it so pleasant an exertion as that of writing verses, in which a sort of impetus is acquired that seems to carry us on whether we will or not, or at any rate makes the movement very agreeable, and enables us to forget the toil in the enjoyment. But if we never labour earnestly except for or with pleasure in the act, we cannot come to much good. What really tries our mettle, both as men and as Christians, is to labour resolutely, when duty calls us, at what we do not like, and by doing this, with the help of God, we acquire not only mastery over the thing we are about, but, what is still more important, a thorough command over ourselves. . . .

315. *To W. H. Gladstone.*

DOWNING STREET,
July 18, 1854.

MY DEAREST WILLY,

At first fatigue, and latterly illness, have prevented me from writing to you on a subject of great moment: I mean your having passed your fourteenth birthday, and having thus arrived at a new stage of your life as a Christian.

The age of fourteen is that which the Church very much recognizes as marking the passage from childhood, properly so called, to a state of fuller knowledge, judgment, and responsibility. At that age, speaking generally, it is considered time to prepare young persons for their Confirmation — that is to say, for a holy rite, instituted by the Apostles of Christ, in which, having taken upon themselves the vows made for them at their Baptism (which, as you know, are set forth in the Catechism as well as in the Office of Baptism), they receive graces from God by the laying on of the Bishop's hands for the fulfilment of that solemn engagement.

But even Confirmation itself is only the introduction to something higher and holier still, the Communion of the Body and Blood of Christ, which ought immediately to follow it, and to be regarded by us as the great source of spiritual life and strength thenceforward unto our life's end. I wish very much to write to you, or prepare something for you on these subjects, but I will not attempt it now: if I can manage it before you come home, I will try to do it so that you shall have it next Sunday: as I hope that you contrive to keep your Sunday as a day of peace.

I will now only say a very few words upon the *preparation* requisite for these great subjects.

Self-examination, a most needful and healthful duty at all times, is especially so at these seasons of special interest and import. It should then take a wider range: we should examine not only the course of the day or the hour by itself, but the course of our whole life, of our thoughts, tempers, desires, language, and acts, *now* as compared with what it was in our earlier years. Are we or are we not going forwards, and towards God? For if we are not going forwards, we may be sure that we are going backwards. It is essential to try ourselves in this matter, as youth comes on, and the enjoyments of the world are more keenly relished, and its snares multiply around us.

I will only suggest to you one or two simple rules by which you may acquire some knowledge useful either by way of encouragement or else by way of warning. A strong-minded mother told her son that whatever deadened in his mind the sense and desire of the presence of God was sin, and should as such be avoided.

1. Is the thought of the presence of God irksome, or is it delightful to you?

2. Are you glad that His eye should see all the inmost thoughts of your heart — should see your faults and weaknesses, that He may mercifully take counsel to amend in you whatever is amiss?

3. Do you find prayer a labour of love to you now, as it was in your childhood?

4. Do you find that you continue to love the House of God, and does your heart understand and answer

to the words of the Psalmist when he says, 'Lord, I have loved the habitation of Thine House, and the place where Thine honour dwelleth'?

5. When you pray, 'Thy kingdom come,' is it the desire of your heart that it should *really* come? that all sins and all follies should be banished from among and from within us, and that Christ alone should rule us all in thought, word, and deed?

I do not wish you to answer *me* yes or no to each of these questions. But I wish you to think them over most seriously for yourself, in calm and silence, as before God: and may He enable you to answer them *now* as you will wish them to have been answered when you stand before the judgment-seat of Christ. . . .

316. *To W. H. Gladstone.*

WORSLEY,
October 1, 1854.

. . . To read much of such matter [daily newspaper] in early youth cloys the palate: it is like eating a quantity of marmalade before dinner. There is such a thing as mental just as much as there is bodily self-denial: and one great branch of it is to impose rigidly upon ourselves the limit both of time and quantity in such reading as tends more to excite than to sustain, form, and strengthen the mind. This, I think, you will already understand, wholly or in part, and if only in part, then I rely upon you to take the rest upon trust — that is to say, profit by your father's experience. [This is] one of the great privileges that distinguishes man from the brutes, each generation of which has to begin afresh in the way of knowledge, and is not allowed to accumulate and transmit any to those that come after. . . .

317. *To W. H. Gladstone.*

HAWARDEN,
October 22, 1854.

MY DEAREST WILLY,
I mentioned to you when we met that we still hoped you might be confirmed during the Christmas

vacation by the Bishop of New Zealand; and the time when you first assume the full responsibilities of a Christian, and likewise enter upon his highest privilege in approaching the altar of Christ to be partaker of His Body and Blood, is so great an era in life that you will readily understand why I wish to make much of it, and earnestly desire that you should make it, as it were, a resting-point for looking backwards, and around you, and forwards. Backwards, to examine what you have been, and pray for pardon and for grace; around you, to consider what you are and are about, and what are your present and immediate means of improvement; forwards upon that broad, mysterious field of life which will now from year to year open upon your view.

As to the first of these three offices, I entirely trust you, and I believe in my heart you will try to discharge it as a Christian should. As to the second, I will suggest to you such rules as seem to me likely to be useful to you; but at the present time I go to the third.

The greatest service, perhaps, that I could render you — at any rate, that about which I am now most anxious — is to bring into your mind *now* what, if you do not receive it at the instance of others, you can hardly of yourself come to know until after many years. You can hardly, from your own reflections and experience, have the least idea as yet of what age teaches us respecting the reality and solemnity of life: the deep meaning, the enduring effects, especially *upon ourselves*, of all we think, say, and do; the immense opportunities of good which God opens to us; the unbounded richness of that field of which I spoke above — the field that all must traverse, but that few will cultivate at all, and that only the choicest saints of God cultivate so that it yields them 'an hundredfold.' It is yet in your power to be among them — may you share in their lot!

It may, however, help you to the perception of these things if you bear in mind the great truth of our condition as Christians. St. Ignatius, a very early martyr, astonished his pagan persecutors by declaring that he was Χριστόφορος — that he bore his Redeemer within him. That sublime privilege, however, he did not mean was his alone; it is common to all the faithful. For, says St. Paul, we are members of His flesh, and of His bones. We are incorporated into Him, and fed by Him — by Him who, though man, yet sits upon the throne of the universe. It is, then, no common destiny to which we are born.

This destiny God gives us certain means and instruments to work out. The first of these is time. You can hardly yet know, but I pray you to believe on credit, how precious it is. As you grow older you will find life so full of deep and varied interests, and of duty to be done, that your time will not suffice for them, and whatever hours you lose now, you will then deeply lament and long for in vain. It is a shocking thing that many persons want, as they say, amusements to kill time, and find their time hang heavy on their hands. How will they, when time is no more, contrive to kill eternity? How will *that* hang heavy on their hands!

St. Paul desires us to 'redeem the time': ἐξαγοράζεσθαι τὸν καιρὸν. This means literally to deal with it as a man deals with a thing which he carries to market. Now, what does he do with such a thing? He tries to get the greatest value for it, to make a profit by it, as a shopkeeper does by his goods, to bring back with him the highest price for it that he possibly can. Now, the price which we can get for our time — the profit which we can make by it — is in duties, in honourable and useful labours done. These are real value for it, since by them we ourselves grow in goodness; for these we may well give it, even as we give money for food.

Now, in order thus to redeem the time, one of the most necessary things is to distribute it: to divide it into parts with care and method, and to give to each part its separate and proper occupation. Relaxations, especially in youth, are not at variance with St. Paul's injunction, if they be adopted and regulated on the one right principle, which is this — to play in order that we may work the better and more cheerfully. And it is quite right to be earnest in play, and whatever we do to try to do it well. But when play is made the business of life, and is so pursued, or so idolized, as to indispose us for work, it then becomes sin and poison.

Method in the use of time cannot be gained without some trouble, nor all at once. At Eton you have a great help towards it in the minute subdivisions of the day for a fixed series of occupations; in the holidays I think you should now try to make a beginning. I venture to promise you that with experience you will find this — that method in application of time gives a double zest to amusement, and that, if a little difficult to learn, it is not less delightful than useful when learned. And this division of time of itself goes very far towards securing its proper use, and giving to our life that constancy and earnestness of purpose without which it can neither be pleasing to God nor honourable in the eyes of men. . . .

318. *To W. H. Gladstone.*

April 22, 1855.

I add first a few words upon what are called *relative* duties — *i.e.*, your duties to others. Do to them as you would they should do to you, and construe this precept liberally. Be strictly just to them; and not only so, but, where is a real doubt, decide in their favour, not in your own. Always put upon their words and actions the best construction they will bear: you will find afterwards that it was the true one in many cases where at the time it seemed to you improbable. While avoiding all outward cringing and arts of currying favour, be most careful to cherish inwardly a habit of estimating yourself, both as to intellectual and especially as to moral gifts, meanly in comparison with others. No two things combine together better than meekness in asserting your rights and resolute resistance against all solicitations to do wrong, with a manifest determination to be governed in your conduct by your own judgment of right and wrong, and not by theirs. Of course this does not exclude deference to authority, age, experience, or superior means of forming a right judgment; but it is rather a rule for the common intercourse of companions. You have, I do not doubt, long known that kindness and a disposition to oblige are necessary parts of the Christian law of love. And that cheerfulness in bearing what is disagreeable, though it costs an effort at first, well and soon repays it by the good-will which it honestly earns.

As to the duties of *self*-government, I add a few words on each of these three:

    1. Self-examination.
    2. Self-observation.
    3. Self-denial.

Give heed to self-examination; use it from time to time: perhaps if used at fixed periodical times, with intervals not too long between them, it will thus be most profitable. It will be of especial use in detecting, and after detection tracking, your besetting sin. When this is found, keep the eye close upon it, follow it up, drag it from its hiding-places, make no terms with it, never remit the pursuit; and so by the grace of God's Holy Spirit may you cast it out. When you have both found what was your besetting sin — that is, the sin *most easily* besetting you — and have by the same grace conquered it, then take the sin which besets you *next most easily*, and deal with it in like manner.

Besides self-examination, which is an act to be done from time to time, form a habit of self-observation. This will come to be a never-sleeping censor and corrector of your actions, always holding the rule of God's law against them, and detecting them when they swerve. The divisions of money necessary in order either to the use or even the waste of it give us without any trouble upon our own part some sense of the relative quantities of it. But the more precious gift of our time is passing through our hands in a continuous and never-ending flow, and its parts are not separated from one another except by our own care. Without this division of it into parts we cannot tell what is little and what is much; above all, we cannot apply it in due proportion to our several duties, pursuits, and recreations. But we should deal with our *time* as we see in a shop a grocer deal with tea and sugar, or a haberdasher with stuffs and ribands: weighing or measuring it out in proportions adjusted to that which we are to get for and by it. This is the express command of St. Paul, who bids us ἐξαγοράζεσθαι τὸν καιρὸν, imperfectly rendered by our version to 'redeem the time': for it means to make merchandise of it, and to deal strictly with it as men deal with goods by which they mean to make a profit, to pursue the same means they pursue — energy, care, watchfulness, forethought, attention to small things — in order that we, too, may make that profit the greatest possible.

319. *To W. H. Gladstone.*

May 12, 1855.

. . . There is such a thing as a foolish pride of knowledge, but this a person must be either very weak indeed or very wonderful indeed to entertain, particularly now when knowledge is so multiplied and extended that any efforts we may make to learn teach us at once (and it is one of their great uses) the vastness of what remains unlearned. In truth, the whole business of study is an excellent moral discipline of patience and humility if we go about it aright. . . .

320. *To W. H. Gladstone.*

HAWARDEN,
November 20, 1855.

. . . I strongly advise *again* that, whether you read much history or little, you should read it *regularly:* make an effort to do so, and I know quite well you will find it practicable. I further advise this with respect to *ancient* history in particular. Ancient history is a far better introduction to modern than modern to ancient. It may be learned at your age more easily, more completely, and more instructively. If you make your plan to read a very moderate portion of ancient history steadily, then as to modern I think you may take such times as offer.

With regard to ancient histories consult your tutor. These things have changed so much since my day that it would be rash in me to advise you. . . .

321. *To W. H. Gladstone.*

February 17, 1856.

When you reflect that your evil thoughts and dispositions, as well as acts, all lie naked and open before the Eye of God, even though they may have escaped the view of man, is this a subject of satisfaction, or of dissatisfaction? Would you have it otherwise if you could, and hide them from Him also? The Christian hates sin, and finding that neither his own nor any other human eye can effectually track it out in him, while he knows it to be the true and only curse and pest of the universe, must rejoice to think that there is one from whom it cannot lie hid — one who will weigh his own case, which he may feel to be to him unfathomable, in the scales of perfect justice and boundless mercy.

But if we are sensible of a lurking wish that we could hide the sad sight of our inner sins from God, this, while it abides, is a fatal sign.

322. *To W. H. Gladstone.*

February 17, 1856.

Beware of taking kindnesses from others as matters of course.

The heart well purged by humility is so deeply conscious of its unworthiness, that to receive acts of kindness always excites some emotion of gratitude, of shame, of surprise, or all three together — of gratitude for the benefit, of shame upon thinking how ill it is deserved, of surprise that our brethren should bestow upon us what we so little merit.

323. *To W. H. Gladstone.*

4, Carlton House Terrace,
February 20, 1856.

... The case of Brutus and his children, if I recollect it right, is one about which there could be no doubt had he lived in Christian times. But men are only responsible according to the light given them, and the light afforded by the religion of Rome was very scanty. We must always beware of judging men who were not Christians by Christian rules. Brutus had the light of natural conscience, and was bound to follow that. In *his* circumstances, the question may be rather a nice one, and I could not speak positively without having all the particulars before me. The presumptions must be against a father taking away the life of his sons; but we must consider whether as a public officer he was specially bound to provide for the safety of the State; whether the guilt of the sons left no room for doubt as to their fate; whether his executing their doom was more effectual in saving the State and the innocent inhabitants from danger; whether the moral effect in deterring others from crime, and in exalting the majesty of law, was likely to be good. After taking all these into view, we may still find cause to say he was wrong; but points of this nature should all be carefully weighed, and must affect the complexion of the case.

324. *To W. H. Gladstone.*

March 12, 1856.

Try and reconcile your mind thoroughly to the idea that this world, if we would be well and do well in it, is a world of work and not of idleness. This idea will, when heartily embraced, become like a part of yourself, and you will feel that you would on no account have it torn from you.

325. *To W. H. Gladstone.*

WILTON HOUSE,
January 21, 1857.

. . . I asked him [Lord Carnarvon] whether there was anything which struck him unfavourably in the examinations [for the Newcastle Scholarship] generally, and he said that certainly there is a defect in point of *accuracy.* I told him that when I was at Eton we knew very little indeed, but we knew it accurately.

The extension of knowledge is an excellent thing, but the first condition of all is to have it exact. I am under the impression, from our Italian reading, that you are trying to keep this always in mind, and I feel most desirous you should, for it is hard to say what an evil the want of it always proves. . . .

326. *To W. H. Gladstone.*

April 25, 1857.

Vanity, unequivocal vanity, sometimes finds vent in self-depreciation. One mode of this is when we affectedly cry ourselves down with a hope — more or less concealed even from ourselves — that others will protest and set us up again. Another mode is when we cry ourselves down as to particular faculties of a secondary order, in order by implication to set up some faculty of higher rank.

327. *To W. H. Gladstone.*

CHEVENING, SEVENOAKS,
May 16, 1859.

. . . When you are at work construing, you should be strictly on your guard against all guessing except such as is allowable. Here, you will say, is a pretty riddle: What *is* allowable guessing? Allowable guessing is such as violates no rule or *principle of grammar or sense*. There may be a word of which I do not know the meaning. I may put in my paper 'I conjecture it to be so-and-so.' It is of little consequence whether I know or do not know some particular 'hard word'; but it is of much consequence that I should not make a guess, which either shows I do not comprehend the general meaning, or else contradicts some law of construction or scholarship. It is very tempting, when we think we have a glimpse of the meaning, to drive right at it; but it is fatal if we cut our way through rules which are in their own nature as *rigid and inviolable* as those of arithmetic. . . .

328. *To W. H. Gladstone.*

11, Carlton House Terrace,
June 14, 1859.

I congratulate you heartily upon your having been elected into the body of students of Christ Church. I never enjoyed any designation in my life so much as that. It is full of incentive, full of comfort, full of honour, and full of warning.

If you look at the chief portraits in Hall, you will see with what manner and calibre of men you are associated. Neither is there any reason why you for yourself should not leave behind you a name with which in after-times others may be happy to claim fellowship: only be assured it must be on the same condition as Nature lays down for all except her prodigies, or, in other words, as God ordains for His children in general — the condition, I mean, of steady and hard work. If I may recommend you a mode in which to inaugurate your studentship, I would say *add an hour to your daily minimum of work.* Besides the good it will do you, it is a double acknowledgment — first to God, who has blessed your exertions; and secondly to the poor old College, to which I must be ever grateful, and whose fame I *fondly* hope you in your sphere will do something to restore and to increase. . . .

329. *To W. H. Gladstone.*

Deanery, Windsor,
November 14, 1859.

. . . I think there are some men who have received from the Almighty an extraordinary variety and versatility of power, so that they can afford to dispense with the benefits of mathematical study. Aristotle was not a mathematician: but the fruits of his mental efforts will perhaps remain unrivalled in their class until time shall be no more. In general it is true that we can none of us afford to dispense with any valuable training that is within our reach, and I think Mr. Hawtrey is profoundly right when he says that Euclid is more important to those who read it with difficulty than to those who feel none: just as our dumb-bells would be of little use to the men of Brobdingnag.

There is no doubt that what your mind will most want before you grapple with the business of manly life is a bracing process: and I also believe that we ought not be in any great hurry, but to give it time, and that you will find, as you go on, a steady increase of power, provided your studies be of a strength sufficient to give *tone*. I am not sure that you may not find the same *preliminary* harshness and repulsiveness in the ethics when you come to them, as you find in mathematics: but I am quite sure that if both were abandoned, or neither really mastered, on that account, you would in all likelihood quit Oxford without having realized above half the benefit she is capable of conferring upon you.

The question whether you have a 'turn' for mathematics is ambiguous and misleading. Comparatively few persons have a 'turn' for anything. Our capacities are chiefly developed out of elements which before culture were not distinctly discernible. Pascal had a 'turn' for mathematics: he drew geometrical figures in the sand; but of ten who come to do them well, scarcely one has originally a 'turn' for them. . . .

330. *To W. H. Gladstone.*

11, Downing Street,
August 1, 1860.

. . . With respect to philosophy, I do not know what may be best according to modern fashions at Oxford, nor do I know what number of books you should take up. But, as far as the value of the books in themselves and for discipline of the mind are concerned, I should recommend you as *three* books Aristotle's 'Ethics' and 'Politics' and Butler's 'Analogy.' You should also read and know Butler's Sermons. I should think you ought now to begin the 'Analogy,' *or* the 'Politics,' if not both. I would read little at a time, making sure that you thoroughly understand and *possess* everything as you go along — not that the two are the same, for the 'Politics' will call more upon memory, the 'Analogy' upon thought.

I cannot say what value I attach to Bishop Butler's works. Viewing him as a guide of life, especially for the intellectual difficulties and temptations of these times, I place him before almost any other author. The *spirit* of wisdom is in every line.

331. *To W. H. Gladstone.*

DOWNING STREET, S. W.,
October 18, 1860.

In my opinion the 'Politics' of Aristotle are much more adapted for discipline to the mind of the young, and especially to your mind, than the 'Republic' of Plato. The merit of Plato's philosophy is in a quasi-spiritual and highly imaginative element that runs through it; Aristotle's deals in a most sharp, searching, and faithful analysis of the facts of human life and human nature. All the reasons that have bound Aristotle so wonderfully to Oxford should, I think, recommend him to you. Were I to determine your study, I should say, Take for the present some lighter specimen of Plato, and nothing more. . . . The 'Politics' will require much from you in thought and energy: I *think* the 'Republic' would be lighter as well as less valuable work. . . .

332. *To W. H. Gladstone.*

11, CARLTON HOUSE TERRACE,
February 16, 1861.

. . . The work of the schools no doubt appals if you look at it in the mass; but if you map out your time — the months as well as the hours — you will find that by distribution it is adjusted, and need not be beyond your strength; though it must be up to your strength, and would lose *more than half its value* if it were not.

333. *To W. H. Gladstone.*

11, DOWNING STREET,
June 2, 1861.

. . . As you grow older you will find more and more how full the world and our life are of opportunity, and how impossible it is that, unless by our own fault, they should seem to present a blank. The real discouragement of life is in our insufficiency for the duties that crowd in on every side, and are still crying out, as it were, that they remain undone. But the consoling and powerful remedy is that nothing is asked of us beyond our power, and that, if more is offered than we can do, it is by way of gracious help to exercise our energies, and so to raise them to the best and highest state of which they are capable. . . .

334. *To W. H. Gladstone.*

11, CARLTON HOUSE TERRACE,
May 15, 1862.

I cannot avoid writing you a line in these last days of your struggle with one or two suggestions, begging you, however, not to *bother* yourself about them, but simply make use of them if you see your way to good by it. One is that in these last days you may do a good deal by using odds and ends of time down to the smallest scrap and shred of it. Things looked at in odd ways and flying moments are often easier to remember by association because they have been so looked at. It is not well to found a course of education on the idea of loading the memory; but *now* is the moment for you to load your memory as heavily as you can without stint — much can be carried for a short distance that cannot be for a long one. It is very convenient at such a time to have the eye able to run over maps and refresh the memory on cardinal or imperfectly known points of geography. Especially at this time I should say work up well all the crack passages: those which concentrate much meaning in few words; those which give characteristic and pointed illustration of the characters of the authors, or of their race, country, or institutions. I think you will find the collection of these passages in my little red books pretty good: they were of great service to me, for which I love them, and I shall love them better if they can now do you a good turn. Finally, believe all my anxiety begins and *ends* with anxiety that you should do your best, and not miss through remissness and want of resolution what you might have got by courage and determination. May God prosper alike, as He shall see best, this and all your efforts!

335. *To W. H. Gladstone.*

HAWARDEN,
October 16, 1863.

. . . It is not easy to deal briefly with the question between Mr. Pitt and Mr. Fox.

I will begin by stating Mr. Fox's great point of superiority. It was this, that he never gave his approval to the Revolutionary War. Mr. Pitt did not give in to the warlike tendencies of the country until they were very far advanced. It was probably not within the power of the man who was Minister to resist them, and the probability is that, if Mr. Fox had been Minister, he also would have yielded.

In perhaps every other point, as far as I can see, Mr. Pitt was superior, though Mr. Fox had, as it would appear, singular fascinations. Both were strong in personal friendships. Mr. Pitt was by far the stronger in private character. Speaking generally and without details, Pitt was a well-conducted and Fox an ill-conducted person.

Pitt was, I apprehend, the better man of business — a great element in the power of an English statesman.

Pitt was a sound and good political economist, in days when that accomplishment was rare, Fox was a very bad one. Pitt had a rare talent for finance, Fox seems to have had little or none.

Pitt had much general prudence, Fox fell into great Parliamentary excesses — in his attacks on Lord North, in his subsequent coalition with him, in his secessions from the House of Commons.

Pitt had a more forcible and commanding, as well as a more business-like and practical, if not a more fascinating eloquence. Lord Lyndhurst, who remembered both, told me how he was impressed in youth by Pitt's dominion over the House of Commons, and felt at a loss to understand how they could be compared as speakers. But the judgment of the world has shown that they at least were sufficiently within range of one another for comparison. Fox at his best seems to have had a grand and transporting fervour.

Lastly, Pitt had in a much greater degree the gift, so difficult to define, of inspiring confidence. In political conflict generally, he proved himself too strong for Fox. But the very great, though very pardonable, error of the Revolutionary War prepared the way for a state of things in which Pitt's so-called followers were to degenerate greatly, and in which Fox's party were to have the honour of associating their name and fame with almost all the great measures of public improvement. Hence the political predominance since 1830 of what is now called the Liberal Party.

Pitt's early career was wonderful. It is the romance of political history. Bolingbroke's first period is the only thing resembling it in Parliamentary annals: but it is at once more solid and more brilliant. It associates reality with the marvellous, and recalls the romance of Charlemagne's Court and of the Round Table, of Orlando and Sir Lancelot. Upon the whole, my impression is that Pitt was the greatest peace Minister that has ever ruled this country.

336. *To W. H. Gladstone.*

HAWARDEN,
October 19, 1863.

. . . The one great error of the war drew Pitt along with the nation into a false position. He became, contrary to the bias of his nature, in some things illiberal (though not in all — witness the question of Roman Catholic Emancipation, and the Slave Trade). In all these things, however, he was less illiberal than the country at large. The struggle in which they embarked speedily became a deadly one. A nation engaged in such a conflict soon grows to be intolerant at home; the majority cannot afford to give freedom of opinion to the minority. Hence the repressive measures which marked Pitt's war administration. All these I consider as belonging to the $\pi\rho\hat{\omega}\tau o\nu\ \psi\epsilon\hat{v}\delta os$: the minor and derivative errors were seminally contained in the great error of the war, and followed in its wake. In resisting them Fox had a corresponding advantage, and played a part which might quite as naturally have been played by Pitt. Perhaps even more so, for when Pitt proposed the Treaty of Commerce with France, Fox described her as our natural enemy. But from the subsequent course of affairs Rogers was enabled to write:

> 'What though with war the madding nations rung,
> Peace, when he spoke, was ever on his tongue.'

The ultimate issue was that, not the Tory party only, but especially the ultra-Tories, called themselves Pittites, and, in the bad domestic administration and policy which they pursued after the war was over, sheltered themselves under the name of Pitt while they were estranging the people by misgovernment from the throne and institutions of the country.

All that latter part of the great and noble-minded man's career is a powerful warning to us weaker men who embark ourselves on the sea of politics, teaching us that there are storms before which we must be driven or drive, and currents that sometimes may carry us whither we neither will nor know. In quiet times, however, this is less likely to be the case. . . .

337. *To W. H. Gladstone.*

BRIGHTON,
Easter Day, April 16, 1865.

. . . It is sometimes necessary in politics to make surrender of what, if not surrendered, will be wrested from us. And it is very wise, when a necessity of this kind is approaching, to anticipate it while it is yet a good way off; for then concession begets gratitude, and often brings a return. The *kind* of concession which is really mischievous is just that which is made under terror and extreme pressure: and, unhappily, this has been the kind of concession which for near 200 years it has been the fashion of those who call (and who really think) themselves 'friends of the Church' (a strange phrase) to make. Early and provident fear, says Mr. Burke (whom you cannot read too much nor too attentively) is the mother of security. I believe that it would be a wise concession, upon grounds merely political, for the Church of England to have the law of Church Rate abolished in all cases where it places her in fretting conflict with the Dissenting bodies; and in the case of Ireland we have *seen* the temporal interests of the Church as an Establishment greatly promoted by the absolute unconditional abolition of Church Cess, which was the Church Rate of that country. I say all this, however, not to form the groundwork of a conclusion, but only in illustration of a general maxim, which is applicable to political questions.

But next, this surely is a political question. Were we asked to surrender an Article of the Creed in order to save the rest, or to consent to the abolition of the Episcopal order in order to obtain a fresh sanction for the parochial ministry, these things touch the faith of Christians and the life of the Church, and cannot in any manner become the subject of compromise. But the external possessions of the Church were given it for the more effectual prosecution of its work, and may be lessened or abandoned with a view to the same end. I need not ask whether they may with propriety thus be compromised, though probably they may, with a view to social good only. But nothing can be more clear in principle than that they *ought* thus to be compromised, when the spiritual good of the Church itself requires it.

Now, we have lived into a time when the great danger of the Church is the sale of her faith for gold. As one large portion of the political world is disposed to tamper with the purity and integrity of that faith under the vain idea of making the whole nation become Churchmen, so another portion of it perhaps yet more seriously endangers the same priceless treasure by clinging with obstinacy to all the temporal incidents of national Establishment. The chain of cause and effect, by which this comes round to spiritual damage, is obvious. In demanding the money of Dissenters for the worship of the Church, we practically invest them with a title to demand that she should be adapted to their use in return, and we stimulate every kind of interference with her belief and discipline in order to that end. By judiciously waiving an undoubted legal claim, we not only do an act which the understood principles of modern liberty tend to favour, and almost require, but we soothe ruffled minds and tempers, and, what is more, we strengthen the case and claim of the Church to be respected as a religious body. This partial but real contrariety of interest between the true life of the Church and its temporal emoluments as fixed by law is already an element deeply entering into the work of modern politics, and before your life has run to its natural length the force of this element will be far more generally and profoundly felt. It may not yet be as visible and sensible to you as thirty-three years' experience have made it to me. With the perception of it which I have, it would be on my part treason to the Church were I to act on the principles with regard to her which are most commonly acted upon by the party in opposition. I am convinced that the only hope of making it possible for her to discharge her high office as Stewardess of Divine Truth is to deal tenderly and gently with all the points at which her external privileges *grate* upon the feelings and interests of that unhappily large portion of the community who have almost ceased in any sense to care for her.

This is a principle of broad application — broader far than the mere question of Church Rates. It is one not requiring precipitate or violent action, or the disturbance prematurely of anything established; but it supplies a rule of the first importance and value for dealing with the mixed questions of temporal and religious interest when they arise. I am very anxious to see it quietly but firmly rooted in your mind. It is connected with the dearest interests, not only of my public life, but, as I believe, of our religion. Again, I say the danger of losing gold is small; that of losing faith is great. At a time when the inspiration of Scripture, and one by one the Articles of the Creed, are brought into question by authority, our great care should be to consider, not how the outer apparatus of the Church should be maintained entire, but whether by judicious modification of it we can strengthen her hands for the purposes to which her Divine commission is addressed. I am in no way anxious that you should take my opinions in politics as a model for your own. Your free concurrence will be a lively pleasure to me, but above all I wish you to be free. But what I have now been dwelling upon is a matter higher and deeper than the region of mere opinion. It has fallen to my lot to take a share larger than that of most around me, though in itself slight enough, in bringing the principle I have described into use as a ground of action. I am convinced that if I have lived to any purpose at all it has been in great part for this reason. It is part of that business of reconciling the past with the coming time and order which seems to belong particularly to our country and to its rulers — to be appointed for them, it is not too much to say, after an especial manner, in the counsels of Divine Providence.

Now, little or nothing of what I have said bears directly upon the course to be taken by you, in the event of your being elected, with respect to Church Rates. But if you embrace the general propositions I have laid down, they will supply you with a point of view from which that course will appear, not indeed necessary, but natural. It will then appear, too, not an unworthy compromise of honour for advantage, but an application of an essentially sound general rule to a particular case in a manner which the nature of that case seems to justify. I believe that every one of my old colleagues, unless it were Lord Herbert, came by degrees to the plan of voting for the Abolition Bill. True, I have not done it myself, for various reasons, but none of them at variance with the view I have here expressed. Indeed, I will go so far as to say that, if obstinate adherence to the present very injurious law is much longer continued, circumstances *might* arrive in which it would become almost imperative to vote for the Abolition Bill *as a protest against it;* though I do not by any means so say to abandon the better ground which I hope you will maintain, that of freedom to concur in some generally fair and reasonable settlement. The great reason for maintaining in some form the Church Rate in rural parishes is not a religious one ; it is to prevent the hardship of making the clergy in such parishes practically responsible for maintaining the fabrics of the churches and the expenses of Divine worship. Reasons of the same order demand the abolition of the present law in parishes of a different character. But reasons more properly religious, and connected with the highest interests of the Church, *may* come to require, as matter of duty to her, the surrender of the whole. That state of things has not actually, I think, arrived. But the permanent duty of securing the Church (not merely the clergy) in her spiritual office should be the first principle of action : and if temporal sacrifices can promote this purpose, they should be made as freely as the shipmaster throws cargo overboard to save the lives of passengers and crew.

In speaking of spiritual compensations for temporal concessions, I do not use words without meaning. Already something has been done towards recognizing and securing the action of the Church as a religious body. In Canada the clergy and people now virtually appoint their own Bishop. The late judgment in the Privy Council, though probably intended for a different end, seems likely to lead to a widespread emancipation for the Colonial Church. In 1852 Mr. Walpole, on the part of Lord Derby's Government, stated that the Convocation could not be allowed to proceed to business ; but the Government of Lord Aberdeen which followed granted the permission. The present Government has already once given the licence of the Crown to legislate — that is, to alter one of the Canons : and is about to give a like licence for a most important object, namely, the alteration of the Thirty-sixth Canon, relating to subscription. The Act of 1854, which gave real self-government to the University of Oxford, was an important step in the same direction. In these measures I have been permitted to take my part : but had I adopted the rigid rule of others in regard to the temporal prerogatives, real or supposed, of the Church, I should at once have lost all power to promote them.

Though this is a very long letter, I will ask you to consider it carefully ; for it contains, however roughly expressed, the results of a long experience. Though I am much younger in political life than the most prominent personages of the day, Lord Palmerston, Lord Russell, and Lord Derby, yet my political life has, I believe, *now* been longer than that of almost any others of the leading men who, during the last century of years, have signalized the annals of the House of Commons. I do not expect that many years will be added to it. Though I agree with the Liberal party, and serve them heartily in general affairs, yet there is partially diffused in that party a tendency to break down the essential landmarks of religion; and should this tendency gain the upper hand and become its rule of action, as it can have no countenance from me, so I think it very probable it may be the means, and not altogether the unwelcome means, of giving me my *quietus*. . . .

338. *To S. E. Gladstone.*

House of Commons,
May 28, 1861.

. . . I feel sure that we have not misled you, and it will now stand to the satisfaction of all concerned that you remain until next Easter. I think you need have no fear about the *relish*. In this world it is very difficult to look onwards to a series of years and of situations with a distinct sense of satisfaction attaching to the contemplation of each. It more commonly happens that we fear to lose what we have, and that we are oppressed with a vague sense of misgiving as to the future. Even in circumstances of the greatest difficulty there is an adequate remedy, which is also the proper remedy in all cases where we feel that the future looks blank and chill. It is in the knowledge that disposal of the events of our life as the greater so the more minute is in the hands of God, and that He always adjusts them as is best for us. Even if we were able to do it for ourselves, we should do it ill, and while we now know ourselves to be unable, we also know that He who loves us so much both can and will do it, and do it better than we can ask or think. . . .

339. *To S. E. Gladstone.*

11, Downing Street,
April 12, 1862.

I see with pleasure and thankfulness your manful efforts, and the real and steady growth of your mind, and I have no anxiety for you about present visible results. It is probable that, if your health and strength are spared, ten or twenty years hence, should your habits of application continue, you will have passed ahead of many who are now ahead of you. The saying of our Saviour is true of the career of intelligence as well as of the spiritual state, 'The first shall be last, and the last first.' God does not put people backwards and forwards arbitrarily; but they who use well the means and faculties they possess, from being behind come to be before, and they who use them ill from being before come to be behind. If an oak could compare itself with a poplar at ten or twenty years old, it would be disappointed; but let a hundred years roll away, and the tables are turned.

340. *To S. E. Gladstone.*

HAWARDEN,
November 9, 1862.

Having recommended to you the use of Palmer's treatise on the Church, I ought to say a word more about it. I do not recommend every opinion contained in it: generally I should say that, with respect to Protestant communions other than our Church, he condemns rather too freely, and does not make allowances enough. But I think the book of great utility for the clear, and methodical, and comprehensive treatment of its subject, and the manner in which it presents to us its fundamental idea — namely, that the Church is not, according to Holy Scripture, an optional association or religious club, but a society or polity founded by our Lord Himself in the persons of the Apostles, and, though not guaranteed anywhere against *all* errors or abuses, nor in particular limbs and portions of it from fundamental corruption, or even extinction, yet that it is ordained to exist as a body visible upon earth, and to maintain the profession of the Catholic or Christian Faith, until the end of time.

341. *To S. E. Gladstone.*

11, CARLTON HOUSE TERRACE,
November 15, 1863.

I often think with regret that you are in a place which, venerable and sound at heart as it is, yet is, at least for the moment, more or less disturbed with controversies. I think they do not cause trouble to your mind, for I trust that if they did you would not hesitate a moment to communicate with me, and would take such advice as I might be able to give you. But I have just been reading Mr. Shirley's sermon, called 'Undogmatic Christianity,' preached at Oxford in May, and I think it not only a most noble and masterly production, but one which is peculiarly fitted to meet the needs of the day. . . . It is all gold, and a very little of it goes a great way. It is a production which once read now may be read again, and thought of hereafter. St. Paul teaches us to put on the whole armour of God, and this sermon is like armour. It is worthy, I would almost say, of being bound up with Bishop Butler.

342. *To S. E. Gladstone.*

LIVERPOOL,
July 18, 1865.

. . . What gives me special pleasure is your affection for dear old Oxford, and your choosing this moment to tell me that she is becoming a precious object to you. I have always cherished a lively hope that this would be so. Continue, my dearest boy, to love her, and to profit, as you have already so much profited, by what she can give you, and you may yet live to do her true and valuable service in the critical times that are coming on. . . .

343. *To S. E. Gladstone.*

11, CARLTON HOUSE TERRACE,
July 17, 1866.

. . . Now about your accounts. I am much pleased with your view and intention. You know this has been the one subject on which you and I have always in a quiet way quarrelled. It has been, for me, absorbed and swallowed up in all manner of satisfaction with respect to other and higher subjects. Not that I think it unimportant. On the contrary, I think it almost, if not quite, essential to one important province of duty — namely, the application of the rule and standard of conscience to the disposal of our pecuniary means. Pray take to it resolutely. You will find it, at any rate after a little while, much more a comfort than a burden. Could I *now* reduce my expenditure to the scale of yours, I would revert to the system of my youth, and put down every penny.

Now about your expenditure. I cannot be displeased with your reproaching yourself — you show a watchful conscience: but I certainly see nothing with which to reproach you. A quiet accumulation of books, though for future use, is not, I think, to be blamed within such limits as you fixed for yourself. This reminds me, however, that I think it was hardly fair in me to lend you Sir A. Grant's 'Ethics,' which he presented me by way of compliment, and not to stand in the stead of a purchase which an Oxford student would and could have made. I rather think you ought to buy a copy.

As regards the prospects of your examination, you do well not to let your mind rest on anything beyond what may lie fairly within your reach. To think little of results, and to work much for them, taken together, make a good rule. Something much more important than the apparent result is in this case involved, and that is the real one, which is to be traced in the state of mind, faculties, and character....

The question about the time for Orders, and the preliminary studies, is too large for me to attempt to dispose of in this letter, or except (I think) upon full communication with you. One thing, however, I would say: If there are particular subjects that press upon your mind so that you feel a practical need of clearer and fuller light with regard to them, *such* matters of controversy I think you may do well in attempting to dispose of without long delay. But it would be a mistake to suppose that by postponing ordination you could make time for going through and settling in your own mind subjects of theological controversy in general. The truth is that any such attempt at settlement would be crude, artificial, and far from durable. You would find that, with the advance of years and ripening of the mind, many new aspects of things would open, and would, as it were, dislocate the frame of thought you had set up. It is that ripening of the mind, which I have no doubt will be granted to you richly, and in which you will find the most satisfactory solutions, by the constant deepening and strengthening with experience of the bases of thought and conviction. I hope I may not bewilder you by the distinction I draw between particular and urgent subjects in which difficulty definitely formed presses for relief, and the large design of reviewing, as it were, the history of thought in regard to the great conflicts by which, as a whole, it has been distinguished. The positive teaching of the best Christian philosophers is that which gives the mind the most effective equipment, and in proportion as this equipment grows more and more effective you will find yourself able to deal more easily, as well as more extensively, with particular subjects. Numberless, it seems to me, are the cases of doubt, distress, and error, from which people would be saved beforehand if they had but a good preparation of the mind. But they go unarmed into the battle. For of arms the best and the *most* important are not those supplied by particular information on each contested subject, but a full possession of the principles and modes of thought by which all subjects ought to be determined.

344. *To S. E. Gladstone.*

11, CARLTON HOUSE TERRACE,
June 9, 1867.

.... With regard to the second question, that of your profession, and the time for entering it, I wish that my brain were more equal than it is to saying all I should like to say. This, I fear, cannot be. But I will go to the point at once by remarking that, as you do not give me your reason for postponing until twenty-five, I have not in full the materials of judgment before me, and so far I speak with reserve. But I confess that I do not see what advantage is gained by the delay, and though I should not dissuade anyone from lay work *before* the clerical age, it appears to me that to choose it afterwards is to choose a post of inferior interest as well as inferior obligation.

The path of a clergyman is not now in prospect as easy as heretofore, because the critical temper and (in part) wayward movement of the age have raised so many questions that they cannot solve. The effect is that this arduous calling is more arduous than ever. But so it is in the present day with every calling of the highest order, and these are very few — only such as deal with the government of man and his higher faculties and destinies. I often feel a comfort in thinking by far the largest part of my work is done. But this feeling, excusable at my age, would be unnatural in youth. And I can say with some confidence that, if the labours and anxieties of a conscientious clergyman are now enhanced, so are his honours and rewards. The greater or more sustained efforts he will have to make are to be made in the service of a Master who counts and records them all until the day when He shall say, 'Well done!' The field of thought is more widely open to a clergyman than ever, and its harvest richer. Depend upon it, whatever murmurings and disputings we may hear, it is still the Gospel of our Lord on which are principally hung the fortunes of the human race; and he who would desire to glorify God on earth during the time allotted to him can nowhere be more certain that every stroke of his hand will tell. Doubtless there is a sapping of the foundations of belief; so much the nobler will be the task of him who toils to confirm, clear, and reinstate them. That is on the speculative side of the clergyman's work, which presents to view the Divine philosophy of religion; but if he prefer the part of Martha, the pastoral and externally active part, or if he embrace both in the plan of his life, this, too, has mounted to an interest in the present day such as it has rarely before attained. Christianity is under strain; but it is like the strain of the good ship in the roaring sea, as it leaps from wave to wave. The immense changes in all departments of life and knowledge put faith on its trial, and apply more stress to that chain which links us to the unseen world. But these are just the very circumstances to call out the high and noble emotions of a devoted service. I admit that for the half-and-half clergyman it will be an evil time. But your nature is earnest, solid, and affectionate; and my belief is that, though you may modestly look with apprehension on the first touching of the Ark, you would with every year of experience become more and more closely attached to your profession. I write to you with a deep conviction that it is no idle venture which is before you. I write also very freely: and I hope you will be, whether by letter or by speech when we meet, as free in return. . . .

345. *To S. E. Gladstone.*

11, Carlton House Terrace,
May 26, 1868.

. . . Probably you are now learning by degrees, yet very effectually, what is the true relation of the individual mind, according to the pure law of reason, to the beliefs and institutions which he, the individual, finds existing in the world when he enters it. Rely upon it, those persons commit a fundamental error of the understanding who think it their first duty to question everything, and begin in every matter from the beginning, as if God had done nothing for mankind as a race; or who set up a supposed contradiction between authority and private reason, whereas one of the true functions of private reason is to comprehend the nature and limits, and to recognize the office, of authority as a πίστις of truth. . . .

Lord Aberdeen, a person of particularly sober mind, once said to me he supposed that no one passed through life without feeling these temptations. This was probably beyond the mark, but it was a remarkable testimony. . . .

I may so far refer to my own experience as to say that, during all my early years, my heart was set on my being a clergyman, that only my father's wish turned me away from it, and that my mind has worked incessantly on the subjects which have tried you. And the upshot is, that it seems to me to be the especial work of sound reason in these times, receiving that light of Divine grace to which you refer so justly, to aim sedulously at discrimination between the permanent and the transitory in matters of religious belief, or between belief properly so called, and the mere opinions which, according to the bias or the supposed needs of each age, tend to gather round it. Of these latter there has been a great shaking in our times; and many have done no more and no better than to substitute a new set of mere opinions for the old — some in one direction, and some in another. But the foundation of the Lord standeth sure; He will find instruments for His work, in His time, and happy are we if we are among them, as I feel a good hope you will be. . . .

346. *To S. E. Gladstone.*

Hawarden,
September 15, 1868.

. . . During very many years my mind has been much directed from time to time to the great subject of the Holy Eucharist. I am a firm believer in the words of our Lord, therefore in the 'objective Presence.' But it is the presence of a spiritual body (see the phrase of St. Paul in 1 Cor. xv.), therefore not according to the laws of a natural body. A local presence I should not have the least hesitation in disclaiming.

When you come here I will show you the MS. notes of a conversation which I had twenty-three years ago with Dr. Döllinger, the first living Roman Catholic theologian: I think they will interest and help you.

There is great fallacy in allowing what are called logical consequences in theological doctrine. Human language is only adequate to a very partial expression of Divine truth; and we must often stop resolutely where the Catholic Faith places us, and decline to follow even arguments of which we cannot at the moment detect the flaw. In this case the sophism lies in the ambiguity of the word 'body,' which is not necessarily to be confounded with or attached to *matter*. . . .

347. *To the Rev. S. E. Gladstone.*

BALMORAL,
September 30, 1871.

... It is only by comparison that our difficulties, disadvantages, and discouragements, can be justly measured. This, which is true of our positions individually, is yet more true of the Church. In proportion as its nature is heavenly, its deflections from the ideal are grievous, and to have seen these deflections in one country and in one form of the Church, only, has often led, and in precipitate or eager minds is very apt to lead, to dangerously hasty judgments.

348. *To the Rev. S. E. Gladstone.*

HAWARDEN,
August 12, 1872.

... With regard to addressing the poor and having to stand upon a level with them, this, I have no doubt, can be acquired. I feel, for example, myself that I could do this now much better than I could have done in early youth, from having had to speak to audiences of different classes, and always with a view to being understood. I know you are sensible of the importance of this subject, which in general the clergy of the Church of England do not thoroughly appreciate. ...

349. *To the Rev. S. E. Gladstone.*

HAWARDEN,
August 14, 1872.

... The entire situation recalls to me the case of Bishop Hamilton in 1854. He was sorely reluctant to take the bishopric — much like you in motives, but he was called to place himself in what was at that juncture a position more arduous than it is now, since the Episcopal Bench is now less sharply divided in its sympathies. He spent most of a Sunday with me, and I think was persuaded by my representations, joined to the desire of his predecessor — Bishop Denison — on his death-bed. I do not think he ever at all repented of having overleapt the obstacles which only his humility interposed.

It has been a great pleasure to me in this important matter that you have let me deal with you as a friend, in perfect freedom, and it is thus that I should always desire and hope to deal with my children. It imposes a special obligation to look fairly at the case, and not with a foregone conclusion. So looking at it I find it grow clearer. You have not sought or desired it; it has come to you. As regards your capacity, you reasonably look to the judgments of others rather than your own; but there can be no doubt at all which way lie the verdicts of those whom you most trust, and who know you best in your clerical capacity. It is a post of greatly increased responsibility, but why? Mainly, though not solely, because it is a post of increased opportunity to serve and glorify God. If the greater station and higher emolument are a trial, they are a trial of that kind which, though it cannot safely be challenged, may be boldly encountered when it has not been sought. The disinterestedness, which you justly think the Church so much needs, may be shown in the handling of money, as well as in the non-possession of it. The opinion of the people about which you ask may perhaps best be shown in the almost universal anticipation that this call must come upon you. . . .

350. *To the Rev. S. E. Gladstone.*

73, HARLEY STREET,
February 8, 1877.

. . . I do not approach the question of the coming Judgment from the same point of view as you do, but I sympathize with those who are, in relation to it, the object of an unjust and unwise prosecution, and I cannot pretend to place confidence in the tribunal, which, I think, does not represent the spirit of the Reformation Settlement.

It is difficult and hazardous to deal in general propositions on these subjects: but I am decidedly of opinion that such questions as the Eastward Position and the Vestments do not justify driving matters to the last issue : that they do not justify what would be justified and required by a Judgment, or a Law, forbidding you to preach the Real Presence or the Eucharistic Sacrifice.

Anything hasty, anything done until after full consultation and aim at general co-operation, would, I think, be a mistake ; but the greatest mistake of all would be resignation — the severing of a spiritual tie on account of temporal action.

Strange to say, but it is material as well as strange, I am very doubtful whether it is meant or understood that a Judgment in one diocese is to rule the whole country. What was the use of giving to each of some thirty Bishops the power to stop a suit, if any one of them was to have the faculty of allowing to go to issue what would rule the question for the whole country?

A great shock has already been given to the principle of Establishment, and the farther they go the severer the shock will be.

It is a time, assuredly, for much thought, much watchfulness, much prayer. I cannot but think God will keep longer what He has kept so long.

351. *To the Rev. S. E. Gladstone.*

73, HARLEY STREET,
March 29, 1879.

. . . I never can wonder at, I may say never can regret, any amount of sombre tints in the picture which an earnest clergyman draws to himself of his work and its fruits. My belief has long been that even the Apostles and the early Church had converted but a small *numerical* portion of society in 300 years, when the change under Constantine led to the bringing in of the masses. But are not these depressing views among the very means by which the quality of the work is sustained, and without which it could not be secured?

352. *To H. N. Gladstone.*

Edinburgh,
September 24, 1864.

My dearest Harry,
 I need not say you have been much in my thoughts since you left us, and not least since, moving northwards, I have lengthened the distance between us. I am looking with much cheerful desire to hear the issue of your examination at Eton. I feel satisfied that, if it is favourable, you will take it as an encouragement to continued exertion, which, depend upon it, is absolutely necessary to us all for a good and useful life. But even if the present result is less favourable than we could desire, it may be of great use if it be taken rightly, for it may tend to bring out increased energy, which is *sure*, sooner or later, to bring its reward.

It was a capital plan by which Willy got you into the same room with Arthur Lyttelton: and on the whole I feel that you make your start at Eton — the greatest event in your life since, as an infant, you were baptized — under very favourable circumstances. Your progress in knowledge pleased me much, and, what is more, it, I think, pleased Mr. Eminson. If any time you feel difficulty, remember that if all things were easy we never should gain strength by practice in them: difficulty is, in truth, the mother of improvement. If anything happens at any time to grieve and dishearten you, remember that such incidents of life do not come by chance ; that they are intended by our Father in heaven to form in us a temper of trust, resignation, fortitude ; and if they begin early, it is that we may early grow stout to encounter the ruder shocks which come in after-life. But I hope and think your Eton life will be both a good and a happy life. You will like the place, the buildings, the playing-fields, all the associations of Eton : you will find good schoolfellows and friends, but you must exercise a choice. . . . Make God your friend, and remember that there is not a whisper addressed to Him which He will not hear and answer. . . .
 Your affectionate father.

353. *To H. N. Gladstone.*

11, Carlton House Terrace,
March 27, 1868.

My dearest Harry,

I am much concerned that my duties here should be so pressing at this moment as to prevent my going down to Eton to-morrow and joining my prayers to your dear mother's that the grace of God may abundantly descend upon you, both in the holy ordinance of Confirmation, and afterwards through all the days of your life. I shall do my best to recollect you from hence; and among other satisfactions I am truly glad that you should be confirmed by the Bishop of Oxford, who far exceeds all the prelates I have ever heard in the wise and devout impressiveness of his administration of that particular rite.

But I look most to what lies within your own breast. It is in the preparation of the heart that the surest promise as to this and every other ordinance is to be found: in the humility and self-mistrust, in the continual looking up to God, the silent prayer of the soul, for help and strength, in the manful resolution, resting on the hope of His aid, to follow right, conscience, honour, duty, truth, holiness, 'through all the changes and chances of this mortal life,' and whether others will walk with us or whether they will not.

May that preparation of the heart, my dearest Harry, be largely and richly yours, and both to-morrow under the Bishop's hand, and afterwards at the altar of Christ, and in every turn and passage of your life, may the best blessings of God descend upon you, for time and for eternity!

Ever your affectionate father,
W. E. Gladstone.

354. *To Miss Agnes Gladstone (Mrs. Wickham).*

Downing Street,
October 17, 1854.

... Your twelfth birthday brings you into your *teens*, and almost shuts the door on childhood.

None of us can stop the flight of Time; but what

by the grace of God can be done is this, that as it passes by it can be made to carry on its wings the best fruit of life — acts of duty done, of conquest achieved over what is evil in us, of love to God and man, of that humility and obedience which are so exceeding precious in the sight of our Saviour.

May these recollections ever be yours, my beloved Agnes : place before the eyes of your mind the image of your Saviour, who once so wonderfully rescued you from death when it was ready to devour you, who is ever ready to save us from our other enemy, sin, so much worse than death, and in whose dear and blessed likeness I trust that you will grow as you grow in years.

355. *To Miss Agnes Gladstone.*

Haddo,
October 4, 1858.

. . . I doubt whether it is well for you to translate from French rather than from English. I think Telemachus not a very good book for the purpose : an historical book would be better, and brief dialogue better than either, and would give more profit with less labour. But further, I think you might do best at present (if Miss Syfert is of the same opinion) to get a further command of translating Italian into English, as well as English into Italian. The benefit of these things is not in substituting one word for another, but in learning how to change the idiom or peculiar form of one language into another.

Be on your guard against introducing the *passive* frequently into Italian. And always consider your sentence as a whole before you begin it, and think in what form it will be most like a sentence of original Italian. . . .

356. *To Miss Mary Gladstone (Mrs. Drew).*

Combe Warren,
April 6, 1884.

Dearest Mary,
You know that when you read to me anything from Lord Acton's letters, they always arouse in me

much interest, but they have never stirred in me surprise until I heard what you read about Dr. Liddon. I understood Lord Acton to say that Dr. Liddon assuredly would not go into the Church of Rome, but that he held opinions or admitted principles which seemed to have that step for their direct and necessary result. Now I know nothing of Dr. Liddon's inner mind, and any assumption of mine about him may be quite worthless. But I had always supposed him to be one of those who may properly be called Anglicans, who pay allegiance to the Church of England (as Manning did before 1850) entirely and exclusively as the Catholic Church, that is as the branch or section of the Catholic Church which in its territorial distribution has become possessed of this realm : and for whom therefore it is no more possible to join the Anglo-Roman Communion, even if they happened to prefer its modes of thought and action, than it would be to transfer themselves out of the family of their own parents, in order to meet the solicitations of another couple who might profess to be, or even might be, more desirable.

This to me has been through all my mature and thinking life the clear and simple and indestructible basis of Churchmanship—and the fact that such a form of thought lives and works among us cannot, I am sure, be unknown to Lord Acton, although I do believe it has been entirely foreign to the minds of very many among those Englishmen who have conformed to the Roman system.

There is another ground on which I should have supposed Dr. Liddon to be severed by an impassable wall of separation not merely from the Anglo-Roman but from the whole Latin Communion : that is the deplorable decisions of the Council of the Vatican, which it seems so hard to exempt from the taint of heresy, though I am aware that this is a stamp which no individual has a title to attach.

Your affectionate father,
W. E. GLADSTONE.

357. *To Miss Mary Gladstone.*

10, Downing Street,
July 1, 1884.

Dearest Mary,

I have read Lord Acton's most interesting letter, and I now seem perfectly to understand his remarks about Dr. Liddon and Rome.

For very many years I have thought that Dr. Pusey was apt, in his mode of handling Roman matters, to abjure or forfeit his historic freedom : and I believe that Dr. Liddon took over a good deal from Dr. Pusey in this and some other matters.

Again I should have a word to say on the comparison which Lord Acton makes between Dr. Liddon and men lately preferred to the Episcopal Bench considered as 'forces.'

It is to be borne in mind that they are so preferred not by a single force but by many. If I am one of them, so the particular Diocese is another, the Queen a third, the Liberal party a fourth. It is the resultant of all these forces which determines the choice.

Men of the highest stamp as a class should undoubtedly be chosen, but it cannot always be the highest man in the class. Bishop Butler had an intellect incomparably superior to that of any Bishop, much more that of any English Bishop, now alive ; but I am not sure that he would have been the best man to place at Bristol or at Durham under the conditions of the northern Episcopate.

Your ever affectionate father,
W. E. Gladstone.

358. *To Miss Mary Gladstone.*

Hawarden,
January 19, 1885.

Dearest Mary,

To my mind the chief and paramount recommendation of the Life of Ellen Watson may be summed up in one word, its nobleness. As a biography it is very incomplete, for it is mainly the history of an intellect. As the history of an intellect, incompleteness still adheres to it; for the biographer, perhaps from modesty, has not set out in detail the influences, and the steps, by which the great transition and the religious transformation were brought about. But the nobleness is in every page, and its features cannot be mistaken. Even in the days when she principally fed upon the joys of conscious mental power, selfishness never lays its paralyzing hand upon her. It is because of this unselfishness that the process so radical is also so gentle; and it is the combination of the intellectual energy with the wealth of purity and love that gives to her conversion a place among the memorable triumphs of the Cross.

Ever your affectionate father,
W. E. GLADSTONE.

359. *To Miss Mary Gladstone.*

10, DOWNING STREET,
May 17, 1886.

DEAREST MARY,

The lesson of Tupper's Life is a very singular and rather touching one — a reproduction of Robert Montgomery's. Him Macaulay killed; nay, drew and quartered him after hanging. Tupper was slain by an article in the *National Review*, as Keats had been slain, for a time, by an article in the *Quarterly*, very inadequately counteracted by the noble 'Adonais.' Tupper's was a hard case, for the public had practised on and developed his bump of vanity, which, according to my recollection, was not very marked at Oxford, where he was a good youth spotted as a 'saint' and little known or heeded. The life is an epic, though a very, very small one. The good-natured article in the *Athenæum* misses all this, and heaps together laughable trifles. If the book misses it, this excuses the review, but seriously condemns the author.

As to the passage which mentions me, fancy has inflamed his statement. It was not an 'Essay' at all, but an attempt to harmonize, as it is called, one or more Gospels. The prize, if I remember right, was not £25, but £10. My reward, as defeated candidate, was a book called 'Jones on the Canon,' well known then, possibly now, the value of which may have been 30s., not £5; three volumes, octavo, plainly bound, and now to be found in the Temple of Peace, if you are curious to look at it, among my octavo books on Scripture, in the eastward face of the middle one, among three stacks of books between the large window and the fire. As to Burton's having asked him for leave to deduct this 30s. or so from the £10, I simply don't believe it: glorifying recollection has deceived him.

I think I shall buy his book. He is a good man, and must have suffered in many ways.

Your affectionate father,
W. E. GLADSTONE.

360. *To Mrs. Drew.*

CANNES,
January 18, 1895.

. . . Since coming here I have been reading, and am now finishing, Zola's 'Lourdes.' An extraordinary book. I suppose the *most* remarkable he has produced. He manifests disbelief, and deals with the miracles slyly, but yet not unfairly, according the fullest subjective credit. There are not less than ten or a dozen separate bits, exhibitions of character and circumstance, all of which are excessively clear and interesting, some of [them] highly refined and beautiful, some very droll. On the whole a very notable work. . . .

361. *To Miss Helen Gladstone.*

11, DOWNING STREET,
August, 1859.

God bless you, my little darling Lena, on this day and on every day! You are, I trust, a happy child; strive to be every day more and more a good one, having continually before you the beautiful and blessed image of our Lord Jesus Christ, in whom is found for young and for old alike the model of all goodness.

If I bid you thus to labour and strive, it is not that I mistrust you, for I am well convinced that by God's

Photo, Valentine, Dundee.

"THE TEMPLE OF PEACE," HAWARDEN CASTLE.
(1) Table for literary work;   (2) Table for political work.

grace you do so labour and strive in prayer and in your daily conduct ; only, I would help you as far as I may both by my words, and by beseeching our Almighty Lord to be ever with you, and to order all things, whatsoever they may be in outward seeming, for your good.

I am so glad to be able to write to you by the post to-day. Best love to Maizie and the rest : and thank Miss Syfert in my name for all she does for you.

Ever your affectionate father,
W. E. G.

362. *To Miss Helen Gladstone.*

WILTON HOUSE,
August 27, 1866.

. . . The journey to Italy which you have in prospect is a great event in your life, or in the life of anyone when made for the first time, but especially if so made in youth. No more powerful stimulus can be applied to the mind and the imagination. You will, I am sure, try to make the best and most of it. It is of the greatest value as an opportunity for self-improvement.

Not but that, indeed, as you will find more and more, the whole of life is rich and fruitful in such, and in all good and noble opportunities. The longer I live, the more I feel that we may all say God hath 'set our feet in a large room.' The duty to be done, the progress to be made, the good to be effected, the store to be laid up for the future, from day to day, from hour to hour, make life a solemn thing, and the first of all our duties is that the life of each of us should have a purpose, namely, the fulfilment of the Divine will, by steady exertion aimed at this object, that so far as depends upon us the sum of sin in the world, and in ourselves especially, shall be lessened by the work of our lives, and not increased. Pursue this end, my dearest child, under an ever-living sense of the presence of God with you, and of your union with Christ, and may you in pursuing it have ever-increasing progress in overcoming evil and infirmity, and in working out the holy will of God.

363. *To Miss Helen Gladstone.*

11, Carlton House Terrace,
November 13, 1869.

. . . I read it [a paper on Ambition] more than once yesterday. It gave me very great pleasure for the ability which it showed, for its powers of analysis, and for the soundness of its moral views.

You will, I am sure, feel what additional force capacity gives to duty. If you can write so well, you are deeply bound to cultivate yourself, so that you may write much better. You are bound to bring care, method, perseverance, in aid of good materials of power. I wish I could help you : it is not in my power to do much, but the little will be done willingly. Remember that I am always ready and glad to be asked any question.

Have you read Bishop Butler? If not, I think you should begin, and read him steadily and strongly with your whole mind at six, eight, or ten pages a day. Dante also ought to do much for you. . . .

364. *To Miss Helen Gladstone.*

Windsor Castle,
November 17, 1869.

One word in addition to my former letter. I advise you to read Bishop Butler in small quantities. He requires a great deal of digestion : there is not a page, hardly a line, which does not afford much matter for thought. . . .

Your affectionate father,
W. E. G.

365. *To Miss Helen Gladstone.*

Walmer,
August 26, 1870.

My dearest Helen,

Although your coming of age to-morrow is not the subject of glittering celebrations, it is an event much noted in the hearts of your parents, and I am sure that the accomplishment of another year will come to you attended with a sense of deeper thankfulness to God at a period like this, when so many, who count no more days than you, are biting and to bite the dust. May every blessing attend you, and never forget that our blessings depend under God upon ourselves, and that none of them, which come from without, can be effectual unless as the appendages of those which come from within ; nor is any life worth living that has not a purpose, or that is not devoted from day to day to its accomplishment. Even in the humblest sphere, and where it has not pleased God to give powers adequate to more than very humble duties, this is an undoubted truth ; and many lives, of which the range is small, are among the happiest and best, because they are most steadily and most completely given to their appointed purpose. But we see in the Parables that our Lord takes as His examples of faithfulness those who are entrusted with a larger store. God has been liberal to you in capacity, and I trust you will render it all back to Him in good works done to your fellow-creatures, in the cultivation of your own mind, and in bringing your whole heart and life into conformity with the blessed Pattern given us. . . .

Ever your affectionate father,
W. E. G.

366. *To Miss Helen Gladstone.*

73, HARLEY STREET,
April 14, 1877.

I am not surprised at your troubles in Political Economy. I would, however, advise your trying Adam Smith, who is very pleasant reading, and who, as far as I can recollect, is *all right* except on Rent and the Navigation Laws. I have already told you I am at some loss to comprehend his being thrust aside in favour of John Mill as text-book.

367. *To Miss Helen Gladstone.*

[This letter was written in between big meetings and speeches in Midlothian. Miss Helen Gladstone had been offered, and had at once refused, the headship of the newly-built Holloway College.]

Edinburgh,
June 19, 1886.

My dearest Helen,

I telegraphed to you yesterday on a matter which is certainly of great importance. Before leaving London, we learned that you had received, from a body of persons highly competent to judge the case, an offer of the principalship of Holloway College. My feelings hereupon were these : First, I had a thrill of delight upon this signal manifestation, this tribute to the work you have done, and the capacity you have shown for more work in a special and very important department. Secondly, a strong hope that it might be found possible for you to proceed onwards, by acceptance, into a yet larger field of service to your fellow-creatures. Thirdly, a sense that the matter could not be settled without much consideration, that the arrangements respecting religion must especially be weighed, and that there might be reasons which might prove fatal to acceptance, though I could not but think it probable that, after having dealt successfully with the religious problem at Newnham, you would not be defeated by it on this great occasion.

On coming here we find that an excess of generosity, and a lofty regard to filial duty, had induced you at once to refuse this remarkable offer. We entreated you to hold your hand. It would not only be erroneous, it would be *wrong*, were you to allow those feelings to balk the purpose of your life. *Your* life has a distinct purpose. After all we have heard and seen, there can be no doubt that you have upon you the marks of a *distinct vocation*. That call is from on high : and I really do not think you have a right to overlook or not to follow the marks of it.

I am not now arguing for acceptance forthwith, but against rejection forthwith, and by implication against the idea that, on your mother's account particularly, you might have to leave Newnham a year hence. I argue against the *ground* of this resignation.

Were you an only child, the case might be different; to what extent I need not inquire, as it is not the point before us. The case stands as between seven children, of whom four are married; and of whom three at present, one permanently, and one with a work that may last for many years, are actually planted at Hawarden, which seems marked out by Providence absolutely for your mother's main residence, and in a great degree for mine. It is evidently a case for division of labour. It seems more than probable that vacations would of themselves enable you to take your fair and your full share. I will frankly say that to me, and I believe also to your mother, it would be nothing less than a cause of standing grief and pain were you, however generous the motive, to commit the error of refusing or quitting a work to which you seem so evidently called, or, as I have already stated it, to balk the purpose of your life.

My conclusion is nothing violent or headstrong. It is simply a plea, which I feel sure you will accept, for the most careful consideration of the subject, and for taking counsel upon, as one of deep importance and of far-reaching consequence.

Before closing I ought to express my sympathy with you as to Cambridge. I admit that in the event of acceptance you would have to make a sacrifice, for you have struck deep roots there. But your place there could be far more easily supplied. What we have all to look at is the accomplishment of God's work in the world by those whom He seems to choose as instruments. What makes me remain at seventy-six in a life which is on all general grounds positively unnatural makes me urge upon you not to hold back, whatever the effort or the sacrifice, from the Divine call, if such it shall appear to be.

   Ever, dearest Helen,
    Your most affectionate father,
     W. E. GLADSTONE.

368. *To Miss Helen Gladstone.*

> KEBLE COLLEGE,
> OXFORD,
> *November 27, 1887.*

. . . Strangely interesting is this place. Great material extension, legislative revolution, intellectual propulsion, abatement or abolition of religious forms, invigoration of religious life, extension of social interests, multiplication of pursuits — all these sever the Oxford of this day from the Oxford of mine. The Oxford of the future may be widely severed from both. Change has been stunning and bewildering ; some evil, some questionable, but none such as either to abate the fame and power of the place or to cut it off from prospects of future good.

369. *To Mr. Edward Wickham.*

> DOLLIS HILL,
> *May 1, 1892.*

MY DEAR EDWARD,
    I said to you a word of good wishes and good will : but I should like to write it also. For the day of your going to school is the first great marked day in your life. I think your life has begun well ; I hope and pray it may continue well.

Let me give you this earnest injunction; strive hard to do your best in everything. Every boy's best is really good in something: and by honest trying he will soon find it out, and will take real pleasure in it, and will be of use to others and to himself, and will never fail to ask God's blessing upon it and upon all he does.

In all our acts, there is no such safeguard as to do them with a sense that they are done in the presence of God, and done to fulfil His will concerning us. Difficulties, taunts, and failures, then come to mean but little to us, except as lessons how to do better, how to try harder, and then they are very helpful : our failures often are our best successes.

But I must not make my little sermon too long, so I only further write, God bless you !
    From your affectionate grandfather,
        W. E. GLADSTONE.

CHAPTER VI

PERSONAL

1826–1896

Mr. Gladstone's chief correspondents in his earliest years were his father and his brother John. For both he had great admiration as well as great affection. His estimate of his father will be seen a little farther on ; of his brother he says : 'My brother John, three years older than myself, and of a moral character more manly and on a higher level, had chosen the navy, and went off to the preparatory college at Portsmouth. But he evidently underwent persecution for righteousness' sake at the college, which was then (say about 1820) in a bad condition. Of this, though he was never querulous, his letters bore the traces, and I cannot but think they must have exercised upon me some kind of influence for good.' I have printed an early letter to this brother (Letter 370) because it shows the interest which Mr. Gladstone, even at Eton, took in ecclesiastical history. To the Evangelicals of that day the Waldenses were the chief link between the Church of the first three centuries and the Churches of the Reformation, and this impression remained with Mr. Gladstone down to his Italian journey in 1832. Then it disappeared, in the light partly of history, and partly of personal acquaintance. A second characteristic which he retained to the end of his life appears in Letter 372. This is, his persistent isolation from religious parties. These early letters show in every line how closely he was associated with the Evangelicals of that day. He admired their characters and he shared their beliefs. But even then he could not accept the party name or the party badge. We have seen him under the influence of a similar feeling in the most exciting period of the Tractarian Movement; in 1865 he tells a correspondent, 'I have never by any conscious act yielded my allegiance to any person or party in matters of religion;' and later still he tries to dissuade a son from saying of himself, 'I am what is called a High Churchman.' It is unnecessary to add that this dislike of religious labels did not hinder him from throwing himself with all his strength into religious controversy when the occasion seemed to demand it.

Even before he took his degree, Mr. Gladstone's mind was greatly occupied with the choice of a profession. Left to himself, he would at once have taken Orders. The reasons which determined him in this direction are set out very fully in the letter to his father which has been printed by Lord Morley. But the strength of his desire is seen even more clearly in one written nearly a month later (Letter 371). His father had shown very plainly what his own wishes were, and, supposing those wishes to remain unaltered, Mr. Gladstone had from the first resolved to make them his own. In this letter he makes a last and vigorous attempt, not to obtain his father's permission — for that was already given — but to change his father's mind. By the end of the year, however, the question was decided. He was not convinced by his father's arguments, but he had no doubt as to what would give him most pleasure. Apparently this deference to a parent displeased some of his friends. At least, a letter written three years later (Letter 374) is mainly a justification of his belief that a father's desire may be one of the appointed ways in which the will of God is made known to men. His conviction that he had made the right choice never varied, though for years afterwards he allowed himself to hope that something might yet happen to close political life against him, and so leave him free to take Orders.

'I was brought up to believe,' writes Mr. Gladstone in an unfinished autobiographical fragment, 'that every Unitarian (I suppose also every heathen) must as a matter of course be lost for ever. This deplorable servitude of mind oppressed me in a greater or less degree for a number of years. As late as in the year (I think) 1836, one of my brothers married a beautiful and in every way charming person, who had been brought up in a family of the Unitarian profession, yet under a mother very sincerely religious. I went through much mental difficulty and distress at the time, as there had been no express renunciation [by her] of the ancestral creed, and I absurdly busied myself with devising this or that religious test as what, if accepted, might suffice.' Of what Lord Morley describes as a 'little sheaf of curious letters on this family episode' I give two (Letters 375 and 376). They show Mr. Gladstone at the highest, and also the latest, point of his Evangelical development, for they were written in the closing months of 1835. In 1836 he renewed his acquaintance with James Hope, and his whole religious future was changed.

Two papers in the Appendix which relate to this process of emancipation may conveniently be noticed here. It was Mr. Gladstone's conviction from a very early period that the 'separation from the world,' which had been so prominent a feature in the early Evangelical teaching, had by this time come to be little better than a shibboleth. The test was satisfied by abstention from certain amusements; it had no value as a universal rule of life. In any circumstances Mr. Gladstone would soon have outgrown so arbitrary a precept, but the process was hastened by his adoption of the Tractarian view of moral questions. Of the purpose of the paper headed 'A Third Order,' and dated March 9, 1838,* I can give no account. It may possibly have been a scheme written for submission to James Hope. Its purpose, apparently, was to replace the Evangelical notion of separation from the world by something framed on definitely ecclesiastical lines. Its author did not propose to make a rule for everybody. He saw how unreal that had become in practice, and how necessary it was to recognize that men's vocations vary with their characters, and that a kind of discipline which is helpful to one may be hurtful to another. The idea may well have come to nothing from the very scale on which it was framed. The foundation even of one such society as Mr. Gladstone had in mind would have needed a very large endowment, and so have come into rivalry with the many other objects which then seemed of importance in the eyes of men to whom Churchmanship had become a reality. The minuteness with which all the details are described must be taken as evidence, not of the progress which the scheme had made at the time when the paper was written, but rather of Mr. Glad-

* Appendix VII. 6.

stone's passion for following out a principle into every particular of its possible application. The paper on Amusements* is of a different character. It is a careful analysis of a popular religious theory, which the writer finds himself compelled by the circumstances of his life either to accept or reject. To accept it in name while disregarding it in practice was not a way out of the difficulty likely to recommend itself to Mr. Gladstone, and in the end it is put aside as merely a partial and arbitrary recognition of 'the need of some systematic self-denial.'

The change from the strict Evangelicalism of these early years is first visible in the project for building an Episcopal chapel at Fasque, the Scottish estate which his father had lately bought (Letter 378). The Scottish Episcopal Church was not in favour with the English Evangelicals. Many of them, when in Scotland, altogether disowned the authority of the Scottish Bishops — mainly on the ground of the supposed Popery of the national Communion Office — and frequented certain chapels which had nothing in common with the Church of either country except that the English Prayer-Book was used in the services. Indeed, for some time after this letter was written Mr. Gladstone defended the Presbyterian Establishment as an exception to ecclesiastical order which could show extraordinary proofs of Divine favour, and some of the arguments he urges on behalf of his proposal are quite consistent with this theory. 'The village kirk,' he says, 'is already crowded,' and the new chapel would relieve 'the pressing demand for seats.' But why should this demand be met by an Episcopal chapel rather than by an enlargement of the parish church?

* Appendix VII. 7.

First of all because there is an obvious advantage in providing Episcopal services for a household 'wholly, or in great proportion, members of the English Church.' So far, of course, the strictest Presbyterian could have found no cause for complaint. The Gladstone family had a right to be Nonconformists in Scotland if they chose. But a missionary idea follows. His father is about to build almshouses for old people, and the Presbyterian Church does not allow the Communion to be administered in private houses. Here is a want which only Episcopal ministrations can supply. The chapel will be equally valuable to the very young, who, according to Presbyterian usage, are not taken to church until they are supposed capable of following an extempore prayer. And then he suggests that, if in addition to the chapel a school were built, 'not in the way of opposition, but of substitution for some one of those already existing in the parish,' the parents 'would gladly afford their children the enjoyment of the blessing of public worship.' If it occurred to Mr. Gladstone that these arrangements were nothing less than a scheme for making proselytes among the very old and the very young, the scruple was at once dismissed in deference to his 'constantly and painfully increasing sense of the inadequacy of the Scottish service to the most essential purposes of public worship.' The church foreshadowed in this letter was some years in building, and was not consecrated till 1847. But Mr. Gladstone's interest in it was a steadily increasing quantity. In the Appendix I have given his own detailed account of the Consecration services,* and for each year between 1846 and 1851 there exist, in his own handwriting, full and carefully

* Appendix VII. 9.

indexed lists of the Psalms (in Tate and Brady's version, which are to be used on each Sunday, with the tunes to which they are to be sung. The number of attendants at each service is also noted, with the name of the minister, and whether he preached in the surplice or the gown.

The church at Fasque was not the only religious undertaking that occupied Mr. Gladstone during these years. In the first freshness of his friendship with James Hope, the two were closely associated in the foundation of Trinity College, Glenalmond. It was to serve the double purpose of an ecclesiastical seminary and a public school on the English model. Both Hope and Gladstone gave largely to the proposed college, and threw into it an amount of zeal — and, on Gladstone's part, of exertion — which attracted large support from outside. 'I cannot now say,' writes Mr. Gladstone to Miss Hope-Scott, 'who was the prime mover in the scheme.' The first mention of it in this correspondence is in the letter of September 8, 1840 (Letter 380). But this was in answer to a criticism by Hope (printed in Mr. Ornsby's book) of a previous letter from Gladstone. 'The nature of the institution,' writes Hope, 'requires us to solve that problem, in these days so difficult, how young men of different ranks and fortune shall have the benefit of a common education without allowing the growth of habits which will be injurious to one or other class — particularly how the clergy shall receive a strict clerical education in contact with, and yet without being secularized by, the laity.' Hope's solution was that up to the age of twelve or thirteen every boy in the institution should be treated in the same way, and this a very simple one. At this point the boys who were meant to take Orders 'should be separated from the rest, and be made to feel throughout that they are under a different discipline ... I know that advantages are supposed to result from familiar habits in early life between the young gentry and the young clergy, but as regards personal character, undoubtedly, I think, to the detriment of the latter.'* Mr. Gladstone's reply (Letter 380) is perhaps, as Mr. Ornsby has pointed out, the earliest indication of the coming divergence of their views. The seminarist theory of training for Orders already finds more favour with Hope than it does with his friend. At this time, however, Mr. Gladstone was necessarily the mainstay of the enterprise. Hope went abroad in September, 1840, but only a month later we hear that five of the Scottish Bishops have given their sanction to the effort, that gifts amounting to about £2,300 are already promised, and that a circular naming £25,000 as 'the smallest sum at all *sufficient*,' and £15,000 as 'the smallest possible—*i.e.*, justifying practical measures' — is in preparation. By this time Mr. Gladstone's attitude towards the Scottish Established Church had a good deal changed. 'In the Kirk,' he goes on, 'matters look more and more ugly from day to day.' (The acute stage of the controversy which ended in the disruption of 1843 was just beginning.) 'It is impossible that our scheme should not be affected one way or both by the crisis ; our business, however, is, as I think, to maintain a position purely negative, and to put forward as our object to supply actual deficiencies of education which grievously cripple the Episcopal Communion. With collateral and ulterior effects we have at this moment, I think, nothing to do; our basis is, existing want, and we are not in a

* Ornsby, ' Memoirs of James Robert Hope-Scott,' i. 210, 211.

condition even to raise the question of aggression, at a time when all the children of our communion, who are educated within Scotland, are actually educated in Presbyterian institutions!'

All this time he is busy with the revision of 'The State in its Relations with the Church,' which he is making so complete that 'the book hardly will know itself again.' He hopes to get through it in the course of the recess, 'but the college is rather a cross-purpose, for it is very engrossing,' and the more so that, while he 'would never have dared to undertake it' without Hope's aid, his absence abroad makes it impossible to refer to him.

In the next two months good progress was made. On the 19th of December Mr. Gladstone writes to Hope, 'The Duke of Buccleugh gives £1,000 with an intimation that he may do more; my father gives £1,000 with the intention of doing, if it be required, very considerably more.' This last gift specially delights him. 'I consider,' he says, 'the manner in which my father has taken up the subject, under all the circumstances, one of the most signally Providential events that has ever crossed my path in life.' But as the scheme became better known a new difficulty presented itself. 'When you come back to this country,' he tells Hope, 'you will find that the general sentiment among those with whom we shall have to deal will be one of backwardness to sanction separate education even in a moderate degree.' This 'backwardness' was a very natural feeling in the circumstances of the country. To the English gentry 'separate' education — *i.e.*, education in schools in which masters and boys were all of the same religion — seemed the natural system, since it was education in and by the Established Church. But the Scottish gentry were largely Episcopalian, and if they wished their sons to have separate education they would have to provide it at their own cost. It was in view of this obstacle that Mr. Gladstone laid so much stress on the 'utilitarian' arguments for the new college (Letter 383). In the end enthusiasm and hard work combined carried the scheme through all its difficulties. Money came in — Charles Wordsworth, the first Warden, giving £5,000 and offering to lend as much more — the site was given in 1842, the foundation stone of the chapel was laid by Sir John Gladstone in 1846, and by 1850 ten theological students and forty-eight boys were in residence.* A passage in Mr. Gladstone's letter to Miss Hope-Scott brings together the three chief movers in the design so happily that I quote it here: 'It was, I think, the undertaking to found Trinity College which gave rise to another friendship that it gave me the greatest pleasure to witness — between him and my father. In 1840 my father was moving on towards fourscore years, but "his eye was not dim, nor his natural force abated"; he was full of bodily and mental vigour; "whatsoever his hand found to do, he did it with his might"; he could not understand or tolerate those who, perceiving an object to be good, did not at once and actively pursue it; and with all this energy he joined a corresponding warmth and, so to speak, eagerness of affection, a keen appreciation of humour, in which he found a rest, and an indescribable frankness and simplicity of character, which, crowning his other qualities, made him, I

* A seminary had existed in Edinburgh from some time in the thirties, and this was transferred to Glenalmond in 1848. The combination did not work quite satisfactorily, and in 1876 advantage was taken of a propitious fire to take the seminarists back to Edinburgh. Since then Glenalmond has been simply a public school.

think (and I strive to think impartially), nearly or quite the most interesting old man I have ever known. Nearly half a century of years separated the two; but your father, I think, appreciated mine more than I could have supposed possible, and always appeared to be lifted to a higher level of life and spirits by the contact. On one occasion we three set out on a posting expedition, to examine several sites in the midland counties of Scotland, which had been proposed for the new college. As we rolled along, wedged into one of the post-chaises of those days, through various kinds of country, and especially through the mountains between Dunkeld and Crieff, it was a perpetual play, I might almost say roar, of fun and laughter. The result of this tour, after the consideration of various sites near Perth, Dunkeld, and Dunblane, was the selection of the spot on which the college now stands. I am ashamed to recollect that we were, I do not say assisted in reaching this conclusion, but cheered up in fastening on it, by a luncheon which Mr. Patton, the proprietor, gave us, of grouse newly killed, roasted by an apparatus for the purpose on the moment, and bedewed with what I think is called partridge-eye champagne.*

Before leaving this period of Mr. Gladstone's life, I will give two letters from Hope to him which show in a very remarkable way the moral temper and the constant subordination of act and emotion to religious duty which they both shared with the early Tractarian leaders. It is in this temper, I think, more than in anything that we must look for the link which bound Mr. Gladstone to their cause. The first letter was

* Ornsby, 'Memoirs of James Robert Hope-Scott,' i. 279, 280. This was the site eventually given by Mr. Patton.

written on hearing of the engagement to Miss Catherine Glynne. Mr. Gladstone's reply to it (Letter 379) will be found farther on.

Lincoln's Inn,
June 11, 1839.

Dear Gladstone,

I hear on good authority that you are going to be married. If this is so, I should be sorry not to be among the first to wish you all the blessings which may be hoped for an engagement entered into, as I doubt not yours has been, in the fear of God, and with a determination of turning every circumstance of life into an instrument for His honour. Marriage is so often resorted to upon light or worldly motives, and so often looked upon by more serious persons as a kind of home and anchorage amongst trials which ought to be guarded against by higher principles, that it is an unusual and a great pleasure to see it entered on under circumstances which allow me to believe that the persons engaging in it look to each other's society rather as a means of more steadfastly serving God than of substituting inferior consolations for those which are alone to be depended on.

I remain, my dear Gladstone,
  Ever yours most truly,
            James R. Hope.

The second letter is Hope's answer to Mr. Gladstone's request that he would be godfather to his eldest son:

Merton College,
June 23, 1840.

Dear Gladstone,

Your request that I should be godfather to your boy is one which I most heartily accede to. I must, however, add a condition which I have before required on such occasions — namely, that you should by your will express your intention that this spiritual relationship shall exist in fact as well as name, and should provide that in the event of your death I may have sufficient control over the child's education to enable me (as far as this will do it) to discharge my trust. He will be my third godchild in life — one is already gone to realize the pledge which he obtained in baptism; and if the rest get as good an inheritance after they have grown out of my care as, I believe, this one has obtained, who had scarce come under it, I shall give up my account with gladness, and shall wish heartily that my own sponsors had as good an one to present.

Of that deep and kind feeling which has led you to select me, and of my association with such a man as Manning in such a charge, I am, I can assure you, very very sensible; and I shall pray God heartily that, when the day comes for all men's thoughts to be known, mine may not appear to have been such as to make you marvel that you should ever have held your present opinion of me.

Pray tell Mrs. Gladstone that as her son and yours is to be henceforth called mine also, I shall consider all mere acquaintanceship to have ceased, and shall insist, if she will suffer it, upon being numbered among those on whom as relations she has a right at all times to depend. To yourself I cannot say more than I have always said since the time when it pleased God to enable me to appreciate your character and principles, and this it is needless to repeat.

I will come up for the baptism whenever it may be, so when the day is fixed let me know.

Yours ever truly,
JAMES R. HOPE.

I have included here some letters which were unavoidably omitted from the chapters to which they properly belong. Thus, the gradual change which came over Mr. Gladstone's mind between 1839 and 1845, in reference to the relation of the State to the Church, is well illustrated by the letter to Mrs. Gladstone in the latter year (Letter 394), if read in connection with one to Manning in 1837 (Letter 377). In the earlier of the two he is profoundly impressed with the difficulty of fighting the Church's battle in Parliament. He who would defend her with any hope of impressing his hearers must state her claims, not in the way in which they appeal to himself, but in that by which alone they can be made intelligible to the House of Commons. But though the task be hard, it is not one from which he ought to flinch. He has but slender hope of success, but it is none the less his duty to apply 'the searching test of Christian Catholic principles' to those numerous measures which are 'calculated to bear powerfully on religion.' Even from the latter part of this very letter it is plain that the severance between him and the Church party in Parliament had already begun. With him the alienation of Church property is no longer a thing to be resisted at all costs. It has become only a change which suggests 'many preliminary inquiries.' By 1845 Mr. Gladstone's thoughts have already taken the shape which they were to retain for the remainder of his life. The 'highest interest of the Church' is not now necessarily bound up with the maintenance of her present relations with the State; it lies, rather, in the cultivation of habitual readiness to put an end to those relations if the State asks too high a price for their retention. The growth of this disposition finds hindrances alike among Churchmen who will give up none of their gold, and among politicians who see in the gold the means of keeping the Church in fetters. Already, too, — more than twenty years before 1868, — Ireland is forcing upon him 'great social and religious questions,' as well as a deepening sense of the courage which it will need to look them in the face and to work through them. The ecclesiastical question is further dealt with three months later in a letter to Manning (Letter 397). Mr. Gladstone was quite alive to the drawbacks of the policy he had made his own: 'The process which I am now actively engaged in carrying on is a process of lowering the religious tone of the State.' But only in this way could the Church be served in the House of Commons. To possess strength there she must have strength with the people. 'As she grows out of doors she will be more felt indoors.' There was a time when some Churchmen dreamed of seeing Mr. Gladstone and Bishop Wilberforce sustain in this country the part which Montalembert and Bishop Dupanloup played in France. But in this same letter we have Mr. Gladstone's opinion that there was never any real parallel between the two cases, and when we recall the various aspects presented by the recent ecclesiastical history of France, we may well doubt whether Parliament has ever been the arena in which the Church has been best served. In Letter 400 Mr. Gladstone returns to the unavoidable disadvantages of his new policy. The admission of Jews to Parliament, for example, *is* a retrograde step. It is a formal departure from the spirit of the text, 'The kingdoms of the world are become the kingdoms of the Lord and of His Christ.' But if they have already ceased to be so in any real sense, what is to be gained by keeping alive 'a hopeless falsehood'? Has not the time come 'to unveil realities'? Mr. Gladstone's attitude towards a policy of Disestablishment was often misunderstood. His consistent repudiation of all idea of making that policy his own led many people to reckon him among the advocates of the State Church. But from 1845 onwards it is more than doubtful whether in the sense that the word 'advocate' commonly bears he could be so reckoned with any approach to truth. The work of destruction would not fall to his lot; it would have, in all probability, to be done some day, but not by his hands. To Mr. Gladstone this was reason enough for putting the subject away from him, except when he was roused to utterance by what he thought some special extravagance on the other side, as, for example, in 1894, when he laments what he calls the 'Establishmentarian fanaticism' of Archbishop Benson (Letter 460).

The journey in the course of which this letter to Mrs. Gladstone was written was important as laying the foundation of that intimacy with Döllinger which is so often referred to in these letters. The notes of a particular conversation will be found in the Appendix,* and possibly it was of value in giving precision to Mr. Gladstone's view of the Anglican doctrine of the Real Presence. It is difficult, however, to believe that upon this question much help from without was needed. There is nothing to show at what time the 'Devotions for Intervals of the Eucharistic Service' were put together, but upon this, as upon Baptism, his convictions seem to date from a very early stage of his religious progress. His entire agreement with the substance of Robert Wilberforce's book upon the Eucharist will be seen in Letter 408, and one written nearly half a century later (Letter 462) shows how unchanged in any particular his belief remained to the end. The friendship with Döllinger, always strong, became stronger after 1870. Naturally, Mr. Gladstone was keenly interested in the Old Catholic Movement, and in the memorandum 'The Vatican Council and the Old Catholics,' written in 1874,† he seems almost to make separation from Rome a matter of duty. Whether Döllinger himself ever went this length is at least doubtful. Possibly as time went on he came to realize how slowly the Old Catholic community grew, and

* Appendix IV. 1.   † *Ibid.*, 4.

how slight a hold it appeared to have upon religion in the country of its origin. At no time, indeed, does he seem to have shared Mr. Gladstone's view that Roman Catholics who were not Infallibilists were bound to leave their Church. Where explicit acceptance of the new dogma was demanded of them, they had, of course, no choice but to refuse it. But there was no need for them to go out of their way to invite attack. To mind their own business and stay where they were, so long as they were left in peace, was the substance of much of the advice he was wont to give to those who consulted him. He used to go and pray in the Roman churches, but he seldom attended any Old Catholic service. The developments that followed the Conferences of 1874 and 1875 were not to his mind, and he preferred the position of a confessor unjustly condemned to that of the founder of a new Church. Accordingly, after 1875 the letters to Döllinger refer rather to the affairs of the Church of England than to those of the Old Catholics.

Here and there we come upon letters referring to Elementary Education. No man was more resolute than Mr. Gladstone in defending the right of the Church to give her own religious teaching to her own children. But he saw from the first the difficulty of maintaining this right in its fulness under a system of State aid (Letter 401). For some years the controversy turned mainly on the Conscience Clause. Indispensable as this is now seen to be, it was at first regarded by many of the clergy as an unlawful concession, though few were consistent enough to go the length of Archdeacon Denison, and refuse a State grant if coupled with such a condition. The letter to Lord Granville written in 1865 (Letter 414) puts with great force the difficulties inherent in any system which gives the State a right of making stipulations as to the nature of the religious teaching given in its schools.

The year 1851 saw a marked change in Mr. Gladstone's correspondence. As regards frequency and intimacy of communication, no friends took the place of Hope and Manning. There is a notable unlikeness, however, in Mr. Gladstone's later attitude towards the two men. Both had been closely associated with him in religious work and religious controversy. Both, as he thought, had taken their hands from the plough and thrown away the highest of human vocations. But the tone of his letters on the occasion of the two secessions is very different. In Hope's case there is an absence of criticism, a pained acquiescence in a mysterious Divine purpose, of which there are but few traces where Manning is concerned. It is not, I think, untrue to say that Mr. Gladstone felt Hope's change more deeply, and Manning's more bitterly. Perhaps the explanation of this lies in the fact that Hope had followed his own course from the first. His Romeward direction dated from the affair of the Jerusalem bishopric, and had only been strengthened by Newman's departure and by the Gorham Judgment. Manning, on the other hand, had for some time been much less of a Tractarian than Mr. Gladstone. He had been neutral in the contest for the Poetry Professorship; he had voted for Ward's degradation; he had preached a Fifth of November sermon which was generally accepted as a veiled attack upon Newman; he had been wholly unaffected by the secessions of 1845. To all appearance, his change in 1851 was the result of the Gorham Judgment alone, and it is easy to understand why the act seemed to Mr. Gladstone so much more precipitate in his case than in Hope's.

The letter to Queen Victoria describing the circumstances of Bishop Wilberforce's death (Letter 428) gives no facts that were not published at the time. I have printed it for the sake of the strong praise it contains of the Bishop's character and work. Mr. Gladstone had not always been in agreement with him, but the occasions of difference between them grew fewer as years went on, and the Winchester episcopate had placed Wilberforce on a higher plane than anything he had previously done. There had been a time (Letter 104) when, as Mr. Gladstone thought, he had not shown the courage the State has a right to expect from the episcopate, when the character he bore among politicians was that of a most able prelate getting all he could for the Church and giving nothing. The Disestablishment of the Irish Church had shown him in a new character — that of a man in great position who knows that there is a time to yield as well as a time to resist. Mr. Gladstone had other friends by whom this lesson had never been mastered. Chief among them was George Denison. In his case, as we see from Letter 419, occasions were constantly arising which forced him to do something for which he would need his friend's forgiveness. Passionate in feeling and expression as the Archdeacon could show himself, he well deserved Mr. Gladstone's praise that there could be no one whom it was more delightful to forgive.

For the most part Mr. Gladstone's gaze was fixed on the present or the future, but in three of the letters in this chapter it turns back to the past. Two of them, written to Mrs. Gladstone (Letters 410 and 411), refer to the death of the Duke of Newcastle — the friend to whom he owed his introduction to the House of Commons, and with whose political career and private sorrows he was afterwards so closely associated. The third is a letter of sympathy to the present Lord Northbourne on the death of his father (Letter 458). It was written in the session of 1893, the year of his victory at the polls and of his defeat by the House of Lords — a defeat which he could not bring his Cabinet to challenge. From 'the chaos of business' he looks back over 'the waste of years' to that unforgotten Roman winter when the two friends were 'enjoying Rome, as it could then be enjoyed,' in the company of those to whom, as it proved, they were to owe so much of the happiness of their lives.

Now and again the reader will come across some characteristic criticisms on books. Mr. Gladstone fully shared in the passing excitement about 'Ecce Homo,' but he did not for a moment fall into the mistake, made even by some good judges, of attributing it to Newman. At the same time, Letter 416 leaves the reader in some doubt whether he thought the book too great to be Newman's, or not great enough. The letter to Messrs. Macmillan given in Chapter III. (Letter 264) goes a long way towards explaining the interest with which 'Ecce Homo' was received. The writer was at first supposed to be feeling his way towards a more complete system of belief. As Mr. Gladstone puts it, what remained was 'not less vital than what had been accomplished.' When it appeared that the author was not likely to go farther in the direction attributed to him, the book came to be judged solely by what it had done, and what was then left of it was chiefly a happy phrase — the 'enthusiasm of humanity'

— and the demonstration that Jesus Christ came not only to preach a present Gospel but to found a Society to which that function was to be committed in the future.

In two letters (Letters 417 and 421) Mr. Gladstone gives enthusiastic expression to his admiration for Walter Scott, and, by an inevitable connection, for Lockhart's Life of him. In these days it is hard for a biography in many volumes to retain the attention it deserves. Happily, this is one of those rare instances in which there exists an abridgment — by Lockhart himself — as good, so far as the necessarily reduced space permits, as the original work. In 1871 Hope-Scott brought out a new edition of this abridgment, and dedicated it to Mr. Gladstone. He gives as his reason that 'from you, more than from anyone else who is now alive, I have received assurances of that strong and deep admiration of Walter Scott, both as an author and as a man, which I have long felt myself, and which I heartily agree with you in wishing to extend and perpetuate.' With Mr. Gladstone this wish rested on 'the conviction that both the writings and the personal history of this extraordinary man, while affording entertainment of the purest kind, and supplying stores of information which can nowhere else be so pleasantly acquired, have in them a great deal which no student of human nature ought to neglect, and much also which those who engage in the struggle of life with high purpose — men who are prepared to work earnestly and endure nobly — cannot pass without loss.' I quote these sentences from Hope-Scott's dedicatory letter both as showing the impression which Mr. Gladstone's opinion of Walter Scott had made upon his friend, and as expressing the serious estimate of life which had been the root of their intimacy. There is a letter of Newman's to Hope-Scott* in which, after describing the trouble it was to him that Scott's works seemed to be so forgotten, he goes on : 'Books are all annuals, and to revive Scott you must annihilate the existing generation of writers, which is legion. . . . Perhaps the competitive examinations may come to the aid. You should get Gladstone to bring about a list of classics, and force them upon candidates. I do not see any other way of mending matters.' It may be doubted whether an appeal to the Civil Service Commissioners would have done much to bring about the revolution in taste which Newman desired. There is better material for hope in the recent multiplication of cheap reprints of the Waverley Novels. They do at least suggest the existence of a new class of readers, for whom Scott still provides healthier interests and nobler ideals than can always be found in contemporary fiction. Few things would do more to help on this happy recovery in public taste than a better acquaintance with the book which was thus blessed by Mr. Gladstone and by Hope-Scott.†

In Mr. Gladstone's latest years his correspondence practically comes to an end. Weakened eyesight, failing health, and a definite and long-cherished idea of the manner in which men should 'slow down towards the close,' combined to lessen the number, though not the vividness, of his interests. But, as if in preparation for this time of gradual withdrawal from that crowded life which had been his for sixty years, he had reserved for his last days two undertakings which, to most men,

* Ornsby, Life, ii. 243.
† Lockhart's own abridgment of his 'Life of Scott' is now to be had in Messrs. Dent's 'Everyman's Library.'

might have seemed fitting employment for their most vigorous time — his edition of Butler, and the founding of St. Deiniol's. 'I find my Butler,' he tells the Duke of Argyll, 'a weighty undertaking,' and, familiar as he was with his author's text, the breaking up of what Pattison calls that 'solid structure of logical argument' into short paragraphs for the convenience of the reader must have demanded a minute attention which old men rarely care to give. The 'Subsidiary Studies,' which fill a whole volume of this edition, are an exposition of his final views on some of the greatest of theological problems. It is here that those who seek for information on these points will find brought together much which they would otherwise have to glean from many occasional articles, only in part collected in the 'Gleanings,' and from a vast number of letters. This is especially true of the question of Future Retribution.

The foundation of St. Deiniol's appealed to Mr. Gladstone on two sides of his character — as a lover of books and as a firm believer in the need of theological learning for the proper treatment of theological questions. What is material to the history of the scheme is already before the world, and all I need do is to reproduce, for completeness' sake, the substance of Mrs. Drew's article in the *Nineteenth Century and After* for June, 1906. Books played a large part in Mr. Gladstone's life, even in his busiest times. As his love for them became known to the dealers who minister to this taste, 'second-hand catalogues rained in by every post, and were always carefully scanned and marked for immediate purchase.' This process of marking for purchase is apt to have one inconvenient result. Books keep coming in, and the space that is to hold them is soon filled. Mr. Gladstone was confronted by this difficulty as early as 1860. In that year 'the housing of the growing library necessitated the addition of a new wing to the Castle at Hawarden.' The building of the 'Temple of Peace' solved the problem for a time, but as this in its turn grew full, a policy of makeshift had again to be resorted to. 'One by one each piece of extraneous furniture disappeared, to make way for low bookcases.' When nothing more could be done in this way, books overflowed first into the vestibule, then into the billiard-room, and finally crowded out the billiard-table. Then some larger plan had to be devised, for the commonplace remedy of ceasing to buy books was not to Mr. Gladstone's mind. At this point, however, another long-entertained desire suggested a way of escape. Mr. Gladstone was not a selfish buyer; he wished his books to be at the service of all who shared his conviction 'that the future of the human race depends in the main upon the great question of belief, and that the most special and urgent of present needs is the need of sufficient means for the effective promotion of Divine learning.' If this need was to be satisfied by his own library, the ultimate destination of the larger part of it must not be Hawarden Castle; but it did not follow that it should not be Hawarden village. If the books were to find a new home, might not the same building provide temporary homes for their readers? At all events, Mr. Gladstone determined to try the experiment, and to try it 'cautiously, tentatively'—and economically. 'In 1889 two large iron rooms, lined with felt and pine, were erected, with six or seven smaller ones to act as studies, on the crest of Hawarden Hill, and the travel of the books began.' To borrow

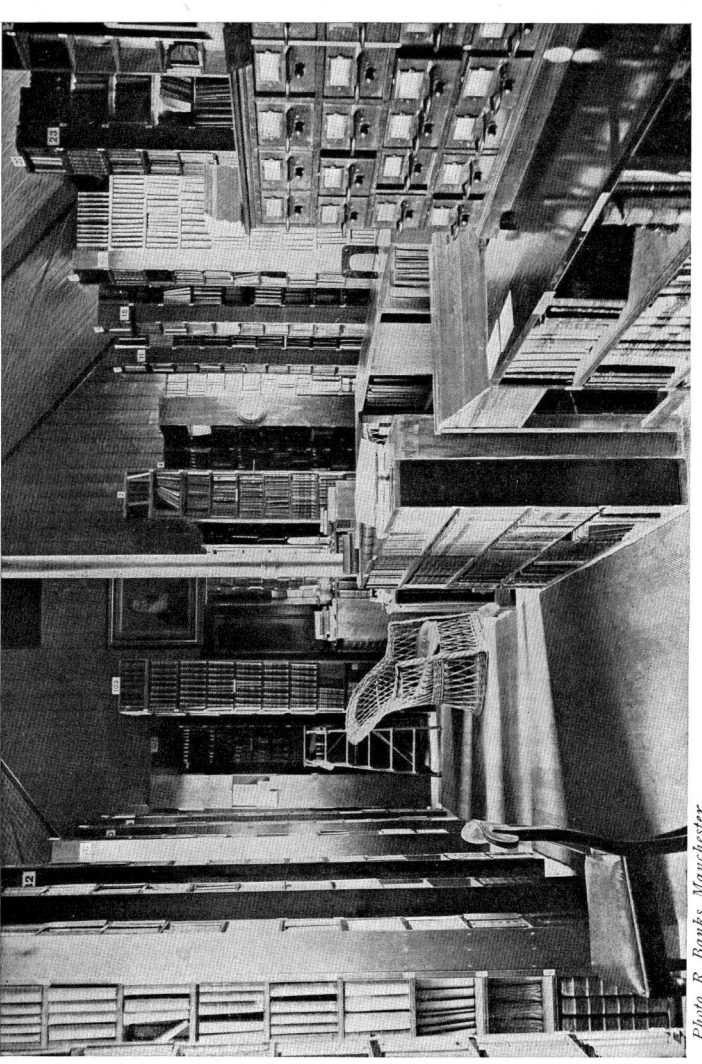

Photo, R. Banks, Manchester.

INTERIOR OF ORIGINAL LIBRARY IN WHICH THE BOOKS WERE PLACED BY MR. GLADSTONE'S OWN HANDS.

a phrase not then in being, it was a personally conducted tour. 'Each book' — and there were 27,000 of them — 'he took down from the shelves, and each packet he strapped up, with his own hands, and no vehicle was ever allowed to leave the Castle without its consignment of book bundles. Arrived at their destination, they were laid upon the floor in the order in which they came, and Mr. Gladstone, unaided save by his valet, and sometimes one of his daughters, went home from Cambridge, unstrapped and lifted and sifted, and placed the volumes one by one in the bookcases prepared to receive them.' This was the beginning of St. Deiniol's, and out of it has grown the spacious library and the existing provision for the accommodation of the students who use it. The founder gave £40,000 by way of endowment; the National Memorial Committee contributed £10,000 for housing the books, and his sons and daughters added another £8,000 for housing the warden and students. The character and object of the institution which has thus been created have been sketched out by Mr. Gladstone himself in a letter circulated among his friends in March, 1896, when it became necessary to provide a recognized head for the new institution.

'In the search for a warden, who will be in Priest's Orders, besides the qualifications of intelligence, character, and capacity to comprehend and forward the spiritual work of the Church, other and more special qualifications are to be kept particularly in view, as follows :

'1. To be engaged in, and to extend the prosecution of, the study of Divine learning.

'2. Aptitude for carrying forward the gradual extension and development of the Library, which embraces as its two main departments Divinity and Humanity, and leaves as yet a great deal to be desired in point of method and of any approach to completeness.

'3. The qualities necessary for attaching and assisting others, who may from time to time become members of the foundation.

'4. To take cognizance of the household cares, as well as to be especially responsible for the religious rules and usages. It is hoped that the household cares would not be burdensome.'

Thus guided and thus administered, St. Deiniol's was, in Mr. Gladstone's hope and intention, to be 'a Clergy House, a House of Rest and Refreshment not rigidly confined to our own Clergy, a House of Study for the glory of God and the culture of man, a House of Mission perhaps for Liverpool, a House of Help perhaps for the parish of Hawarden,* and, of course, a House of Prayer and Worship.'

370. *To John Gladstone (brother).*

ETON COLLEGE,
Sunday, January 29, 1826.

. . . There is a very interesting article in the last number of the *Quarterly Review*, written, I believe, by Southey, on the Vaudois or Waldenses—whose numbers now amount to only, I think, eighteen thousand. They have alone kept the faith pure and undefiled from the age of the Apostles — and their piety is not shaken by length of years — but they are extremely poor, and the clergymen have the greatest difficulty in educating

---

* Mr. Gladstone's idea seems to have been that Liverpool and Hawarden should be helped only in the case of Disestablishment and Disendowment. As long as the Church retained her property she would be able to provide for her own needs.

their children for the Church. It is pleasing to think that their tenets and Church government are the same as those of the Church of England. They are the parents of all the reformed Churches, and more especially the cradle in which our own was fostered. I think it is stated that Wickliffe came from among them. The head of their Church was formerly called a Bishop ; when Mr. Gilly, the author of a work on their condition, etc., visited them some years ago, he found that they had exchanged the name of Bishop, as less suitable to their humbled condition, for that of Moderator. His [the Moderator's] stipend amounted only to forty pounds a year — the summit of his wishes being an hundred and twenty ! Father Peyrani, the Moderator of whom I speak, they describe as a perfect gentleman, but, of course, in indigence — not repining at his condition, but speaking with evident satisfaction of the likeness between his Church and the Church of England. They have frequently, with rustic weapons, made a most heroic defence against the Catholics, and defeated their regularly organized armies — animated by the spirit of *true courage.* I need hardly tell you that the Romanists take every opportunity of oppressing them. Altogether I do not know a more interesting people. I hope that the English will not suffer their parent Church to fall to ruin, while we send our missionaries into remote and comparatively strange parts of the world. I spoke yesterday in our Society. We have also got a valuable acquisition in a fellow of the name of Selwyn — one of the cleverest fellows here. In fact, altogether I have the pleasure of announcing that we are in a very flourishing condition. . . .

371. *To John Gladstone (father).*

CUDDESDON,
August 29, 1830.

. . . In the first place, I believe that employment to be, of all others, the highest and the noblest, however honourable and praiseworthy others may be, which has for its object the bearing of the great embassy from God to man, the communication of the tidings of salvation. Eighteen hundred years have now elapsed since our Saviour bled for us upon the bitter cross. The tree which He planted grew gloriously at first, and indicated, in a manner not to be misunderstood, its high and holy original by its rapid increase and holy fruits. But how small a portion of the work has been performed which He commanded to be done. 'All nations' are not yet baptized into the faith of the crucified Jesus, but, on the contrary, a large proportion of the race of Adam have not heard His name; while of those who bear His name, how many are there who bear His name alone? To go, then, forth into this world, lost, alienated, apostate — this world, once great and glorious, and to become great and glorious again by the mercy of God, and thro' the instrumentality of man — this is a province which must by all surely be allowed to be an exalted one, as to me it seems to transcend all others in dignity and usefulness, not because a man may not serve God in other professions, with a conscience cheerful, free, and pure, but because here *I think* he is admitted to the high honour of serving Him in that mode which is, of all others, the most efficacious and direct. Thus much for the *dignity* of the profession; another not less urgent but more awful plea is, in my view, its necessity: that constraining necessity which results from the present condition and future prospects of the human race. When I endeavour to view my condition apart from all artificial disguises, all extraneous considerations, I cannot but see that I am one of a sinful race, who were made like God, with capacities for knowing, loving, serving Him, but are fallen like the sun of the morning into the depths of sin, misery, and darkness. Then I hear of the redemption of the world by Christ, of His lowly birth, His life of sorrow, and His death of shame, and the infinite and inestimable value of that sacrifice proves to me at once the two fundamental propositions of religion: first the wretchedness of the condition to which we have fallen, to *require* so costly an atonement; secondly, the extent of the love of God to *give* it, and the loftiness and majesty of those capabilities which could render man the object of this transcendent love. I deem, then, that if I, a drowning man myself, may be permitted to lend a hand to one in the same condition with myself; if I, a guilty and trembling sinner may hope to look to God as a reconciled Father, and may communicate to another, alike in guilt and alike in fear, the same abundant and efficacious means of delivery; that so we shall escape that fire, that torture, naturally inherent in all sin, those pangs of remorse without repentance, those cravings of passions never to be gratified yet never to be stayed — all that fearful accumulation of horrors which awaits those who continue in their natural state of alienation from God.

I feel that I know little of anyone, and perhaps least of all of myself; but still if I may presume on *any* feeling or bias of my mind, if I may believe in the reality of *any* of those impulses which sway my being, I cannot help believing that the glories of this picture, of God reconciled and man redeemed, are such as must continually, by God's grace, grow upon my sight, and kindle day by day into a more and more celestial brightness. Therefore I am willing to persuade myself that, in spite of other longings which I often feel, my heart is prepared to yield other hopes and other desires for this — of being permitted to be the humblest, as I am the vilest, of those who may be commissioned to set forth before the eyes of man, still great even in his ruin, the magnificence and the glory of Christian truth. Especially as I feel that my temperament is so excitable, that I should fear giving up my mind to other subjects, which have ever proved sufficiently alluring to me, and which I fear would make my life a fever of unsatisfied longings and expectations. . . . It tortures me to think of an inclination opposed to that of my beloved father — and more of carrying that inclination into effect. . . .

I have here [Cuddesdon] been reading for the first time in my life ten hours a day or more — not that the quantity of work is by any means excessive, but the quality is not agreeable throughout — indeed it could not be expected that it should be. I have so culpably indulged my natural aversion to mathematics up to the present time, keeping up a merely nominal study of them, and doing everything regarding them with the utmost negligence — in addition, too, having a bad memory in all matters, but most atrocious in these. For myself I would gladly give them up, but as my father wishes that I should go on with them, I must endeavour to regain some of the ground I have lost, and if I be too late, must put off my degree till next November. . . .

372. *To John Gladstone (brother).*

LEAMINGTON,
Thursday, December 30, 1830.

. . . I will take this opportunity of endeavouring to lay before you explicitly the state of my own prospects which, I think, cannot have been clearly stated to you before, from the expressions which you use in your last received letter (I have not it at hand, but it is the same in which you name the transfer to the Druid) ; though I do not know whether your impressions were derived from my own letter on the subject or from any other. But the circumstances as I understand them are these : My dear father, with [his] usual affectionate indulgence, is anxious that I should follow the bent of my own inclinations, though also anxious that those inclinations should coincide with his own : of these desires he postpones the second to the first. On the other hand, both from natural duty and from those, if possible, stronger obligations which such extreme kindness imposes, I feel exceedingly solicitous to come to no decision which shall in any way interfere with his wishes, although to the general question which was the most useful I could then give no other answer than the one I did. Having given that answer, I had done all that I was bound to do, or justified in doing — for they are the same in matters such as these. This view of the subject was the one which appeared to me the true one ; but I have neither the right nor the desire to act upon it in opposition to a parent's wishes : especially as on the one hand I am convinced that neither duty nor happiness are at all confined to any one station or condition of life, and that acceptable and free service to God may be rendered by those who are so disposed in one as well as another. People say, indeed, that you are to follow the will of God in these things, but that will must have channels of conveyance, and what more natural one than the wishes of a parent? And, on the other hand, it seems to me that in the present age there is a dangerous and increasing laxity on the subject of certain social obligations: not social obligations in general, but those where there are relations of inferiority on the part of the inferior party. I mean that the duties which differences of age and the condition of sonship impose are frequently overlooked and generally more or less neglected, and I bitterly regret to say that this neglect is found in too large a proportion among those who are called the religious world. Now, *God forbid* I should pretend to consider myself as possessed of the privileges, exalted as they are, of true Christian religion: and God forbid (I trust I am not impious in saying) that, if I were, I should attach myself, in the way which I think too generally prevails, to this 'religious world' which I have mentioned. I mean this: it is an honour — it is the highest honour — to claim kindred and relationship with the faith of those who are practical believers in the crucifixion of our Saviour, in their entire inability to justify themselves, in the perfectness and abundance of this atoning power, in the need of the implantation of a new principle of action — the love of God — in the place of that which we have, some wholly all too much, by nature, the love of self (or, indeed, of any created being), *if independent* of the love of the Creator. This is the true bond of union between men, essentially and in its nature eternal. Why? Because it is altogether founded upon the *approximation* of those whom it unites to the nature and image of Him whose unchangeableness and eternity are necessary. The bonds of flesh *cannot* endure when flesh itself is no more. But this bond of union is, as it seems to me (may God reprove me if I am wrong), to be altogether different from that incrustation of party badges and symbols which the remaining corruptions of human nature, and no other cause, have, I fear, superinduced upon a portion at least of the religious world. To return to the point from whence I started, I fear there is no inconsiderable neglect of the duties above mentioned among the members of this 'religious world,' and it would be a blow to whatever hopes I might entertain of attaining to its privileges did I not attempt, when enabled, to keep free of those abuses which have been unhappily joined with them. I hope I have made the matter understood, at least as far as [I am] able : and you will see that it rests in abeyance. . . .

373. To John Gladstone (*father*).

VERONA,
Monday, June 25, 1832.

. . . As to myself, as our return is now coming in sight, I am thinking about my own matters after arrival in England ; for I should hope to get to work soon. What my *views* are, I take this opportunity of submitting to you for your approbation, correction, or rejection. Naturally enough, one's mind is turned with concentrated interest to that class of questions which seem most to be agitated in one's own time, and with most effect on the peace and happiness of mankind. These seem to me to be the *principles* which bind society together, direct the mutual conduct of governor and governed, and determine their relations. To these, which I believe are now very rarely made a subject of serious inquiry, it is my desire, should that desire meet your approbation, to turn ; and herein to embrace mainly two kinds of reading : the one, legal and historical, as law and history bear upon this question ; the other, the works of those authors who have investigated the same subject in a more general and abstract form. My firm belief is, according to my means of judging, that these topics are not less neglected than they are intimately blended with the happiness of mankind — and, in the relation of instruments to an end, with the final triumph of that religion in the world, whose propagation, I trust, will ever be the dearest desire of my heart, and the ultimate end of all my actions, in as far as they are placed beyond the imperative control of circumstances. I trust this will appear to you in conformity with what is right, and with the sentiments formerly expressed, which you were good enough to approve.

374. *To O. B. Cole.*

ALBANY,
August 12, 1833.

MY DEAR COLE,
. . . I acknowledge, because it is impossible to deny, the soundness of your principle of action, which I understand to be this: that the will of man as a final cause or supreme law of action is utterly and essentially sinful, because the will of the Creator must of right be the supreme law to all but rebellious and apostate creatures, and the ultimate object in which all their efforts find their consummation and satisfaction. Alas! I would that this noble and elevated philosophy had as effectively planted itself in my heart, as it easily and fully approves itself to my understanding. But we are now concerned not with the actual, but with the proper consequences of this principle, in the establishment of which we seem to be at issue. Now my belief, and that belief which seems to bring me into collision with you, is this: that the doctrine of the Bible, while it unquestionably prescribes one principle of action, does nevertheless embrace a much more extended subject-matter than many are led to suppose. To communicate the will of God to others, I confess, or rather I would maintain, naturally and forcibly strikes us as the loftiest function to which His creatures can be called. Then there are many ways of communicating that will, and perhaps those which are the most obvious and direct may not be always the most comprehensive or the most permanent in their effects. But in its humbler forms, of example always and of entreaty or admonition as power may be given, it stands forth as an indefeasible duty and privilege of every Christian. From this even now — and I impute it to you even though I may seem to impute along with it an erroneous judgment of your understanding — you, the self-condemned, do not hold yourself absolved, or you would not have written the letter which lies before me.

I know, or think I have gathered it from you in conversation, that you admit the universality of the operation of Christian principle, and that beautiful peculiarity which belongs to it, of investing with true sanctity even the humble and ordinary offices of daily life : as, for example, that our Saviour did the will of God, even as He sat at meat in the house of the Pharisee ; that the Christian women would be doing the will of God, who meekly obeyed the directions of St. Paul, indicating to them a lowly and a silent path of duty ; that even Onesimus went to do the will of God, when the Apostle remanded him to the performance of the labours of servitude, undignified except by the spirit dwelling in him upon earth even amidst his menial toil, and by his title to the glory of Christ's inheritance in heaven. How wide then is the vineyard of the Lord, and how true it is that He is the God of all our nature, and that He wills all that tends to its progression — for it is *His* own work and not ours — provided only the law of proportion amidst its parts be maintained, and all be governed and directed for the fulfilment of His will by our spiritual advancement in the knowledge and likeness of Him. But I conjecture that your position is this—if I may be bold enough to put words into your mouth, for the sake of making myself understood : 'I admit that God has servants of ten thousand ranks for as many various functions. Each man is blessed in the performance of the work to which he has been called ; but I have rejected the work to which I was called, therefore, by your own rule I am no longer an heir of blessing.' Now I will make my reply to this, though conscious that I may perhaps be replying to my own argument, and not yours. My reply is this : Admitting, for argument's sake, that you were called to labour in a higher office, and admitting, for the same reason, that you refused and deserted your duty, and lost the blessing attached thereto — yet I say that so long as in your bodily and mental conformation there remains any jot or tittle of any kind of power, which may enable you in any way to perform any one of those ten thousand functions, from the highest to the lowest, so long you are *called* to its performance. You may maintain inward persuasions to be a more direct call, but you are not one who can deny that God calls by circumstances *also;* that his Providence mingles itself in all the shifting events of this world of shadows, and *speaks* by those events, palpably and intelligibly, and in a manner such that we are responsible and guilty if we answer not: well then, to apply this argument, in your mind *are* faculties capable of ministering — in a degree, if you choose, infinitely minute — still, capable of ministering to the glory of God — how *can* you escape the obligation of using them? You hold the argument of final causes — you infer the existence of a Divine volition from the *applicability* of certain instruments to certain ends: but what would become of that noble and irrefragable argument if the mute creatures of God had rebelled like ourselves against the laws of their existence — if the applicability everywhere existed, but nowhere the application? So long as you maintain that you are debarred from doing the will of God — that is, from performing duty, having at the same time a spirit capable in no mean degree of appreciating the harmony of His visible works and the benevolence of His loftier unseen designs, are not you, I say not in the condition, but in the determination and intention of one who oversets that primary law which even the elements of the most infantine and immature religion absolutely need for a foundation whereon to raise a future and more ample structure? Surely, then, you are still called: if not by visions of heavenly glory, or by sweet accents heard in the calm of your soul, still, though the manner be sterner and more magisterial, by a title equally imperative, by the essential character and capabilities which God has communicated to your being? — there is no link of adamant so strong as that moral law which binds in an indissoluble union the instrument fitted for a purpose, and the purposes for which it is fitted. You cannot, you do not deny, that the instruments and the purposes both exist: wherefore are they not brought together? . . .

375. *To John Gladstone (father).*

ATHOL CRESCENT,
November 30, 1835.

. . . The use of all the means it has been in my power to employ upon the subject of religion has led me long since to a conclusion, which gathers strength from the lapse of years : that in the doctrine of redemption alone has Christianity any adequate foundation, and that by this is meant, not Divine assistance to our weakness, nor Divine protection to save us from external foes, alone, but the *purchase* of our souls by Jesus Christ, and the power of His Spirit to cure the radical *disease* of our wills and hearts. And, further, that these truths ought to become the great and governing principles of daily life. As, therefore, a great disparity in worldly circumstances, or a great discrepancy in natural dispositions, renders a marriage unfit, and in consequence unhappy, in an earthly point of view, so, as it appears to me, the belief of the great truths of redemption on one side, and their not being received upon the other, presents a case of difference as great, and in subject-matter infinitely more important than the foregoing in a spiritual point of view. Union, then, before this difference has been removed, appears to my mind not in conformity with the principles of our faith, and, as a necessary inference, not a happy event, but, until those circumstances are altered, a cause of regret. . . .

So far as I understand the question now, it is not whether my convictions are to influence another's conduct, but whether they are to govern my own. I have reconsidered them again and again : most willing am I to devote any time, and in any manner you may wish, to their further investigation. My presence at the marriage is, of course, at your option ; but it would be as wrong there, as elsewhere, so to speak or act as to falsify my belief.

For the present, then, I must be content with inquiring what there is that I can do without giving the lie to my conscience. Within those limits, I need hardly say, it only needs to be pointed out.

Believe me, I have not chosen for my conduct . . . a rule which I should shrink from applying to myself. In writing to ——, which (having your approbation) I propose to do in a day or two, it will be my duty to express my humble but full concurrence in the rule which they adopted of requiring unequivocal evidence of conformity in religious belief as a preliminary to entertaining the question of marriage

— of conformity more comprehensive and minute than any which has been thought of in the present instance.

It has the appearance of selfishness thus to introduce my own far less important case : but I have no other way of giving testimony to the fact that my feelings are not based upon a disposition to sacrifice recklessly the peace of others to mere speculations of my own.

376. *To John Gladstone (father).*

EDINBURGH,
December 26, 1835.

. . . There is indeed one thing that I can do, and that is I can see now that I might have written a letter quite as consistent with truth, and less likely to be felt objectionable, than that which I did write. I might have written to this effect : to have wished him, as God knows I do, every blessing, to have admitted my want of means to comprehend the grounds of *his* satisfaction, and to have expressed a belief that he had arrived at it by means of more ample information than he had transmitted by letter. I am quite persuaded that I might have written thus to him more properly and less offensively, and I am therefore ready, and more than ready, to express my regret for my choosing a course of inconsiderate harshness, a fault which I have in the course of my life had but too many occasions to regret, and which I well know to lie deep in my character. All this I could consequently do now, but it would be more satisfactory and entire if I could have been enabled, not only to express my conviction of my own fault, but also the reestablishment of a full confidence that my opinion itself was formed on defective and insufficient grounds. If, however, you are of opinion that it is in vain to look for the assurance which I have earnestly desired, and that still my writing to the *above* effect will give any satisfaction, I will not delay doing so a moment after hearing from you. . . .

377. *To the Rev. H. E. Manning.*

BETCHWORTH, DORKING,
March 29, 1837.

MY DEAR MANNING,
. . . I fully believe with you that there is in the public councils of this realm, and especially in the House of Commons, where, after all, the brunt of the social battle is to be borne, a 'most blessed calling' open to us, a work which does indeed cry aloud for men to work it, and that is the application of the searching test of Christian Catholic principles to those numerous measures of the time which are in form or substance or both calculated to bear powerfully on religion. But there are few men in the kingdom the joint state of whose minds and hearts would permit them to discharge that function : and I fear their mental composition is for the most part of too fine a texture readily to undergo the rude handling of a popular election, and the subsequent contact with party combinations and with every form of worldly motive. It must require a large gift of grace, to have strength for carrying unharmed through the crowd so precious and so delicate a burden. It is no reproach to our party leaders that they fail to develop in their public speeches what the study and the cloister have only rewrought out in this country within the few last years : for I think that that form of Christian feeling which we now want as applicable to statesmanship, involving a mixed and justly proportioned regard to the body and spirit of institutions, is one different from personal piety even where combined with intellect, still more different from any combination of secular motives, only realized by a few persons under the most favourable circumstances, requiring time to spread over and tinge the general sentiment of the nation, and less likely to prevail in proportion as persons are in contact firstly with the excitements, secondly with that pressure of detail, which are the accompaniments of all politics, but especially so of those of our own day and time. And let me observe this further : there is a great obstacle to this development in the peculiar nature of that description of

speaking which is required in the present day. It is not now as it was in ancient times, when the orator addressed his audience from the elevation of a mental *bema* as well as a physical one ; he must now stand upon the floor — believe me this is no fanciful analogy — he must, having the part of a debater in the House of Commons to discharge, place himself upon a level with his audience, his mind with their minds ; study their accessibilities accurately and narrowly, seek to lead their wills and not trust to a tone of command, to a mere display of intellectual power, or to the influence of rank or character or experience, in anything like the same degree to which it would formerly have been safe. In fine, it is of the character of a debater to be peculiarly subject to impressions from his audience, to be passive before and while he is active, to be oppressed by the sense of their antipathy while he is seeking to rouse or create their sympathy. Now if this be true, and, as all the world knows, the standard of the religious sympathies of the House of Commons, is not the distance immeasurable between that frame of mind, and that frame of language, in which a debater can be intelligible, so to speak, to this audience, and those on the other hand in which he must needs be himself in order fully to realize the conception of the Christian Faith and the Christian Church ?

For myself I avow that, taught as I have been in a sound and also an awakened University, and blest as I am with friends who, from positions less disturbed, supply me from time to time with views of unmaimed and uncontaminated truth, it were a sin indeed if I did not look forward with desire at least, though with slender hope, to a struggle with these difficulties ; but it would also be a blindness grosser than that of which I am conscious if I did not see that I have never yet succeeded at all in carrying myself upwards during a speech to that region of pure principle, and at the same time retaining the sympathy of the hearers. When the handling of obvious and everyday considerations is at an end, and when after the time for argument, should come the time to rise into the expression of feeling, I cannot describe to you the sensation of faintness and incapacity which oppresses the mind ; it tries to fly, and finds itself laden with wings of lead, and the only refuge of the tongue is in some bald and general commonplaces. This is sad truth : and yet what you say is true, that, so far as the principle of an Establishment is perceived in the House of Commons, on our side at least, it is honestly, warmly, loyally, felt by a class of men either religious or at least high-minded, and they will always respond even to the feeblest appeal upon such a subject.

Nothing that I have said is intended as in the nature of an exception to any view which you have taken : and I shall always be glad when you are inclined to open to me those yet unfolded sentiments upon this subject to which you advert.

Now with reference to the doctrine of alienations of religious property. I did not, so far as I am aware, commit myself upon the rectitude of such alienation in *any* case — unless you think that I did so virtually, by remarking that it might be consistent with maintaining the principle of a National Establishment : and I instanced the period when half the land was in the possession of the Church as affording the example of such a case. What more we are bound to do, as men and as a nation, than simply to maintain the principle and practice of such an Establishment, is, I think, an *ulterior* question.

Upon your general doctrine I am not prepared to give a decided opinion : but it seems to me to suggest many preliminary inquiries — *e.g.*, what is the nature of the consecration proposed to be untied : and whether it were really and unmixedly to the direct religious worship of God. And whether the alienation be to purposes capable of receiving a Christian character — *e.g.*, education : and charity in all its forms. Whether, if it be wrong in all cases to alienate, it were wrong to stop the bequests of lands on their way to the treasury of the Church, as was done, and I think properly, by the Statutes of Mortmain. Whether there be so broad a line of distinction between the devotion of which you speak, and that devotion of his property along with every other gift, not merely a nominal, but a real though an indirect one, which every Christian owes to God. Whether this line were not evidently much broader under the Jewish dispensation. Whether the argument therefrom would apply as

strongly where the proportions were greatly exceeded. Whether the consecration had been made by persons really competent — *i.e.*, not under delusion. In short, there is great difficulty in applying any very broad abstract principle to a creature so essentially concrete and conventional as property. But after having stated all these questions, which might issue either into mere bubbles or into serious considerations, I still come to nearly the same point as yourself, because I never contemplated the distinct case of alienation to sheer secular uses, and I feel that no diversion of any kind should take place except at the point, if there be a point, where the purposes themselves are hindered by the bulk of apparatus for working them out. We both admit a class of mixed uses — *e. g.*, feeding the poor: yet alienation for this would, I think, be sacrilege before the higher purposes were satisfied, though charity after it. But, I think, further we should erect a Propaganda with the excess of our own Church property rather than divert it (were there any). But this is beyond the mere principle of a National Church.
                         Your sincerely attached
                              W. E. GLADSTONE.

378. *To John Gladstone (father).*

FASQUE,
October 29, 1837.

When the idea of building an Episcopal chapel was lately mentioned amidst the light conversation of the dinner-table at Fasque, it passed off in a manner suitable rather to the occasion (for which I, as the introducer, am responsible) than to the subject itself. It has certainly struck me that there are reasons for it, which you would deem *serious* at least, whether they are or are not in your view *sufficient;* and having once been led almost involuntarily to allude to them, I cannot help wishing to give them the advantage of a more intelligible statement: and I only premise that I do so trusting to your invariable indulgence, and of my own motion alone, no other person being aware that I write this letter.

As regarded the point to which you alluded in jest —

namely, my contributing to the expense — I revert to it in earnest for the purpose of stating that it would afford me cordial pleasure to do so, both as a means in general of doing good, and also because in the particular instance it would tend towards supplying one of *your own* wants, which are the only ones that you ever fail to meet, while you more than satisfy those of all around you. In a few months I believe there will be near £3,000 at my credit in the books of the House; and if I were allowed, on the ground above stated, to devote £1,000 of this towards the object in question, I should be ready and desirous to do it.

Next I will endeavour to set aside two objections which might offer themselves to the proposed plan. The first, that it would seem to be an interference with the Kirk of Fettercairn; the second, that it would not afford sufficient employment for a clergyman.

With reference to the first (as some might consider it of weight), I should observe that the population of the parish is increasing: and that it already appears to be quite beyond Mr. Whyte's powers of visiting when we take into view its considerable extent. I never enter a cottage where I do not find testimony, in general volunteered, to this fact. The village kirk is already crowded, and does not, I believe, supply the full amount of seat-room for which the heritors are legally liable.

As regards the second, my idea certainly is that it would be desirable on every account for the clergyman of an Episcopal chapel, if built at or near Fasque, to have some additional occupation or study besides that immediately connected with his cure: and that this would readily be supplied by his taking pupils. A desirable tutor, anywhere in England, has no difficulty in getting them, and the remuneration is considerable. In Scotland I cannot help thinking such a person would be still more in request: and a better situation could hardly be conceived.

I shall now endeavour to enumerate some of the positive advantages which I think would accrue, and that not simply according to my own views (for to them the acquisition of an Apostolical ministry and ordinances within easy distance is alone enough), but as I think they might strike observers in general.

How can I omit, in the first place, to speak of yourself, and for the reason I before gave, that *you* will neither speak nor think of yourself ? You have, I trust in God, a considerable proportion of many successive years of health and vigour to spend at Fasque. I have often heard you lament the comparative meagreness of the Scottish worship, and owing to its peculiar nature it is now wholly beyond your reach. In the place you have made so commodious and delightful, may you not remain without the privilege of participating in the ordinances to which the Divine promises belong !

As next in order I take your household. They are, and are likely to continue, wholly or in great proportion members of the English Church : and one can hardly say less than that it is *desirable* to place the services of that Church within their reach : nay, that it would be so were those services only on a level in point of advantage with those of the Scottish Establishment. Besides which, as I take it for granted, they would not have to go so far even as now to Fettercairn, and in proportion they would be able to attend with more regularity.

The next point that I would mention is one connected with the almshouses you are about to build. The old people are a class much to be felt for here as regards their spiritual concerns. The discipline of Presbyterianism does not allow the Communion to be administered to them in their own houses. It would be no small advantage, surely, to have a minister who (where they desired it) could avail himself of a wiser system. But further : that class in an uncertain climate are very liable to be cut off from public worship by any inclemency of weather : and they soon become disqualified for traversing the distance between many of the cottages on your estate and Fettercairn. The present opportunity would enable you so to adjust the relative situations that these aged and commonly forlorn persons should, amidst your other bounties, have to bless your name for the secure enjoyment of the most valuable gift they can possess on earth.

I believe there is little doubt that they would be glad to avail themselves of the services of the English Church. At least, I can testify that in every case I have known they have accepted the English Prayer-Book *with joy,* or even solicited it *with eagerness.*

Descending to the very young from the old, one cannot fail to observe with pain how very rarely they are taken to church in this country for a period of several years after they become capable of appreciating, in the heart at least, if not the understanding, our beautiful and simple Liturgy, although doubtless incapable of properly following an extempore prayer. Now, if a school were connected with this chapel, not in the way of opposition, but of substitution for some one of those already existing in the parish, I cannot but believe that the parents would, in many instances, gladly afford their children the enjoyment of the blessing of public worship which would thus be at their command.

As regards other attendants, besides your household, the young, and the old, of course I do not contemplate, *at once,* any considerable number : nor do I more than mention that we have been, as you know, at times forty in number within your own walls : nor that our neighbours at Fettercairn and at Thornton are Episcopalians : but the members of our communion are likewise spread, and not thinly, through the people. I have never made it my business to ascertain them, but casually I have found on your own estate Wilkie, one of your tenants, and his entire family : the mother of another, Bruce. Old widow Fraser, at the Old Mains, for twenty-five years attended the Laurencekirk Chapel, but now cannot go to the village, and therefore goes nowhere. Close by Craigneston Bridge, Mrs. Mollison, again, is Episcopalian. Crabb, the tailor, and his family (but he has removed, for a time at least, to Brechin), and the Exciseman of the village, were all that I knew in Fettercairn. These, however, you will observe, are known to me, not by search for the purpose, but as it were by accident.

Of course the erection of such a chapel would be a relief, as far as it went, to the pressing demand for seats in the parish church, which, if unrelieved, will soon, I suppose, lead to a demand for its enlargement. The expense, according to the rates of building here and the local facilities, could not be great. If a school for children were added, I fancy it would support itself.

The right description of clergyman would be, I should think, a young man in English Orders, and his emoluments (of course not of a nature to locate him here for a *great* number of years, which would be quite unnecessary) would be, say, a small endowment, a house, a proportion of the weekly collections, and the payments of pupils.

I have thus endeavoured to lay before you the case upon its own merits, and without attempting to create a favourable inclination on your part by raising up voices in its support; and if I have not expressed a willingness to lay out upon the proposed undertaking a greater share of what your extreme bounty has enabled me to save, it has been from the recollection that other places and objects have their claims. Individually I am perhaps less interested than others in the realization of the plan, for to me it is no great hardship under any circumstances to go to Laurencekirk: though I will not deny that I may have been partly stimulated to its proposal by a constantly and painfully increasing sense of the inadequacy of the Scottish service (without any disparagement to Mr. Whyte's efforts individually, which seem to me to do him great credit) to the most essential purposes of public worship.

I hardly know whether it be worth while to suggest as a modification of this plan, or as a commencement for it, that possibly an arrangement might be made with Goalen to give a single service here on the Sunday besides his duty at Laurencekirk, for this seems of at best doubtful practicability.

Of our afternoon prayers in the dining-room, it is enough to say they do not seem to me in any sense worthy to be called a substitute, unless we were *necessarily* debarred from the reality.

And now it only remains to ask your pardon for having at so much length stated my own insignificant opinions, and to express a trust and prayer that they may be dealt with, not according to any wishes of mine, but to their own merits and the substantial interests involved.

    I remain, my beloved father,
        Your ever-affectionate son,
            W. E. GLADSTONE.

379. *To J. R. Hope.*

6, Carlton Gardens,
June 11, 1839.

My dear Hope,
  Accept my sincere thanks for your faithful and friendly letter : I love it far better than merely smooth and thoughtless congratulations. You will, I hope, soon know my wife, and try her by the test you propose ; unless I am mistaken, the genuine graces of her character — and of course I speak not of human graces alone or chiefly — will abide it. We have both much need amidst the kindness that pours upon us ; and I more in proportion, as I am less worthy to have our thoughts directed to the Cross, and to the Man of Sorrows upon it. Pray for us that we may be enabled to bear both our griefs and our joys so that they may work out in us, and by us, the purposes of God. I rely much on your friendship. I hope you will never shrink from admonishing me, and that my attachment may grow with your fidelity.
  God bless you now and ever, and believe me,
Your warm friend,
W. E. Gladstone.

380. *To J. R. Hope.*

Hawarden Rectory,
September 8, 1840.

My dear Hope,
  . . . I agree very much in the general spirit of your remarks respecting the details of the institution, and in most of the observations themselves. I think, however, that it would not be wise to separate the clerical pupils so soon as you propose. For fifteen or sixteen I should say seventeen or eighteen, thinking it desirable to keep lay boys until the natural age for their repairing to the Universities. I am rather persuaded that their last years at the college would be the best : but if it were not so, we might discourage their remaining a little by taxing them higher. Neither do I like the proposal that the exhibitioners who are to be candidates for Orders should sleep in a common apartment. I think that a certain measure of privacy is very

advisable and very sacred for persons who have grown to the full use of all their faculties. I have been considering the education of the laity all along, not only as a great object, but as quite co-ordinate to the other in importance, and greater in *bulk*. A very small establishment indeed would enable you to educate as many candidates for Orders as the Church in Scotland is likely for some time to require: but without such a school for the laity as we contemplate, I think the means of extending Church principles in Scotland will be greatly crippled; for at present the clergy are without *access*, almost, to the gentry, unless in a few exceptional cases. I am afraid that your plan of early separation would startle people much, and should wish the general aspect of a school to remain elevated indeed, but undisturbed. There is no such separation as you mention in the Anglo-Popish colleges, I believe: and surely it is early enough at seventeen or eighteen. All these, however, are matters in which we may compare our ideas with each other and with friends hereafter, so as either to agree or to differ without impeding the pursuit of our great common object: the time has not yet arrived for dealing with them definitively, as you observe.

With respect, however, to the general problem — how to unite in a common education persons paying different rates of charge, without arrogance on the one hand and debasement on the other — I look to attaining that object by dividing the foundation scholarships partly into exhibitions for those who are to be clergymen, and partly into rewards of merit, open to competition by the whole body of the school. I should hope that this would keep them in the same relation of moral *superiority* as the studentships at Christ Church have with respect to commonerships. . . .

381. *To Lord Lyttelton.*

LONDON,
March 5, 1841.

. . . I received yesterday a letter from Girdlestone enclosing copies of the same papers which you have sent me. It is a very difficult subject: and it appears to me that, of the two points contrary to G.'s view, the expurgation of the text is far more questionable than Christianizing the notes. As respects the latter branch, I see no obstacle that ought to prevent it: only it should be done by very judicious men, who will not run out into sermons in their notes: they should be in my view dryly and succinctly done. But to me it seems that expurgation is liable to many objections, although I admit the use of the entire text is by no means free from them. It is a happy circumstance that, of the classical books otherwise most apt and most in use for boys, there is hardly any one except Horace which raises the question: and the quantity of expurgation requisite in him is limited. The amount being small and the quality very bad, I do not see why in mere school Horaces the omissions should not be made: but I do not see that it could be extended much farther. In such a case as that of Juvenal entire satires must be omitted: and instead of publishing Juvenal purged, it would be better, it seems to me, to select certain satires only for boys to read first. Even in the tenth, however, there must be an omission, but, if I recollect right, only one. As to applying the process to the whole of Aristophanes, it is, I imagine, hopeless: but a play or two might be selected for the initiation of boys, and disencumbered. It seems to me quite fallacious and visionary to talk of publishing a number of authors, or any general edition of the classics, on this principle: it goes upon the supposition, which I imagine would prove totally false, that young persons, up to the age at which they have gained an acquaintance with a considerable range of classical authors, would hereby be kept free from the notions it is desired to avoid.

But, after all, what I should most like to have upon this important subject would be the judgment of a good and sensible man who had been extensively conversant with the education of youths where it had been conducted upon the principle of expurgation. I cannot deny or palliate the fact that mischief does arise from the present practice: and though I much doubt whether, generally speaking, natural appetite and curiosity together do not greatly outrun information thus acquired, and anticipate any temptation it may bring, yet if a practical man could be found to say, 'I have seen much of boys educated this way and also that, and I find the one class much purer than the other,' I should willingly choke my own suspicions.

This question connects itself very much with a larger question respecting young boys, and the expediency of sending them to public schools. There is no doubt that it places them *early* in contact with danger: the question is, whether upon the whole of the process of entering life the *aggregate* of danger is hereby increased or diminished. My own strong conviction is, that to send a bad or a weak boy to a public school is madness: but that every boy who with a true principle of love to his Redeemer has any firmness or tone of character is better there than anywhere else. On something of the same consideration I believe we must be content to act with reference to false principles and corrupting passages in the classics. Nay, further, is it not to be recollected that the principle of expurgation, narrowly viewed, is capable of application even to the Bible, almost as much as to those authors whom I have named? It might also be applied to all unchristian passages in all authors that boys are to read, though in various degrees.

If I were a juryman obliged to make a verdict on pain of starvation, I should say, 'I think it impracticable to carry the principle of expurgation of the classics to any considerable extent, but can see no harm in applying it to such works as are put into the hands of young boys before they begin to range freely in their reading. . . .'

July 4, 1841.

382. *Part of a Circular giving an Account of the Proposed College.*

In order more fully to inform parties who are unacquainted with the details of the 'higher English Education' mentioned in this Circular, it has been thought expedient to specify the chief particulars of the Education alluded to.

These are:

1. The union of religious teaching and of habits of public worship with secular instruction.

2. The regulation of conduct out of school-hours, whether by the general discipline of the system, or by superintendence within boarding houses.

3. The general teaching of reading, writing, and arithmetic, of the English, Latin, and Greek languages, of history, ancient and modern, of mathematics, of science, moral and physical, and of the doctrine of the Church, according to the gradual capacity of boys from the age (say) of eight up to the age of eighteen.

Also the supplying means of instruction in foreign languages, drawing, and music to those pupils whose parents may desire these accomplishments.

The advantages above mentioned cannot at present be procured in a combined form by Episcopalians in any public institution in Scotland, and yet it is upon their combination that the chief value of each particular depends.

Thus historical, classical, and scientific instruction, to be safe, must be guarded by religion : doctrine to be held otherwise than as a theory must be interwoven with the elements of general knowledge and find a practical support in religious exercises ; and, again, lectures in all branches, Catechisms, and acts of public worship, must have their deficiencies supplied, their effects combined and assisted and the regular use of them enforced by domestic discipline and the continual superintendence of authority.

In the chief English schools this union of means either is, or, according to their Constitution, ought to be attained, but at a cost (to speak roughly) of not less than from £100 to £200 and upwards per annum besides the expense and inconvenience attendant upon the distance from Scotland at which these schools are placed. In the proposed institution it is calculated that both board and the general Education above described might be furnished at from fifty to seventy guineas per annum according to the age of the pupil or less than one half of the expense in England.

It is also thought that the foundation of a new establishment would afford facilities for a fuller development of the system than can always be ensured in England.

383. *To J. R. Hope.*

LIVERPOOL,
August 9, 1841.

MY DEAR HOPE,
Since I last wrote to you it has appeared to me that we are, in point of fact, extremely strong in utilitarian arguments for the Scotch College. That the soil of Scotland is admirably adapted for the growth of patient, earnest, and able persons fitted for the office of teaching is clearly shown by a fact notorious to us all, namely, that England is at this very time importing schoolmasters by scores from beyond the Border: in other words, we in England want a great number of persons to undertake a laborious and scantily remunerated function, and at the same time absorbing all that our own region can supply, we are obliged to depend upon Scotland to enlarge our store. Now, just let us consider that English schoolmasterships, such as are now drawing Scotch masters to fill them, are *better paid* (or quite as well at the very least) than the clerical cures in Scotland for which we wish to provide: surely, then, upon the genuine principles of free trade, and setting aside every argument for encouraging home growth as such, it is clear that Scotland is better fitted than England for yielding the class of persons we want, inasmuch as she is now an exporting country of such persons, while England is an importing one. I think that this topic is capable of being handled with great truth and effect, and that some of our refractory or reluctant friends will surely see that talent and character available for a teaching function are to be had cheaper and more easily in Scotland than in England.

Nor can it be said in answer to this that the Scotch are a Presbyterian people, and that the class now trained for schools would not take advantage of the College: it is notorious that many of them come into Church schools in England, which is scarcely compatible with the supposition that none of them would use a Church seminary in Scotland.

I have here *grazed* another topic, viz., that the College ought to be a training-school for schoolmasters too, and that by its means we have a prospect of regulating the Bell bequest according to the intention of the founder, which I imagine is hardly done at present: but the argument is of wider scope, and goes upon the anomaly of coming to a *dear* country to supply a cheap one which is already itself supplying that dear one, by reason of its dearness, with (economically speaking) the same commodity. . . .

      I remain always,
        Your attached friend,
         W. E. GLADSTONE.

384. *To the Archbishop of Canterbury.*

        AUDLEY END,
     Sunday, November 21, 1841.

MY LORD ARCHBISHOP,
  It is probable your Grace may have received about this time a letter from Bishop Skinner, the Primus of the Episcopal College in Scotland, requesting your Grace's countenance and support to a design for founding an educational institution, for both lay and clerical training, in that country.

  I shall not presume to offer any pleading on behalf of a project which, I trust, will be more effectually commended to your Grace's notice by the documents which Bishop Skinner undertook to forward: but having been in the first instance, together with Mr. James Hope, responsible for the suggestion, I venture to furnish some slight information respecting it.

  The moving cause with us, I am bound to state, was not ambitious or aggressive intention, but an earnest desire to supply the Episcopal Communion in Scotland with an organ of the first necessity for her internal welfare. She is as yet destitute of the means of rearing her own children, and to provide adequate instruments for this purpose will require all her disposable energies for a length of time.

  And I am glad to say that, so far as I know, this scheme has not in any respectable quarter been misconstrued into an attack, open or covert, upon the Church Establishment of Scotland.

  The only circumstance, I conceive, that could make it wear that aspect would be its failing to obtain public, general, and (so to speak) authoritative support in England.

It was received at the outset by the Scottish Bishops with a cordial approbation of its principle and aim: by some influential parties among the laity with indifference, or even aversion: by others with satisfaction, as the Duke of Sutherland and some more; and it pleased God that from the very first it should be cordially welcomed by some persons, such as the Duke of Buccleuch and the late Lord Lothian, who had both the will and the power to place it on a stable footing. The Queen-Dowager has also granted her patronage.

From what I know of the existence of such dispositions in Scotland, I may venture to assure your Grace that, humanly speaking, the scheme will proceed: though of course the difficulties to be encountered, and the comprehensiveness of its utility, will depend very much on the quality as well as the amount of support which may be acceded to it.

Mr. Hope, I know, partakes with me in the desire that we may be understood to claim no other share in the proceedings connected with it than would be open to any other individuals anxious to aid them, and indeed, as to myself, my occupations will not allow of my paying them more than an occasional and rare attention. On every ground we trust that it may be identified in the utmost possible degree with the Church herself, by having a basis of principles neither narrower nor less defined, and by being placed under the control of the Scottish Bishops.

At present I think it may be asserted with truth that the design stands well in the general opinion north of the Border. We trust, however, to receive important aid from England, especially from the approval of the rulers of the Church and from great institutions connected with it. We have reason to believe that very favourable dispositions exist in the Committee, for example, of the Christian Knowledge Society: but I may, perhaps, be pardoned for suggesting that no circumstance could so favourably introduce our appeal in England as if your Grace should think fit to make a specific recommendation on behalf of the projected college to that Society.

I may further submit that, should your Grace be so inclined, it would be an important advantage that the Committee should be in possession of your Grace's mind on the subject at its meeting on the 29th, or at the latest on the 6th, in order that the requisite notice might be given at the meeting of the Society on the 7th, and the matter entertained definitively at the January meeting.

I remain, . . .
W. E. G.

I have also written to the Archbishops of York and Armagh.

385. *To Mrs. Gladstone.*

FASQUE,
August 18, 1842.

. . . You do not seem to be much disturbed by the neighbourhood of this turn-out, which I hope may cause no commotion beyond the edge of the manufacturing district; but in itself it is formidable. This is the time when we may reflect on the thorough rottenness, socially speaking, of the system which gathers together huge masses of population having no other tie to the classes above them than that of employment, of high money payment constituting a great moral temptation in times of prosperity, and then reductions in adversity which *seem* like robberies, and which the poor people have no discipline or training to endure.

386. *To the Rev. W. G. Ward.*

WHITEHALL,
November 23, 1843.

MY DEAR WARD,

Let me thank you for your note, which renews our direct intercourse after so many eventful and changeful years. It is but little that I have to say in reply, but I felt a dislike to the appearance of indifference which silence would have borne, considering your direct appeal. Be assured that I thank you for your frankness, while I must beg you to excuse my own.

If you are desirous to find 'any one good thing about the English Reformation' before you publish; and if you ask me to point out what may correspond with that condition, I am driven to the answer that the way to that discovery may lie through an operation upon your own mind: as if on a lowering, stormy day a person said to me, 'I see nothing but clouds; show me the daylight,' he would force me to conclude that there was something in his vision requiring to be dealt with. Anxious 'to see as much good as you can in all movements,' you find 'in the English Reformation itself,' and not merely in the motives of its instruments, 'as nearly unmixed wickedness' as 'the intrinsic inconsistency of human nature' will allow. I am most certain that you would not knowingly judge either of men or things in an inequitable mode or spirit: but of what you have done unconsciously I confess to a very different opinion.

For my part, without going farther, I see in the free use of Scripture by the Christian people at large, not for controversy, nor for dogmatic accuracy, nor for the satisfaction of the understanding, but for its milk and meat, the food of the spirit, one undeniable object and fruit of the English Reformation which appears to me not to correspond to the description of 'nearly unmixed wickedness': and the sense of that which I deem an immense though a much-misused blessing is, I confess, quickened when I remember what substitutes for that celestial gift are supplied in some other Christian lands.

But I am not so vain as really to suppose that it can lie with me to point out to a much more competent and experienced person anything that has not already met his view. I do not draw consolation, in the perusal of your note, from any such hope, for it would indeed be anything rather than a reproach to you that what I had said carried no conviction, or rather no suspicion, to your mind.

I lean much more on the belief, which your kind expressions confirm, that it is possible for persons to seek the truth, while they differ concerning the way to it, under such conditions, both of faith and temper, that they may have an union in and by virtue of that search, real though not yet fully realized: and that, where it is so, the subjects of that relation may wait with content and thankfulness for the day of being made perfect in peace.

    Believe me always,
      Very sincerely yours,
        W. E. GLADSTONE.

387. *To Mrs. Gladstone.*

      13, CARLTON HOUSE TERRACE,
       Sunday Evening,
        January 21, 1844.

. . . I am going to end this day of peace by a few words to show that what you said did not lightly pass away from my mind. There is a beautiful little sentence in the works of Charles Lamb concerning one who had been afflicted : 'He gave his heart to the Purifier, his will to the Will that governs the Universe.' But there is a speech in the third canto of the 'Paradiso' of Dante, spoken by a certain Piccarda, which is a rare gem. I will only quote this one line :

   'In la Sua volontade è nostra pace.'

The words are few and simple, and yet they appear to me to have an inexpressible majesty of truth about them, to be almost as if they were spoken from the very mouth of God. It so happened that (unless my memory much deceives me) I first read that speech upon a morning early in the year 1836, which was one of trial, although the meaning of the event that made it such has since been made manifest, and it wears in retrospect a character quite different ; and I was profoundly impressed and powerfully sustained, almost absorbed by them. They cannot be too deeply graven upon the heart — in short, what we all want is that they should not come to us as an admonition from without, but as an instinct from within. They should not be adopted by effort or upon a process of proof, but they should be simply the translation into speech of the habitual tone to which all tempers, affections, emotions, are set ; that as, in a time of gaiety, the lively consciousness of a state of enjoyment revives again and again, so in the Christian mood, which ought never to be intermitted, the sense of this conviction should recur spontaneously, that it should be the foundation of all mental thoughts and acts, and the measure to which the whole experience of life inward and outward is referred. The final state which we are to contemplate with hope, and to seek by discipline, is that in which our will shall be *one* with the will of God : not merely shall submit to it, not merely shall follow after it, but shall live and move with it even as the pulse of the blood in the extremities acts with the central movement of the heart. And this is to be obtained through a double process : the first, that of checking, repressing, quelling, the inclination of the will to act with reference to self as a centre — this is to mortify it: the second, to cherish, exercise, and expand, its new and heavenly power of acting according to the will of God, first, perhaps, by painful effort in great feebleness and with many inconsistencies, but with continually augmenting regularity and force until obedience become a necessity of second nature.

And these two processes are carried on together. Your abundant overflowing affection as a wife leads you to wish we were together, while duty keeps us apart. You check that affection, school and subdue it — that is mortifying the individual will. That of itself is much more than the whole of what is contemplated by popular opinion as a Christian duty, for resignation is too often conceived to be merely a submission not unattended with complaint to what we have no power to avoid ; but it is less than the whole of the work of a Christian. Your full triumph, as far as that particular occasion of duty is concerned, will be to find that you not merely repress *outward* complaint — nay, not merely repress inward tendencies to murmur — but that you would not if you could alter what in any matter God has plainly willed ; that you have a satisfaction and a comfort in it because it is His will, although from its own native taste you would have revolted. Here is the great work of religion : here is the path through which sanctity is attained, the highest sanctity. And yet it is a path evidently to be traced in the course of our daily duties ; for it is clear that the occasions of every day are numberless, amidst the diversities of events, upon which a true spiritual discrimination may find employment in discerning the will of God, and in which also the law of love and self-denial may be applied in the effort to conform to it both inwardly and outwardly so soon as it shall have been discerned. And thus the high attainments that have their crown and their reward in heaven do not require, in order that we may learn them, that we should depart from our common duties, but they lie by the wayside of life ; and every pilgrim of this world may, if he have grace, become an adept in them.

When we are thwarted in the exercise of some innocent, laudable, and almost sacred affection, as in the case, though its scale be small, out of which all this has grown, Satan has us at an advantage ; because when the obstacle occurs we have a sentiment that the feeling baffled is a right one, and in indulging a rebellious temper we flatter ourselves that we are merely, as it were, indignant on behalf, not of ourselves, but of a duty which we have been interrupted in performing. But our duties can take care of themselves when God calls us away from any of them, and when He interrupts the discharge of one it is to ascertain, by the manner of bearing the interruption, whether we are growing fit for another which is higher. To be able to relinquish a duty upon command shows a higher grace than to be able to give up a mere pleasure for a duty ; it shows a more practical discernment of the Divine will to distinguish between two things differing only in measure, than between one which has a manifest stamp of God upon it and another which is but remotely related to Him, or what is commonly (and hazardously) called indifferent.

Monday.

Thus far last night. To-day I only add that what precedes is with me speculation, not practice. . . .

388. *To Lord Medwyn.*

FASQUE,
October 5, 1844.

. . . As at present informed, I could not participate in any application to Sir Robert Peel and the Chancellor of the Exchequer for an increase of the

Photo, Chidley, Chester.

MR. GLADSTONE, 1897.

grant to the Episcopal Communion of Scotland, even upon the very modest scale which you propose — namely, by the simple change of a biennial into an annual gift of £1,200.

My reasons are various, and in part, but in part only, have reference to myself personally. I think that every new grant, and in its degree every augmentation of a grant, to an unestablished body of Christians, is a new relaxation of the connection between Church and State : and that I am a very unfit person to take part in any such proceeding : although I am far from saying that I regard you, for example, as bound by the same ties. At the same time I cannot help thinking that all our brethren in Scotland should well consider the effect of any effort they may make upon the claims, especially when regarded as exclusive claims, of the Church in England, and especially in Ireland.

I pass, however, to more general reasons. What claim can we urge upon Parliament? Loyalty is a duty, and does not entitle the loyal subject to have his religion endowed. Shall we, then, plead the Apostolic title of the Bishops? I for one am ready to urge it, except to the State : because, if that argument be good for anything to the State, it is good to the extent of claiming the whole property of the Presbyterian Church Establishment. But of course, in making such a request as you propose, our friends would carefully disclaim any such idea, and would ask the money as a free and almost an eleemosynary gift. I have a considerable repugnance to seeing the Episcopal Communion of Scotland seek, by the mouth of those who for such purposes are her organs, for public support *in formâ pauperis*, because I think it has some tendency to lead us to undervalue, or even to disavow, our unassailable ecclesiastical position. The pretension to represent spiritually the ancient Church of the country is serious and respectable while it is urged soberly and not compromised by those who hold it ; I should see no compromise in accepting what the State might tender ; I do not at all presume to limit others who may feel themselves free in conscience to go farther : but I am so satisfied that the strength of our Church is intrinsic, and lies in the principles of her construction, that I am extremely loath to run any risk of restraining the free expression of those principles for the sake of a new pecuniary grant which you very probably would not obtain, and which if obtained might be a pledge of silence and of servitude.

I am by no means for premature and inconsiderate assertion of the claims, in a religious view, of our Church, but it is my earnest desire that she should keep in her own hands the whole question as to the time and mode of opening them.

It may occur to you that these opinions are not less fatal to the acceptance of the present grant than to an application for doubling it. But I am under the impression, confirmed by the construction I put upon your letter, that the present grant is the bounty of the Sovereign, not of the Legislature, and that it was given by the Crown out of moneys which would otherwise have been available for the use of the Crown. If this be so, it stands upon a ground wholly different; and if we could go with a prospect of success and with general prudence to the Sovereign as a member of the Church to ask her bounty, to this my objections would not apply. I was not aware that the vote was now made by Parliament; but if it is, my view is not altered, for I apprehend that Parliament takes over, as charges upon the Treasury, burdens which may have been laid on the Crown revenue while it was in the hands of the Crown.

We cannot plead that we are a numerous body in Scotland. We can plead that we were established: but look to the effect of this in the other two countries.

Still, I confess to you that I have reserved my strongest grounds of objection for the last place. I do not think there is on the face of the earth a greater scandal than the state of the pecuniary resources of the Scottish Episcopal Communion, when compared with those of its individual members. We are few in numbers, but we have a greater proportion of members in easy circumstances, and even of great possessions, than almost any other existing body of Christians. We have also a ministry of which the hierarchical structure rather tends to increase than to diminish the just measure of its demands for pecuniary support. With these facts staring us in the face, taunted with them as we are in the public journals, we are to resort to the State for assistance upon the ground of the poverty of our Church. Might we not more fitly cut off one-half or three-fourths of the wages of our domestic servants, or the allowances of our children, and then ask the State to contribute to the relief of *their* poverty? A friendly Minister might be satisfied to decline our application in silence, I confess that I think a hostile one would not rest content without a bitter taunt upon ourselves.

Poverty, undoubtedly, in our Bishops and clergy we can show, along with wealth in ourselves, and the ownership of perhaps half or more of the soil of Scotland. True, this is no relief to the wants of our clergy, I am not now arguing, God forbid, against our taking some measures to improve their circumstances: but I think if we go to the State, and are put upon an exposition of the state of the facts, we shall prove effectually that there never was an instance of more undeniable ability on the part of a religious community for the proper sustentation of its clergy, and never an instance of half so disgraceful neglect.

But let me here insert one word to assure you that, while I speak thus warmly, and perhaps vehemently, of ourselves as a body, I honour not the less but the more, on account of the general neglect of duty, those few who have laboured to remove the evil: those few of whom the honoured name you bear claims so large a proportion.

Always understanding, then, that my remarks relate to the body, I proceed to say that the worst part of the whole matter, darker even than the shame of the visible state of our clergy as to their subsistence, is the proof which our penuriousness affords of spiritual languor, of indifference to the blessings of the communion of the Church, of disposition to adhere to the good things of this world, and to part with no share of them which we can contrive to retain — I was going to say, which we can contrive decently to retain, but the qualification may be dispensed with in word, for we are not careful to observe it in act.

Now, I have a serious apprehension that an increase of the existing grant by the State, as an act independent of our own exertions, while in its immediate effect it would tend to mitigate the existing mischief, would have a more extensive and permanent effect in hiding from us our own misconduct, and in increasing thereby the deadness of conscience which is the real root of it.

And now I must intreat you to forgive me for having written with this freedom — a freedom consistent, as I trust, with the highest respect both for your character and for the motives with which you urge the claim of the Church, and also with a full consciousness that I am ill informed and ill qualified to come to conclusions upon the subject even for myself, far less to influence others. Indeed, the plainness of speech, perhaps in excess, which I have used, is in no way warranted by my slight personal acquaintance with your lordship. It has not been my habit to obtrude these sentiments upon others not intimately known to me, but you will forgive me for feeling that there was a bond of brotherhood between us which would supply the place of ordinary intercourse; and after *you* in your position had thought fit to make a request to one from whom the Church has a right to demand all such services as he can render, and from whom you might, I think, very naturally presume that you would meet with encouragement and co-operation, I felt myself on the one hand compelled to decline sharing in your intended proceeding, and on the other hand not less unequivocally constrained to avoid shrouding my views and motives in language of formal etiquette, and I determined to state strongly what I think strongly, and to trust to your indulgence for a favourable construction.

But now I am well aware that there is nothing more justly offensive in matters of this kind than the character of an objector, who intercepts the benevolent intentions of others and substitutes nothing for them. And your lordship's letter gives me a good opportunity to mention that I for one have long been looking for an occasion to do something towards providing fitter means of support for our clergy. In the first design of Trinity College I thought we were sowing for the future, by endeavours to supply such a training as would teach the next generation in our Church something of the value of their position and something of the blessedness of being allowed to contribute towards her temporal support. And at this moment I am most anxious that we should, if possible, wind up our Trinity College subscription, in order that we may clear the ground for a fresh effort to raise a fund towards the endowment of our bishoprics.

Individually I am quite prepared with my contribution towards such a fund; but it is necessary to await the moment when there may be a reasonable hope of obtaining the co-operation of a sufficient number.

You are the first person to whom I have presumed to mention this subject in such a manner, and I am led to do it because it seemed incumbent on me to show that in declining, and even I would venture to say dissuading, the course you would follow, I did not propose acquiescence in the present miserable state of things, but entertained the hope that good examples may be given, and may find imitators as God shall permit; and the belief that the Church will find her best support, under His Providence, in the due appeal to those motives which are most intimately allied with our personal relation to her, and to the ordinances which it is her office to dispense. . . .

389. *To Mrs. Gladstone.*

13, CARLTON HOUSE TERRACE,
Sunday, November 24, 1844.

. . . For years have I been talking about discipline, and now some opportunity and hope of help in it appears to have come into view. My conscience is weak, and wants aid — not to say that it is crooked, more than you know or can know, and wants a straight rule for its correction. The laxity of habits which my occupations entail forms another good reason for taking some means to ascertain that it does not degenerate into a mere pretext for self-indulgence. I am quite at ease also in this matter, as the movement is one not only within, but almost required by, the injunctions and spirit of the Church.

It often occurs to me what a blessing it will be to our children if they can be brought up in the habit of constantly disclosing the interior of their minds: then that is met by the thought that while thus governing them we should — or at least I should — also have made already some provision still nearer home. This seems to me so healthy and so simple that I confidently anticipate its appearing so likewise to you, and I say nothing, therefore, with the view of obviating apprehension or suspicion. If the eye be steadily fixed on the salvation of the soul, how precious does every real help appear! How do we love the holy songs of the Church, which are such helps! Let us, then, love other true helps also, though not of such unmixed exterior sweetness. . . .

390. *To Mrs. Gladstone.*

CALAIS,
September 25, 1845.

. . . I had heard so much against Calais, which I have never seen before, that I am rather pleased with it. It is exceedingly clean, and the view of it from the sea on entering the harbour has a good skyline, with three tower-spire projections, of which only one, however, belongs to a church. But that is rather a striking building — Notre Dame. I found service going on, and made such notes as I could. It seems to be the only church in the town within the walls; there was a function going on, and a sort of officer to keep order, who, I am sorry to say, smelt strongly of spirits, and looked them too. There is an elaborate marble screen behind the altar, dated 1622, much of the style of our monuments of that period, but with the figures much more modernized and affected — in fact, like those of the time of Louis XIV. and Charles II., as they appeared to me. A fine organ, but harsher than our old ones, pealed valiantly from one end; at the other, two priests or singers (*cantores*) chanted one on each side of an enormous trombone that completely drowned them, played by an unchurchlike-looking man in slippers — the one whom I saw taking snuff liberally between his responses. When I see the amazing accumulation of gestures and evolutions, almost dancing-masterlike, of their priests in celebrating service, it never fails to prompt a Puritanical reaction in my mind. But let us give due weight to the fact that their congregations are so attentive. There were some fifty present to-day, and they appeared absorbed in their work. I was a little surprised to see in the *affiches* of prices for chairs that a stall in the choir may be had for five francs a year, that being properly the clerical part. The charge for chairs at funerals is very high — several francs — varying according to the hour. . . .

391. *To Mrs. Gladstone.*

MUNICH,
September 30, 1845.

. . . I passed Strasburg without seeing it: as it was Sunday, I was not sorry to be prevented, by the necessity of setting off at once for the railroad (between Kehl and Carlsruhe), from getting a sight of it, which must under the circumstances have been a mere sight, and no more like a spectacle than a Sunday employment. It is impossible, however, not to receive some general impressions from the character of these South German churches, so different from ours, though in pointed architecture one is surprised at their great size, and particularly their height. The interiors (two) that I have seen have a kind of solemnity and grandeur; and yet it is not rich, it is not sublime, it is not heavenly, it does not *move* one to rapture as the best interiors of our cathedrals do, or would do if they were as they should be. In Augsburg there is a singular arrangement of the altars — they are all placed against the pillars of the nave, one to each, looking westward, and none along the sides of the church. In the cathedral here I was sorry to see an arrangement new to me, on a principal altar. In the centre, between the candlesticks, was a figure of the Blessed Virgin without our Lord. Then with each candlestick was an angel kneeling towards the figure in the middle — this is very *strong*. In this country, generally, by the roads I see few images, except of our Lord upon the cross — which, I think, Arnold wished to see in England. This city seems to be one in which art and munificence have been contending vehemently against great natural disadvantages. It is a dead flat, hot, cold, wet, and foggy — my experience is not good for much, but it has poured with rain almost all to-day. The architectural character is not interesting : there are a number of great public buildings, but they do not make a whole such as one finds in the towns of the Middle Ages. Of the pictures, whether fresco or others, I have as yet seen almost nothing.

Yesterday evening, after dinner with two travelling companions, an Italian *negoziante* and a German, I must needs go and have a shilling's worth of the Augsburg Opera, where we heard Mozart ('Don Giovanni') *well* played and very respectably sung. To-day I have spent my evening (for I write just before bed, and this will go to-morrow) differently : in tea and infinite conversation with Dr. Döllinger, who is one of the first among the R. C. theologians of Germany — a remarkable and very pleasing man. His manners have great simplicity, and I am astonished at the way in which a busy student such as he is can receive an intruder. His appearance is, singular to say, just *compounded* of those of two men who are among the most striking in appearance of our clergy — Newman and Dr. Mill. He surprises me by the extent of his information, and the way in which he knows the detail of what takes place in England. Most of our conversation related to it. He seemed to me one of the most liberal and catholic in mind of all the persons of his communion whom I have known. To-morrow I am to have tea with him again, and there is to be a third, Dr. Görres, who is also a man of eminence among them. Do not think he has designs upon me. Indeed, he disarms my suspicions in that respect by what appears to me a great sincerity.

392. *To Mrs. Gladstone.*

MUNICH,
October 2, 1845.

. . . On Tuesday after post I began to look about me: and though I have not seen all the sights of Munich, I have certainly seen a great deal that is interesting in the way of art ; and having spent a good deal of time in Dr. Döllinger's company — last night till one o'clock — I have lost my heart to him. What I like, perhaps, most, or what crowns other causes of liking towards him, is that he, like Rio, seems to take a hearty interest in the progress of religion in the Church of England, apart from the (so to speak) party question between us, and to have a mind to appreciate good wherever he can find it. For instance, when, in speaking of Wesley, I said that his own views and intentions were not heretical, and that, if the ruling powers in our Church had had energy and a right mind to turn him to account, or if he had been a member of the Church of Rome, I was about to add he would then have been a great saint, or something to that effect, but I hesitated, thinking it perhaps too strong, and even presumptuous; but he took me up and used the very words, declaring that to be his opinion. Again, speaking of Archbishop Leighton he expressed great admiration of his piety, and said it was so striking that he could not have been a real Calvinist. Then, he is a great admirer of England and English character, and he does not at all *slur* over the mischiefs with which religion has to contend in Germany. Lastly, I may be wrong, but I am persuaded he in his mind abhors a great deal that is too frequently taught in the Church of Rome. Last night he spoke with such a sentiment of the doctrine that was taught on the subject of indulgences which aroused Luther to resist them; and he said he believed it was true that the preachers represented to the people that by money payments they could procure the release of souls from purgatory. I told him that was exactly the doctrine I had heard preached in Messina, and he said a priest preaching so in Germany would be suspended by his Bishop.

Last night he invited several of his friends, whom I went to meet at an entertainment which consisted first of weak tea, immediately followed by meat supper with beer and wine and sweets. For two hours was I there in the midst of five German professors, or four and the editor of a paper, who held very interesting discussions. I could only follow them in part, and enter into them still less, as none of them (except Dr. Döllinger) seemed to speak any tongue but their own with any freedom — but you would have been amused to see and hear them, and me in the midst. I never saw men who spoke together in a way to render one another inaudible as they did — always excepting Dr. Döllinger, who sat like Rogers, being as he is a much more refined man than the rest. But of the others I assure you always two, sometimes three, and once all four, were speaking at once, very loud, each not trying to force the attention of the others, but to be following the current of his own thoughts. One of them was Dr. Görres who in the time of Napoleon edited a journal that had a great effect in rousing Germany to arms. Unfortunately, he spoke more *thickly* than any of them. . . .

393. *To Mrs. Gladstone.*

MUNICH,
Sunday, October 5, 1845.

. . . Last night it appeared that Gilbert Lewis was in this hotel — so the Somerses sent him a message and suggested his performing service, for which he was quite willing, the regular clergyman being away. We failed, however, in getting the keys of the usual chapel, or I dare say we should have had Holy Communion. However, we have had prayers in a room in the inn, and about eighteen present — much better than nothing. We have them again at three: meantime I have heard a sermon at eight in one of the churches, and hope to hear another at five. Of the first I have made a record, and also of a most interesting conversation with Dr. Döllinger — I am to have yet one more evening with him, please God, to-night. I know that not even my saying so much about him will make you uneasy for me. But lest the thought should be suggested to you, let me tell you the effect of my conversations with him is confirmation and corroboration in our position as members of the Church in England, though it delights me to find so good and able a man in the Roman Church whose statements command so much my assent and sympathy.

I hear the guns firing for these great festivities: agricultural show, races, and what not. On another day I should have been glad to see them: as far as the races are concerned, they belong to those things which I would do here, but not in England; not because we should have two standards for two countries, but because one comes here to inquire and see (or, in my case, being here one should a little inquire and see), and because I believe they make among this people a very innocent amusement. . . .

394. *To Mrs. Gladstone.*

BADEN,
October 12, 1845.

. . . In my wanderings my thoughts, too, have had time to travel: and I have had much conversation upon Church matters, first at Munich, and since coming here with Mrs. Craven and some connections of hers staying with her, who are Roman Catholics of a high school. All that I see and learn makes me more and more feel what a crisis for *religion* at large is this period of the world's history, how the power of religion and its permanence are bound up with the Church, how inestimably precious would be the Church's unity — inestimably precious on the one hand, and on the other to human eyes immeasurably remote — lastly, how loud and how solemn is the call, upon all those who hear and who *can* obey it, to labour more and more in the spirit of these principles, to give themselves, if it may be, clearly and wholly to that work. It is dangerous to put indefinite thoughts, instincts, longings, into language which is necessarily determinate. I cannot trace the line of my own future life, but I hope and pray it may not be always where it is — not that it may now cease to be so, nor while a reasonable hope remains of serving God there to more purpose than elsewhere: but that that hope may come to an issue, if it be His will. I see too plainly the process which is separating the work of the State from the work of Christian faith. Even now as a consenting party, in a certain sense and relatively to certain purposes, to that process of separation, I am upon the very outside verge, though with full consciousness, and an undoubting support from within, of the domain which conscience marks to me as an open one. I have a growing belief that I shall never be enabled to do much good for the Church in Parliament (if at all), except after having seemed first a traitor to it and been reviled as such. I mean that it is now for the highest interest of the Church to give gold for freedom; but there are so many who will not allow the gold to be touched, even though they value freedom, and so many more who will have the Church keep all the gold that it may be the price and the pledge of her slavery. Ireland! Ireland! that cloud in the west, that coming storm, the minister of God's retribution upon cruel and inveterate and but half-atoned injustice! Ireland forces upon us these great social and great religious questions—God grant that we may have courage to look them in the face and to work through them. Were they over — were the path of the Church clear before her as a body able to take her trial before God and the world upon the performance of her work as His organ for the recovery of our country — how joyfully would I retire from the barren, exhausting strife of merely political contention. I do not think that you would be very sorrowful? As to ambition in its ordinary sense, we are spared the chief part of its temptations. . . .

395. *To Archdeacon Manning.*

HAWARDEN,
Sunday, December 28, 1845.

MY DEAR MANNING,
. . . I write respecting your sermons, and in their bearing on myself. . . .

You teach that daily prayers, the observance of fast and festival, and considerable application of time to private devotion and to Scripture, ought not to be omitted, *e.g.*, by me : because, great as is the difficulty, the need is enhanced in the same proportion, the balance is the same.

You think, very charitably, that ordinary persons, or such who have a right general intention in respect to religion, give an hour and a half to its direct duties; and if they add attendance at both daily services, raising it to three, you consider that still a scanty allowance while some sixteen or seventeen are given to sleep, food, and recreation.

Now, I cannot deny this position with respect to the increase of the need — that you cannot overstate. But I think there are two ways in which God is wont to provide a remedy for real and lawful need — one by augmenting supply, the other by intercepting the natural and ordinary consequences of the deficiency. I am desirous really to look the question full in the face: and then I come to the conclusion that, if I were to include the daily services now in my list of daily duties, my next step ought to be resignation.

Let me describe to you what has been at former times, when *in London and in office*, the very narrow measure of my stated religious observances: on weekdays I cannot estimate the one family prayer together with morning and evening prayer at more than three-quarters of an hour, even if so much. Sunday is reserved, with rare exceptions, for religious employments, and it was my practice in general to receive the Holy Communion weekly. Of daily services, except a little before and after Easter, not one in a fortnight, perhaps one in a month. Different individuals have different degrees of facility in supplying the lack of regular devotion by that which is occasional, but it is hard for one to measure this resource in his own case.

I cannot well estimate, on the other hand, the amount of relaxation which used then to accrue to me. Last year I endeavoured in town to apply a rule to the distribution of my hours, and took ten for sleep, food, and recreation, understanding this last word so as to include *whatever* really refreshes mind or body or has a fair chance of doing so. Now my exigencies for sleep are great. As long as I rise feeling like a stone, I do not think there is too much, and this is the general description of my waking sense, in office and during the session, but I consider seven and a half hours the least I ought then to have, and I should be better with eight. I know the old stories about retrenching sleep, and how people have deceived themselves: with me it may be so, but I think it is not. I have never summed up my figures, but my impression is that last year, upon the average, I was under and not over the ten for the particulars named — I should say between nine and ten. But last year was a holiday year as to pressure upon mind and body, in comparison with those that preceded it. Further, people are very different as to the rate at which they expend their vigour during their work — my habit, perhaps my misfortune, is, and peculiarly with work that I dislike, to labour at the very top of my strength, so that after five or six hours of my office I was frequently in a state of great exhaustion. How can you apply the duty of saving time for prayer out of sleep and recreation to a man in these circumstances?

Again, take fasting. I had begun to form to myself some ideas upon this head; but I felt, though without a positive decision to that effect, that I could not and must not apply them if I should come again into political activity. I speak now of fasting in quantity, fasting in nutrition; as to fasting in quality, I see that the argument is even strengthened, subject only to the exception that in times of mental anxiety it becomes impossible to receive much healthy food with which a sound appetite would have no difficulty. The fact is undoubted; it is extremely hard to keep the bodily frame *up* to its work under the twofold condition of activity in office and in Parliament. I take it then that to fast in the usual sense would generally be a sin, and not a duty — I make a little exception for the time immediately preceding Easter, as then there is a short remission of Parliamentary duties.

I need not, perhaps, say more now. You see my agreement with you, and that I differ, it may be, where the pinch comes upon myself. But I speak freely, in order to give scope for opposite reasoning — in order that I may be convicted if possible, as then I hope also to be convinced.

There is the greatest difference, as I find, between simple occupation, however intense, and occupation with anxiety as its perpetual accompaniment. Serious reading and hard writing even for the same number of hours that my now imminent duties may absorb, I for one can bear without feeling that I am living too fast; but when that one element of habitual anxiety is added, Nature is spurred on beyond her own pace under an excessive burden, and vital forces waste rapidly away. I should be more suspicious of myself than I now am in the argument I have made, were it not that I have had experience of occupation in both forms, and know the gulf between them.

I ought to have added the other *sting* of official situations combined with Parliament. It is the sad irregularity of one's life. The only fixed points are prayers and breakfast in the morning, and Sunday at the beginning of the week. It is Sunday, I am convinced, that has kept me alive and well, even to a marvel, in times of considerable labour; for I must not conceal from you, even though you may think it a sad bathos, that I have never at any time been prevented by illness from attending either Parliament or my office. The only experience I have had of the dangers from which I argue, in results, has been in weakness and exhaustion from the brain downwards; it is impossible for me to be thankful enough for the exemptions I enjoy, especially when I see far stronger constitutions — constitutions truly Herculean — breaking down around me. I hope I may be preserved from the guilt and ingratitude of indulging sensual sloth under the mask of wise and necessary precautions.

Do not trouble yourself to write at length, but revolve these matters in the casuistical chamber of the mind, and either before or when we meet give me an opinion which I trust will be frank and fearless.

There is one retrenchment I could make: it would be to take from activity outwards in matter of religion, in order to give to prayer. But I have given a misdescription. What I could economize is chiefly reading: but reading nowadays I almost always shall have to resort to — at least so it was before — by way of repose. Devotion is by far the best sedative to excitement: but, then, it requires great and sustained exertion (to speak humanly and under the supposition of the Divine grace) or else powerful external helps, or both. Those mere dregs of the natural energies which too often are all that occupation leaves are fit for little beyond *passivity* — only for reading when not severe.*

---

* Later in life 'Cardinal Manning recognized the danger of a preacher usurping the office of a spiritual director of souls. In one

Reading all this you may the more easily understand my tone sometimes about public life as a whole. Joy to you at this blessed time and at all times
     Your affectionate friend,
       W. E. GLADSTONE.

396. *To Archdeacon Manning.*

13, CARLTON HOUSE TERRACE,
March 10, 1846.

. . . I see but two modes in which the available resources of the Church are likely to receive material increase — over and above certain modes of increase now in operation under statutes or other arrangements already formed ; these are : (1) The episcopal and part of the capitular estates, and (2) the free and systematic resort to voluntary contributions.

As to the first, I am afraid I am right in the supposition that the old spendthrift modes of managing ecclesiastical estates are still generally in vigour, so far as relates to Bishops and to many Chapters : that there is still, to this extent, the same inducement to provide for the life interests of actual holders by waste of prospective resources, and that so long as it continues it must, one may almost say it ought, to produce the same effects.

In my opinion it is visionary as matter of fact, and unwarrantable as matter of right, to ask Parliament to interpose for any purpose which regards the Church *in formâ pauperis*, until she has thoroughly husbanded her own pecuniary means and applied them to the best advantage. There may be some remote risk in centralizing the management of episcopal and capitular estates, there may be some derogation to temporal dignity in interposing such a system of control over and above the will of life-incumbents as is necessary for thrift — let us have as little of these evils as possible : but we must, I think, and ought to have that of which they may be the accompaniments — a thorough excision of the old system of management

---

of his autobiographical notes he confesses 'that as an Anglican he had treated subjects in the pulpit which properly belonged to the confessional' (Purcell, i. 439).

and a *bona-fide* effort to obtain from the property all that it can justly be made to yield.

But what next? Supposing this done, can the Church then seek for public aid? I think not. She would be met at the door of Parliament — (1) by the allegation that half of the population of the United Kingdom do not belong to her communion: (2) by the question, Who are you and what are you? The first of these constitutes a formidable opposition; the second is far more formidable — it would carry division, and with division dismay, into her own ranks. She has become in the popular view so hybrid; her mind is so variously apprehended on this side and on that; the just jealousies of the people of England have been so fearfully aroused by the development of Romanizing elements among her members, that she is no longer an unity for the purposes of political combat.

But the evil does not stop there. Neither you nor I should much lament shutting the door upon the prospect of Parliamentary Church extension. The sorer evil, for which also the late movers to the Church of Rome have also in my belief mainly to answer, is that they have brought into fatal prejudice and disrepute that most innocent, most simple, most effective, nay, let me add — for so it is — that somewhat Protestant and Presbyterian mode of supplying the wants of the Church, by churchlike appeal to the voluntary liberality of her members. The sore point in the use of the offertory seems to be collection from pew to pew — the common practice, I believe, of multitudes of Presbyterian congregations every Sunday in Scotland. But being favoured here by those who favour Rome, and who favour her as Rome, it seems to be now placed under general ban, to hold its ground in some places where it had been introduced before the general suspicion of Romanism put the Church in a flame, but the hopes of its progress and extensive prevalence to be indefinitely postponed. This is very sad and very disheartening. Nor do I think we shall live to see this prejudice effectually removed, except by new modes of action. The last twelve or fifteen years have, I think, afforded us an example of what Froude declared the Reformation to be — the limb is badly set, and must be broken again before it can get sound. In some way or other the Church must descend into the ranks of the people, and find her strength there, and build up from that level. If she can really unfold great energies in that region, prejudices among the classes having property will be too weak to hold their ground. Asceticism itself, provided it be an active and missionary asceticism, will become a source of popular as well as of inward strength. To some this would seem at the best very remote speculation; but I confess that whatever it may be, when I look deliberately at it and compare it with other modes and schemes of human improvement now in vogue, as to its utilitarian aspect, the question arises, Why does not every one who wishes well, or thinks that he wishes well, to his kind, betake himself to this path of duty?

397. *To Archdeacon Manning.*

13, CARLTON HOUSE TERRACE,
Sunday, April 19, 1846.

MY DEAR MANNING,
 . . . I blame myself for never having clearly stated to you the original and cardinal ideas upon which I proceed. Had I done this thoroughly, we should sooner have found out our real proximity of view. But the truth is, that to deal properly with a question of this kind requires certain mental habits as well as will, and those habits, with me never well matured, are now of course utterly disorganized.

Still, let me repair one omission, and beg you to observe I am not claiming privilege or relief: first of all, because that possibility of change in my outward career, which is all that I claim, may never realize itself; secondly, because the claim rests upon a different basis — namely, on this, that the process which I am now actively engaged in carrying on is a process of lowering the religious tone of the State, letting it down, demoralizing it — *i.e.*, stripping it of its ethical character, and assisting its transition into one which is mechanical. This it is which makes me feel that the 'burden of proof' lies on the side of the argument for remaining in public life; and that the purposes which warrant it for me — *i.e.*, for one in whose public life office or executive government is an element — must be very strong and very special in order to make good the conclusion.

I agree with you that, in all probability, the Church will hold her nationality, in substance, beyond our day: I think she will hold it as long as the monarchy subsists, and that that will last when we are gone, though it is difficult to look at the little Prince of Wales without a sigh.

So long, undoubtedly, the Church will want political and Parliamentary defence. But it is quite another question in what form that defence can be best conducted. I have seen the popular cause of Ireland at its strongest, when the popular leaders have even contumaciously absented themselves from the business of the House of Commons. The Dissenters have no members for Universities, but their real representation is better organized by far, in proportion to its weight, than that of the Church: and yet it is not formally organized at all. A knot of men professing and claiming everything, engaged in constant resistance and protest, like Montalembert [and Dupanlou] in France, present to view a method of advocacy which may be well united to a country like France, and to a state of acute active hostility between the Church and the State. But that is not likely to be our case for a long time to come, and my belief is that strength with the people will, for our day at least, be the only effectual defence of the Church in the House of Commons, as the want of it is now her weakness there. It is not everything which calls itself a defence that is really such. There are kinds of defence that excite jealousies far beyond their power to repel, and thus cause more danger than no defence at all. As the Church grows out of doors, she will be more felt indoors. She has already, as you justly say, the educated classes: therefore she has the *personnel* of Parliament: what she needs is beyond it, to make that *personnel* effective. But I cannot conceive the possibility of her lacking the means of representation in that region in full proportion to that which is to be represented, and which now, I think, demands the application, to speak generally, of all available energies for its replenishment.

These truths must be held 'in solution,' but the day

for them to be 'precipitated' may be nearer, or may be farther, than any rational conjecture now formed would serve to show.

My impression has been that Hope is beyond being affected by the Jerusalem Bishopric either one way or the other ; but if you think otherwise, and particularly if you know anything to the contrary, it is a fact so important that I hope you will give your mind to the case, and consider what you can do towards bringing Gobat's case out fully. From some little things lately seen and heard, I have comforted myself with the belief that Hope's mind was more settled.

Believe me always,
Affectionately yours,
W. E. GLADSTONE.

398. *To Archdeacon Manning.*

HAGLEY,
March 9, 1847.

MY DEAR MANNING,

. . . I suppose that there is a region between high health on the one side and ill-health on the other, which is the region proper to the exercise of abstinence: and that deviation either way should at once be marked and corrected. I mean that as high animal health shows that there is not abstinence in the proper sense, so the first appearance of ill-health shows that we are approaching danger and incapacity for duty, and that this *first* appearance should be cared for and removed, that we may be put back into a condition for duty. Is this right ?

Since I came back here I have received your tract for Lent, and I feel about it as everybody else does. But I wish it could have had your name, as, though the authorship is known, it is not notorious, and it is not so known as to recommend the tract through as wide a circle as it would otherwise have ranged over. There is another question important at the present time [the time of the Irish famine] : I mean that relating to the use of animal food. Persons seem now to suppose that to economize flour and bread is everything. No doubt it is the first and most important ; and for this reason I do not suppose it is desirable to keep Lent by total abstinence from animal food. Nor, indeed, do I think it is a good mode generally, at least for persons not living very privately, because it attracts attention : and it is quite plain to me that restriction of the total quantity of food may be made, and is likely to be made, more effectual in the way of abstinence than an abstinence from animal food as such, which at most is no better than a contraction of quantity. It is worth, however, reflecting now that, if the attention of all the consumers of meat should be concentrated only on the notion of economizing flour, this would cause a greatly increased consumption of meat ; by raising the price of meat it would directly stimulate the breeding and feeding of cattle, and would thereby tend greatly to diminish the aggregate quantity of food available for man ; because there is, I believe, no doubt that we might have a much larger *total* of subsistence from the earth if we consumed no animal food. These considerations seem to become important when we reflect that the present scarcity cannot well be temporary. Even if we have abundant crops of all kinds, the quantity one may fear of unsold land in Ireland, and the exhaustion of stocks through the present pressure, will keep food more or less high — at least, until after the harvest of 1848. But again, it is fearful to remember that our harvests usually move in cycles, that from 1842 to 1846 inclusive we have had no *bad* harvest, and that there are due to us now, according to the usual cycles, a majority of bad harvests in the next three or four years. So that, if we look at natural circumstances only, they show the likelihood to be that of severe and continued pressure.

But it will not do to look at such circumstances either as sole or as principal agents. Here is a calamity most legibly Divine ; there is a total absence of such second causes as might tempt us to explain it away; it is the greatest horror of modern times, that in the richest age of the world, and in the richest country of that age, the people should be dying of famine by hundreds, and we, the English community, have scarcely as yet got even the feeblest notion of this horror in its aspect to us. No mere giving of money will do, it can only be met by national and personal humiliation. To have balls and operas for the distressed is bad and rotten in principle at all times ; but at this time it seems like a judicial blindness, a defiance of the Divine wrath, a looking up into the very face of God, and saying, 'Thou hast called us to weep, and, lo, we laugh.' How can the handwriting be made clear against us if it is not clear now? To give money is very well, to economize flour is very well, because these go to diminish the quantity of actual suffering, the external range of the evil; but they do not touch its root; we want the heavy hand of God lifted from off the land, and so long as we ourselves personally continue in our usual tone of thoughtless joyous or ambitious life, we cannot be in a tone to ask or in a state to receive the boon. But I find I am preaching to you, of which I had not the remotest intention when I sat down to write. The question, however, for us is, What shall we do when at the end of this week we resume our household cares in London? As to my servants, I have put them on board wages, making them a small allowance *over* on account of the dearness of provisions. I can now exhort them vigorously to save and spare, and I am political economist enough to believe that it is a sound and sure way of relief to increase the quantity of food in the market by lessening what is taken out. As to ourselves, we have some difficulty from the circumstance that my mother-in-law will be with us, and, as she is an invalid and nervously so, [this] will prevent our being quite as thrifty as we could be for ourselves alone, But the most difficult question is as to entertainments. I feel that not only in Lent, but during the continuance of this visitation, people ought, if possible, to be set free from every entertainment which is either of a gay and ostentatious kind, or which causes waste of food. But the degree and manner in which this principle can be worked out I am not as yet clear about. I shall be very glad if at any time you can give me your thoughts and advice. There will be time to think, for I hope the question will not arise in any serious form before Easter. We have not, however, thought it expedient to adopt any *rule* of refusing all invitations through Lent, although we do not give them.

Your affectionate friend,
W. E. GLADSTONE.

399. *To Archdeacon Manning.*

LONDON,
March 20, 1847.

MY DEAR MANNING,

. . . This is not the first time that it has happened that we have approached questions from different sides, and on that account, to say nothing of the other reason of my doing it much worse, have expressed ourselves very differently when our real meanings were not far apart. I hope and believe this must be the case in the present instance, though ever since a walk to St. Peter's in December, 1838, we have had some shades of distinction in our views of the element of human freedom, its proper scope and action, in the Christian system. I have the belief that the earliest constitution of the Church was in its spirit singularly free, and that it would be happy for us, and would imply the real strengthening of the hands of authority, if weight *could* again be given to it as was then given. In the case before us, I have written under the belief that the twofold system of compulsory confession for retrospect, and direction for prospect, not, or scarcely less, compulsory, do in practice so work as very frequently and extensively to take out of the hands of the individual Christian the chief care of and therewith the chief responsibility for, his own conduct, and that *therefore* it is that in this country, notwithstanding our sins and miseries, the moral sense upon the whole is at this moment more generally clear and strong than in the lands where the Roman Church bears sway.

But I am sensible that I do not write on this subject with the weight which is due to any dispassionate judgment concerning it: for my own convictions upon it are in an immature and half-developed state — I mean in its relation to my own conduct. For I should reply much more aye than no upon the question whether my own conscience is not one of those to which the Church refers as having been unable to bear the weight of its own government, and as accordingly requiring not advice only, but the aid which confession and the grace which absolution gives. The period of relief from distraction which I now enjoy I hope will, as it certainly should, enable me to shape definitely my own resolutions about it, and to take them to a definite issue, whatever that issue may be. But I must say that in all my reflections about it I have felt the pressure of the reasons in its favour had reference to my own peculiar case, and by no means connected themselves with its appearing a general rule which ought to be obeyed by every normal mind. . . .

400. *To Archdeacon Manning.*

LONDON,
Sunday, March 12, 1848.

MY DEAR MANNING,
 . . . It is always a pleasure to write to you, but it is an effort, too, because there is so much — so very much — that I should like to pour out before you ; and for a long time back I have had no energies to spare, nearly all my works have been works of anxiety, I have not had strength or elasticity to look any duties except those nearest hand in the face. Care has been very heavy upon me, and in some new and unaccustomed forms. You may remember one day, as we walked back from St. Mark's, my telling you something as to my general views about the disposition of such property as I had or might have, and how they were qualified by my having become involved in a great iron mining and manufacturing concern which was opened many years ago by a reckless agent unduly trusted. . . . A concern in bankruptcy with £250,000 of liabilities, a vast and complex business to be recast, very heavy and early demands to be provided for, large sums of money to be borrowed and realized, and a constant uphill fight to be carried on against difficulties which are to all appearance all but and only not insurmountable : these are the additions now made by the dispensation of God to the usual engagements of my life, which have at all times for many years back seemed to be quite adequate to my very middling strength. How I get on with them I hardly know ; they often make me faint and sick at heart, for there is something in having to deal with the case of another, for whom you may not take the resolutions you would in your own case, that gives a peculiar form to the problem

and the working of it. But do not suppose that I presume to talk of it as an affliction — it is a weight much more than a pain. . . . My recent experience of our little Agnes's struggle between life and death, and my remembrance of the rebellious temper of my heart when I thought that God had evidently marked her for the world of spirits, and of the sharpness of that conviction, enables me, if not to describe, at least acutely to feel the difference between the two. I cannot pray or wish that this should be removed; I have never seen the working of the prudential and moral laws of God's providence more signally exhibited. I fully own the signs of His Fatherly wisdom and love; were the task taken away from me, I think it would leave me light-headed, such a difference would it make in the pressure on my daily existence, and all I can presume to wish or pray is that it may please God to give me a little more strength to carry the charge so full of admonition. All this, which, as you will readily see, is very private in its nature, I have only been led to state in order to explain to you what really demanded explanation — namely, the reason why I have so often flagged and failed to discharge an office of friendship to you in your absence, and, in an absence from such a cause as yours, by trying to bring a little of the world in which we live and of its events and interests before you. . . .

As to public and Church affairs, there are so many and of so much interest that I scarcely know how to touch them in what remains to me of time and space. The course of things, you see, has brought me at once into collision with my constituents about the Jews, and into a pretended collision about the Roman Catholics. As to the former, I agree with everything that you say; it is a decided *note* of retrogression in the matter of that text, 'The kingdoms of the world are become the kingdoms of the Lord and of His Christ'; but there is *a* point at which it becomes not politic only, but obligatory, to let down the theory of civil institutions — namely, when the discrepancy between them and their actual operation has become a hopeless falsehood and a mischievous and virulent imposture. It was time, I think, to unveil realities, though in every case by unveiling you are apt, for the first effect, to confirm; but you open new sources of hope by throwing the minds of men into a more natural and genuine attitude, to think and to labour in fields that are not and cannot be exhausted. I have published my speech with a long preface, and I have the consolation of knowing that it has mitigated the displeasure of some excellent men, while in other cases I hope a form of thought has been suggested which will exercise hereafter an influence in modifying its course among the clergy. None of these things can be done without a painful wrench. Though the National Club tried to get up a requisition against me and failed, yet some weeks ago I was informed on good authority that if I vacated I should be opposed and beaten. It may still be so, but that, of course, does not move me; I am deeply and energetically convinced that I have acted *for* the Church, and that any other vote from me would have been decidedly injurious to her; and if Oxford should reject me on such a ground, painful as the reverse would be, I shall, I trust, take it cheerfully, and believe that that, too, will work for good, though in a way very different from the one imagined by those who might inflict the blow. Let me add that Hope, Lyttelton, R. Palmer, and some others, to whose judgments I assign much weight, had come separately to my conclusion.

As to the revived 'war of investitures,' I think the remonstrant Bishops will be prepared to stickle for some provision which shall secure a power of equitable and canonical objection when the question comes to be stirred. But it seems to be thought, and I for one undoubtedly think, that the Church has decidedly gained by the proceedings, except as to having Dr. Hampden for a Bishop, which, though serious, is not *the* great question involved, so we are content to wait a while. Meantime the Government are in great difficulties, and have blundered sorely with their finance; we are obliged (I mean the ex-official corps) to lend what help we can towards bringing them through. The case of Lord John and the Church is now, I fear, fixed for ever. To the Church, as she is Apostolic and as she is dogmatic, he will conscientiously do the very utmost of evil that he dare. And this, I must say, ought to have been foreseen by those who rushed into his train last summer, and who (in my judgment) then and at other times have done Peel so much injustice. . . .

401. *To Archdeacon Manning.*

6, Carlton Gardens,
July 6, 1849.

My dear Manning,

I do not see any immediate prospect of a discussion in Parliament about National Education. I am also far from desiring to hasten one, for I know well by experience that, whatever pleasure persons may have out of doors in reading speeches made in the House of Commons by those who sympathize with them, a question touching spiritual or clerical power is never mooted there in opposition to the Executive Government without damage to the idea of such power and a diminished disposition to recognize it as the result. All *such* discussions should be contemplated as preludes to the severance of Church and State, remote perhaps but yet true and substantial preludes, and it is a misfortune that many persons regard them as mere flourishing of trumpets, and, sensible of the inspiring effect on their own minds, assume that they have no other or at least no different effect. But this is a lecture which you do not want, and which those who do want it will miss. Therefore εἴηται.

I fear I cannot undertake by an engagement now to be formed to adhere in the House of Commons either to the principle that the whole extent of the former liberty of the Church in constituting schools is to be preserved under the system of aid from the State, or to the particular application that it is necessary to retain a liberty of giving them a constitution by which all matters in dispute shall be referred to and settled by the Bishop. Indeed, I would suggest to you to read the correspondence, which has just been published, between the Privy Council and the Roman Catholics before *you* determine finally to insist on that liberty. I was before, as you may remember, not disposed to think it essential, I am even less disposed to stickle for it now. The Bishop has no strength to spare for purposes lying beyond his sphere; and a strict *bona-fide* definition of the spiritual sphere and restraint of his authority, as a general rule, within it in all new arrangements, I conscientiously think to be for his interests, since, being already too weak for his spiritual and ecclesiastical work, he has evidently no spare force to spend upon other questions where he will be brought into collision with portions of the local communities interested in schools.

You will perceive that the concession to the National Society would at once be followed by a similar grant to the Vicars Apostolic. The liberty thus given would be sometimes used among us, almost always among the Roman Catholics. I should be sorry to see that system at work in Roman Catholic schools aided by the State.

To obtain liberty for the Church is the object for which I should think it the highest, almost the only, honour and delight to spend and be spent. But by this I understand liberty in the English sense, liberty under rule, and the whole question is what rule is admissible or desirable, what freedom will tend to or is required for the real development of your religious system. . . .

Your affectionate friend,
W. E. GLADSTONE.

402. *To Mrs. Gladstone.*

FASQUE,
September 11, 1850.

. . . Without more information about the poor suicide, I can say nothing but that these cases raise the most painful questions for clergymen. I incline to think that as a general rule the cases of suicide, where there is a legal verdict of insanity, are less difficult than some other cases of sin where there is no verdict. A clergyman as a public officer must not always set up his own impressions, though reasonable, against a public authoritative declaration, though unreasonable. But don't suppose I am condemning — I suspend my judgment. . . .

403. *To Mrs. Gladstone.*

FASQUE,
May 2, 1851.

By dint of some rather hard work and the use of my two legs, I got back from Trinity College to breakfast this morning, having left it late last night. The day was a very interesting one, and you are right in saying you would have wished to be there rather than at the grand show in London. . . .

Trinity College looked finer than ever — the chapel is a beautiful structure : the chanting, done entirely by the masters and the scholars, was most living and effective, and I do not doubt the whole institution is taking root and gaining solidity as well as prominence. We had a large body of communicants with the Scotch office. Four of the Bishops were present. Dean Ramsay preached in the morning ; I cannot say I was satisfied with the sermon, but the part about Hope was most graceful and most touching, and would, I think, have pleased him, as it did me deeply. Of course the thought of him dashed a cup otherwise very joyous with bitterness. My father's fidelity to Trinity College in all tempers and circumstances is really a moving circumstance of his old age.

404. *To J. R. Hope.*

6, Carlton Gardens,
June 22, 1851.

My dear Hope,
Upon the point most prominently put in your welcome letter, I will only say you have not misconstrued me. Affection which is fed by intercourse, and above all by co-operation for sacred ends, has little need of verbal expression ; but such expression is deeply consoling when active relations have changed. It is no matter of merit to me to feel strongly on the subject of that change. It may be little better than pure selfishness. I have too good reason to know what this year has cost me, and so little hope have I that the places now vacant ever can be filled for me, that the marked character of these events in reference to myself rather teaches me this lesson : the work to which I had aspired is reserved for other and better men. And if that be the Divine will, I so entirely recognize its fitness that the grief would so far be small to me were I alone concerned. The pain, the wonder, and the mystery is this, that you should have refused the high vocation you had before you. The

same words, and all the same words, I should use of Manning, too. Forgive me for giving utterance to what I believe myself to see and know: I will not proceed a step farther in that direction.

There is one word, and one only, in your letter that I do not interpret closely. Separated we are, but I hope and think not yet estranged. Were I more estranged I should bear the separation better. If estrangement is to come I know not: but it will only be, I think, from causes the operation of which is still in its infancy, causes not affecting me. Why should I be estranged from you? I honour you even in what I think your error; why, then, should my feelings to you alter in anything else? It seems to me as though in these fearful times events were more and more growing too large for our puny grasp; and that we should the more look for and trust the Divine purpose in them, when we find they have wholly passed beyond the reach and measure of our own. 'The Lord is in His holy temple: let all the earth keep silence before Him.' The very afflictions of the present time are a sign of joy to follow. 'Thy kingdom come, Thy will be done,' is still our prayer in common: the same prayer in the same sense, and a prayer which absorbs every other. That is for the future: for the present we have to endure, to trust, and to pray, that each day may bring its strength with its burden, and its lamp for its gloom.

Ever yours, with unaltered affection,
W. E. GLADSTONE.

[The following is the letter to which No. 404 is an answer:

14, CURZON STREET,
June 18, 1851.

MY DEAR GLADSTONE,
I am very much obliged for the book which you have sent me, but still more for the few words and figures which you have placed on the title-page. The day and month in your own handwriting will be a record between us that the words of affection which you have written were used by you after the period at which the great change of my life took place. To

grudge any sacrifice which that change entails would be to undervalue its paramount blessedness; but, as far as regrets are compatible with extreme thankfulness, I do and must regret any estrangement from you — you with whom I have trod so large a portion of the way which has led me to peace; you who are *ex voto* at least in that Catholic Church which to me has become a practical reality admitting of no doubt; you who have so many better claims to the merciful guidance of Almighty God than myself.

It is most comforting, then, to me to know by your own hand that on June 17, 1851, the personal feelings so long cherished have been, not only acknowledged to yourself, but expressed to me. I do not ask more just now — it would be painful to you. Nay, it would be hardly possible for either of us to attempt (except under one condition — for which I daily pray) the restoration of entire intimacy at present; but neither do I despair under any circumstances that it will yet be restored.

Remember me most kindly to Mrs. Gladstone, and believe me,

Yours, as ever, most affectionately,
JAMES R. HOPE.]

405. *To J. R. Hope.*

FASQUE,
September 23, 1851.

MY DEAR HOPE,
Apart from his very high general qualifications for the headship of an University, I should not have supposed Dr. Newman to be particularly qualified for the Irish meridian, but I am little in a condition to judge.

I am glad and thankful to hear of the application, as a probable event, of any portion of your time and attention to the history and prospects of religion, and its relations to human society, whether in Ireland or more at large. I hope, whatever share you give to that singular country, you will let me plead with you to allot a corner in your mind to a question every day growing more difficult and formidable, that of the temporal dominion of the Pope.

You will think I have interpolated these sentences to hide or soften the nakedness of my replies to you. I know but few good books about Ireland, and am not sure that I can recollect all even of them. Those which now occur to me as *decidedly* good in their kinds are —

Mathison's 'Six Weeks,' privately printed.
Spenser's (Edmund) Tract.
Sir W. Petty's Tracts.
Sir J. Davies's History, or Historical Tracts.
The 'Drapier's Letters.'

I must also recommend Charles Greville's 'Past and Present Policy.'

The only historians, I think, that I have made much acquaintance with are Leland and Plowden, with Mant, Dr. Phelan's account of the Irish Church, and Todd's 'Church of St. Patrick,' for Church matters.

Do not overlook Bishop Jebb's Life, and the correspondence with Knox in parts. The *Times* Commission of course you will remember; and in Swift you will find curious matter, such as the declaration that the Roman Catholic population never could possibly come to be of political importance.

You should, of course, read the 'Letters of Columbanus,' G. C. Lewis on Irish Disturbances, Wyse's 'History of the Catholic Association,' Lord Clare's speeches on the Union ; and there is much interesting matter connected with the history of the Veto negotiations that has its bearing on the question of the Titles Bill. A good deal of this is to be found in Parliamentary Reports and Evidence, but I cannot supply references.

There is, however, a Report on Education in which Sir F. Lewis took part, about the year 1812, which has had much influence and should be read. . . .

     Believe me always,
      Affectionately yours,
       W. E. GLADSTONE.

406. *To R. J. Phillimore.*

FASQUE,
December 12, 1851.

MY DEAR PHILLIMORE,

I well know where you are always to be found in the day of mourning, and even so kind and affectionate a letter as you have sent me causes me no surprise. You, however, do no more than truly appreciate the fact with regard to my father's position. Though he died within a few days of eighty-seven, with little left either of sight or hearing, and only able to walk from one room to another or to his brougham for a short drive, though his memory was gone, his hold upon language, even for common purposes, imperfect, his reasoning power much decayed, and even his perception of personality rather indistinct, yet so much remained about him of one of the most manful, energetic, affectionate, and simple-hearted among human beings, that he still filled a great space to the eye, mind, and heart, and a great space is accordingly felt void by his withdrawal. But it is all well, and this does not cut like some other forms of natural grief.

I have got and read the Bishop of Salisbury's Charge. You know, no man better, my immeasurable soreness and disgust with reference to those matters in England, and will therefore know I mean something when I say that Charge did me good, and (without entering into this or that particular) seemed to me thoroughly worthy of his high moral tone (what a rarity that is!) and solid sagacity. I don't write to him about it, for it rather seems always to me an impertinence to write to a Bishop about his Charge.

Ever affectionately yours,
W. E. G.

407. *To H. E. Manning.*

DOWNING STREET,
August 7, 1853.

MY DEAR MANNING,

With you, I hope, not even my date will belie me, when I say that I received with deep interest your letter of April 5, and was most thankful for the assurance with which it concluded. Indeed, to express that thankfulness is the chief aim with which I write. I rejoice to be in your prayers at all times, and especially at the time you name, when prayer assumes its vantage-ground. Your intercession can have no ingredient of harm for me, nor even mine for you. Let us continue to meet in the Presence of the Eternal. If that which was is cut away, yet this, the best part of it, invisibly remains. I, indeed, shall never recover the losses I have sustained, and sustained at a time when the pressure and strain of life were becoming heavier upon me from year to year. But, then, I fully know it was the enjoyment, not the bereavement, that was undeserved. I never was worthy to associate with you; and now, if we could associate, perhaps you would find me less so than ever. What I still have is far more than I can appreciate or use aright. What I most lament is not my loss — it is that hands, once so strong to carry sword and shield, now carry them no longer in the battle, the real battle of our place and day. I grudge you the rest which you say, and which I do not doubt or question, you have obtained; I would it were at an end. Never can I in this world see or think of you, or you of me, but this must be the pivot on which all our thoughts must turn. That, I think, you know well; and when you speak of the wide field of intercourse still left free to choice, as between us two, you speak what is to me a riddle. But I know also that you speak in kindness and affection, which darkens sometimes, as well as sometimes clears, our view.

I remain,
Ever your attached friend,
W. E. GLADSTONE.

408. *To Archdeacon (Robert) Wilberforce.*

HAWARDEN,
October 31, 1853.

MY DEAR WILBERFORCE,
When you left us I had not begun your book [on the Eucharist]; nor have I yet finished it: I have, however, read the first nine chapters and glanced at the eleventh; and though I am little fitted to say anything at all about such a work and such a subject, I cannot any longer forbear; indeed, I have found silence very difficult to maintain even up to this point. Speaking generally — and to make this reservation seems paltry in such a case — I really cannot tell you either how I admire it as a great effort of comprehensive knowledge and masterly skill, or how thankful I feel

that the poor Church of England, and I as a member of it, ought to be for a gift so wonderfully suited to her uses and her needs. With the anticipations I entertained as to the propositions you would have to defend, I *was* a short time ago greatly astonished at the circumstance which you mentioned, and which I had noticed — namely, that there was no uproar, and even no controversy, about the work: but since I have read, and witnessed the *manner* in which you have set out the doctrine, my surprise has vanished. Your method of proceeding by what is positive rather than by what is polemical has the effect of placing you *within the guard*, so to speak, of opponents. Again, the nearness of the subject to men's thoughts and lives, from the fact that you are dealing with a matter of universal duty, gives you an advantage and a power such as you have never yet had: and I cannot remember the appearance of any work of theology from which I should expect anything like the same amount of real revival and progress, both in doctrine and in the habits of thought by which doctrine is embraced and assimilated, that yours, I trust, is destined to produce.

If there is an especial feature of the book which beyond all others gives it strength, it seems to me to be this, that you have maintained so faithfully the historical or traditional character in it, and have theorized so little: except in those parts where theory was appropriate, and even necessary — viz. the *rationale* you have given of the Lutheran and Calvinian opinions, and of the tendency of various schools in the Church from particular circumstances to derange the equilibrium of the true doctrine.

What appears to me least satisfactory as matter of argument is what relates to the 'natural' conditions of Christ's glorified Body: nor can I feel sure ground under me in the formal distinction of the *Res* and the *Virtus Sacramenti*, nor understand that the life and power of the Lord's Body, which I suppose you do not in any case separate from His Soul and Divinity, is not in itself a grace, and the highest grace. It looks as if the doctrine of universal participation really grew up out of anxiety to maintain the substantive and objective effect of consecration, and was used by way of an outwork to it.

I dare say that after so great and prolonged an effort your mind feels a necessity of unbending, and an instinctive aversion to further labour upon the book: but quite apart from reopening any serious (much less vital) question, I hope you will still, when you can, look to every subsidiary and minute point of order and expression, in order that so great and signal a work may not stop short of its perfection.

Have you had any Roman opinions upon it, and to what effect?

I remain,
Affectionately yours,
W. E. GLADSTONE.

409. *To J. R. Hope-Scott.*

CORFE,
February 17, 1859.

MY DEAR HOPE-SCOTT,
Your letter of November 3 has lain by me these three months, never forgotten and never answered. But the day for my turning homewards is now close at hand, and this reminds me not any longer to delay what I ought to have done before.

There is nothing intrusive, and nothing painful for me to read, in what you tell me of the blessings which your wife derived from her religion. There are few unalloyed pleasures in this world; but, surely, to hear of a faith which grasps the unseen and the future with the firmness of a hand laying hold on the sensible objects proper to it, and to hear of this, too, in the case of a person so near to my thoughts and feelings, could not but be one of them. Why should either of us grudge to one another the precious gift, 'the substance of things hoped for, the evidence of things not seen,' because God has chosen or permitted for its conveyance a medium which is not according to our choice or understanding? Nay, forgive me if I go one step farther, and ask whether anyone reading those sentences in your letter would not have said that their tenderness was mingled with mistrust, and that we, too, never could have known one another well and closely.

Be assured it is with an unmixed joy that I see

you clinging to the Divine dispensation, and covetous of the treasure it conveys — not that it teaches what is new concerning you, but only that it gives a new assurance of what is old. Be also assured that you cannot pain me by what you may say : my pain lies in this, that we have so much unsaid, that free speech is impeded between us, and certainly not in any use that you could make of it. But I turn from a subject which it is equally difficult to open and to close, with expressing the hope that we may both be moved by the lamentable circumstances of this world to live the more in that world where all is peace.

I trust that you have been spared anxiety about your children, and that you have been able to make good arrangements for them as far as any arrangement can be good which aims at supplying such a void as it has pleased God to make for them. . . .

W. E. GLADSTONE.

[The following is the letter to which No. 409 is an answer :

ABBOTSFORD,
November 3, 1858.

MY DEAR GLADSTONE,

I was uneasy at not having written to you, and hoped you would write, which you have done, and I thank you much for it. An occasion like this passed by is a loss of friendship ; but it was not, nor is, easy for me to write to you. You will remember that the root of our friendship which struck the deepest was fed by a common interest in religion ; and I cannot write to you of her whom it has pleased God to take from me without reference to that Church whose doctrines and promises she had embraced with a faith which made them like objects of sense to her, whose teaching had moulded her mind and heart, whose spiritual blessings surrounded and still surround her, and which has shed upon her death a sweetness which makes me linger upon it more dearly than on any part of our united and happy life.

These things I could not pass over without ignoring the foundation of our friendship ; but, still, I feel that to mention them has something intrusive, something which it may be painful for you to read, as though it required an answer which you would rather not give. So I will say only one thing more, and it is this: If ever in the strife of politics or religious controversy you are tempted to think or speak hardly of that Church — if she should appear to you arrogant or exclusive or formal — for my dear Charlotte's sake and mine check that thought, if only for an instant, and remember with what exceeding care and love she tends her children. . . .

And now good-bye, my dear Gladstone. Forgive me any word which you had rather I had not said. May God long preserve to you and your wife that happiness which you now have in each other; and when it pleases Him that either of you should have to mourn the other, may He be as merciful to you as He has been to me.

Yours affectionately,
JAMES R. HOPE-SCOTT.

410. *To Mrs. Gladstone.*

HAWARDEN,
October 19, 1864.

. . . So that brave heart [the Duke of Newcastle] has at last ceased to beat. Certainly in him more than in anyone I have known was exhibited the character of our life as a dispensation of pain. This must ever be a mystery, for we cannot see the working out of the purposes of God, yet in his case I have always thought some glimpse of them seemed to be permitted. It is well to be permitted also to believe that he is now at rest for ever, and that the cloud is at length removed from his destiny. . . .

411. *To Mrs. Gladstone.*

CLUMBER,
October 26, 1864, *night.*

. . . It is a time and a place to feel, if one could feel. He died in the room where we have been sitting before and after dinner — where, thirty-two years ago, a stripling, I came over from Newark in fear and trembling to see the Duke, his father — where a stiff horseshoe semicircle then sat round the fire in evenings, where that rigour melted away in Lady Lincoln's time, where she and her mother sang so beautifully at the pianoforte in the same place where it now stands. The house is full of local memories.

I have no doubt that in these last weeks he told a good deal piecemeal to Dr. Kingsley. He said this: 'I cannot now look to gain the place which I once hoped to gain, but I think I may live to be of great use to the Queen, particularly about the Church; she is not well advised about the Church. Or if I do not do this, yet I shall have plenty to do among my own people here. . . .'

412. *To the Rev. C. J. Glyn.*

11, Carlton House Terrace,
February 4, 1865.

. . . You think (and pray do not suppose I make this matter of complaint) that I have been associated with one party in the Church of England, and that I may now lean rather towards another. You are in every way entitled to form your own judgment upon my acts and declarations: you have done it heretofore, I doubt not, with perfect fairness of intention, and I have no other desire than that you should continue to do the same; but I will never make professions which must in themselves be general and vague, and can hardly fail to be suspected and equivocal.

There is no one about whom information can be more easily had than myself; I have had and have friends of many colours — Churchmen High and Low, Presbyterians, Greeks, Roman Catholics, Dissenters, who can speak abundantly, though perhaps not very well, of me. And further, as Member for the University, I have honestly endeavoured at all times to put my constituents in possession of all I could convey to them that could be considered as in the nature of a fact, by answering as explicitly as I was able all questions relating to the matters, and they are numerous enough, on which I have had to act or speak.

Perhaps I shall surprise you by what I have yet

further to say. I have never by any conscious act yielded my allegiance to any person or party in matters of religion. You and others may have called me (without the least offence) a Churchman of some particular kind, and I have more than once seen announced in print my own secession from the Church of England. These things I have not commonly contradicted, for the atmosphere of religious controversy and contradiction is as odious as the atmosphere of mental freedom is precious to me ; and I have feared to lose the one and be drawn into the other, by heat and bitterness creeping into my mind. If another chooses to call himself, or to call me, a member of this or that party, I am not to complain. But I respectfully claim the right not to call myself so, and on this claim I have, I believe, acted throughout my life, without a single exception ; and I feel that, were I to waive it, I should at once put in hazard that allegiance to Truth which is at once the supreme duty and the supreme joy of life.

413. *To T. D. Acland.*

HAWARDEN,
August 20, 1865.

MY DEAR ACLAND,
In consequence of your letter, mentioning the Bishop of Worcester's [Philpott] Charge, I wrote to the Bishop, and he very kindly sent it me. I have read it with attention : and I think it deserves what you say of it, and more. Irrespective of coincidence of opinion on this or that particular topic, it leaves upon the mind a deep impression as to both the abilities and the character of the person who could write it.

It is not by way of deduction (*i.e.*, diminution) from what I have said, if I ask what the Bishop means in p. 29 by 'the enactment of law which prescribes written formularies as the sole test of soundness of doctrine, and the sole rule of teaching for our clergy.' What enactment of law is this ? Do you know where it is to be found ? That men may be found who believe in such an enactment, and some of them those who have figured as judges in ecclesiastical questions, is very possible : but unless I am much mistaken, there is no such enactment, and no such principle in our law. And unless I am again much mistaken those who have erroneously proceeded on the assumption of its existence have also laid down the astounding proposition that *Scripture* is of no authority in the Church of England to determine faith or duty, except where it is incorporated into, and interpreted by, the Prayer-Book or the Articles.

Another point. The Bishop states his sense of the danger of setting up a body of men to declare what is the doctrine of the Church of England. I feel that there is very serious danger in such a proceeding : and there is also, perhaps, a good deal of just objection to it in principle. Again, he dwells with force and justice upon the principle of applying to the temporal rights of an incumbent the same narrowing rules which govern criminal judicature in general. This seems to me difficult to deny. But I do not, so much as the Bishop apparently does, find the question exhausted by considerations of this class. For I suppose the business of a Church is to teach and maintain the truth : and I do not see that the constitution of the Court of Appeal makes the same effectual provision for attaining the great end of such a Court — namely, the correction of false doctrine — as it makes against *collateral* abuses which might aid in the prosecution of that end.

For example, the late judgment (wholly disowned, as *I am told*, by Lord Kingsdown) deals with two subjects. On one of them, the inspiration of Scripture, the Bishop has explained his views. It would require an immense amount of the famous non-natural expedient to bring them into unison with the declarations of the Judicial Committee. On the other point the Bishop has said nothing : but on that other point I will say that that judgment appears to me simply to deprive words of all their meaning. Consequently I ask myself, What is the use of a penal judicature to the Church of England, if, upon matters lying at the root of religion, it is simply, by applying the rules of criminal justice (however properly), to give the authority of law to a set of negative propositions without any positive security for the faith of the

Church; while on the other hand we are to derive our comfort, and our guarantee for the public standard of belief, from expositions like that of the Bishop in his Charge on the inspiration of Scripture, admirable indeed as it appears to me, but still entirely without the authority of law already given to the propositions it is evidently intended to correct?

The conclusion towards which these considerations would seem to point is that it is very difficult to maintain religious doctrine in these days by means of penal law. But penal law is with us correlative to laws of exclusive privilege, power, and emolument, which are enjoyed by the clergy. I individually could live, as I have lived in Scotland, without any of these. But I am not willing to consent that the clergyman shall, under pretence, or with the honest allegation, of the love of freedom, or upon any other plea, escape from his obligation to preach the system of doctrine he has engaged to preach, and yet remain in the enjoyment of all the legal privilege, power, and emolument, which he received upon condition of that obligation. The pursuing of this rule of freedom without limit, which is the matter now really at issue, will ultimately be fatal to any national establishment of religion. And as long as you have a national establishment (perhaps longer) you will not be able to get rid of penal judicature. But, if we are to have it, how is it to be so regulated as that it shall not place the authority of law practically on the side of that which it is the business of law to prevent, and except with a view to the prevention of which we should all say that it would be much better that law should have nothing at all to do with the matter?

In a word, would it not appear that the rule necessary for the maintenance of religious teaching is one thing, and the rule necessary to guard the civil rights of an accused person is another? And that it is the business of the clergy principally or specially to guard the first, that of the laity exclusively to secure the last? (The same considerations will apply in a great degree to cases of clerical immorality; in these, however, there is little fear of perversion of justice from prejudice or extraneous motive.) I frankly own I do [not] see my way at present to the framing a Court which shall at once give to Christians, humanly speaking, a fair security against the destruction of their faith, and to accused incumbents an assurance that they shall not be deprived of their livelihood except by a trial conducted on the same principles as in other cases of misconduct. I think, therefore, there is a great deal in what has been said by Archdeacon Sinclair, who in his Charge, after showing how easily Hume would have escaped condemnation for his 'Essay on Miracles,' intimates that the *spiritual* office or the *benefice* may seem to require in cases of appeal different modes of dealing.

Many thanks for your kind words about Oxford to your attached friend,

W. E. G.

414. *To Earl Granville.*

Court Hey,
October 9, 1865.

My dear Granville,

. . . Provision, I understand, is required to allow the withdrawal of the children of Dissenters from instruction in the 'formularies and doctrine' of the Church of England. What does this mean? If it be limited to instruction given *ex proprio* in Church doctrine, it is an immediate corollary to the exemption from formularies; but this limitation of meaning is too important, I think, to be left as matter of inference only. And there arises the question whether it would or ought to satisfy the Dissenting argument.

But suppose the schoolmaster is reading with his boys the third chapter of St. John, and he explains the passage relating to Baptism in the sense of the Prayer-Book and Articles: the Dissenter would say, 'This is instruction in the doctrine of the Church of England.' Now, it is utterly impossible for you to tell the Church schoolmaster or the clergyman that he must not in the school explain any passage of Scripture in a sense to which any of the parents of the children, or at least any sect, object: for then you would in principle entirely alter the character of the religious teaching for the rest of the scholars, and in fact upset the whole system. The Dissenter, on the other hand, ought (in my opinion) to be entitled to withdraw his child from the risk (if he considers it such) of receiving instruction of the kind I describe. But would the conscience clause secure to him this right? Would not a very awkward wrangle arise upon the question whether *bona-fide* exposition of the Scripture text, incidentally touching doctrine in which the Church of England differs from some other body, is to be considered as 'instruction in the doctrine of the Church of England'? It would not be desirable to leave the decision of such a question to an executive and political department with fluctuating views.

It appears to me as if the right of withdrawal ought to embrace the whole or any part of the religious instruction, or of what the parent considers to be such. You are strong on this ground : but weak, as I think, when you use language which gives even the faintest colour to the imputation that your real meaning is, under cover of protecting exceptional consciences, to invade the integrity of the instruction which is to be given to the mass of the children. . . .

415. *To Lady Mary Herbert (Baroness von Hügel).*

11, CARLTON HOUSE TERRACE,
January 28, 1866.

MY DEAR MARY,

I wish it were in my power sufficiently to make known to you the earnestness of the interest which we feel in all that concerns you, both for your dear parents' sake and for your own, placed as you are in your early years, in years usually so free from care and the sense of responsibility, in a position which makes such calls upon you as many go through life without being required to meet.

But God, who has caused you through no act of your own to find yourself so placed, has abundant means to make it even easy for you, were it His will, to fulfil your duties. And if He does not thus give you ease, if, as may well be the case, your spirit sometimes droops for a little while, this is not because He loves you little, but because He loves you much. For though He never sends trial without being ready also to send strength to bear it, yet it seems His will often to charge us quite up to the strength He gives; and this in order that the fruit of the trial may be the richer for us, that faith may be strengthened by exercise, that reliance upon Him may be more certain as in the ever-deepening sense of our own weakness we feel more and more the need and the all-sufficiency of the strength He gives.

I need not tell you that you will find your labour prosper in your hands in proportion as you live near to Him, in all the ways He has appointed — in His Blessed Sacrament, in the solemn prayers of the Church, in the private and even, if I may so say, in the unspoken prayers which, amidst all the occupations of life, will ascend from your own heart. As He gave Solomon the precious gift of wisdom, so I trust He will give it to you, that you may know how to live in all love and in obedience to your mother, and yet may also know how to maintain your loyalty to the Church. Need I remind you that, while you pursue your appointed path, the prayers of your friends, too, will ascend to heaven for you, and with the more encouragement because the past seems already to show them that you do not shrink from duty, arduous as it is and may be. Just as in every other exercise excellence is attained by difficulty, so here, in proportion as the strain is great, the purpose of God in your favour is high; and the effect upon your own character, and through your character on your life, will, I hope, be blessed.

Little as your youth ought to be perplexed with controversy, yet it may happen that difficulties may be thrown in the way of your understanding; and in any matter relating to the Church of England you would, I think, find it useful to refer to Palmer on the Church — not because he is certain to be right in all he says, for indeed there is a certain harshness in his judgment of some Protestant bodies, but because it is a work of great force and remarkable clearness, with excellent method and much knowledge, presented in a very accessible form. I am sure it is a book which your father would have approved for such an use, and which you might wisely employ in case of need, now that you have become in this great matter (a humbling but an inspiring thought for you), as long as present circumstances continue, the chief guardian of his wishes.

All intelligence of you at all times will be most acceptable to us, and if at any time you can make me of use, believe at least in my willingness, or rather in my earnest desire, to afford you any service.

Believe me, my dear Mary,
Your very sincere friend,
W. E. GLADSTONE.

416. *To Sir F. Rogers, Bart.*

WINDSOR CASTLE,
February 25, 1866.

MY DEAR ROGERS,

I have read, or rather reread, those fine sermons, and will return the volume to-morrow, which you so kindly lent me; but, though with a great deference to your opinion, I hold firmly to my own, that the 'Ecce Homo' cannot be by Dr. Newman. I please myself with thinking that in this busy age, quick at sapping and dissolving, but commonly not masculine enough in thought to construct, the author of this volume may have been sent among us as a builder, and may perform a great work for truth and for mankind.

I have called the two sermons 'fine.' It is a poor word for them. I do not know if Newman's style affects others as I find myself affected by it. It is a transporting style. I find myself constantly disposed to cry aloud, and vent myself in that way, as I read. It is like the very highest music, and seems sometimes in beauty to go beyond the human.

It is a *kind* of beauty far above the ordinary beauties of style, like the drawing of Raphael compared with the drawing of ordinary painters. It calls back to me a line in which I think (but it is long since I read it, Dante describes his own *religious* ecstasies: 'Che fece me da me uscir di mente.'

And yet (I do not know if you agree with me) I think Newman is not, and never was, a philosopher — a philosopher, I mean, in the sense of Butler.

He has not the balance of mind, and his aspects of

Photo, Numa Blanc Fils, Cannes.

MR. AND MRS. GLADSTONE, CHÂTEAU THORENC, CANNES,
FEBRUARY, 1898.

truth are partial : he is not well settled on a centre of gravity, his plumb-line is not true.

I think there is nothing more characteristic of the unphilosophic mind than impatience of doubt and premature avidity for system. That seems to me (especially after the revelations of the 'Apologia') to have been Newman's snare all along. No man can grasp truth entire. Butler took it in fragments, but his wise instinct enabled him so to lay each stone that it would fit in with every stone which might be well and truly laid in the double light of thought and of experience. He is now in his second century, and his works are at once younger and older than when he wrote them : older, because confirmed by the testing operations of other minds, younger, because with not only fuller and broader, but with, so to speak, more flexible foundations adaptive to the present and the coming needs of the human mind. Newman also laid his stones ; but at every period of his life he seems to have been driven by a fatal necessity to piece them all together, to make a building of them, and he has made half a dozen; and when the winds blew and the floods beat they gave way, and if the one he now inhabits seems to him firmer than the rest, I do believe it may be the result of little else than weariness of mind at so many painful efforts and (to a man of his intense feelings and perceptions) so many sad collapses. And yet, for one, I say boldly that since the days of Butler the Church of England reared no son so great as Newman.

It would seem the Almighty, ever bringing good from evil, has given him a work to do where he is : may it prosper in his hand !

Believe me,
Most sincerely yours,
W. E. GLADSTONE.

417. To J. R. Hope-Scott.

PENMAENMAWR,
September 7, 1868.

. . . With great delight, and under fascination, I have been treading (in mind) much ground familiar to you, and have been upon a regular perusal of Lockhart's

Life of Scott from end to end. I am already reflecting with concern how soon I shall probably reach the last page of the last volume. . . .

418. *To the Bishop of Oxford (Wilberforce).*

November 20, 1869.

My dear Bishop of Oxford,
One extorted word to say I have seldom read anything with more pleasure, or more emotion, than the address to you from the clergy of your now vanishing diocese, and your reply. You have not known me as a flatterer, and so I the more freely say it makes the heart bound to feel that even in this poor world truth and justice sometimes claim their own; and thank God it has not been in the power of jealousy or cowardice or spite, or any other evil creature, to detract one jot from the glory of that truly great episcopate, the secret of which you have written alike in the visible outward history of the Church and in the fleshy tablets of the hearts of men. May the undying, unabated courage with which you now gird yourself for the work elsewhere feed you with the bodily strength which I am well assured is the only quality for it that can ever fail you! I wish I had been an Oxford clergyman qualified to sign.
Do not write, but when you chance to have occasion, I shall *then* only like to know how many signed.

W. E. Gladstone.

419. *To Archdeacon Denison.*

July 14, 1870.

My dear Denison,
I deeply regret the occasion which has called forth your note, and I trust you may yet be spared for many years. But I write a line, unfortunately in great haste, to say that I do not think you have given me any occasion to exercise the virtue of forgiveness; but if you had, I think there could be no one towards whom it could be more easy and delightful to put in practice. . . .

W. E. G.

420. *To Mrs. Gladstone.*

HAWARDEN CASTLE,
January 7, 1871.

I found in Dryden yesterday a line *most* suitable to be addressed to you on that day,

'And ever be thou blest, who liv'st to bless,'

and it is worth sending now, if a day too late.

I did not pass unnoticed what you said of sleep, and I act upon it. My general rule is to take all my frame will accept. Hence freshness in the morning for the day's work. . . .

421. *To Dean Ramsay.*

August 8, 1871.

. . . I wish I could convey to you adequately the regret with which I find myself cut off from any possibility of joining in the tribute to be paid to-morrow to the memory of the first among the sons of Scotland. He was the idol of my boyhood, and though I well know that my admiration is worth little, it has never varied.

In his case the feeling is towards the man as much as towards his works. Did we not possess a line from his pen, his life would stand as a true epic. I will not say I think him as strong in his modern politics as in some other points, but I find my general estimate of the great and heroic whole affected in the slightest degree by this point of qualified misgiving. If he is out of fashion with some parts of some classes, it is their misfortune, not his. He is above fluctuations of time, for his place is in the Band of the Immortals. The end of my letter shall be better worth your having than the beginning. A fortnight ago I visited Tennyson, and found him possessed with all the sentiments about Scott which your celebration is meant to foster. . . .

422. *To the Rev. Sir G. Lewis.*

September 24, 1871.

... I have now finished your brother's book on Authority, which on coming here I have made it one of my first, or rather my first object to read, in the limited portion of the day which my correspondence leaves at my disposal. I am astonished that such a book should have been confined to so moderate a circle of readers, and that it should have never reached a second edition. It exhibits all the writer's patience, tolerance, calmness of mind, and sound sense, his discerning observation and his wide knowledge. I am truly obliged by your kindness in giving me an opportunity of perusing it, and I shall pursue my search for a copy which I may call my own with increased determination. ...

423. *To Mrs. Gladstone.*

On the Rails,
October 11, 1871.

At ten this morning I had a moving farewell. The Dean himself (Ramsay), with everything about him, forms a really beautiful picture of life : the evil, the poison, the disorder of the world, seem expelled. All is full of love and sweetness. I was most unwilling to say good-bye. But if I had stayed more days, I should have been just as unwilling at the end of them. ...

424. *To the Archbishop of Syra.*

August 18, 1872.

... From my recollections of Your Grace's mission to England, I am very sensible of the large and conciliatory view which you take of ecclesiastical questions, and I feel confident that you would not, without strong cause, recommend a course to be hastily adopted which might end in a formal schism between the Russian and Bulgarian Churches on the one hand, and the ancient and venerable communions which look to Constantinople as their centre of unity on the other. Your Grace will, however, understand that it is difficult for me, at this distance, at once to recognize a necessity for running such fearful risks, especially as, according to all I learn, the violent partisans on the Bulgarian side are themselves disposed to precipitate the sharpest issue to the controversy. I enter very much into Your Grace's views as to any aggression of the Panslavist against the Hellenic element, either in religion or otherwise. But while, as a Christian, I must cordially desire the union of all your Churches, I find myself led to a similar form of feeling by my duty as a Minister. We in this country are anxious for the peace of the Levant. To this end it is material that there should be harmony between the Ottoman Porte and the Christian Churches within its dominions, But for this purpose it seems to me also much to be wished that more Churches should be in harmony with one another, since, if they are at variance, foreign Powers may be tempted to step in, and, under cover of religion, to promote political aims, of a nature adverse to peace, by taking up some one of the rival interests and working it against another. This has been known to happen in other days, through differences between the Greek and Latin communions — differences which far more, I suppose, than any other cause brought about the downfall of the Byzantine Empire. The evil will, I fear, be greatly aggravated if permanent discord spring up among the orthodox Churches themselves, and it would be especially sad, in these days of so many perils to religion, that a schism should be established among those who agree together in matters of faith. Had I therefore (which I have not) any power in this deeply interesting question, my aim would be first to procure the intervention of a little time, which, by allaying heats, cures so many disorders, and then to see whether it was quite hopeless to procure from the Bulgarian Church a due observance of the rights of the Patriarch and the Eastern Church, before proceeding to extremities. . . .*

* For the substance of the following note I am indebted to a friend:
 The Bulgarian schism is one of a series of similar incidents which have occurred in nearly every country that has shaken off the Turkish

425. *To the Ven. Sir G. Prevost.*

November 30, 1872.

. . . I think I mentioned to you at Hawarden the course taken by Dr. Pusey towards me at the time of Dr. Temple's appointment, when his long-suffering gave way. A fortnight ago I passed a night at Oxford, and heard through Dr. Liddon that Dr. Pusey would be glad to see me. I called on him, and was received with all his old accustomed warmth and kindness. I thought it would be well to make this known to you. Considering his age and labours, I thought he looked well. . . .

426. *To Lord Lytton.*

May 13, 1873.

. . . I cannot resist the impulse to add one letter to our correspondence respecting 'Kenelm Chillingly.' At broken times (as is my wont), and in the Easter holidays, I read it, and it pleased me so much in so many ways that, after some delay, I feel obliged to write a hasty word. First, I am delighted with the high aim and purpose of the book. It is aimed at making men nobler and better; not, as is so commonly the case with the novels of the day, at inducing readers to work through three volumes for the sake of the morbid excitement they afford by exhibiting, in

---

yoke. Ecclesiastically these countries were all exarchies of the Patriarchate of Constantinople, but since their emancipation they have rejected the control in things spiritual of a subject of the Sultan, and have declared themselves autocephalous. Thereupon the Patriarch has excommunicated them and pronounced them in schism. Hitherto he has always come, mainly under Russian pressure, to recognize accomplished facts, but in the case of Bulgaria there was a longer delay than usual owing to her being a part of the Sultan's dominions, and now that she is independent her relations with Constantinople are embittered by the conflicting jurisdictions in Macedonia. The Russians have all along been in communion with both Churches.

varied or unvaried combination, the vices, follies and weaknesses of society. Next, all this is done with a most remarkable abstention from the introduction of bad, base, and contemptible characters, even by way of contrast. In foregoing this contrast, the artist deprives himself of much factitious aid, and his dispensing with it, and yet attaining his end, is a great achievement. Next, I cannot too highly express my feeling about that ethereal sketch of Lily. She reminded me, in a different sphere and surroundings, of Ariel as a work of art. And, lastly, I think it a master-stroke that Kenelm and Cecilia Travers are left in the possibility and evident likelihood of union, but are not as a fact united ; for I have never seen a case when a transferred affection was satisfactorily handled in a work of imagination. Forgive me for troubling you with these few words, in a matter full of interest to you, of eulogy not less sincere than it is insignificant. Most gifts ought to be made in life ; but this work was surely made for a posthumous bequest, to remain a centre of pure and genial recollections for all who knew, honoured or loved your father. . . .

427. *To Mrs. Tyler.*

July 19, 1873.

. . . I know that an occupation may be real, steady, and permanent, without what is termed 'a profession.' The essential thing, I think, is that in some form or other there should be an occupation corresponding to that description. The habits of this age and country dispose us to look with far too great indifference upon the evil, I would almost say the misery, of a life without adequate employment. Is not this the talent hid in a napkin ? Is it not really worse than many things which at first sight appear worse than it ? You are, I am sure, acting for the welfare of those in whose happiness you are bound to take so deep an interest, when you contend that this great want ought to be supplied. And supplied it can be, without doubt, since Providence has supplied for every one of us a work in the world, and has given us sufficient means of discovering what it is. . . .

428. *To the Queen.*

House of Commons,
July 22–23, 1873.

Mr. Gladstone has had the honour to receive Your Majesty's interesting letter on the death of the Bishop of Winchester. He could, if it were needful, bear an independent testimony to the truth of much of what Your Majesty has said respecting that great prelate. Of his special opinions, Mr. Gladstone may not be an impartial judge : but he believes there can be no doubt that there does not live the man, in any of the three kingdoms of Your Majesty, who has, by his own indefatigable and unmeasured labours, given such a powerful impulse as the Bishop of Winchester gave to the religious life of the country. And that affectionate disposition which he testified before Your Majesty after the death of the illustrious Prince Consort was ever ready to soothe and share the sorrows of the humblest of your subjects. Mr. Gladstone went yesterday with Lord Granville to Abinger Hall, where the Bishop lay dead. The inquest was short and almost painfully simple, though conducted with perfect propriety. The shock to Lord Granville's mind and nerves from the terrible sight which he saw had not wholly passed away. The jury, of course, went to view the Bishop as he lay, and Mr. Gladstone had his last sight of him on earth. The countenance was calm, but full of the marks both of his labours and of his powers. There were slight marks — dots they might be called — on one side of the forehead and nose, where the face, partially protected by the hat, had met the grassy ground in rolling over. There was a heavy bruise at the base of the hinder part of the skull, but this Mr. Gladstone did not see. The hat was exhibited to the jury quite crushed. There seems to be no doubt that death was caused by the dislocation of the vertebræ of the neck, on which the whole force of this heavy fall was discharged, and that it was instantaneous and absolutely painless. After the inquest Mr. Gladstone went to see the spot, where it is but too easy to understand the manner of this catastrophe. A rough cart-track passes straight down a rather, but not very, steep descent. On the left is grass, and the ground inclines downward also towards the line of the cart-track. Upon this descent there is a dip almost in the shape of a horseshoe, about 18 inches deep on the side near the cart-track, and shallower away from it: where Lord Granville (probably) rode, it is almost imperceptible. The Bishop, riding down at a slow canter, seems not to have taken up his horse, and the animal, though a very sure-footed one, not finding the ground meet it as it stepped, lost its footing, and came (as the groom says) on its knees. It had risen at the moment when Lord Granville, who was slightly ahead, looked round upon hearing a dull, heavy sound, and saw the horse standing up, the Bishop lying at full length motionless, with tranquil countenance, his arms by his sides, and his feet in the direction in which they were proceeding. The scene was quiet, rural, and pretty, but without any wide view or other circumstance to absorb attention. Thus, a slight and momentary carelessness in riding seems to have been the cause of this great calamity. To these details, in which Mr. Gladstone has thought Your Majesty would feel an interest, though the whole of them may not be new, he will only add that the extent and depth of feeling which has been shown, both in the neighborhood and in London, are even beyond what he could have anticipated. There appears to be a widespread desire, which Mr. Gladstone shares, that he should be buried in the Abbey: of which, though but for a limited time, he once was Dean, and where his honoured father lies.

429. *To the Rev. G. Williams.*

November 27, 1873.

... I scarcely know what to say of the loss of Lord R. Cavendish. First, it is so heavy that it can hardly be described without seeming exaggeration. Let us, however, forget ourselves, and be glad that that tender and ripened spirit is at rest, and has no longer to feel or witness the buffetings of this agitated world. ...

430. *To Mrs. Gladstone.*

HAWARDEN CASTLE,
Easter Morning, April 6, 1874.

. . . The anti-Parliamentary reaction has been stronger with me even than I anticipated. I am as far as possible from feeling the want of the House of Commons. I could cheerfully go there to do a work, but I hope and pray to be as little there as possible except for such an aim. In London I think we were too much hustled to speak leisurely or effectually of the future. It will open for us by degrees. . . .

There is one thing I should like you to understand clearly as to my view of things, for it is an essential part of that view. I am convinced that the welfare of mankind does not now depend on the state or the world of politics : the real battle is being fought in the world of thought, where a deadly attack is made, with great tenacity of purpose and over a wide field, upon the greatest treasure of mankind — the belief in God and the Gospel of Christ. . . .

431. *To Earl Granville.*

HAWARDEN,
December 7, 1874.

. . . The religious question generally — which we could manage while we were in power — has now passed out of our hands, and is a great difficulty in *my* way. What in this province the next session may bring about, I cannot tell. But the Church of England has been brought to the brink of a most serious crisis, which may take the form of schism, disestablishment, or both. It is, I believe, still avoidable ; but only by an amount of self-command, high-mindedness, and circumspection, on the part of the highest Church authorities, very different from that which they exhibited during the last session. While the question remains unclosed, any strapping up of the relations between the party and me can only, I fear, constitute a new danger. . . .

432. *To Lord Acton.*

HAWARDEN CASTLE,
December 18, 1874.

MY DEAR LORD ACTON,

1. When you were putting in caveats and warnings, you did not say to me, 'Now mind, this affair will absorb some, perhaps many, months of your life.' It has been so up to the present moment — and it evidently will be so for some time.

2. But for me it is nothing, compared with what it is for you. And I assure you I have asked myself much and many times what was my duty to you, and others like you. And my answer to myself has been this:

(*a*) To move others, if I could, to take up their position abreast of you. For, in such a position, *Defendit numerus.* I have laboured at it, but as yet without effect.

(*b*) By carefully watching my own language, and making no attack on the Roman Catholic religion *such as a Roman Catholic was required to hold it before July*, 1870. To this I have endeavoured rigidly to conform. A furious and inveterate Protestant foe of mine, Dr. Porter or Potter, of Sheffield, has pointed this out in print. I might deviate by accident. If I do, pray pull me up. Of course I do not, and cannot, hold myself tightly bound as to reserves of language in speaking of the Roman authorities who have done all this portentous mischief. You perhaps saw a letter of mine in the papers to some Nonconforming ministers. It was intended to mark out my province. Unfortunately, they had misread 'clearly,' and printed it 'merely.'

(*c*) By curbing myself from all endeavours to turn to account this crisis in the interest of proselytism. This has applied chiefly, I may say in confidence, to my communications with my sister.

3. A thousand thanks for the admirable passage about Dr. Döllinger; I enclose my projected rendering of it. I would also print the original.

4. His words to me in English on the point you mention were to the effect that he despaired of any

satisfactory change under the ordinary working of the Roman Curia, though it might, however, come by 'crisis or revolution.' But you doubtless have heard from him in German which in these nice matters is better. . . .

433. *To Mrs. Gladstone.*

11, Carlton House Terrace,
January 9, 1875.

. . . Do you not see that the opinion of a man like E. Talbot, so far as it has force, tells the other way? The very thing that unfits me to lead the Liberal party on Church questions — namely, anticipated differences from them — recommends me in his eyes, under the idea that I am to make that party less un-Churchlike than it would otherwise be. . . .

434. *To Dr. Döllinger.*

23, Carlton House Terrace,
July 24, 1875.

My dear Dr. Döllinger,

. . . As the meeting at Bonn is nigh at hand, I lose no time in acquainting you with the exact state of my sentiments.

I regard the idea of returning to office at any future time with aversion, and, as old Time fights on my side, I also conceive it to be in a very high degree improbable.

Still, as long as I do not leave Parliament, I am under many restraints, from the impossibility of totally avoiding its business, and from the moral ties which still unite me with all my old colleagues. I remain in free and familiar intercourse with them, and I share their counsels whenever they desire it.

With some risk and much criticism, I assert my liberty up to a certain point, but beyond that point I could not go without making a change for which the time has hardly arrived. And I think, as you providently and considerately suspect, that it would not be expedient for me to take an actual part in the meetings at Bonn.

At the same time, I recognize as freely as I did last

year your title, in your arduous and hopeful work, to every kind of moral support which it may be in the power of any of your friends to give you. If you think that, in view of the presence of the Eastern prelates or representatives, I can in any way strengthen your hands, I could contrive to come to Cologne, or some spot in the neighbourhood of Bonn, and could pay a visit to that place *unofficially* on the day before the Conference, or on any morning or afternoon while it continues, but so as not to interfere with the proceedings, and could see you and any other persons, as you might think it desirable. In the newspaper it might fairly be stated that I had on such a day come over to visit you, my old and revered friend. Please to consider this and to let me know your wishes.

I know money must be wanted for some of the purposes in view, and I should gladly send (or bring) a hundred pounds.

Very sincerely do I hope that you will have some good Englishmen present to take part in the proceedings. If you cannot have the Bishop of Winchester and Dr. Liddon, why not have the Bishop of Salisbury (Dr. Moberly) and the Dean of St. Paul's (Dr. Church). I think they would not refuse a line from you. I would back it up if this were your wish. But I trust you have not lost the Bishop of Winchester (Dr. Browne), who is so much and so justly respected: I mean his presence, for I am sure his heart is with you.

I do not think that the controversy on Ritualism in this country threatens you, at present, with any difficulty. And I anticipate a continually increasing measure of sympathy with the endeavour to work out a scheme of concord on the basis of the dogma and faith of the undivided Church.

Even your proceedings in Germany are scarcely more interesting than the tidings from Italy, and the proceedings of the peasantry in the three parishes of the Mantovano. I was also greatly delighted with the debate in the Italian Parliament, and I had some days ago an opportunity of speaking pretty freely to Prince Humbert, who is paying England a visit. . . .

435. *To Dr. Döllinger.*

73, HARLEY STREET,
May 29, 1876.

MY DEAR DR. DÖLLINGER,
  I send you by post the proof-sheets of a paper I have written for the *Contemporary Review* of June. It aims at setting out, in a manner very slight and very rude, the principal courses of thought concerning religion at the present time. It can give you no information. But, if you look at it for a moment, you will, without going through the several divisions, see the general distribution I have made, and will understand in what way it is that I think that it may perhaps be of some use among my countrymen.

Père Hyacinthe is in London, and thinks of holding one or more Conferences (in which I believe nobody confers) on the 'religious question.' He asked my opinion, and I recommended this. He seems a man of upright mind, and his wife is a pleasing and sensible woman, with a good deal of apparent energy, and a real religious character — though many, and I among them, think he made a serious mistake in dispensing himself from his vows to marry her. His ecclesiastical position seems to be that of the Old Catholics: he waits and longs for a provisional Episcopal Government, and then a reform in the Latin Church; having no idea that a schism, properly so called, can have warrant or prosperity. I understand privately that he has communicated in the Church of England, but I have no authority to say so. He assures me that he gets much private benediction and encouragement from within the Roman Church : and seems to estimate rather highly the number and importance of those who are waiting for the death of the present Pontiff as *the* crisis of the present controversy.

While contemplating with the deepest interest the progress of the work you have carried forward on the scientific area at Bonn, I look rather anxiously also to the practical side and the Christian provision made, and to be made, for persons who resist or cannot accept the innovations of Vaticanism.

It still seems to me the reasonable opinion that, if the old Catholic body is to thrive, and is to avoid the snare of Erastianism so injurious to the Jansenists, the *via prima salutis*, the most available and probable means for durability, and security, will be such a re-establishment of relations with the Eastern Church as will allow that Church in all or some of its branches to take part in some consecration or consecrations of Bishops to assist Bishop Reinkens and continue his work.

I hoped and believed Archbishop Lycurgus would be the instrument for achieving this work, and I trust God may raise him up a successor. . . .

Always affectionately yours,
W. E. GLADSTONE.

436. *To Mrs. Gladstone.*

HAWARDEN,
December 29, 1876.

. . . God be thanked that we have been spared so long to mount the hill of life together, and to reap such a harvest of love and blessing in our children, a harvest which even seems to grow richer from year to year, and to give every confidence that the increase will continue. During what remains of life may we come ever nearer in spirit, and may I be less unthankful for all God has given me in you to love and honour. . . .

437. *To James Phillips.*

HOLMBURY,
April 8, 1877.

SIR,
I fear I can render but little service, yet I should be glad to aid in removing, if it might be, risks which you name, and each of which is in its own way so grave.

I know of no rule which forbids a Christian to examine into the preternatural agency in the system called spiritualism.

But it seems to me his duty —

1. To refrain from dabbling in a question of this kind — that is to say, making a shallow and insufficient examination of it.

2. To beware of the assumption that, if the signs are real, the system has therefore of necessity any claim to more than an acknowledgment of this reality.

3. To remember that, on the principles of Christian religion, a bad preternatural agency, or a misleading one, is not shut out from the range of possibility.

4. To avoid in so solemn a matter the spirit of mere curiosity, and to be assured of having in view an useful object. Universal knowledge is not possible, and we are bound to choose the best and healthiest.

I may add that an inquiry of this kind seems to me much more suited for a mind in a condition of equilibrium than for one which is disturbed. If the storms and gusts of the day have in any way shaken your standing ground, is it not the first and most obvious duty to make an humble but searching scrutiny of the foundations? I speak as one who is deeply convinced that they will bear it, and that God has yet many a fair plant to rear in this portion of His garden.

With all good wishes, I remain, sir,
Your faithful servant,
W. E. GLADSTONE.

438. *To Dr. Döllinger.*

WOBURN ABBEY,
October 23, 1878.

MY DEAR DR. DÖLLINGER,

I am very grateful for your letter: for I was afraid that I might have intruded unwarrantably upon your time. And I am also greatly pleased to find you think my main propositions right. I need hardly say I agree with you that the subject requires a much fuller elucidation. Indeed, I consider my paper as no more than a provocative to serious and searching inquiry.* My object, really, was to broaden the field of discussion, which has heretofore been sadly narrow when the questions raised have touched the polemical interests of the Roman and Protestant causes respectively. I have described with truth the slavish traditionalism with which the Reformation is still largely regarded in this country. Not merely for the

* 'The Sixteenth Century arraigned before the Nineteenth,' *Contemporary Review*, October, 1878.

sake of justice to the Church of Rome, but even in our own interest, it is time to vindicate a true historic freedom against this servile temper. What may be called Protestant idolatry — for example, idolatry towards the letter of Scripture, and even of its translation used among us (a most noble work) — has undoubtedly opened a broad road in our time for the incursions of unbelief.

In describing the fourteenth century as early days, etc., I meant to throw the stress on the word *culture*. This I suppose to have begun just before Dante, and therefore I thought Boccaccio might be called as belonging to its early days. I quite understand the isolation of the 'Decameron,' Petrarch representing another and better side of 'Humanism.' I will take care, should the opportunity offer, to give the greater fulness and roundness to my statement, of which it stands in need. Meantime I am glad not to have seen objection seriously taken on the Anglican side to what I have said about the loss which reformed Christianity has suffered in respect to such matters as prayers for the faithful departed, and the Eucharistic sacrifice.

It is much otherwise as to the silly and effeminate criticisms which have been showered on a single sentence in my article in the *North American Review*, where I have said that at a future time America may, and probably will, carry away the commercial primacy which we at present hold. When Chancellor of the Exchequer in 1866, I dealt largely with this subject in a Budget speech, and no one objected; but with all the arrogance and rhodomontade of the last few years there is connected a vein of morbid weakness which comes out in these feeble criticisms. . . .

Believe me, in unabated reverence,
Your affectionate friend,
W. E. GLADSTONE.

439. *To J. Morley, Esq.*

October 27, 1880.

. . . I also read with great interest a few days back the *Pall Mall Gazette's* article on the High Church Party in the Church of England; agreeing, I think, with what is said until I came, near the end, to a statement that they were wrong in not leaving the Church. This, I think, from the writer's point of view, would have been just, if he had said they ought not to leave, but to disestablish and disendow (if they could). As it is, the allegation requires of the High Churchman that he should contravene a fundamental article of his belief — namely, that our Saviour, through the Apostles, founded an institution called in the Creed the Holy Catholic Church, to be locally distributed throughout the earth, that it is matter of duty to abide in this Church, and that for England this Church is found in the Church of England. I do not well see how, with this belief, he is to go out of it. . . .

440. *To the Rev. Malcolm Maccoll.*

HAWARDEN,
March 27, 1881.

. . . What I want to have, on the basis of Palmer's work, is a setting forth, according to the methods which theological science provides, of the *Civitas Dei*, the city set on a hill, the pillar and ground of truth, the Catholic and Apostolic Church, the *Fortsetzung der Fleischwirkung*, exhibited, not as against Nonconformists, nor even principally as against the Jesuit, aggressive Church of Rome, but as a positive dispensation, a form divinely given to the religious idea, which challenges with authority, but agreeably to reason, the assent of the rational and right-minded man, in competition with all the other claimants on that assent. I want some solid scientific work which shall set up historical or institutional Christianity to takes its chance in that mêlée of systems dogmatic and undogmatic, revealed and unrevealed, particularist, pagan, secular, antitheistic, or other, which marks the age.

Having spent fifty years of adult life in this mêlée, I find the method I describe the most rational of all, and I wish that there should be a textbook of it for the help of doubtful or uninstructed minds.

Also that this textbook, founded on the principle I have described, should apply the principle, for the benefit of Englishmen, to the case of the English

Church, under the shadow of which our lot is providentially cast.

441. To G. A. Macmillan.

Hawarden,
April 10, 1881.

. . . 'Hymns Ancient and Modern' ought some day to receive a drastic purgation. But I am less tolerant than the Dean.

The 'Jacob's Dream' is indeed a true and very fine poem, especially the earlier part of it. But the 'Jesu, Lover of my Soul,' though a general favourite, I cannot and will not admire. Why, on the other hand, has Mr. Goldwin Smith left out those noble, those wonderful verses of Scott in the Lay, 'That Day of Wrath, that Dreadful Day' — almost the noblest sacred verses since the *Dies Iræ*, of which they are sometimes wrongly called a translation?

442. To J. H. Shorthouse.

Hawarden,
December 5, 1881.

I thank you very much for your interesting paper upon Wordsworth's Platonism.

You say that the effect of his teaching is a sacred peace. Your words remind me of words used to me by Sir James Stephen in the Colonial Office nearly fifty years ago. He said 'Wordsworth is the most sabbatical book I know.' With both sentiments, or both forms of the one sentiment, I strongly sympathize. He has been a great teacher and a great blessing to mankind.

I am glad to see, from the form of your tract, that the spirit of Baskerville is not wholly expelled from its convenient haunts.

443. To John Murray.

Hawarden,
January 23, 1882.

I must not omit to send you more than formal thanks for the gift of Mr. Beckett's able book.

The calamity (I cannot use a weaker word) which it was written to avert is, I trust, no longer impending; undoubtedly he has given us an additional security against it.

The English nation, while they retain their senses, never can assent to such a substitution as this.

The Revised Version cannot be *corrected;* the work will have to be begun anew on other principles, and the good work will have to be picked from out of the mass of trashy alterations. Such is my surmise.

444. To Dr. Döllinger.

HAWARDEN,
September 1, 1882.

MY DEAR DR. DÖLLINGER,

. . . I trouble you with a letter from myself on a fact of some interest in ecclesiastical history. I do not know if you have ever had an opportunity of seeing Archbishop Hamilton's Catechism. He was the Primate of Scotland in 1552, when the reforming movement in England went at a headlong pace. A synod was held by the Archbishop, and this work was put forth as a norm for teachers rather than an instruction to the laity. It is, I apprehend, important as showing what doctrinal and ecclesiastical language was thought advisable by a National Church at that critical moment. The work became exceedingly rare. I saw a copy in the University Library of Edinburgh twenty years ago, and urged its republication, offering in case of need to get it done at Oxford. They paid no heed. But an Edinburgh bookseller has now republished it in a rather costly form. I think you would esteem it to be of some importance. It expounds ably and fully the Decalogue, the Creed, the Lord's Prayer, and the *Ave Maria.* It presents several salient points for notice, especially that, in setting forth the substance of Christian teaching, it nowhere notices the supremacy, or primacy, or jurisdiction, of the Pope, but speaks simply of the Church.

In treating of the Eucharist, it lays down sharply the scheme of substance and accidents, and of reception in one kind. On the other hand, it avoids the *phrase* Transubstantiation, it habitually speaks of God's Board, and it hardly touches the doctrine of sacrifice, *only* saying: 'It is called the Sacrifice of the Altar, because it is a quick and special remembrance of the Passion of Christ, as it is said in the Evangel of St. Luke, *Hoc facite in meam commemorationem.* It seems generally to be composed with much ability, and in a pious tone.

You have heard, I believe, that a recast of Palmer's book on the Church is in progress. I have done what I could to promote it. I have some apprehension lest it should be made rather too much a defence of revelation, instead of a treatise on the Vehicle provided by Divine ordinance for bringing home its provisions. I look, however, to the republication, and to mitigations in it which will be real improvements, with lively interest; for I believe its reproduction will be an event of great importance for the future of the Church of England and of religion in this country. I understand your advice will be sought: and I earnestly hope and pray you will not withhold it. I believe it will have large Episcopal countenance.

I would it were in my power to renew those personal communications with you which, of late especially, but also from the first, have been to me a source of so much pleasure and advantage. But I am a slave to the heavy undertaking which has lain upon me, without remission, almost ever since I saw you. Much, thank God, has been done. Even Ireland has improved, and is improving. In Egypt, naval and military operations have, thus far, gone beyond our expectations.

If you write to Bishop Strossmayer, pray convey to him the assurance of my continuing affectionate respect: and accept the same for yourself from the bottom of my heart. May every blessing rest upon your life and work!

Ever yours,
W. E. GLADSTONE.

445. *To Mr. R. Ornsby.*

HAWARDEN,
October 15, 1883.

I received the proof-sheets on Saturday, and I now return them. I must not claim any credit for despatch:

once taken up, it was hardly possible to lay them down. You will find on the margin a few insignificant pencil notes; but I have not a single exception to take on my own behalf. I am glad to see that they contain some marks of the deference which I always paid him, though they may not directly show that that deference was founded on a sense of his superiority even more than upon affection. But I never could be an impartial judge of him : he possessed that most rare gift, the power of fascination, and he fascinated me.

In reading these proof-sheets I could not confine myself to the narrow scope of the request which induced you to send them. I could not but look to the biography itself, and I rejoice to see from every page of it that a wise choice has been made of its writer, and that, unlike many works now published under that title, it is to be a real, a careful, and a living work.

Still, it raises in my mind the question whether there should not be, if there can be, some other memorial of James Hope in a republication of some of his own remaining works. Is it quite out of the question to make a small collection and reprint of them ? Would not what he has left on colleges and foundations be of much permanent value ? I do not doubt the justness of your selections, but can they truly represent the whole ? In saying this I bear in mind that few men are so inadequately represented by their external distinctions. Eminence at the Parliamentary bar is not eminence in the English nineteenth-century life ; and to the attainment of this eminence, as a visible sign, he was limited by his own choice. I feel that it is hazarding much for me to make this suggestion. His secession placed so terrible a rift between us (except in feeling), that without doubt I lost in a great degree the perspective of his life. But I am sure you will in any case pardon me, and ascribe my boldness to the desire that full justice should be done him.

The work when it appears must in any case be received as one of deep religious interest; but I am sure your wish would be that, through him also, Religion should reassert her hold upon the world.

Before reading these sheets, I was not aware that his friendship with Cardinal Newman was a late as well as a rapid growth. I now see that in the very month in which he tendered to me (p. 107) a very remarkable engagement, he came under another attraction far more powerful, which after a comparatively short time disabled him from fulfilling it, and made him resolutely close his ears to anything I could urge upon him.

I am exceedingly struck by your remarks in p. 179. There is, I believe, much deep truth in them, and they still further deepen the belief I have always rather specially entertained as to the amount of that profound and diversified influence which the Tract Movement, and its singular sequel, have exercised upon academical as well as ecclesiastical and religious history.

446. *To R. Ornsby.*

HAWARDEN,
October 20, 1883.

I need say but little on your interesting letter beyond this, that your subject has too much hold upon me to allow of my reckoning very minutely any time I may spend upon it. I may be misled, but it still appears to me that, even if no piece is forthcoming except the speech of 1840 and the article which carried away Cardinal Newman, their publication *in extenso* would constitute a splendid funeral oration for the old collegiate system, of which it is worthy, and which I fear it never can receive in any other form. I do not now recollect his writings on the Jerusalem Bishopric but I have no doubt they must be important.

It is a subject the revival of which in any shape is painful to me, but I cannot help wishing before all things that the debt of justice to him should be paid.

The religious interest of the book is perfectly safe, but religion in this age has a special interest in exhibiting all that was great in men who have believed, and have wrought their belief into their life, as he did.

Pray make sure about his politics. My impression had been that he was a Tory to the last. I do not know whether to ascribe in any degree to his influence the change which took place in the Duke of Norfolk's politics during his lifetime.

447. *To Sir H. Ponsonby.*

HAWARDEN,
November 4, 1883.

... The celebration of a Luther Festival seems perfectly natural in Germany, where he is a great national hero, and not merely a theological or ecclesiastical combatant. There he has acted powerfully upon, and given much of its tone to, the whole thought of the country. But, as I think, to make the celebration here is above all things to stir up the embers of religious controversy, and the religious controversies of one age are never wholly satisfactory to the mind of another. In Germany the name of Luther is associated with the widening of thought; here the attempt rather is to tie it down to a particular form, and thus to narrow it. Agreeably to this, I see in the printed list the names of the most vehement anti-Maynooth men.

448. *To the Rev. C. H. Spurgeon.*

10, DOWNING STREET,
June 18, 1884.

MY DEAR SIR,
  I cannot avoid writing a line to offer you my hearty congratulations upon the approach of a day full of interest to many who stand beyond the circle, wide as it is, of your immediate hearers, followers, and denominational brethren.

I believe that both you and I belong to the number of those who think that all convictions, once formed, ought to be stoutly maintained, and who would therefore be called strong denominationalists.

But without prejudice to this persuasion, and outside the points by which our positions are marked off, there happily abides a vast inheritance of truth which we enjoy in common, and which in its central essence forms, as I rejoice to think, the basis of the faith of Christendom. I therefore ask to unite my voice with the voice of thousands in acknowledging the singular power with which you have so long testified before the world 'of sin, of righteousness, and of judgment,' and the splendid uprightness of public character and conduct, which have, I believe, contributed perhaps equally with your eloquence and mental gifts to win for you so wide an admiration.

449. *To the Rev. C. Beard.*

HAWARDEN,
August 23, 1884.

. . . I very seldom volunteer a letter: indeed, now that I think of it, this is hardly volunteered. It is, I may say, extorted from me by the singular merits of your Hibbert Lectures, with which I have only just become acquainted. I have nearly finished the delightful task of reading them, and I should run to great length were I to say all I think in their praise.

I have never read anything so good, in so brief a compass, on the English Reformation, still probably the least understood of all.

It is not, however, mere concurrence of opinion (varied rarely by dissent), nor even the great power and richness of the volume, which most impress me. It is the large and generous spirit of the book, and the gift it shows of bringing out the nobleness of mixed characters, a gift which must be allied with something ethically similar in the writer.

After saying this, I wish to put in a plea for St. Augustine. I cannot think he ought to be put in a leash with Luther and Calvin, except as to what was best in them. His doctrine of human nature is substantially that of Bishop Butler; and he converted me about forty-five years ago to Bishop Butler's doctrine.

I will not trouble you further, though I am tempted, sorely tempted, to ask whether *you* really think there is a true antithesis between authority and reason. I know it is a favourite phrase. All systems have their slang, but what I find in almost every page of your book is that you have none.

450. *To G. W. E. Russell.*

HAWARDEN,
October 13, 1884.

... I remember a young Tory saying at Oxford he could not wish to be more Tory than Burke.

He was perhaps the maker of the Revolutionary war; and our going into that war perhaps made the Reign of Terror, and, without any 'perhaps,' almost unmade the liberties, the constitution, and prosperity, of our country. Yet I venerate and almost worship him, though I can conceive its being argued that all he did for freedom, justice, religion, purity of government, in other respects and other quarters, were less than the mischief which flowed out from the reflections. I would he were now alive. ...

451. *To T. G. Law.*

HAWARDEN,
October 15, 1884.

On understanding that it would be agreeable to you, I have written a short introductory notice to precede your admirable preface, and have received for it the imprimatur of Bishop Stubbs. Pray note fearlessly anything in it that you may find wrong.

I venture a criticism on one phrase which you have used in p. xxxvi. After saying, 'this saving faith consists in intellectual assent, with fear, hope, repentance, and complete self-surrender added (the Lutheran *assensus et fiducia*).'

Will the words in the parenthesis hold good? Is not the *fiducia* of Luther a fixed confidence of having received the gift of pardon and justification? I do not like to trust my rusty recollections. But, as far as they go, nothing less than this is the Lutheran *fiducia*: whereas I should say the description here given singularly resembles that furnished by the English 'Homily of Justification.'

452. *To Lady Russell.*

HAWARDEN,
December 14, 1884.

. . . A very clever man, a Bampton Lecturer, evidently writing with good and upright intention, sends me a Lecture in which he lays down the qualities he thinks necessary to make theological study fruitful. They are courage, patience, and sympathy. He omits one quality, in my opinion, even more important than any of these, and that is reverence : without a great stock of reverence, mankind, as I believe, will go to the bad. I might add another omission: it is caution — a thing different from reverence, but an apt handmaid to it, and the proper counterpoise to the courage, of which certainly there seems to be no lack.

453. *To Dr. Döllinger.*

HAWARDEN,
May 27, 1888.

MY DEAR FRIEND,
On coming hither for the Whitsun holidays, I found a double pleasure prepared for me in receiving the book you had kindly sent me. It lay firstly in the token of your recollection, and next in the proof of your continuing vigour. I have begun it with the essay on Madame de Maintenon, for a strong attraction draws me to the whole Louis XIII.-XV. period, as one of the most instructive and memorable, although one of the most odious, in history. I found your disquisition profoundly interesting, apart from its marvellous freshness and fulness. It seemed to taste of the mountain streams that fill the Lake of Tegernsee. The woman herself has been placed by you on a very high pedestal, in point both of talent and of piety and personal unselfishness. But was her country, though her country was the world, better or worse for her existence ? I am not certain, from your three or four last sentences, what would, on this issue, be your verdict. She was art and part in the whole vast mass

of the transactions of the reign of Louis XIV., for thirty years or more, which were one long conspiracy against liberty both political and moral, against peace and justice in Christendom, and against the whole principle and the very idea of legality in France. You have weightily noticed the connection between 1685 and 1793, and the enduring and as yet unexhausted vitality of the terrible bequest of that Sovereign and his abettors to the world. That she was a well-intending Christian is all the better for her : but I ask whether she was a benefactress to the world. Perhaps, but for her, her husband might have lived to the end a life as foul as that of Louis XV., but this does not, I think, in any way suffice to redress the balance.

I have lately undergone the shock of a most painful surprise in being introduced to the novels of Zola, through the medium of a book called 'La Terre.' It is a brutally realistic account of the life or supposed life of a provincial and rural community in the district of La Beauce. Exaggerated it must be, I hope grossly: but the delineation is close and first hand, and the question arises, What must be the state of a population about whom such a book could be written?

Canon MacColl tells me that you share a desire, which has been expressed here, that I should write something on the reign of Elizabeth for the long-suspended recast of Palmer's book. Although I feel incredulous as to his report, I may try to comply. Reading over Palmer's section on the reign of Elizabeth, I should think it might stand ; but in a short supplement I might try to show how much she did towards restoring a Church system that had become seriously dilapidated in the later years of Henry VIII. and under Edward VI., and had been replaced under Mary simply by the action of the Papal Power.

It is, however, enormously difficult for me, while I remain in the political sphere (as it brings me fresh work every day), to do anything requiring any width of survey or re-examination.

I have, however, recently written two articles, one published in America and one here, touching on the sceptical movement of the day. The first I have not seen in type ; of the latter I venture to send you a copy.

In vain I long for an opportunity of conversing with you on the state of things here, in which even when I first knew you, in 1845, you took so warm and living an interest. As regards the Church, the picture is really brighter than some time ago I could have hoped to see. The Bishops, speaking generally, govern with dignity, unity, and wisdom. The strength of the office and its traditions subdues for the most part any minor eccentricity (so to call it) of the man. The clergy are to a large extent efficient and devoted: more bold in their mission, but almost always in harmony with their parishioners. (How I wish you could see one large parish here, of which my second son is the Rector!) Further, I am assured that in Oxford, which is a kind of heart's core to the country, there is among the candidates for Fellowships, who are the flower of the University, a strong current of inclination towards Holy Orders: almost a novelty since the great secession of Newman. . . .

May health, strength, and all inward light and joy, be long continued to you, and let me remain,
Affectionately yours,
W. E. GLADSTONE.

454. *To Lord Acton.*

LONDON,
April 29, 1890.

MY DEAR ACTON,

 . . . In the matter of the Old Testament, all the little I can gather, either by reading or by reflection, tends to the strong belief that, whatever the changes of form may have been, the older books, the essential substance, has been wonderfully well preserved.

I have always had a strong conviction that the Israelites never could have carried the *pith* of their religion through the 1,000 years between Moses and the Captivity unless it had been walled in by a strong institutional system.
Ever yours,
W. E. G.

455. *To Mrs. Church.*

BRIGHTON,
April 6, 1891.

MY DEAR MRS. CHURCH,
 I have not written to you since your great bereavement, but I am now really unable to refrain from giving you the trouble of reading this letter. For I have just read through your husband's 'History of the Oxford Movement.'

To call it able, and extremely able, is to say little. It is much more than that. It is a great and a noble book : few indeed are the books to which the first epithet can be applied, and fewer still can claim, and rise to, the level of the second. It has all the delicacy, the insight into the human mind, heart, and character, which were Newman's great endowment ; but there is a pervading sense of soundness about it, which Newman, great as he was, never inspired.

In its small compass, and without the advantage of his final touches, it is a chapter of real Church History, and for the first time it supplies a really historical record of a period and a movement certainly among the most remarkable in the Christendom of the last three and a half centuries — probably more remarkable than the movement associated with the name of Port Royal, to which he is fond of comparing it ; for that has passed away and left hardly a trace behind, but this has left ineffaceable marks upon the English Church and nation. Nay, they have gone much farther, and the ulterior consequences, I admit, have been very mixed, but with these I have nothing to do — I write only of the faithful, penetrating, high-minded recorder.

Many personages, such, for example, as Froude, Hampden, Ward, have been here set in frames from which they will, I think, never be dislodged. The one case of severity in the book is the treatment of the Board of Heads. I am sorry to say it is deserved. Yet I cannot help thinking there must be something more to plead on behalf of Dr. Hawkins.

Whatever other memorials there may be, your

husband can have no higher monument than this work.

With our united and warmest good wishes,
Very sincerely yours,
W. E. GLADSTONE.

456. *To Lord Acton.*

10, DOWNING STREET,
September 19, 1892.

MY DEAR ACTON,

. . . My lecture at Oxford, planned several months ago, is to come off in October. Now that it is on paper, I could much have wished for the advantage of perusal by you. But it is not yet *verbally* quite complete: and I should not like to trust it to the post.

One or two points of literary conscience I may submit to you.

1. I have got together tolerably the great Oxford men of the Middle Age. I have difficulty in doing the like for Paris: though Budinszky's book gives the foreigners who *repaired* thither to teach or learn. I do not know if you can tell me any names — besides William of Champeaux, Abelard, Stephen Langton.

2. I have given Cambridge the credit of a trio unapproachable by Oxford for the seventeenth century — in Milton, Bacon, and Newton. Will European opinion justify placing Bacon by the side of the other two? Evidently Locke had much greater influence, but I could not *pit* him against Bacon. I should think that as philosopher Boyle came nearer Bacon.

3. I have been reading Zart. He does not even mention Butler. I think you believe that Kant does. He is honourably mentioned by Lotze, but I think only as an apologist. . . .

Ever yours,
W. E. GLADSTONE.

457. *To Lord Acton.*

HAWARDEN,
September 26, 1892.

. . . 1. I have failed to make my point clear about Oxford. I speak of *rearing* only. As to men who, apart from rearing, studied and taught, the position of Paris is overwhelming. 2. Barrow was indeed a great man. He died under fifty, and had not the chance given to blockheads like me. The world knows little of him. Cambridge had also a strong fifth in Bentley, *summus ille Bentleius* as he is, I think, classically called by German scholars. 3. In dealing with Butler, are you not dealing with his sermons? Only? To me he seems a great moral discoverer, as you say Martineau makes him. Bravo Martineau! I want to know when did Time produce a greater — perhaps so great a — teacher on the laws of moral action as between God and man? And all action (not 75 per cent., as M. Arnold says) is moral. . . .

458. *To Lord Northbourne.*

HOUSE OF COMMONS,
February 9, 1893.

MY DEAR WALTER,

Absorbed and distracted as I am at this time by the pressure of business, I cannot longer delay saying a few words on your dear father's death. It is to me, as it is to my wife, an event which reaches back so far. With it seems to totter the fabric of more than half a century's recollections, which for me began in the winter of 1838, when your mother, in her youthful beauty, was enjoying Rome as it could then be enjoyed, together with her parents. Unless memory deceives me, that winter laid the foundations of his marriage, as it did of mine, and it is united with this present death by a long, unbroken line of this warmest friendship. Even from out of the chaos of business I look back along it, and see how bright it stretches into the distance along the waste of years. If the responsibilities of a man are to be measured, in some not in considerable part at least, by the excellence of his parents, then you, my dear Walter, have them in such [abundance] as is shared by few. A long life has in my case been coupled with a wide acquaintance : but among all the friends I have known, I could not, the light of this our Christian civilization, easily point to a more happy or more normal life and death than that of your father. I feel, indeed, as if I ought not to be here and writing about him, but rather to have preceded him. Here, however, I am, and being here I feel that this honour (?) has been given you by God, that in your case the pains of privation, which I know must be sharp, are singularly set against what I may almost call a far more exceeding and abundant store of consolation which we remotely, though warmly, and you in close proximity, and almost without limit, must draw from the retrospect of his gifts, his virtues, and his graces. Peace be with him — the peace of the just, the peace of his Redeemer. And what can I wish for you and yours but the heart and the strength to follow him?

Yours, with true affection,
W. E. GLADSTONE.

459. *To the Rev. Dr. Fairbairn.*

HAWARDEN,
October 15, 1893.

... Childhood and boyhood placed me in very close connection with the Evangelicalism of those days, and very notable it was.

In one collateral point I think you give it more than it deserves. It had large religious philanthropy — *e.g.*, in missions — but little political philanthropy. The great case of Wilberforce was *almost* purely an individual case: nor was he more against slavery than Dr. Johnson. Speaking generally, I am sorry to say, the Evangelicals of that day were not abolitionists. They left that honour to the Nonconformists, most of all to the Quakers. Their Toryism obstructed them, as it does now.

Buxton, I admit, did a great work, but was, I think, hardly a Churchman. Wilberforce, on the other hand, was a warmly attached one, and of a beautiful and heavenly character.

460. *To the Rev. Stephen Gladstone.*

DOLLIS,
May 5, 1894.

... Painful indeed is the Archbishop's establishmentarian fanaticism.

Many things could I say on this latest and singular

passage in my life. I will only say one. Never did
I see more plainly the Divine handwriting. Here had
I been scheming for twenty years to get out of public
life without dishonour, and never could make any
approach to it. Then comes in the providence of
God, and arranges to set me free by means of this
cataract! from which in its turn I have good hope of
being set free in a short time; and all this has been
done, O infinite mercy, amidst universal outburst of
kindness and goodwill at the end of my long contentious life. Praise to the Highest in the height, and
in the depth be praise.

461. *To Mrs. Church.*

HAWARDEN,
December 11, 1894.

MY DEAR MRS. CHURCH,
My powers of vision are now a good deal
restricted: but I have read through, on and since
Sunday, the delightful volume which you have been
good enough to send me, and which I hope and believe
will enchain many another besides me. It surpasses
all my expectations, though these were at a high
pitch. It has, I think, only one fault — there is too
little of it — the fault opposite to that of modern
biographies in general.

There is, indeed, a consideration which ought to
restrain me from speaking much about it, and that is,
that I receive in this book at every turn so much more
than is my due. But I look back with thankfulness
on the efforts which I used to draw him towards the
centre of Church life. I think I was guided in them for
the benefit of others by a wisdom higher than my own.
Measured in *quantity*, the sum total of my knowledge
of him was always limited; and it was certainly very
small, though clear and strong, at the epoch when I
dunned him into St. Paul's. It seems that for once
a kind of divining-rod was entrusted to my hands.
The Church of England has within the last half-
century lived through the extremes of difficulty and
peril. In reading such a book as this, we see what
were the qualities which God ordained to be the
means of her deliverance.

The Preface, the paper by Canon Scott Holland, and Dr. Barrett's affectionate sketch, are in their several ways of exceptional value, though the last is but brief.

It would have been right, I think, to make mention of occasions on which, in vain, I solicited him to allow me to recommend him for a bishopric.

I do not know whether I ever named to you either of the following circumstances :

Dean Wellesley was in the habit of receiving at his house most of those who preached before the Queen at Windsor. Himself no mean judge, he told me that he placed Mr. Church (as he then was), in a spiritual sense, before *all* the others. Again, a constant reader of the *Guardian* in those days, I observed with gratitude the wonderful skill and great indulgence with which, through a series of years, it handled the tender subject of my sayings and doings. I was led to suppose Mr. M. Bernard to have been the author of these comments, and after a long continuance of them I wrote to thank him. In reply he disclaimed it, and used language which led me to suppose it was your husband to whom I was indebted.

He speaks so humbly of himself in conjunction with Cardinal Newman. Doubtless the genius of Newman has given him a throne which is all his own. But surely the Dean was by much the weightier and the wiser man.

You have been elected, dear Mrs. Church, to great privileges, and to the great sorrows which, under the Gospel, are their appropriate accompaniment. Among and even above them all, I feel sure, must ever tower the blessed recollection of your husband.

Believe me, with our affectionate good wishes,
Ever yours,
W. E. GLADSTONE.

Your dear daughter will know from this letter what my husband thinks of *her* share in this work.
Affectionately yours,
C. G.

462. *To the Rev. G. F. Hodges.*

Christmas Day, 1894.

Rev. and dear Sir,

I am much obliged by your kindness in sending me your treatise on Bishop Guest and Articles XXVIII. and XXIX., which appears to me, if I may presume to say so, to be a succinct but substantial contribution to theological history. It supplies deficiencies which must be felt by readers of the common 'Life of Guest.'

I venture, however, upon two remarks:

1. I have always been impressed with the idea that the word 'given' in Article XXVIII. is decisive on the whole matter. It entirely shuts out the confused and confusing doctrine of a mere Presence in the receiver, and it embodies the whole force of the word 'objective.' It reduces, I cannot but think, any inferences even from the title of XXIX. (if that title had authority) to a secondary position.

There is no more remarkable feature, I suppose, in the movement of the last sixty years than the firmer and larger grasp which has been obtained of Eucharistic doctrine.

2. I notice that you make a rather free use of the term 'Consubstantiation.' This seems to be meant merely as a mode of expressing a belief in the Objective Presence such as excludes Transubstantiation. But I would respectfully suggest for consideration whether it is a convenient term for the purpose; whether it is a safe term generally; and whether it is not open to the charge of attempting to define the mode of the Presence which our divines, I think often justly, boast that our Church avoids.

I remember very well that in 1845 Dr. Döllinger spoke with me on the Anglican idea, and I told him that we believe (or were bound to believe) in the Real Presence. 'Oh,' he replied, 'then you accept Consubstantiation,' which I wholly disclaimed. I may be wrong, but my idea is this: That the term 'Transubstantiation' is a term highly technical, and turning altogether upon the distinction between substance and accidents; that this intrusion of purely metaphysical matter into the domain of faith is mischievous and dangerous; and that the phrase 'Consubstantiation,' which changes the preposition, is open to the same objection.

Forgive me for offering these suggestions. I venture to add that we are busied here with the foundation of a library partly theological, that we hope it will be useful to those who desire rest with study, and that, if at any time you should desire to make use of it, all needful information will be supplied by Rev. H. Drew, now Warden, or by the Rector of Hawarden.

Yours very faithfully,
W. E. GLADSTONE.

463. *To the Rev. J. H. Bernard, D.D.*
(*Dean of St. Patrick's.*)

HAWARDEN,
November 10, 1895.

I have referred to the admirable passage in p. 21 of your sermons (for the gift of which I trust you received my thanks), and I need hardly say it has my entire concurrence. There is, I think, a way in which the 'Analogy' may have ministered to scepticism without implying any fault. I suppose the difficulties of Theistic belief to be strong and real. But he seems to state them with great force, and sets his arguments by the side of them. When this twofold representation comes before one who has been positively but vaguely instructed in Theistic doctrine, the objections have all the freshness and force of novelty, which the affirmative arguments necessarily want, and which the higher class of minds are attracted to. But by the weighty considerations you have suggested, minds of a more ordinary class who have got their belief, such as it is, without trouble, resent the trouble that Butler gives them, and punish him by superficially attaching value, which is disproportionate, to the pleas of his adversaries. I hope this may not seem fanciful.

I gather from the work of Miss Dawson that Butler has a recognized place in your University studies. But perhaps it is only on the theological side. His deposition in Oxford was a cruel act, perhaps the worst determinate result of the great anti-Newman reaction.

464. *To E. S. Purcell.*

BIARRITZ,
January 14, 1896.

DEAR MR. PURCELL,
Your biography of Manning reached me on Saturday. Formal thanks would be out of place with reference to such a book, or I would give them. My powers of reading, always slow, have in the new state of my vision become slower still. But by throwing over all else, I have perused, I think will care, the 600 pages which you give to the Anglican period. I will divide what I have to say, and my numbers 1, 2, 3, will be in inverse proportion to their importance.

1. Your range of time and subject is large, your statements of necessity almost innumerable. I find a good many errors, though *none* of a nature to impeach your general care and trustworthiness. Also the words in Italian want overhauling. I know them to be usually a source of trouble with our printers.

2. This is the challenging head. I am myself the subject of it. Pray tell me — (1) Did you ever obtain my leave to publish my letters? (2) In what way had you access to them? I have no recollection of lending them.

Next, I read with surprise Manning's statement (made first after thirty-five years?) that I would not sign the Declaration of 1850 because I 'was a Privy Councillor.' I should not have been more surprised had he written that I told him I could not sign because my name began with G. I had done stronger things than that, when I was not only Privy Councillor, but official servant of the Crown — nay, I believe Cabinet Minister. The Declaration was liable to none (in my view) interior objections. Seven out of the thirteen who signed did so without (I believe) any kind of sequel. I wish you to know that I entirely disavow and disclaim Manning's statement *as it stands*.

And here (alone) I have to ask you to insert two lines in your second or next edition : with the simple statement that I prepared and published with promptitude an elaborate argument to show that the Judicial Committee was historically unconstitutional, as an organ for the decision of ecclesiastical questions. This declaration was entitled, I think, 'A Letter to the Bishop of London on the Ecclesiastical Supremacy.' If I recollect right, while it dealt little with theology, it was a more pregnant production than the Declaration; and it went much nearer the mark. It has been repeatedly republished, and is still on sale at Murray's. I am glad to see that Sidney Herbert (a *gentleman* if ever there was one) also declined to sign. It seems to me *now* that there is something almost ludicrous in the propounding of such a congeries of statements by such persons as we were — not the more, but certainly not the less, because of being Privy Councillors.

It was a terrible time, aggravated for me by heavy cares and responsibilities of a nature quite extraneous: and far beyond all others by the illness and death of a much-loved child, with great anxieties about another. My recollections of the conversations before the Declaration are little but a mass of confusion and bewilderment. I stand only upon what I *did*. No one of us, I think, understood the actual position, not even our lawyers, until Baron Alderson printed an excellent statement on the points raised. And now I turn from this rather repulsive position of the subject; of some interest, perhaps, to me, but otherwise of little weight or moment.

3. Very different is the case when I turn to your biography and to the subject of it. The part I have read must have been for you the most critical, the most difficult, of the whole. So it (*i.e.*, the period) was for me: afterwards I had Manning's at arm's length.

Now here I have so much to say that I hardly know where to begin. Were it not from a sense of justice and duty to you, I think I should not begin at all.

You have produced, I think, by far the most extraordinary biography I ever read, and have executed a work of (I think) unparalleled difficulty with singular success. I have not been interested in it, I have been fascinated and entranced. You have maintained firmly your own principles, which I take to be Ultramontane; and yet, to the poor outlying Church of England, you have been equitable, generous, and kind. Accept, I pray you, this sincere tribute for what it is worth, however little that may be.

All my communications with you while you were writing were of a nature to make me hopeful: but you have greatly surpassed my expectations. All this I write not knowing yet what I have to encounter in the remaining 1,100 pages. Of course there may be differences and great ones; but so there are already, most of all in what you write of Dr. Döllinger — as to whom, let me say that my knowledge of him, let me say my friendship with him, dated from 1845, when (you perhaps will smile) he formed my mind on the Holy Eucharist, and gave me a good piece of my theological education.

So much for the *biography*. But I approach with fear and trembling the remaining subject, that of the biographee. Some things I can say without much apprehension. For example, I have formed the opinion that he went too fast and too far in introspection, and did himself very serious mischief by formulating the results in writing. For I do not agree with you that diaries afford the most trustworthy evidence. In them there is, I always feel, an interlocutor—namely, myself, the worst of all interlocutors.

I presume to think he was either wholly wrong, or went much too far, in garbling this evidence by excisions and lacerations. Why did he not, like that great and noble, and not less simple than great and noble, St. Augustine, write his 'Retractationes'? (This paragraph should have preceded the last.)

Further, I can even venture into the sphere of intellectual judgment. Your book even raises my estimate of Manning's talent, which was always very high. It greatly lowers my estimate of his wisdom, his power of forming a comprehensive judgment.

Here I pause with my censures. Yet one thing I must add. You have, with a manly force and frankness, threaded the labyrinth of the 'double voice,' and have offered its apology. But I fear that apology in no way covers the memorable declaration of 1848 made to me in St. James's Park.

Here I really pause. The immense gifts of his original nature and intense cultivation, his warm affections, his life-long devotion, his great share in reviving England, but above all his absolute detachment, place him on a level such that, from my plane of thought

Photo, Sir Benjamin Stone, M.P.

LYING IN STATE, WESTMINSTER HALL, MAY 26–28, 1898.

and life, I can only look at him as a man looks at the stars.

Even so, my difficulties in contemplating him are grave. On the whole I leave him, in the spiritual order where Bishop Butler leaves all the unsolved, and apparently unsolvable, problems of the natural order — to Him, namely, who ordained them; in the never-dying hope of what lies beyond the veil. You have so pierced into Manning's innermost interior that it really seems as if little more remained for disclosure in the last day and when the books are opened.

     Believe me,
       Sincerely yours,
         W. E. GLADSTONE.

APPENDIX

THE contents of this Appendix are taken from an immense mass of notes and memoranda extending over the greater part of Mr. Gladstone's career. As indications of the direction of his thoughts, they are at least as valuable as his letters. I have arranged the extracts in an order roughly corresponding to that of the preceding chapters.

I. — CHURCH AND STATE

No. 1 is an account of a conversation with Lord Ashley in 1837. If Lord Shaftesbury kept any similar record of this conversation, he may in after-years have looked back to it as giving the first hint of the coming severance between Mr. Gladstone and himself. Though they were both devoted supporters of religious establishments, Mr. Gladstone's Parliamentary instinct was already opening his eyes to the difficulty of defending them in the House of Commons on the high theological ground taken by his friend.

The next four papers refer to the Reformation Settlement, taking that term as applying to the whole process of change between 1532 and 1666. The most interesting is the careful and sympathetic study of Queen Elizabeth, whose ecclesiastical policy always had a special attraction for Mr. Gladstone.

No. 6 appeared originally in the *North American Review*

for December, 1889, and was afterwards reprinted as a leaflet for private circulation. It is given here as the latest and fullest statement of Mr. Gladstone's views on divorce.

No. 7 is a list of Mr. Gladstone's seventeen nominations to the Episcopate.

1. CONVERSATION WITH LORD ASHLEY.

(March 17, 1837.)

Yesterday I had the following conversation with Ashley on the subject of my speech delivered the night before.* It was in the Carlton Club; he seated himself opposite (but close) to me. I spoke of the Division, and regretted that he had been unable to speak. He said: 'Now, I will tell you what, Gladstone, you made an able speech, but you disappointed me. I expected that you would have taken up the question on higher grounds; but you did not, and I was much grieved at it.' I expressed in the first place my great obligation to him for this truly friendly conduct; and I begged him to particularize wherein lay the defects which had given him pain. He replied: 'This measure cuts up by the roots all our national homage to God, which is the meaning of a Church Establishment. If it be passed, we separate ourselves as a nation from Him. It is true you spoke about the principle of a National Church, and alluded to the spiritual destitution of the country, but you did it in the same cold manner as——. What could be more flat and void of feeling than his description of that destitution? Now you have many gifts and advantages, and you may become a considerable man in this country, and one of God's most efficient instruments; and I am sure you had it in your heart to say more than you did say in last night's debate, and so I said when conversing on the subject with several others as we walked home. You did not give that high tone to your speech which I had expected from you; I am sure you will excuse my saying it.

'Then, as to your quotation from Polybius, I must say I

---

* March 15, 1837, in support of Church rates.

thought it altogether misapplied. The notion of the heathen gods as producing the same result with the revealed Gospel! I will tell you the remark my wife made upon it, and I thought it a very sensible one. She said: "Why, if that religion could have produced such effects, they will naturally ask where was the need of Christianity." It is true that Polybius writes as you quoted him, but his statement is not true, and if you examine the Roman character you will find it fraudulent, selfish, and hard-hearted, and their policy towards other nations the most grasping and oppressive on the face of the earth.'

I have here condensed what he said; for I could not faithfully portray, and I was unwilling to caricature by an attempt at detail, that warm and noble eloquence of feeling with which he spoke of those highest and deepest truths which are at the bottom of his whole life and conduct; and I proceed to my own reply.

'As regards the Polybius,' I said, 'I am confident it was merely the want of a fuller explanation which has caused your present impressions, and that upon your own principles, with which I concur, I could show that I was not fundamentally wrong. My meaning was this: On looking at the Roman institutions, I find they had a principle of vigour and of permanence which belonged to no other in those times; and that the phenomena presented by them require the assignment of a gigantic cause which alone is adequate. Then I find the man who, of all writers of the period, most united philosophy with practical habits, discovers that cause in the extraordinary degree to which that religion, though false, was brought home to the mass of the people and interwoven with all public concerns. I grant you that the Romans were fraudulent, selfish, and hard-hearted; but I say, compare the individual character of the Roman with that of the Athenian, or other ancients in general, and you will find him less fraudulent, less selfish, and less hard-hearted than they — I meant in early times. Now, I say this is fairly ascribable to the influence of their religion, which, blind, false, and degraded as it was, had nevertheless this efficacy, that it tended to impress his mind with the idea of a power beyond himself, and to carry his desires beyond himself, concentrating them upon the glory of the state. This I do not call a right principle, but it is better than the principle of mere self-worship; and thus we show not only, like Bishop Warburton and others, that the principle of religion was found by lawgivers to be the only one capable of binding together social institutions, but that in the case where those institutions were of the most effective structure, we find coexisting with that fact an extraordinary degree of attention to religion. Then comes the argument *a fortiori* for the influence and use of revealed truth. I admit my reference to it was brief and obscure ——'

A.: 'Yes, your quotation was looked upon as the end of your speech, and immediately after it they began to talk ——'

G.: 'But I felt I had been unconscionably long. And, further, I feel this: it is comparatively easy to speak in the House of Commons on matters merely secular, but as you ascend higher into the region of principles, the work of expressing what you feel in the face of a popular assembly becomes incomparably more delicate and difficult. So much for Polybius. Now, my dear Ashley, for the remainder of what you have said, I concur in every sentiment; I bow entirely to your animadversion; I did desire, and intend, to state your own very words that the plan went "to rob God of His honour and the poor of their right"— but it was with this as with many of my best intentions and desires. I am striving to learn how to speak, but I have not yet acquired the effective use of memory in the face of such an audience, nor my self-possession so as to express with any fulness what I feel. The words wholly escaped me. In every speech I have ever made, and more in proportion as the subject was a lofty one, I have painfully had to feel how entirely I have failed of realizing even my own conception of the subject, and much less the subject as it really is. I therefore only hope that this fault may hereafter be less weighty. I admit its existence to the full.

'But pray tell me whether you had any affirmative objections to the speech; whether you thought that in what I *did* say there was anything of untruth or of unworthy compromise?'

He assured me, nothing of the kind. 'Then I trust you are satisfied with my avowal of the want, which I cannot too much lament.' He expressed himself quite so. Mr. Goulburn came up while we were speaking about Polybius; praised that part of the speech which described the vacillation of ministers, and objected to the citation. I thanked both very heartily; and, admitting the want of elucidation, said I thought the ground-work of the idea in my mind came from St. Augustine's 'De Civitate Dei'— at least that it was that book would *permit* me to think and say. Mr. Goulburn went away. Ashley and I sat writing for a little. When I had concluded, I rose, and, to attract his attention, said 'Good-day.' I shook him warmly by the hand, as the simplest way of offering my thanks to this true and high-minded friend, and he replied, 'God bless you.' May blessing be upon him. Now what a character was this — he would not join in the tones of compliment and congratulation without showing me how sadly I had fallen short of my duty. Of what value is such a friend! I felt with him in all that he said; and yet, had he not said it, that feeling would have fallen asleep in my mind, I should have indolently acquiesced in the less courageous sentiments of others, and should have lost the advantage of remembering hereafter the previous deficiency, and of being thereby incited to use every effort for the purpose of supplying it. Would that such were the acknowledged law of friendship, and its universal practice!

He spoke of himself in depreciating terms; of his having omitted to acquire the power and practice of speaking, and of its being now too late. I entirely demurred to this low estimate; I have never heard him speak, except with latent clearness and general effect. He spoke of retiring from Parliament. I replied: 'God forbid!— unless you go thence to some still more extensive sphere of usefulness.' I had in my mind, whether wrongly or not, the desirableness of his appointment to some important government abroad. Some effort must be made for religion in our colonies.

2. FACTORS IN THE ENGLISH REFORMATION.

(Undated.)

There were, then, I apprehend, originally three main elements or factors in the English Reformation.

The first of these was the old national sentiment of resistance to foreign domination, which had long found its most frequent provocation in the ambition and rapacity of the Roman See. Of this sentiment Henry VIII. made himself the exponent, and directed all its force to the purpose of strengthening the Crown against the Papacy. The closest union between the Crown and the National Church was one obvious method of attaining this end. The formation of such union might have been difficult if the idea of separate and cross interests between the parties had as yet been raised. But in the struggles of Church and State before the Reformation, whether it were Dunstan, or Becket, or Anselm, the champion of the Church always betook himself to the Papal Chair, and was regarded as fighting the battle of that Chair. The entire National Church had often been seen contending against the Pope and resisting his extortion; it had never been so seen in conflict with the Crown, but only some member or members of it, and then always in alliance with Rome. Thus it appears that Henry had the materials of resistance ready made for his use; and that the traditions of the country had predisposed the Church in a manner favourable to the civil power.

The second of these elements was, a growing inclination on the part of enlightened Churchmen towards reform. Only one generation before this sentiment had had a noble representative in Savonarola. It had been conspicuous in Dean Colet; it had moved Bishop Fox to found the College of Corpus Christi at Oxford, under the impression that if he established a religious house it could not stand; it had prepared the sagacious Gardiner and the pious Tunstall for no inconsiderable changes, and had brought them into the arena to contend against the Papal Supremacy before the sovereign lifted a finger for the purpose. It is needless to relate how many illustrious men of the Continent were under similar impressions, and were disposed to a thorough reform of the Church which should yet be a reform conducted upon ancient and canonical principles. To this class of minds I believe that Cranmer, Ridley and Parker essentially belonged. It is true that this latter divided from those first mentioned or the survivors of them. But this is the fate, almost universally, of middle parties in times of violent change. It is in the main by two great armies of opinion or force as the case may be that at such periods the destinies of mankind are brought to their decisive issues; and it rarely happens that the right and the wrong of these great arbitraments are so clearly divided, or remain so steadily with the same side from first to last, as not to leave room for differences of opinion among those who with general but not uniform concurrence occupy the intermediate ground. Thus under Charles I. we at first find Hyde and Falkland united in opposition to the Court, we then perceive them on adverse sides, and at last they are reunited in support of the Crown. So Laud, without doubt, had he lived in Parker's time, would have gone to a given point with the Reformers: Parker had he lived in Laud's would have made a firm stand against the Puritans. We must estimate men not only in their relation to the circumstances and parties of their own time, but likewise in the relation of those circumstances and parties to the circumstances and parties of other periods.

This spirit of enlightened and circumspect reform placed between opposite dangers each of the most fearful kind necessarily when developed in action presented to the common view some appearances of indecision: first because such is its besetting infirmity or vice, and secondly because its very virtue is sure to be mistaken in times of crisis and of overpowering passion.

Those who were governed by it were numerically weak. Their contest really was with the more violent of both parties. In the Church of Rome it is too plain that they were obliged to succumb both at the Papal Court, in the Council of Trent, and among the nations on that side. In the Protestant countries generally, they could scarcely be said to make head. In Scotland there is not a vestige of them, at least among the Reformers. In England only they acquired a powerful and ultimately a prevailing and determining influence over the fortunes of the Church. They attached themselves to the civil power, and made concessions to it, which did their work for their day, although that day has now gone by, and we must now, as they did, endeavour to make the best provision for the future of which the time and our materials admit. Although few they had knowledge and the gift of governing; they were also men of pure and Christian character if not of the loftiest strain of piety. They sat at the helm, and a little strength of theirs swayed the violent and brute forces that tossed and drove the vessel, and turned them to account.

The third powerful element of the Reformatory movement in England was that known by the name of Lollardism, which afterwards formed the basis of Puritanism in all its forms. In its ultimate developments this spirit was relatively to the ecclesiastical order what the spirit of Wat Tyler and Jack Cade was relatively to the temporal authority: a spirit originally roused by oppression and abuse to a righteous indignation, then carried by it beyond self-control, then associating with itself all the elements of turbulence and passion, and finally acquiring a bent and tendency utterly destructive of all positive religion. Such developments, it is needless to say, are commonly gradual and in their details far from uniform. It would be absurd to combine the name of Lord Cobham with such ideas as these; but in Wicliffe we may easily discern the groundwork of these destructive tendencies, the want of the discriminating mind and the strong sense of the positive truth bound up in the subsisting Christian institutions which are essential to the true reformer in religion and which separates between him and the instigator or tool of movements having their goal in unbelief.

3. THE THREE ANGLICAN SETTLEMENTS.

(January 25, 1883.)

In the period of transition from the Roman obedience to the Anglican system, there were three distinct settlements or resettlements of the affairs of the Church and the religion of the country.

The first was in the reigns of Henry VIII. and Edward VI. The second under Elizabeth.

The third under Charles II.

The two intervals between them were themselves revolutionary: the first undoing the whole work of Henry VIII. and Edward VI., except that it could not replace the destroyed ecclesiastical establishments; the second exhibiting the triumph of Puritanism wrought out through civil war.

Of the three settlements, the first covers by far the largest arc in the wheel of ecclesiastical revolution. In its earliest portion it was marked by violence, rapacity, servility, the establishment of State power over religion, notwithstanding some theoretical reserves, in the harshest and most sweeping fashion, and extreme peril in the civil sphere, even to the elementary principles of that freedom which had distinguished England under the Plantagenets.

It was, however, in its first division, under the sceptre of Henry VIII., eminently national as to its main religious outline, which alone, probably, the nation apprehended. It embraced the correction of grossly superstitious abuses, the extrusion of the Pope as a troublesome and mischievous alien from the active exercise of jurisdiction within the realm, the permission, by no means unrestricted, of access to the Scriptures as a means of combating both Papalism and priestcraft, and a firm adhesion to the substance of doctrine and tenet as these had been received.

Under Edward VI. all the restraining forces that had slackened, and occasionally, even, for a time reversed, the movement were withdrawn; the greed of unscrupulous governors and the fluctuating instability of the mind of Cranmer, rendered only more dangerous by his great talents, placed both ecclesiastical and civil authority on the side of unlimited innovation. Viewing the distance of the second Prayer-Book from the first, we may speculate with curious wonder on the question, What would have been the distance between the second and the third? But that there would have been a third, the men continuing in their places who made the second, there can hardly be a doubt.

And apart from all speculation, it may be allowed that the living system of the Church, at the end of the reign of Edward VI., required only the continued operation of the prevailing policy to be simply a wreck. If the walls and gates of the city on a hill remained, there was no disciplined garrison to man and to defend them.

The year 1553 exhibited in England the nadir of the Church system. The year 1661 notes the normal elevation at which the returning tide arrived. As a constitutional and political scheme, it remains in substance till the present day.

The two great agents of this reaction were Elizabeth and Laud. To neither of them are we indebted for any portion of our civil freedom. But they were, humanly speaking, the creators in one sense of Anglicanism : the two great agents, without any rival or even any second, by whom, in the world of action, it became a reality, and established itself as one, and not the least weighty and significant, of the standing, immovable facts of Christendom.

The ecclesiastical activity of Laud is on the surface of history, and all that is censurable in it has been abundantly censured, while it still awaits that meed of praise to which, from the Anglican point of view, it is thoroughly entitled.

But the activity of Elizabeth was many-sided, and the dazzling brilliancy of her position as the Island Queen cast her ecclesiastical operations and policy into the shade.

She, too, has yet to receive the honour due to her for steadily refusing to allow the Thirty-nine Articles, the great polemical document of the English Reformation, to assume the rigid form of law until the violent and rash proceedings of the Pope against her throne and person compelled her to let her subjects close their serried ranks as against a foe utterly implacable.

But there is one other point of view from which the conduct of the great Queen has to be regarded in its relation to religion.

Taking, as she could not but take, the year 1553 for her

starting-point, she found the Church system lying in ruins around her; but it has not been sufficiently observed how many of its stones she picked from the ground and put together, so that the fabric rose again from the ground and became once more a place of shelter and of habitation.

(1) The title of Supreme Head, which, as understood under Edward VI., must have been speedily fatal to Church life was abandoned, and that of Supreme Governor, which fairly exhibits the normal relation of the Crown to a Church nationally established, was substituted for it.

(2) A virtual sovereignty in the Church, first delegated by Henry VIII. to a single layman, and after his fall exercised by a Council, which under Edward VI. was almost wholly lay, and was from being purely civil in glaring contradiction to the great Preamble of 1532, was severed from the machinery of civil government, and exercised (with much restraint and only as a penal power) through a High Commission essentially ecclesiastical.

(3) The Commissions which were taken out by Bishops under Harry and his son were abandoned under Elizabeth.

(4) The principle of election for Bishops was revived by the restoration of the *congé d'élire*, in lieu of the simple nomination enacted under Edward VI.

(5) The Convocation again came to be summoned by writ of the Archbishop, instead of meeting simply under the order of the Crown, as in the time of Edward VI.

(6) The demand of that body in 1547 to receive the royal permission to proceed to business, and to share in the settlement of doctrine and worship, had been unceremoniously set aside, but the Elizabethan Convocation settled the Thirty-nine Articles as they stood until they became the subject of a statute.

(7) When that period arrived, the Queen, by a stretch of power, inserted in Article XX. what is, perhaps, the most pregnant clause they contain, '(The Church) hath authority in controversies of faith.' As to the means, they were no doubt irregular, nor is it needful to hold the Act as valid, but it expressed the true mind of the Church, and became perfectly regular under the final settlement at the Restoration.

(8) The external regulation of worship reposed in her hands by statute was subject to ecclesiastical concurrence, and, if exceptional in form, was intended and was used in the sense of the Church.

(9) In the statutory definition of new heresy, the judgment of the Church was included as a necessary condition.

(10) According to the contention of Palmer, the act of the reign most violent in appearance — namely, the deposition of the Marian Bishops — was ecclesiastically valid, inasmuch as they had extruded from the sees persons regularly possessed of them without canonical condemnation, *or* refused an Oath of Supremacy founded on a valid act of the English Church, and not repealed by lawful authority.

NOTE. — I do not here inquire what warrant or apology may be shown for the proceedings under Henry so far as the element of violence is concerned. There may have been a mass of superstitious practice, so welded together by use and traditional encouragement that it could not be corrected in detail, and could only be touched with effect like an igneous rock by a blast as of gunpowder.

4. FRAGMENT ON QUEEN ELIZABETH.

(Undated.)

The experience of my life has impressed me with the belief that, of all the classes of human characters (and they are many), politicians present to us those which are the most complex. I use the phrase as the most comprehensive which the subject supplies, and as including alike Sovereigns, Ministers, popular leaders, all in short who are neither figureheads nor clerks, but who wield wholesale power or influence over the destinies of men as they are associated in civil life. Of this most complex class, if the problem were to name the most complex personality, it might not be easy at a venture to fix upon a likelier candidate for the place than the great Queen Elizabeth. Perhaps the most remarkable in the long line of English Sovereigns, she attracts and she repels. She does both in an uncommon, an abnormal degree. It must, perhaps, be admitted that in the main she attracts by what she did, and repels by what she was. She is, I think, still among

> 'Th' inheritors of unfulfilled renown'

in this respect, that the depths of her character have not yet been so thoroughly sounded as to explain by what amalgam its strange and staggering contrasts were cemented into a personal unity. It seems plain that she inherited in a marked manner both from her father and her mother, and that the drastic experience of her childhood and her youth, which has been set forth in the instructive work of M. Wiesener,* may go some way to explain how the sources of feeling in her heart were dried, and the powers of her mind schooled into a persistent energy which made them equal through her long reign to all demands in a state of things as complex as any known to history.

I am not about to attempt what I have described as the still unaccomplished work of dealing with her character, a work which is far beyond me. But her actions, apart from her character, have contributed largely towards making the people of England what they are—in the phrase (I think) of Cardinal Wiseman, 'an imperial race.' I make no apology for treating those actions as her own, and not as done in her name by the great, able, and powerful statesman with whom it was among her greatest merits that, more than any other Sovereign, she was surrounded. And I proceed to deal briefly with a department of her policy which, as it appears to me, has not yet received sufficient attention, and which, unless I am mistaken, is strongly marked with her individuality. I mean her policy with respect to the Church.

And here I note a difference between the ecclesiastical and the civil order. In the State she had great men for her servants. Her father, Henry VIII., had lived among great prelates. Not to reckon the reforming Bishops, he had known Wolsey, Fisher, Warham, Tunstall, who taken together make an illustrious generation. The Elizabethan Prelates, with the exception of Parker, who may have been a Burleigh on a smaller scale, are not men of more than

* 'La Jeunesse d'Élisabeth.'

moderate dimensions. Though a few were men of learning, the strange lapse into ultra-Calvinism in the Lambeth articles does not allow a very high estimate of their mental calibre; and many of them were in religious accord more with the Puritans whom they had to put down than with the ecclesiastical system which their office bound them to administer. Heath, the deprived Archbishop of York, had led the Parliamentary opposition to the Elizabethan statutes. But the Queen used to visit him after his deprivation. Probably her great intellect kept her in sympathy with an able as well as an upright man.

In one sense Queen Elizabeth may be termed a survival. She was a reformer rather after the pattern of the reign of her father than of the Edwardian period, when the direction of the Church of England was given over into the hands of foreigners; when Lutheran, Calvinist, and Zwinglian contended among themselves for the possession of this fair portion of the vineyard; and when the Lutheran influence, once powerful, fell into the background as the type of an insufficient and still semi-Popish Reformation. It is said, and it seems probable, that a third form of Prayer-Book was in preparation, to replace the second, when the King died. It is plain that these years do not represent the deliberate adoption of a defined position, or the preparation of a stationary camp for defence; but a ship on the bosom of the stream, with no fixed destination as to moorings.

The performances of this period, and still more its promise and its potency, drove back into the Roman party in a mass men of the colour of Tunstall and of Gardiner, who represented in the main the sentiment of nationalism dominant in the reign of Henry VIII. The Queen [Mary] was thus emboldened to destroy the work of her father not less than of her brother, and made the first year and a half of her reign a deliberate conspiracy against the nation. England had hardly had a taste of the Prayer-Book of 1552, and was not for the most part intolerant of the older worship, but had heartily concurred in the abolition of the 'usurped jurisdiction,' and does not seem to have been scandalized at the petition in the Litany to be delivered 'from the tyranny of the Bishop of

Rome, and all his detestable enormities.' The Protestant sentiment was suppressed, but in its suppression was immensely sharpened by the violent persecution which broke out in full force.

5. FRAGMENT ON THE RESTORATION SETTLEMENT.

(Undated.)

(1) As the authoritative basis of the Catholic Faith was determined, after a century and a half of controversy, by the four first Œcumenical Councils and the reception of them in the Church at large, so, after a period of nearly the same length, the authoritative basis of the English National Reformation was determined by the Church and State after the Restoration in a canonical manner.

(2) The succession of Bishops having been carried without breach of continuity from pre-Reformation times through the reigns of Henry VIII. and his successors, the other transactions of those reigns, however interesting and important in themselves, are not essential to, and do not form any part of, this final and authoritative settlement.

(3) In the conditions of this settlement, as they are set forth in the Prayer-Book and the Articles, there are, both by way of omission and of commission, particulars which vary both in the region of theological opinion and in that of practice, from the current doctrine and discipline of the Latin Church, and in a lesser degree from those of the Churches of the East; but there is no such variation (*a*) in any matter regarded by the National Church of England as *de fide*, nor (*b*) in any matter of doctrine determined by any Œcumenical Council, nor (*c*) has the Church of England anywhere claimed for itself a final authority in the interpretation of Scripture, or of historical tradition, superior or equal to that of the Church of God at large, to which the promises are made.

(4) The Church of England then exercised an authority which was competent in its sphere, to make arrangements adequate to the emergencies of a divided Christendom, but which in principle were provisional and not absolute; and her

action as a Reformed Catholic Church is attested by these circumstances :

(*a*) That she teaches the faith of the Creeds under the same secondary conditions of tenet and practice as were adopted by her in the sixteenth and seventeenth centuries, without abatement or corruption under the testing experience of three centuries and a half.

(*b*) That in this character she has accepted, and humanly speaking fulfils, her mission to the English-speaking race throughout the world.

(*c*) That she rears elect souls within her to a standard not inferior in Christian attainment to that of any other Christian Church at this day, so far as it is given to the human eye to perceive.

(*d*) That, if separations have grown up around her, her situation in this respect, relatively to those of the English tongue, is no worse than that of the Latin Church relatively (and this is the analogous case) to the Christian world.

6. THE QUESTION OF DIVORCE.

REPLIES TO THE FOLLOWING QUESTIONS.

(1889.)

(1) *Do you believe in the principle of divorce under any circumstances?*

(2) *Ought divorced people to be allowed to marry under any circumstances?*

(3) *What is the effect of divorce on the integrity of the family?*

(4) *Does the absolute prohibition of divorce where it exists contribute to the moral purity of society?*

I undertake, though not without misgiving, to offer answers to your four questions. For I incline to think that the future of America is of greater importance to Christendom at large than that of any other country ; that that future, in its highest features, vitally depends upon the incidence of marriage ; and that no country has ever been so directly challenged as America now is to choose its course definitively with reference to one, if not more than one, of the very highest of those incidents.

The solidity and health of the social body depend upon the soundness of its unit. That unit is the family; and the hinge of the family to is be found in the great and profound institution of marriage. It might be too much to say that a good system of marriage law, and of the practice appertaining to it, of itself insures the well-being of a community. But I cannot doubt that the converse is true; and that, if the relations of husband and wife are wrongly comprehended in what most belongs to them, either as to law or as to conduct, no nation can rise to the fulfilment of the higher destinies of man. There is a worm in the gourd of the public prosperity; and it must wither away.

(1) On the first of the four questions I have to observe that the word divorce appears to be used in three different senses. First, it is popularly applied to cases of nullity, as in the world-famous suit of Henry VIII. This sense has only to be named in order to be set aside, since the finding of nullity simply means that, in the particular case, no contract of marriage has ever been made.

The second sense is that which is legally known, in canonical language, as divorce *a mensâ et toro* — from board and bed — and which is termed in the English statute of 1857 judicial separation. The word is employed apparently in this sense by our Authorized Version of the Bible (Matt. v. 32: 'Whosoever shall put away his wife, saving for the cause of fornication, causeth her to commit adultery: and whosoever shall marry her that is divorced committeth adultery'). The Revised Version substitutes the phrase 'put away.' The question now before me appears to speak of a severance which does not annul the contract of marriage, nor release the parties from its obligations, but which conditionally, and for certain grave causes, suspends their operation in vital particulars. I am not prepared to question in any manner the concession which the law of the Church, apparently with the direct authority of St. Paul (1 Cor. vii. 10: 'Unto the married I command, yet not I, but the Lord, Let not the wife depart from her husband'), makes in this respect to the necessities and the infirmities of human nature.

(2) The second question deals with what may be called

divorce proper. It resolves itself into the lawfulness or unlawfulness of remarriage, and the answer appears to me to be that remarriage is not admissible under any circumstances or conditions whatsoever.

Not that the difficulties arising from incongruous marriage are to be either denied or extenuated. They are insoluble. But the remedy is worse than the disease.

These sweeping statements ought, I am aware, to be supported by reasoning in detail; which space does not permit, and which I am not qualified adequately to supply. But it seems to me that such reasoning might fall under the following heads :

That marriage is essentially a contract for life, and only expires when life itself expires.

That Christian marriage involves a vow before God.

That no authority has been given to the Christian Church to cancel such a vow.

That it lies beyond the province of the civil legislature, which, from the necessity of things, has a *veto* within the limits of reason upon the making of it, but has no competency to annul it when once made.

That according to the laws of just interpretation remarriage is forbidden by the text of Holy Scripture.

[I would here observe :

(*a*) That the declarations of the Gospel of St. Mark (x. 4 : 'Moses suffered to write a bill of divorcement, and to put her away. And Jesus answered and said unto them, For the hardness of your heart he wrote you this precept. But from the beginning of the creation God made them male and female. For this cause shall a man leave his father and mother, and cleave to his wife ; and they twain shall be one flesh : so then they are no more twain, but one flesh. What therefore God hath joined together, let not man put asunder. And in the house His disciples asked Him again of the same matter. And He said unto them, Whosoever shall put away his wife, and marry another, committeth adultery against her. And if a woman shall put away her husband, and be married to another, she committeth adultery') ; and St. Luke (xvi. 18 : 'Whosoever putteth away his wife, and marrieth another committeth adultery : and whosoever marrieth her that is put away from her husband committeth adultery'); and of St. Paul (1 Cor. vii. 10) make no exception whatever.

(*b*) That the language of St. Matthew prohibits absolutely the remarriage of a woman divorced or put away (*apolelumenēn*, not *tēn apolelumenēn*).

(*c*) That the reservation found in St. Matthew only is reasonably to be referred to the special law of Moses, or what is here termed *porneia*.]

That, although private opinions have not been uniform even in the West, the law of the Latin Church, and also of the Anglican Church, from time immemorial, allows of no remarriage.

[Divorce with liberty to remarry was included in the *Reformatio Legum Ecclesiasticarum* under Edward VI.; but that code never received sanction. In all likelihood it was disapproved by Queen Elizabeth and her advisers.]

That divorce proper, without limitation, essentially and from the time of contraction onwards, alters the character of marriage, and substitutes a relation different in ground and nature.

That divorce with limitation rests upon no clear ground, either of principle or of authority.

[In England it was urged, on behalf of the Bill of 1857, that adultery broke the marriage bond *ipso facto*. Yet when the adultery is of both the parties, divorce cannot be given ! Again, it is said that the innocent party may remarry. But (1) this is a distinction unknown to Scripture and to history, and (2) this innocent party, who is commonly the husband, is in many cases the more guilty of the two.]

That divorce does not appear to have accompanied primitive marriage. In Scripture we hear nothing of it before Moses. Among the Homeric Achaians it clearly did not exist. It marks degeneracy and the increasing sway of passion.

(3) While divorce of any kind impairs the integrity of the family, divorce with remarriage destroys it root and branch. The parental and the conjugal relations are 'joined together' by the hand of the Almighty no less than the persons united

by the marriage tie to one another. Marriage contemplates not only an absolute identity of interest and affections, but also the creation of new, joint, and independent obligations, stretching into the future and limited only by the stroke of death. These obligations where divorce proper is in force lose all community, and the obedience reciprocal to them is dislocated and destroyed.

(4) I do not venture to give an answer to this question, except within the sphere of my own observations and experience, and in relation to matters properly so cognizable. I have spent nearly sixty years at the centre of British life. Both before and from the beginning of that period absolute divorces were in England abusively obtainable, at very heavy cost, by private Acts of Parliament; but they were so rare (perhaps about two in a year) that they did not affect the public tone, and for the English people marriage was virtually a contract indissoluble by law. In the year 1857 the English Divorce Act was passed, for England only. Unquestionably, since that time, the standard of conjugal morality has perceptibly declined among the higher classes of this country, and scandals in respect to it have become more frequent. The decline, as a fact, I know to be recognized by persons of social experience and insight who in no way share my abstract opinions on divorce. Personally, I believe it to be due in part to this great innovation in our marriage laws; but in part only, for other disintegrating causes have been at work. The mystery of marriage is, I admit, too profound for our comprehension; and it seems now to be too exacting for our faith.

The number of divorces *a vinculo* granted by the civil court is, however, still small in comparison with that presented by the returns from some other countries.

7. EPISCOPAL APPOINTMENTS.

(1) Archbishop Benson owed his elevation to the Episcopal Bench to Lord Beaconsfield, and was promoted to the Archiepiscopal See of Canterbury by Mr. Gladstone.

Archbishop Thomson was raised to the Bench and promoted to York by Lord Palmerston.

(2) The Bishops.

Lord Palmerston	Lord Derby	Lord Beaconsfield	Mr. Gladstone
1. Pelham (Norwich). 2. Philpott (Worcester). 3. Ellicott (Gloucester). 4. Harold Browne (Ely, translated by Mr. Gladstone to Winchester).	1. Campbell (Bangor). 2. Claughton (Rochester, afterwards St. Albans).	1. Lightfoot (Durham). 2. Atlay (Hereford). 3. Magee (Peterborough). 4. Jones (St. David's). 5. Thorold (Rochester). 6. Maclagan (Lichfield). 7. Ryle (Liverpool).	1. Temple (Exeter, and London). 2. Moberly (Salisbury). 3. Goodwin (Carlisle). 4. Hervey (Bath and Wells). 5. Mackarness (Oxford). 6. Fraser (Manchester). 7. Durnford (Chichester). 8. Hughes (St. Asaph). 9. Woodford (Ely). 10. Wilberforce (Newcastle). 11. Lewis (Llandaff). 12. Wilkinson (Truro). 13. Stubbs (Chester). 14. Ridding (Southwell). 15. Carpenter (Ripon). 16. King (Lincoln). 17. Bickersteth (Exeter).

I. — THE OXFORD MOVEMENT

THE Oxford Movement supplies but four papers. The first is only a fragment of what seems to have been meant to be a longer study of the nature of the Episcopal Commission.

The second and third deal with the Thirty-nine Articles, with an interval of forty-six years between them. The earlier in date is really a softened version of Newman's famous tract; the later begins as though the writer had intended to go over the same ground in the light of further knowledge, but it soon becomes merely a damaging criticism of a single Article — the Thirteenth, or rather of its title.

The resolutions embodying Mr. Gladstone's suggested substitute for the Public Worship Regulation Bill are reprinted to explain the references to them in vol. i., pp. 388–391.

1. CHURCH GOVERNMENT — GENERAL.

(Undated.)

Among the mass of ideas vaguely afloat in the Christian world there is no more shallow misconception, and perhaps there are few more widely entertained, than the belief that the question between the ancient constitution of the Church and the various forms which have prevailed in the greater part of the Reformed communities since the sixteenth century is a question of Church Government. It is analogous in this view to the controversy between our monarchical, aristocratic and democratic forms of government in the civil order.

FUNERAL PROCESSION FROM WESTMINSTER HALL TO THE ABBEY,
MAY 28, 1898.

Now it cannot be said that the question is wholly detached from that between the respective forms of civil government, because this ancient and once uniform system is essentially based on the concentration of principal power in single hands. This statement does not fully exhibit the essence of the case which turns upon our principal power — the power of ordination — by which the Church is supplied with a succession of persons formally entitled to administer her highest offices. It is only through the exercise of this power that the Church has any permanent constitution at all. The highest ministering functions are thus confined within certain limits. If they were promiscuously given by each individual at his own option, this would not be so much a constitution as a chaos.

The constitution of the National Church of Denmark is episcopal, but, be this good or bad as an internal arrangement, no one supposes that it makes the smallest essential difference between that Church and the sister Lutheran Churches in Germany.

The constitution of the Latin Church, on the other hand, is stringently monarchical, especially from the time of the Vatican Council; but neither the Orthodox Church of the East, nor the other Eastern Churches, nor the Anglican Church, are in any sense monarchial, except as to their Diocesan constitution. As bodies they recognize some combined authority which unites the Diocesan Churches together, and places them under an authority wielded by many.

The question is one for which as to its essence we can derive no analogy from the case of civil government. The civil governor leaves his office vacant by death or otherwise, and it is refilled according to the conditions of the particular constitution, but he has nothing to do with the designation of his successor. Whereas, in an Episcopal Church of the ancient form, the authority of all the present Bishops is derived by express commission from those who preceded them, and the authority of those who are to follow them will be derived in the same formal manner from the present Bishops. And the chain of διοδάχαι mounts farther upwards from century to century. It is traceable in the British Sees, for instance, up to very early dates, commonly giving the first foundation of the See. But much more is asserted or presumed. The Bishop who was the first in each See came there by express commission from the Bishop of some other See, and it is held that this method of historical succession began with, and has been regularly continued from, the Apostles. They, it is plain, did not invent the commission, but received it from our Lord Himself, who was pleased to incorporate it in the Baptismal Charter at the first foundation of the Church. It had been so under the old dispensation. The question between Moses and Aaron on the one side, and Korah, Dathan, and Abiram on the other, was not whether the people of God should be governed by one or three, or any given number, but whether they should be governed by men whom God had given charged with an express commission to govern them. Even in the case of the prophets, they allege as their authority for prophesying not the mere action of the private spirit, however earnest and sincere, but a palpable order, an intelligible message from the Most High, analogous perhaps to that internal but well-defined operation by which St. Paul was enabled to distinguish between the commands of the Holy Spirit, which he was to deliver, and the recommendations which he thought it fit in certain cases to offer on his own account. 'To the rest speak I, not the Lord.' And this Apostle has laid down the principle in the broadest manner which requires an external commission capable of being tested like any other matter of fact as necessary in order to the full and legitimate appointment of the preacher of the Gospel. 'How shall they hear without a preacher? And how shall they preach except they be sent?'

The object here in view is not to establish the fact of this historical devolution of the ministerial charge, but merely to point out that this is the great — might we not say the sole — matter at issue in the argument as to what is necessary for the legitimate constitution of the Church. To place this question in the fullest and clearest light, let me refer to the statement of St. Jerome respecting the Church of Alexandria, where, as he states, it had been the custom of the presbyters to select and empower their own Bishop.

If we assume that St. Jerome was historically correct, the meaning of this would be that the Alexandrian presbytery had received from those above them and before them an authority so to act. Otherwise we should place him in contradiction with St. Paul, for if a man may not preach with authority except under a commission, how could he govern; how, above all, could he constitute other governing authorities by delegation except under such a commission? If it can be shown that there exists anywhere a duly ordained presbytery, which has through an historic channel been empowered to appoint its own Bishop, and to vest in him the powers of consecrating and ordaining, the acts of such a presbytery would have to be acknowledged as having their base in the Apostolic succession, and then, indeed, the question of the distribution of Church power in Alexandria might have come to be, what no such question now is, a question of Church Government.

But there remains to be considered a very important question. The mere question of the form of government in the Church appears to be of some weight, but of no commanding weight. The question of transmitting ministerial authority through an historic channel by acts which become a regular subject of record is of a different nature. If we consider the Church merely as a society, there is no necessity for it, since other societies have existed, and now exist, without it. Why, then, was it (apparently) embodied by our Lord in the Baptismal Charter? Why has it been so constantly believed and maintained in the history of Christian belief and practice?

When the Gospel went forth into the world, there were great — aye, terrible — odds against it.

*   *   *   *   *

2. RULES OF CONSTRUCTION FOR THE THIRTY-NINE ARTICLES.

(August 11, 1847.)

(1) That according to reason, as well as according to the Declaration, the Articles ought to be taken in their literal and grammatical sense.

(2) That within the natural meaning of words, or their literal and grammatical sense, a diversity of sentiments is admissible.

(3) That so much and no other diversity of sentiments ought to be taken to be conformable to the intention of the authority requiring the subscription.

(4) That the history of the period supports the proposition that room was intentionally left for some, and in particular points for considerable diversity.

(5) That the character of the compilers and of the revisers supports the same proposition.

(6) That the same proposition imports no reproach to their honesty or ingenuousness, and pays a high tribute to their wisdom.

(7) That damnatory and repudiatory clauses in a formulary imposed by way of test, being of a penal and restrictive nature, ought to be construed in the most favourable sense of which the language will justly and naturally admit.

(8) That the 'literal and grammatical sense' will be determinable in the main from the Articles, and indeed from the passages themselves.

(9) That the inquiry, What construction of a given Article or passage, within the limits of that sense, is preferable? must be governed by proofs and presumptions drawn from —

> (a) The authorized formularies of the Church of England.
>
> (b) The other laws, and the established and approved usages (as opposed to casual and licentious custom), of the Church of England.
>
> (c) The doctrines and principles of the Catholic Church.

(10) That Holy Scripture has the whole sovereign authority, and the scale above given has reference to the best mode of fixing the sense of Scripture and its application in the particular case.

(11) That no weight is to be given to the private opinion of the subscriber, or even of the compilers, in contravention of proofs or presumptions drawn from any of the above-named sources.

3. THE THIRTY-NINE ARTICLES.
(*December* 31, 1893.)

The Thirty-nine Articles walk (as it seems to me) at times along the edge of a precipice, yet without actually tumbling down.

I have signed and could sign them. The *imponens* is the English Church. If the framers were the original *imponentes*, I should not like to be bound to all their opinions.

The titles of the Articles are not, I believe, part of the Articles. Had they been imposed, I think I must have kicked scores of years ago at the Thirteenth, which, according to the title, would affirm that all works done 'before justification' have the nature of sin. In the body of the Article this is predicated, not of works before justification, but of 'works done before the grace of Christ and the inspiration of His Spirit.' That is a different matter. For the grace of Christ and the inspiration of His Spirit may reach infinitely farther than what we 'forensically' term 'justification': whether this was or was not present to the minds of men under the many narrowing influences of the Reformation controversy. Is there, then, no good among heathens and non-Christians? Take the self-sacrifice of Regulus, an imperfect but true martyrdom. Take the deaths of the two brothers in Herodotus, after drawing the car of the god. Take the hymns recently published by Professor Newman. Our Blessed Lord is, alas! studiously expunged from them: but it would (so far as I see) be absolutely profane to deny that they contain true piety.

We are not, however, wholly extricated from difficulty. The Article is not content with its dogmatic assertion: it adds the reason why works done before an access of grace have the nature of sin. It is because they 'spring not from faith in Jesus Christ.' No: and as I would not venture to make any assertion about any works done before the 'grace of Christ' has had some access to the soul in its now faulty and degenerated condition. No direct difficulty, then, arises upon the words of the Article. But they throw a curious light upon the ideas of the framers. Let us consider the matter logically. Certain works have the nature of sin. Why? Because they are not founded upon faith in Christ. Therefore in the minds of the framers all works have the nature of sin, which are not founded on faith in Jesus Christ. That means a faith consciously founded upon Him. Therefore it would seem they thought all works sinful except such as were performed (of course I do not refer to those of the elder covenant) out of a faith consciously resting on this ever-blessed name. This has an aspect somewhat horrible.

These works, says the Article, have the nature of sin. What, then, is sin? Is it not voluntary conflict with the will of God? But in the Litany we speak, and I suppose correctly, of our 'sins, negligences, and ignorances.' The last term denotes what we absolutely did not know. Our negligences are ignorances in thought, or omissions in action, of what we ought to have known and might have known. For both of these we ask pardon from God. Yet would it not be overstern to say that all our ignorances, for example, 'have the nature of sin'? Is it intended to lay down the doctrine that everything that falls short of perfection, in so far as it falls short of perfection, being undoubtedly imperfection, is therefore also sin? Sin is indeed a terrible and an awful thing, especially in an age which seems so largely to have blunted the edge of the old conceptions about it, and which seldom, I fear, hears it denounced as it deserves. But may it not be very seriously questioned whether to stretch the notion of it beyond its true and exact conception, while it seems to aim at loftiness and dignity of tone, is the true way for those who desire to see the hatred of it made vigorous and intense? The result may be, not so much stringency of dealing with elements comparatively innocent, as confusion and laxity in our mental apprehension of the monster-mischief, and a consequent coolness and slackness as to the remedial means necessary for putting it down.

4. THE PUBLIC WORSHIP REGULATION BILL: MR. GLADSTONE'S RESOLUTIONS.

(July 9, 1874.)

(1) That in proceeding to consider the provisions of the Bill for the Regulation of Public Worship, this House cannot do otherwise than take into view the lapse of more than two centuries since the enactment of the present Rubrics of the Common Prayer Book of the Church of England; the multitude of particulars embraced in the conduct of Divine Service under their provisions; the doubts occasionally attaching to their interpretation, and the number of points they are thought to leave undecided; the diversities of local custom which under these circumstances have long prevailed; and the unreasonableness of proscribing all varieties of opinion and usage among the many thousands of congregations of the Church distributed throughout the land.

(2) That this House is therefore reluctant to place in the hands of every single Bishop, on the motion of one or of three persons howsoever defined, greatly increased facilities towards procuring an absolute ruling of many points hitherto left open and reasonably allowing of diversity; and thereby towards the establishment of an inflexible rule of uniformity throughout the land, to the prejudice, in matters indifferent, of the liberty now practically existing.

(3) That the House willingly acknowledges the great and exemplary devotion of the clergy in general to their sacred calling, but is not on that account the less disposed to guard against the indiscretion, or thirst for power, or other fault of individuals.

(4) That the House is therefore willing to lend its best assistance to any measure recommended by adequate authority, with a view to provide more effectual securities against any neglect of, or departure from, strict law, which may give evidence of a design to alter, without the consent of the nation, the spirit or substance of the established religion.

(5) That in the opinion of the House it is also to be desired that the members of the Church, having a legitimate interest

in her services, should receive ample protection against precipitate and arbitrary changes of established custom by the sole will of the clergyman, and against the wishes locally prevalent among them; and that such protection does not appear to be afforded by the provisions of the Bill now before the House.

(6) That the House attaches a high value to the concurrence of Her Majesty's Government with the ecclesiastical authorities in the initiative of legislation affecting the Established Church.

III. — OXFORD ELECTIONS

The letter from Charles Wordsworth to Hope is given as a reasoned example of the Extreme Church and State theory which underlay much of the opposition to Mr. Gladstone's claim to represent his University in Parliament. The two circulars that follow also belong to the election of 1847, and between them constitute a pretty complete defence of his political action up to that time. The farewell address to the electors in 1865 is added.

1. CHARLES WORDSWORTH'S VOTE IN 1847.

Rev. Charles Wordsworth to James R. Hope.
                    Trinity College,
                        Glenalmond, Perth.

My dear Hope,

You have done me a very great kindness in endeavouring to convince me that I may conscientiously vote for Mr. Gladstone, for the difficulty I feel about it has been a constant source of uneasiness and pain to me; as indeed *you* may well suppose, knowing as you do, better than almost anyone, the very strong grounds of all kinds, public and private, which I have for wishing not only to vote for him, but to support him in every way to the very utmost of my power, and if I shall not eventually do so it will be the most distressing step of the kind which I have ever had occasion to take, and one which I would gladly do anything that I could, without a sacrifice of principle, to escape. For many years I looked upon Gladstone, and often spoke of him to others, as *the man* to save the country, or rather *the nation;* it was thought almost — if I may speak so strongly — his mission from God to do so— to *save* it in the only way in which I believe it is to be saved (under Providence) upon the principles of the Constitution in Church and State; but in an evil hour, as I think, his faith failed him. Fascinated by the practical ability and power of Sir R. Peel, he lost sight of his own position; and at last, from the high ground which he *fancied* to be untenable, but *was* not more so than high ground has often been before in faithless times, and will be so no doubt again, he leapt like Curtius into the gulf, and what is far worse, he drew the Church of England along with him. Such is the language which my revered father often used during the last year of his life in speaking of Gladstone, and you will not wonder that it made a deep impression upon me, knowing as I did the pain it gave him to speak so of one for whom he entertained the highest possible regard and esteem. Had Gladstone abided by his own principles, instead of falling in with the no-principles of Sir R. Peel and of the House of Commons, how different would have been his position, and the position of parties at the present time! But, not to indulge in painful reflection upon the past, What is to be done *now?* Are we still to have no rallying standard — no solid ground to stand upon again? Let it be that we have no certain or clear principles for the government of our Colonies, circumstanced as they are so differently, and occupied as they have often been in unprincipled ways, is the same to be the case with the Mother Country? — with England? with Ireland? with Scotland? Am I, at all events, as a member and minister of the United Church of England and Ireland, not to *aim at* a uniformity in religion in the three countries, without which upon no sound principles can they properly form one kingdom? More especially, am I to help to aggravate our present inconsistencies by relinquishing still farther the ground of the Constitution, so as to render it impossible, eventually, for our Sovereign to be crowned, or our Parliament assembled with any sanction of religion? With Scotland Presbyterian and Ireland neutral (in the eye of the State), what right, it may well be argued, can we have to claim the use of the Prayer-Book for any State occasion whatever? Ireland has been for many years, and is still, in a most wretched condition, both religious and political, worse probably since the passing of the Emancipation Act than it was before, certainly not better, and yet what politician was there that supported that measure who did not assure us of a very different result? The fact is, no statesman since Perceval's time has even thought of acting honestly by the Church of that country. It has been established only to be kicked and insulted, and eventually robbed. Who, having any faith in God's word, wonders that such a country so governed should be a thorn in our side? And what sincere member of a Church protesting against Popery can think that the true remedy for such evils is to be found in strengthening the hands of the Popish priesthood? But I beg pardon — some sincere members of our Church do think so, and others think that the Church might do as well, or perhaps better, both in England and Ireland, without any connection with the State. I can only say to both opinions, God forbid! for I believe *He does forbid*. Gladstone himself has taught me to say so, and as he, moving in the turmoil of politics, claims for himself to see political expediences or *necessities* which I cannot admit of, so I, living in another atmosphere, and subject to experiences, as I think, of another kind, am bound to act upon them as I best may; and in this case I am able to do so with greater confidence in that I do nothing but appeal from Gladstone, the member of an ungodly House of Commons and colleague of Sir Robert Peel, to the same Gladstone 'beneath the shades of Hagley,' the wise philosopher and pious divine. Not a year ago he himself told me he had abandoned his first principles because they had found so little support in the country, especially among the clergy. I answered I thought he had done so without reason, for the *support was there*, and only wanting to be called forth. If he will now tell me, or allow me to understand that he returns henceforth to his own principles, and means to act upon them on all occasions faithfully and unflinchingly, *he shall have my vote and interest with more pleasure and satisfaction than I can express;* otherwise, after the conversation to which I have referred, he cannot but *misinterpret my support* as withheld from that which I approve, and given to conduct and to principles which I then described as faithless, and which

I must still object to as strongly as ever. The unhappy condition of things to which you refer in the latter part of your letter I can see plainly enough, but yet I am not altogether without hope when I consider what a change has come over the spirit of our Church during the last fifteen years — a change still going forward, and which, if we have but one man of power and principle to fight the battle as Gladstone *might* fight it in the House of Commons, may bring about still more astonishing results in the next fifteen years to come.

But however this may be, I certainly do not think that we shall be likely, *on the whole*, to mend our bad practices by plunging deeper into *false principles;* nor am I desirous of seeing the Church more pure on the terms which you propose — viz., of the State becoming more irreligious. Rather I protest against any such notion. What God (as I believe) has joined together let no man put asunder.

I am, my dear Hope,
Ever yours most sincerely,
CHARLES WORDSWORTH.

2. DRAFT RESPECTING VOTE ON WARD'S CASE.
(*June* 11, 1847.)

Mr. Ward's book, entitled 'The Ideal of a Christian Church,' when it came to my notice in the autumn of 1844, appeared to me to be a work written with honesty of intention upon a subject of the greatest importance, but, at the same time, to constitute from the opinions it contained, and from the mode of their announcement, an outrage upon the first principles both of public decency and of duty to the Church.

I had ever before, I believe, undertaken to censure any work through the medium of the press, but I thought it my duty, or felt myself impelled, to write a review of Mr. Ward's work, and to tender it to the editor of the *Quarterly Review*, mainly for the purpose of exposing the writer as having proved himself totally unfit to handle such questions by the exhibition of almost every fault (except personal dishonesty) of which he could in a book be guilty; but partly also to suggest caution and discrimination as to the form of any measures which might be adopted against him. I declined, on account of the pending question at Oxford, to inquire whether his work was consistent with even the letter of his obligations as a clergyman and a member of the University. I disclaimed, however, the slightest objection to enforcing, in their substantial meaning according to history and authority and with the provident securities of law, those subscriptions which are required from clergymen and from the members of universities.

Soon after my article had been published in the *Quarterly Review* of December, 1844, Mr. Ward, in his 'Address to Members of Convocation,' expressed in print his intention of replying to it so soon as the question pending at Oxford was over, which was not done, probably owing to a subsequent change in his views of his position.

Having been acquainted with Mr. Ward at Oxford, and having a great repugnance under such circumstances to censures which are anonymous as between the writer and the subject of them, I made it known to Mr. Ward that I was the author of the review at the period when it issued from the press.

In the meantime I had perceived, to my great sorrow, that a censure had been proposed at Oxford in terms (independently of some other objections not inconsiderable, but of less moment) directly denying the *bona fides* of Mr. Ward. I felt at once that, having censured him publicly and severely in the way of discussion, and believing his *bona fides* could not properly be questioned by Convocation, it would be an act of gross cowardice on my part to refrain from acquitting him of a charge of which I believed him to be innocent. It is not advancing any claim to the praise of forethought if I state that I was, of course, aware that in discharging this act of justice I should expose myself to many, and, on the part of remote and imperfectly informed observers, not unreasonable suspicions.

I remember observing at the time to a gentleman nearly connected with a leading person at Oxford that I thought Mr. Ward well deserved censure, but that, on the ground

I have now stated, I could not concur in the censure proposed. He replied that he could venture to assure me that it was not intended to impeach Mr. Ward's honesty. I answered that, as a judge, I must be guided by the meaning of the words, and that the term *bona fides* went directly and exclusively to the question of inward sincerity. At the same time, I do not doubt that the majority of Convocation viewed the motion in the light which he suggested, and attached to the words a sense which, as I thought, they could not bear.

I am aware that there may be at first sight something paradoxical in refusing to affirm the dishonesty of a man who teaches doctrines like that of the non-natural sense sure to beget dishonesty in others. But first I thought that a question of inward motive was unfit for the cognizance of a human tribunal, and especially of a large and promiscuous body. Secondly, I believe more perhaps than most men in the capacity of the human mind for self-delusion, and I thought Mr. Ward infatuated without being dishonest.

The votes given on the respective sides were naturally, though most inaccurately, termed votes 'for or against' Mr. Ward; and since my own was described under the former appellation and indefinitely associated with the doctrines of the book, as well as with the subsequent acts of its writer and of others, I regard it as a subject upon which every member of Convocation who may desire it is entitled to receive the fullest explanation. This, as far as memory and hasty reference would enable me, I have now endeavoured to give.

3. ELECTION CIRCULAR, 1847.

COMMITTEE ROOM,
July 26, 1847.

In consequence of the occurrence, very unusual in an University contest, of an attack upon Mr. W. E. Gladstone by the committee of the opposing candidates, Mr. Gladstone's committee have placed the paper which contained it in his hands, and have received the accompanying notice of it, which, under circumstances so peculiar, they think it fit to publish, more particularly as they trust and believe it does not contain a word which reflects on the principles, capacity, or conduct of his opponent, Mr. Round.

13, Carlton House Terrace,
July 26, 1847.

I extract the principal assertion contained in a circular of the 19th, which has this day been put into my hands, and which is signed William Harrison, Charles Sumner, Edward P. Hathaway, and I add my observations upon them:

'1st. — The object of the Dissenters' Chapel Bill was to secure to certain Socinians the undisputed possession of property which was never intended for them.'

I argued in Parliament that this proposition was entirely false; that the property affected by the Bill generally was intended to be held by persons who repudiated all creeds and human impositions, and drew their opinions for themselves from the Holy Scriptures; that there was no evidence to show it to be the desire, even of the original associates (to call them founders would be, generally, an abuse of terms), to make the profession of particular doctrines a condition of succession to them in the possession of the chapels and their appurtenances; and that, therefore, the Socinians were really entitled to what they held. I supported this argument, in great detail, by historical evidence; no man then or since replied, or brought counter evidence in Parliament or elsewhere to my knowledge; and to this hour I rejoice in having been permitted to take part in the performance of a great act of justice.

'2nd. — The courts of equity were compelling them to relinquish this property.'

This also is untrue. It was shown in the House of Commons — and without an effort, I believe, at reply — that the case of Lady Hewley was entirely distinct from that of the chapels, because Lady Hewley did refer in her trusts to particular doctrines which were in the nature of tests, whereas the Chapels Bill was expressly intended for cases where there was no such reference.

'3rd. — The Bishops were unanimous in opposing it.'

This is also untrue.

I find two divisions recorded in the House of Lords.

In the first of them no Bishop opposed the Bill.

In the second of them the names of those who opposed it are not recorded, but two Bishops supported it. I have a letter from a third prelate, than whom no one, perhaps, commands more universal confidence, dated July 17, 1844, in which he states his 'conviction of the justness and propriety of the Bill,' and adds, 'that he was unable, on account of absence from London, to be in his place on the occasion.'

If it be asked, What, then was the object of the Bill? I answer, It was to prevent litigation by establishing *at once* an issue which was definite and just, instead of leaving the question liable to perpetual agitation, without hope of settlement.

'4th. — Mr. Gladstone supported the Maynooth Bill, believing it to be opposed to the views of the people of England.'

This is true. However willing I had been upon, and for many years after, my introduction to Parliament to struggle for the exclusive support of the national religion of the State, and to resist all arguments drawn from certain inherited arrangements in favour of a more relaxed system, I found that scarcely a year passed without the fresh adoption of some measure, involving the national recognition and the national support of various forms of religion; and in particular, that a recent and fresh provision had been made for the propagation from a public Chair of Arian or Socinian doctrines. The question remaining for me was whether, aware of the opposition of the English people, I should set down as equal to nothing, in a matter primarily connected not with our but with their priesthood, the wishes of the people of Ireland, and whether I should avail myself of the popular feeling in regard to the Roman Catholics for the purpose of enforcing against them a system which we had ceased by common consent to enforce against Arians: a system, above all, of which I must say that it never can be conformable to policy, to justice, or even to decency, when it has become avowedly partial and one-sided in its application.

'5th. — Mr. Gladstone voted against the censure on Mr. Ward.'

This is true. In that censure two propositions, totally distinct, were unhappily combined. The first of these condemned his opinions and proceedings: the second declared his personal dishonesty. I was ready to condemn the opinions and proceedings, as I stated at the time to persons of influence, connected, as I believe, with the framing of the motion against him; and as I had, indeed, already done myself, to the very best of such capacity as I possessed through the medium of a powerful organ of opinion, the *Quarterly Review* for December, 1844. I was not ready to declare Mr. Ward's personal dishonesty; without presuming to judge for others, I thought that question was one not fit for the adjudication of a human tribunal.

In conclusion, I humbly trust that Mr. Harrison, Mr. Sumner, and Mr. Hathaway are not justified in exhibiting me to the world as a person otherwise than 'heartily devoted to the doctrine and constitution of our Reformed Church.' But I will never consent to adopt, as the test of such devotion, a disposition to identify the great and noble cause of the Church of England with the repression and the restraint of the civil rights of those who differ from her. I shall rather believe that it may more wisely, more justly, and more usefully be shown, first by endeavours to aid in the development and application of her energies to her spiritual work, and next, by the temperate but firm indication of those rights with which, for the public good, she is endowed as a National Establishment.

4. FAREWELL ADDRESS.

TO THE MEMBERS OF CONVOCATION IN THE UNIVERSITY OF OXFORD.

Hawarden, Chester,
July 18, 1865.

Gentlemen,

After an arduous connection of eighteen years, I bid you respectfully farewell.

My earnest purpose to serve you, my many faults and

shortcomings, the incidents of the political relation between the University and myself, established in 1847, so often questioned in vain, and now at length finally dissolved, I leave to the judgment of the future. It is one imperative duty, and one alone, which induces me to trouble you with these few parting words: the duty of expressing my profound and lasting gratitude for indulgence as generous, and for support as warm and enthusiastic in itself, and as honourable from the character and distinctions of those who have given it, as has in my belief ever been accorded by any constituency to any representative.

   I have the honour to be, gentlemen,
    Your obliged and obedient Servant,
      W. E. GLADSTONE.

IV. — CONTROVERSY WITH ROME

The Controversy with Rome plays so large a part in the Letters that there is not much left for an Appendix. The Conversation with Döllinger gives a very full account of Mr. Gladstone's position in reference to the Eucharist. Upon the effect of consecration his faith was unalterably fixed, but all speculation as to the mode in which this effect was wrought seemed to him rash and unprofitable.

It would have been well for Europe if the plan of a reconciliation between the Papacy and the new Italian Kingdom, sketched out in the Memorandum on the Roman Question, had found favour with both parties. But only a very hearty acceptance of it by the Pope would have recommended it to Cavour, and of this there was never the least chance.

The conversation with Pius IX. had no theological or political importance, but it shows Mr. Gladstone in pleasanter relations with the Pope than the stress of controversy often permitted him to maintain. The Memorandum on the Old Catholics may be taken as the high-water mark of Mr. Gladstone's hopes on their behalf.

1. CONVERSATION WITH DR. DÖLLINGER, 1845.

Munich,
October 4, 1845.

Yesterday I had a conversation with Professor Döllinger on several questions of religion to the following effect, and I put it on record because of the pointedness of its results.

He spoke of the question of images as one on which there

were great differences between the Church of Rome and that of England: I said not in regard to the formal and net doctrine, but to the practical system in the former Church; and then added that the points on which that system presented the greatest obstacles to communion were, I thought, the worship of images, the invocation of saints and particularly that of the Blessed Virgin, and the purgatorial indulgences.

He smiled, and said as to the last it was a subject scarcely existing or scarcely sensible for them in Germany. Then he stated the meaning of purgatorial indulgence to be this: that the Church offers her prayers for the deceased person in the belief that they are beneficial to him, but without defining the effect upon his state. I said: 'Then, I was right in supposing that yesterday you referred with reprobation to the preaching of Tetzel and his associates, because they told the people that their gifts were to be followed by the release of souls from Purgatory.' Yes, he said that was the case. 'Yet surely,' said I, 'indulgence is a judicial act, is it not?' 'As to the living, but not as to the dead,' he replied. 'The jurisdiction of the Church is over the living; it terminates with the grave. For the dead she can only pray, and she cannot measure the result of her prayer.' Upon this he expressed himself as most positive.

I then asked: 'I conclude that with you all prayer for the dead is conditional upon the supposition that the person departed in a state of grace, although the condition may not be expressed?' 'Undoubtedly,' he said. 'We,' I replied, 'you see, who travel in Roman Catholic countries, do not see the signs of that condition, but everywhere see prayer absolute in appearance.' He said no Catholic can be misled upon that point.

To my inquiry (earlier in the conversation) what was the meaning of indulgence to the dead for so many days, or other periods of time, he answered it was still the application of the prayer of the Church for them for forty days.

(There are, indeed, difficulties left behind. Practically as they manage prayer for the dead, is not the result that all men are regarded as subjects of prayer under no condition at all, or one insensible — all who die ostensibly in the communion of the Church as no worse than in purgatory? And if so, must not the effect of this upon many living be immensely to diminish the force of the thought of death as the closing up of their moral account?

(And as to the indulgences, an indulgence is taken from some proclaimed paper of terms by someone living on behalf of a dead person. There is no act of the Church subsequent to, it may be, the printing of the paper with the conditions. Is it, then, meant that the force of the petitions of the Church for the peace of the departed is, unconsciously to those who offer them, distributed according to indulgences which have been obtained by other parties, so that the effect of the prayer is thus separated, systematically and by anticipation, from the consciousness of those who offer it? There is something slippery in this, yet it seems capable of an explanation.)

I said to him: 'I wish you could have heard sermons which I have heard, particularly two to which I have adverted, in Italy and Sicily; and to know what your view of them would be. In a sermon at Naples I heard the preacher found himself on these two main propositions: (1) That the Blessed Virgin differed essentially from all created beings whatever in that their gifts and graces were finite, whereas hers bordered upon the infinite; the words used were "Toccano a' cancelli del infinito." I know it is difficult to give a metaphysical meaning to this sort of medium between finity and infinity; but the practical force of the sentiment is clear and positive enough. The second was that the Blessed Virgin Mary was invested extrinsically with all the attributes of the adorable Trinity — infinite power, infinite wisdom, infinite love.' He replied, with a little straining — then corrected himself, and said with a great deal of straining — 'the words might be made to bear a tolerable sense; but taking them as they stand, I should say they border upon blasphemy.' I said: 'Toccano a' cancelli della blasfemia.' He replied yes; that no such thing would be tolerated here. I answered: 'Then, you see, this has some bearing upon that matter on which you press us so much, the unity of doctrine.' He seemed a little touched, and made no reply, but that it must be the neglect of the Bishops. I answered I hoped it might be so (meaning, I feared they either did not wish or, *more* probably, did not dare to disturb such teaching).

We passed to the subject of the Eucharist, and I ventured to suggest to him that perhaps in the last resort it would be found that the great difficulty between the two Churches would be found to lie in the predication by the Church of Rome of the cessation of bread and wine. He said he thought he could not approximate without a more defined doctrine of the Real Presence by the Church of England. I said our difficulty was not in believing the Real Presence in the Eucharist, but in believing the unreality of the signs. He said: 'If you admit that the elements become the body and blood of our Lord, it follows that they are not what they were; they have lost their identity. That upon which their identity rests we call substance, so that if you believe in the real presence you must believe in the cessation of the substance of bread and wine, although, on the other hand, in every point that meets the sense they are just as real as ever they were.' I said: 'Forgive me if, in reply, I state that our objection is to these deductions founded upon questionable, overbold, and even, perhaps, fantastic metaphysics; and that I know to some of the best among us the doctrine of the Church of Rome seems chiefly noxious from the rationalizing character which it seems to us to have. By rationalizing, I mean not giving reasons in support of faith, nor giving elucidations of matter of faith simply, but giving such reasons and such elucidations of a matter of faith as are injurious to faith in some other manner or matter.' To this he assented. Then I said: 'Do not suppose we draw objections *ab impossibili*. The objection, as it seems to me, is this: here is a sacrament; we have it defined as consisting of two *parts*, the outward visible sign and the inward spiritual grace. If you overset the reality of the sign, you overset the reality of the sacrament by destroying one of its essential parts. Now, are bread and wine the signs, and therefore essential parts, or are they not? And, if so, must not they still be real bread and wine?' 'It depends,' said he, 'on what you mean by reality;

in respect to all that you see and feel, and to all their nutritive qualities, they are as much bread and wine as ever. But with all this, their substratum may be changed. Thus, St. Paul teaches us that there is a σῶμα πνευματικὸν, and we know that in this glorified or spiritual body our Lord dwelt upon earth for forty days. In this body He passed through the closed doors or the walls, and entered the chamber where the Apostles were sitting. At the same time St. Thomas put his hands in the hole of his Lord's wounds. Could he, then, properly have argued that because he had thus touched he had been assured of the reality of the flesh which he touched, and therefore knew it could not have passed through the doors or walls?' I replied: 'No; and I can advance no such argument at all. We stand upon the ground that the elements are declared in Scripture to be bread and wine when consecrated. Therefore we hold they must be real and true, as other sensible substances. I should set out from this that God has given us certain faculties and certain objects for them; and although He has not provided us with such means of assurance as are infallible (for in what process *may* not error as a possibility intervene? — to this he assented) but with such as are intended, and adequate, to give certain conviction. I by no means place the evidence of the senses higher than that which belongs to our mental perceptions; but I take them as a great, Divinely-ordained channel for receiving a part of those impressions through which God works upon and with us. I am therefore bound to guard the authority of this evidence, on account of its relation to our knowledge and convictions in general, and therefore to all belief. According to me, it seems we must hold not only that certain attributes which we perceive in the consecrated elements are real, but that these make them real bread and wine; and that which is presented to our senses not only is real, but also is that by which the things are what they are, is *the essence*.' 'No,' said he, 'there you are wrong; independently of doctrine I believe all metaphysicians and chemists will tell you that there are in matter attributes that escape us — and thus that the whole essence is not presented to us.' 'I was wrong, undoubtedly,' said I; 'I should have spoken thus, that the attributes which we perceive are of the essence, belong to it, and constitute, to us, the ground of predicating it.' He said: 'You know that we were at one time accused of making the Eucharist a *phantasmagoria*, and of teaching that these attributes were mere appearances.' I said: 'That is by no means the allegation I have made: I have always believed your best divines at least allowed the reality of the accidents; but what right have they to put down as accidents those things which are to us the only evidence of the essence, when in the particular case Scripture calls them, and therefore fixes upon them the character of, the essence? But I am not to say because the nature of bread remains, therefore the nature of our Lord's body is not there; nor yet am I to say that it is there with the bread in the manner of consubstantiation.' 'No doubt,' he said, 'it was happier when the early Church in the energy of faith could dispense with definitions; and the Greek Fathers do speak of bread and wine as remaining after consecration.' 'So also Pope Gelasius,' said I. 'Yes,' he added; 'but heresy arose, and what could the Church do? She was obliged to give metaphysical definitions respecting the Trinity, which may not be abstractedly desirable from the imperfection of our knowledge. So she must do the same in the case of the Eucharist when the Real Presence is denied.' I replied: 'I know that the alleged parallel between the definitions on these two subjects is a common, and a most plausible, and to me, if the fact be true, a conclusive, argument; but I cannot find the fact to be true. I find the greatest difference between the Nicene definition in defence of our Lord's Divinity and the definition expressed by Transubstantiation.' He did not seem disposed strongly to press the parallel, and in matter so high I readily refrained from explaining my meaning. 'But,' said he, 'all matter has a spiritual character, a spiritual part, as it may be glorified.' 'A spiritual susceptibility,' said I. 'Yes,' he replied. 'It is in that respect that the elements are changed in the blessed Eucharist. In another sense they are certainly real. This,' said he, 'is, I am sure, an exposition allowed in our Church.' I answered: 'Would it, then, be allowable to speak thus (I had before put to him this point: Scripture calls the holy elements by the names of bread and wine; the Fathers do the same. The Church of Rome will not allow it, unless in a figure—on which he did not give a definite reply): There is a higher region of creation, and there is a lower one dependent upon it and receiving life from it; in that lower region the consecrated elements (which are related to both) are still bread and wine; in the higher one they are no longer such, having spiritually become the body and blood of our Lord?' 'Yes,' he said. 'Surely,' I replied, 'much would be gained if these things were understood.' He agreed. And the conversation was of great comfort to one who views the unity of Christians as I must do. Perhaps on such a question it should be remembered that Dr. D. spoke in a tongue not his own, although he understands it extremely well.

When we bid farewell he said: 'Well, we are in one Church by water — upon that I shall rest.' I said: 'It is my happiness, if I may say so, to be allowed to go farther.' I must indeed carry away with me a very lively sense both of his kindness, and of the great value of intercourse with him; and I must say of the breadth of those grounds of agreement which I find with such expositions of doctrine as those to which I have here referred.

Dr. D. also asked if there was not for us great force in the fact of the adhesion of the Eastern Church on Transubstantiation? I said: 'Yes; but we did not conceive the Eastern Church to take quite the same position with regard to it.'

Sunday, October 5, 1845.

In the foregoing conversation of October 3, Dr. Döllinger spoke with a particular positiveness on his statement of the doctrine of purgatorial indulgences as the proper doctrine of the Roman Catholic Church. He said, I think: 'I have been twenty years in theology, and I am sure I cannot be wrong.' On the Real Presence he only spoke of his exposition as allowable.

He adverted to the doctrine of sacrifice, and said some of our divines seemed to resolve it into the material sacrifice of bread and wine, which was rather a judaizing notion. I said I supposed we were taught the doctrine of a double sacrifice in the Holy Eucharist, the *first* that of the elements as fruits of the earth. He replied: 'Yes certainly; but that first is only in respect of the higher character to which they are to be elevated.'

Of my very long conversations of former days with Dr. D. I shall only record certain fragments delivered by him.

He expressed a strong opinion that if the Church of England were to work upon the people with effect, the character of our preaching must be changed to the kind without book — except in the case of the higher classes.

He thought it a great felicity of the English people that they were in many things less technical and systematic than other nations, and yet practically quite as effective. I pleaded this when he remarked on our want of systematic theology, and he did not wholly repudiate the plea.

He had read my article on Ward, and said certainly Ward could not complain of it.

He had read Manning on the Unity of the Church, and admired it as a work of talent, but thought it quite unsatisfactory because it did not make out the case of internal unity of doctrine in the English Church, of which he thought we must feel the want much more acutely than the want of external unity.

He conceived that as our theology strives to become systematic, the Catholic and Puritanical elements in it will come into sharper collision, will both become systematic and rend us in pieces.

Here I must give my reply: it was that the Puritanical element had been once cast out of the English Church and was a reintroduction — that we had a Church divinity independent of it — that it was not within our Church properly a system but an impulse, working loosely and diversely through a very heterogeneous mass of opinions, often on the verge of heresy or in it, but yet not often held in an heretical spirit — that a few years ago, say before Tract CX., it was in course of rapid absorption — that on the whole I still believed and trusted it would be absorbed, and indeed developed as to its sound part in a Catholic system, but that undoubtedly since the romanizing turn in the Oxford Movement it had become more obstinate, and had made efforts to rally into order and system, which if effected, I agreed, must destroy us.

He thought it a great misfortune that there should be a close and constant conflict in detail between the Roman Church and ours, as tending to quicken the sense of differences and to subdue that of agreements.

He said the habit of his Church on the Continent was from the known sympathies of Cranmer and others with the Continental reformers to assume that we were essentially a portion of the same body, though we had kept much nearer to the Church of Rome.

He clearly understood from me that in my view the secessions in detail to the Church of Rome were the great obstacle to the realization of a Catholic character among the members of our Church, and that England never would be reunited to the rest of the Western Church through the agency of the Roman Catholic body there as an aggressive system apart from and in conflict with the actual Church. Should not I have gone one step farther and also stated the conviction that if a conflict was now caused in the Church of England, and a merely Protestant character fastened upon her, the opposite element being cast out or reduced to comparative impotence, still the hope of reunion would have been lost, so far as it was dependent upon us?

2. MEMORANDUM ON THE ROMAN QUESTION.

(March 27, 1863.)

The simple and unconditional union, for every civil purpose, of Rome with the Italian Kingdom, as its natural, necessary, and only possible, capital, is desired by every friend of the cause of Italy, and is regarded as the proper consummation of the constructive work.

That consummation being for the moment impossible, it becomes a matter of importance to consider whether a separation can be made between the essential parts of that union, which may be necessary and sufficient for the purposes of a true political unity, and the adjuncts by which, in a more favourable state of circumstances, it would naturally be attended.

It may be difficult for a distant observer to measure accurately the intentions or the wishes of the Emperor of the French with regard to Italy. What appears plain, however, is simply this: that he has arrived at an *impasse;* he is pledged to reconcile the claims of the Italians with those of the Pope, and yet he has been unable to suggest any plan which has given satisfaction to *either* party. It seems right to believe that his views are generally favourable to Italian unity and nationality; and, if they are so, then it may with some confidence be assumed that he would be inclined to examine with impartiality, and even with favour, any plan bearing upon its face some tolerable semblance of reason.

Can such a plan be suggested? What is the maximum (such is the question to be solved) of dignity, of security, and of political and pecuniary independence, which can be secured for the Pope compatible with the paramount object, on the other side, of obtaining for the Roman people the full enjoyment of the political and civil rights possessed by their fellow-countrymen, and for Italy that practical possession of her capital which is essential to the cause of order, freedom, and good government in that country?

The objection always urged by the friends of the existing state of things in Rome to the surrender of the temporal power is this: that the Pope must not be the subject of anybody.

But all mankind are divided into Sovereigns and subjects, so that those who cannot be subjects must be Sovereigns.

Sovereignty, however, may be either sovereignty of dignity or sovereignty of administration. The former is called *suzeraineté,* and is compatible with a variety of particular arrangements appertaining to the dignity and advantage of the Suzerain.

Let us suppose, then, the first notion of a plan to be that the Pope is to be Suzerain of Rome and the rest of his territories, and that the King of Italy is to be his Vicar, invested by a permanent, irrevocable instrument with all the ordinary power of civil government over the inhabitants.

What seems to be requisite, on the other side, is that the Suzerain should be secured in all the circumstances necessary for his ease, dignity, and personal inviolability.

He is not to be the subject even of the law, such is the demand. For all his personal acts, he must enjoy an entire immunity from restraint and from penalty.

It seems plain that if this can be conceded and secured, there remains no decent plea, much less argument, for the retention of the temporal power. For the highest advocate of it must admit that it is not necessary in itself, but only on account of its insuring such immunity.

The difficulty in conceding immunity of this kind may be considered as relating, for practical purposes, not to the personal but only to the official acts of the Pope.

His prerogatives, which are properly spiritual, have a thousand points of contact with the established political order, and with the civil interests of the people; and the regulation of the reciprocal relations at these points of contact, though it does not seem to have been found difficult in Eastern Christendom, has constituted for a long period of time a difficulty of the first order within the present and former limits of the Latin Church.

What is required on behalf of the Italian kingdom is, not to take security for the just and reasonable exercise on all occasions of the spiritual powers of the Pope, but simply to prevent them from being so used as to invade the province of civil government.

It seems worth while to consider whether the double object of an absolute unconditional inviolability for the Pope, and the plenitude of temporal rights for the head of the Italian kingdom, might not simultaneously be attained by a method somewhat resembling that which has been worked out in English history as respects the person of the Sovereign.

The maxim that the King can do no wrong has there been reduced, within the political sphere, to an absolute and practical truth.

All the Acts of Government in England require the countersignature, or other intervention, of the Minister of the proper department: except only the choice of a new administration.

Nothing done by the Sovereign, however contrary to the laws or to public right, would be punishable : but the person or persons who concur, and whose concurrence is necessary in order to complete the act, are fully amenable. And this security is deemed ample under all circumstances.

An arrangement equally simple and effective could probably be made were the Pope willing to agree to act only with the concurrence of ecclesiastical ministers or servants, selected and dismissed at will by himself.

We must perhaps assume that he would refuse to be party to such an arrangement.

But it may still be thought that absolute personal inviolability might safely be conceded to him, if not only everyone who should illegally obey him, but every counsellor by whom he was surrounded, and every agent who might be employed, ministerially or otherwise, in giving effect to any illegal act, remained responsible to the law. This, after all, is the substance of the English arrangement, which has a special distinction in the means taken to determine at once who those counsellors and agents are.

The Pope would then stand in regard to Italy, to *all* Italy, as he now stands in regard to the Italian kingdom within its present limits, or as he stands in regard to France or England. He may issue a deposing Bull : he may do acts that in themselves, if done by a British subject, would be acts of treason or sedition : we cannot touch him : but we can touch any and every one who shall obey him.

In the interest of His Holiness it does not appear why this inviolability should not be as effective as the temporal sovereignty, a mere fragment of which he does not enjoy but possesses, and which the lapse of every day helps to undermine. Nor in the interest of Italy is it clear why the dangers attaching to such immunity might not be for every practical purpose neutralized substantially in the same manner as in the case of the civil sovereignty of England, even if without the same perfect facility and simplicity of arrangement.

That such inviolability would with the utmost natural and inherent propriety be attached to a Suzerain appears pretty clear.

There remains the question what would be the security for its being duly observed by the Italian kingdom. But this question applies alike to *all* conditions which might be stipulated on the Pope's behalf. His palaces, churches, revenues, and the local precinct which might be formed into a kind of sanctuary for him — all these would have to be covered by the same security, and any security adequate for them would also be adequate for this additional condition.

It hardly belongs to the purpose of this memorandum to treat of a point which is not peculiar to it, but belongs to the subject at large. It has, however, seemed to the writer of it that the best security for an arrangement of this kind (and to the *very* best that can be had the Pope is in justice entitled) would probably be found in an European Act, to which all the Powers, signatories to the Treaty of Vienna, should be parties along with the Italian kingdom. Any breach of the stipulations by the King of Italy would then be a *casus belli* for any of these Powers. Their number would be the Pope's best defence, for in proportion to their number would be their diversity of interests, on which he must greatly rely: and his best chance of having what are termed the Catholic Powers in general on his side in any given case would be their being combined with Powers out of the Latin Communion, instead of being left to intrigue among themselves for preponderance of interest and favour.

It would be not a little singular if the Pope, who began by holding under the temporal Sovereign, were to end by the temporal Sovereign's holding under him.

3. MEMORANDUM OF A CONVERSATION WITH HIS HOLINESS POPE PIUS IX. ON OCTOBER 22, 1866.

Cardinal von Reisach having signified to me that it would be according to rule to ask an audience of the Pope, I wrote accordingly to Cardinal Antonelli on Friday, and received on Saturday a courteous note in reply, naming Monday at half-past twelve. At that time accordingly I repaired to the Vatican in household uniform. I found the Pope dressed with great simplicity in white: the apartment and its furniture were of the same character. He sat on one side of an oblong table. When I had bowed and kissed his hand, dropping on one knee as before the Queen (an operation in which he took my hand himself), he motioned and asked me to sit down on a chair placed over against him. Mr. Russell had told me that it was his wont, notwithstanding this invitation, to stand: I therefore begged permission to do 'as I should if before the Queen.' But he said: 'If the Queen ordered you to sit, you would sit.' 'Allora,' I said, 'Santo Padre non mi resta altro che di ubbidire: *Roma locuta est:*' quoting the famous words of St. Augustine in a well-known case against the Donatists, I think. The Pope smiled, and finished the sentence, *causa finita est.* He then asked about the Queen's health, and where she was: and observed on the etiquette maintained in the Court of England, which he said also had subsisted in the 'piccola nazione' (such, I think, was the phrase) of Piedmont, but not among the Courts of the other Italian princes with their more impulsive peoples. He observed on the superior practical ability of the Piedmontese, as exhibited in Cavour, and he likewise understood in Menabrea, now at Vienna; but thought there was a general want of power in Italian administrators, including Ricasoli, who, he said, had never returned to Florence since Custozza.

He spoke of England and its general course in the past in terms of great honour: he spoke of the *primato* she had obtained among nations. Also of the vast extension of the Empire: of her having a *gamba* here, and another there, all over the earth.

The exceedingly genial, and simple, and kindly manner of His Holiness had at once placed me at my ease, and I entered freely into the conversation. I observed that the etiquette of Courts was of especial use in a country like England, where wealth was so rapidly created, and where the movement into the forward and upper ranks of society was active in proportion. When he came to the extension of our Empire, I replied: 'Santo Padre, ne abbiamo troppo, di queste gambe. Abbiamo troppo da fare e per questo non le facciamo troppo bene.' He replied he understood we had representative governments in our Colonies. Yes, I said, and it was not in their internal government that serious difficulty arose, but in the false position into which they might bring us with Foreign Powers. But this very variously. Australia, for instance, created no difficulty : British North America much, in contact with a most powerful and energetic people, and ill able, not at all used, to defend itself, while for us its defence while incumbent by honour would be a most difficult and critical operation. He hoped that Fenianism was not formidable. I said not in Ireland, but mixed with the colonial question it might be so in America. I said I looked on Ireland and British North America as involving our greatest difficulties for the future : that in Ireland they might be due to our own fault, but in British North America rather to a false position. He spoke warmly against Fenianism, and declared the decided hostility to it of his clergy in Ireland, which hostility, in any point that might come before him, he always approved and seconded.

He said the Irish Bishops were true to the existing order of things, though in some points they would wish for change, and in some points I replied *hanno ragione*. I then explained the state of the University Question, and the steps taken by the late Government.

At an early period of the conversation he had spoken of himself and of Italy. He, too, wished, he said, to promote peace, conciliation, settlement ; quoted the *il faut s'entendre*, *bisogna intendersi*, urged upon him by *questi mediatori*, the French : a *buon principio*, I replied, but all depended on the development and application. Well, he said, he was most ready to receive anyone who might be sent to him by the Italian Government, though he did not think they should conclude much. I said it would at any rate be *il primo passo*. The previous failure, he said, was not the fault of Vegezzi, with whose conduct he said he had every cause to be satisfied.

He did not lead me farther than this into Roman affairs, and though looking for an opportunity I did not see any that offered itself consistently with due respect and my intention to volunteer nothing. But on the affairs of Italy he spoke rather largely and very freely, and I not less freely in return.

With regard to the unity of Italy he made no objection in principle, but even seemed to admit it theoretically, and to allow that there were practical advantages in it. But he spoke of the present state of things as deplorable. He distinctly complained of the conduct of the Italian Government as inimical to religion. In one place he said: 'I direttori di questo movimento sono Anticristiani.' I replied: 'Santo Padre, non è vero che questi sarebbero piùttosto i direttori per così dire sotterrandi, mai non quelli che guidano il popolo : il popolo d' Italia non è irreligioso.' No ; he said, the people of Italy is Catholic, but the conduct of the Government is adverse to religion. I said, that according to our view in representative Governments, there was a power and a tendency to cure their own faults ; that the constituency in Italy freely choosing those who form the Parliament should, and would, impress upon the Parliament its own convictions, especially being, as I understood it was, formed of an intelligent class of persons. I trusted, therefore, that respect for religion would be maintained by the State if it lived in the people. He admitted the general and powerful tendency in these days towards representative Government ; expressed no feeling adverse to it, but said that in Italy the elections were not really free ; there was such a timidity or indifference in the good, and such a *sfrontatezza* of the bad.

He spoke also of the strong traditionalism of the various parts of Italy. There would be Naples, with its 600,000 inhabitants (*sic*) ; Venice, with its recollections of the Doges — he specified nothing else. I said that these tendencies to localize and separate did not appear to be paramount in the Italian Parliament ; that as I understood, both commerce and education had made great progress at Naples ; that undoubtedly the difficulties of Italy were great, most of all, perhaps, in connection with finance (he said there was infinite and unpunished peculation); that there ought to be great and vigorous reform and reduction ; that it was not for me to estimate the forces and probabilities this way or that, but that I could not fail to see what great benefits would flow from the unity of Italy to Europe. She would in the first place by becoming a nation shut off a battle-field on which

Austria and France had been able to pursue their aims, would stop a series of constant intrigues, and would substitute for a standing weakness and cause of danger a strong State necessarily pacific and conservative (he seemed to assent, observing 'with the Alps for its boundary') that could not entertain ambitious aims. He threw in that there would be questions about the Tyrol and Trieste, but seemed to allow my reply, that the claim for the latter would be too unreasonable to be seriously urged, and that the former must be a question within the narrowest bounds.

I must say that what he dwelt on *most* was the necessity of time for Italy to consolidate itself, referring, very properly, to the cases of Spain, France, and England. At the same time he hoped that instead of the present evils it would attain to a little tranquillity, respect for religion, and especially *un poco d' ordine*, and that *o forse una lega o forse una nazione*, a solution would be found. This was the only distinct reference to any alternative involving the severance of Italy. He made no mention of the deposed families; none of the religious corporations. He complained, as an example, that Archbishop Polding had been imprisoned on suspicion when travelling through Turin. This seemed a very strong case; but he added that his release was immediately ordered from Florence.

I should have said that when I referred to difficulties connected with our Colonies, he replied he supposed it was for that reason that we gave up Corfù. I said yes: the occasion was perhaps not very good, but the spirit of the people was Hellenic; and we had no interest or plea which would justify us in disregarding in their case the principle of nationality, which within certain limits was a good principle.

I thought he began to feel we had had enough of Italy when he most graciously asked if I had not brought my wife and family to Rome, so that I inquired whether they might be presented to him, when he said he should have much pleasure in seeing them to give them his blessing. He also received with kindness and warmth a message from my sister, and made a reference to works of mine. He then expressed his willingness to do anything to promote our comfort in Rome, and I in retiring could not avoid tendering a marked expression of my thanks for his condescending kindness towards a person so unworthy as myself. The interview lasted about three-quarters of an hour.

4. THE VATICAN COUNCIL AND THE OLD CATHOLICS.

(September 30, 1874.)

(I.)

(1) The adoption of an erroneous proposition touching Christian belief, or *circâ fidem*, by a Christian Church is a very serious matter at best.

(2) Its adoption as *de fide*, as a thing to be believed for necessity of salvation, is a thing far more serious.

(3) But this act becomes tremendous in its consequences when the particular Church, or Churches, however extended, claim the entire authority of the Church Universal.

(4) And, lastly, when they teach as matter of faith that the authority so claimed embraces infallibility *in such a manner* that the seal of infallibility is set to the proposition in question by the act of its adoption. This is, on the part of such a Church, a repudiation and breach of duty, in vital matter, to be repaired only by repentance. And this is the truth in every word, with the dogma of Papal Infallibility recently adopted by the Vatican Council.

While, however, the decree of Papal Infallibility considered with a view to practical effects leaves a door open to much equivocal argument by the condition that in each case the utterance of the Pope shall be *ex cathedrâ*, the Council has provided another more ready and effectual arm against the private conscience, in another of its decrees, which has not received the attention it well merits.

It has decreed that the acts of the Pope may not be questioned, and that his orders must be obeyed. This is without qualification or exception.

There is no *ex cathedrâ* here: and by this decree the consciences and actions of the faithful are effectually bound, in all cases where they might have escaped from the reach of the other, in so far as it shall at any time please the Pope, or those who from behind move the Pope, to bind them.

It is easy to perceive how the power hereby given might be used in reference, for instance, to the temporal power of the Pope.

Prayers might be ordered for its restoration.

It might be declared vital to the independence of the Church, and thus mediately to Christianity itself.

To impugn its necessity or its legitimacy might be prohibited under pain of mortal sin.

In what manner could the meshes of *this* net be escaped?

(II.)

The Old Catholics, if I understand them aright, are by no means Protestants, nor are they Rationalists in disguise; but they are men who believe as the moderate, Cisalpine, or Gallican divines and members of the Western Church generally, always believed, and as the Council of Constance in effect decreed; and who will not be bound to an article of the Christian Faith which they know to be novel, and therefore to be false as an article of faith; even if it were true, which they hold it not to be, as a proposition.

Reformers doubtless they are, but within the limits compatible with the maintenance of their ancient faith: that is to say, within the province of discipline, which, however, according to high Roman authorities, is a very wide one: and if of doctrine also, only of such doctrine as has never been truly accepted by the Church.

It seems to me, however, probable that they are in one sense too good for the age in which they live; an age for the taste and apprehension of which not only things abstract, but things remote, are as if they were not.

At the same time, in Germany, the roots of intellectual life are vigorous, and the legitimate authority of human reason, as a factor in life and conduct, is thoroughly naturalized in idea and practice.

These men are, eminently, if not exclusively, the professors of historical Christianity; and the desire, disposition, and capacity, to maintain the basis thus defined will not easily die out among them.

It seems highly probable that they will seek strength in a quarter where they may legitimately obtain it, namely, by union with the Eastern Church, immediately represented by the See of Constantinople. Of the two more serious points of distinction between East and West, one, the Papal Supremacy, is already virtually disposed of : and there seems no reason why the other should not be adjusted provisionally on the footing marked out at Bonn, or one resembling it. The services, usages, and local privileges and powers generally, would remain intact.

(III.)

It appears to be indubitable in principle that the great duty of Church communion, when it calls us to consider between conflicting claims, likewise provides us with the rule by which those claims are to be decided. We are not to consider — if we act on Catholic principles — what communion best suits our tastes. Nor even what communion is, by the usages it follows or the promises it holds out, most liberally furnished for the supply of our personal religious needs. It is, 'What communion holds the titles of the Apostolic Church? For this end it must produce to us the original charter of the day of the Ascension : and it must teach the Christian Faith — perhaps we should say more specifically the faith of the undivided Church — without diminution and without addition. For where these marks are, God has set His hand : and where He has set His hand, our souls will be best trained and moulded : and we have no more right to go elsewhere than the child to leave the house of his parents because he happens to know some other house where the father is richer or the mother fairer.

Neither must it be an intrusive Church. But this does not touch the case as between the Old Catholics and the Church of Rome, to which alone these remarks apply.

V. — CONTROVERSY WITH UNBELIEF

I HAVE printed the paper on Future Retribution of 1864 rather than that of 1879, because, though the latter is of later date, it is only part of what was probably meant to make either a review article or a book, and was left in a very confused state. Nos. 3 and 4 are given mainly for the perennial interest of the questions they deal with.

For Mr. Gladstone's matured views on this question, the reader must go to the 'Studies Subsidiary to the Works of Bishop Butler,' part 2, chaps. i. to iv.

1. FUTURE RETRIBUTION.

(November 13, 1864.)

When we address ourselves to the questions connected with the administration of the Divine justice in the world to come, we seem to be encountered by a preliminary consideration. Who and what is the creature that calls upon the Divine Being to unlock His stores and render an account of His government under any heads which it pleases the interrogator to select? What is the moral standing, what is the competency, of those who require these matters to be explained to their plenary satisfaction?

Now, this preliminary consideration, if legitimate, is important; and if important, it suggests as very worthy of note the fact that it is so seldom entertained, or even noticed. In general, each man quietly assumes the judge's chair, and proceeds to deliver therefrom his oracles.

Again, we ought the less to shrink from giving a due weight to this topic, because, after all, we must ourselves, being parties, be also judges in the case. It is pretty sure that we shall not rule it in a manner unfair to our own true claims. It is somewhat probable, indeed, that we shall do the very reverse, and that we shall finally pass from the preliminaries to the case with too favourable an estimate of our position. Still, whatever, within the confines of truth, may be done towards reducing that estimate is so much gained.

Let us take our departure from that which seems to be beyond doubt, the immeasurable distance between the Framer of the world and ourselves. Viewing this distance, we may well say it is reasonable to anticipate that the problems connected with the Divine government over us will require for their complete comprehension some intelligence higher and more powerful than ours.

If, indeed, the Almighty has thought fit by any special means, such as we term revelation, to give us a knowledge of things future and unseen different in degree or in kind from what the general resources of our being would have afforded us, then we may rationally expect first the full benefit of that inspired knowledge on the matters which the revelation embraces, and secondly, and less directly, a general elevation and bettering of our faculties. When, however, we go beyond the limits of the revelation (and *a fortiori*, if indeed we were without one), it does not appear that our capacity of judgment upon the matters now under view is essentially altered. We approach them, to say the least, with imperfect integrity and with imperfect force.

But labouring under this double imperfection, with an inadequate standard of right and inadequate means of bringing points of right to the test of that standard, can we expect that Truth will so perfectly unveil to us all her secrets as to dispose of all our difficulties? May it not be the case that even if there be a perfect solution for every single problem, even if all is without qualification 'wisest, virtuousest, discreetest, best,' and if that solution could be displayed to us in the present state of our faculties, we might still be far from able to comprehend it, and to us it would be imperfect and so far bad, and this not by reason of its faults, but by reason of its perfection?

Let us seek analogies in the world of nature and experience.

No civilized nation would allow its criminals to legislate for crime, or would consent to be bound by their judgment on this branch of its jurisprudence; for the criminal element in them would be justly held to disable them from the uniform or sure perception of right as against themselves. The analogy seems to be plain, for criminals, though they would have a selfish bias, are not wholly and absolutely corrupt. But if there are those for whom it is too harsh, let us seek for others: let us take the ward under his guardian, the child under its nurse, the animal under its guide. From these in their several degrees we may perceive how vain it would probably be to expect that the scheme of the Divine government, if it were exhibited to us, or accessible by us as a whole and in all its grounds, could as a whole and in all its grounds be thoroughly intelligible by us.

Thus far as to the competency of the race: but now a word on that of the individual. Each of us personally has his own account with the Most High, and is in a certain sense alone in the universe with his Maker and his Judge. In what attitude is he to stand before that great Being? Not only as a creature of limited powers, means, and opportunities, but as one who has corruptly or negligently failed to make the best of that use, which was in his power, of these limited powers, means, and opportunities. 'I know,' he may naturally say, 'that I am a sinner: I constantly confess that I am a miserable sinner. Over and above all mere circumstances of disadvantage, I well know that I have failed to do, not only what I ought to have done, but what I might have done, and that I have done, not only what I ought not to have done, but what I might have avoided. Therefore, O Lord Most High, I come to the pursuit of Divine knowledge with an eye dimmed and blurred, and the exhalation of my sins lies as a cloud between Thee and me. But whatever be the abstract problems of my condition as a member of the human race, this I know, that in relation to my personal desert it is one of extraordinary grace and favour. I at least am within the area enlightened by the Sun of Righteousness: I am on every side hedged in by the influences and appliances of grace: I am ever solicited to be saved: this earthly dispensation is made subservient and ministerial to the interests of my soul: all events of joy or sorrow come to me charged with purposes of love and beneficence: no question can arise upon the law of my personal condition, except how the Lord can have been so patient with me, so indulgent, so liberal towards me.' Whatever be the case with the benighted, this surely, or something like this, is the strain of thought and language that ought to be addressed to the Most High by the bulk of such as take these themes in hand.

By way of answer to this, it may perhaps be urged that God has in a certain sense made us the judges of His own justice. For the principles of Christian doctrine make their appeal to us, and find their entrance into us, by means of the elements of truth and right which still abide in the perceptions of men, in the ground and soil of the heart. It is obvious, however, to reply that it does not follow, because God has assigned a certain office and duty to these perceptions, to which they must be presumed competent, that they are also competent to other offices and duties, such as the ransacking of the whole of the Divine government, which he has not assigned to them.

2. THEISM.

(September 3, 1893.)

There are certain propositions which seem to lie at the root of the great theistic question, and also to be almost or altogether incontestable.

The visible frame of things in which we live appears to supply copious proofs that it is the work of a Maker, and that that Maker is possessed of power and wisdom to which we can assign no limits, and of an abounding and predominating goodness.

Yet there is much in things outside us, and there is more in our condition as human beings, of which we cannot give a rational or satisfactory account. Not only is there waste in creation, which appears to be a disproportion of means to end, but there is, altogether apart from human agency, both pain and the fear of pain suffered by the innocent; while all creatures are likewise overhung by the saddening mystery of death.

Acute and crushing misery is, however, chiefly referable to human agency, and to that part of human agency which is sin, or departure from the will of God. So that we have to say that if man inflicted no ill on his neighbour the world would as a rule be a happy world, and the suffering inflicted by natural agents would only constitute the rare exception.

It would also appear that, of the evil done by man, much is due rather to weakness than to an original and determined depravity: and though he is not compelled to do wrong, yet he is often placed in circumstances of weakness, temptation, and pressure, such that, in exercising the functions of moral choice, he finds the scale that inclines to evil heavily weighted against him.

Hereupon arise in the human spirit most grave questions difficult to repress. Why are not the scales of moral choice equally or even favourably weighted? Why is wickedness allowed to afflict the innocent or unoffending? Why is strength so often on the side of wickedness? Why is evil in the world outside its recoil upon the agent of evil? And lying behind all these the deeper question yet, Why is there a sufferance of evil in the world at all?

In dealing with the problem presented to us by the presence of pain, Paley suggests to us that it is a happy world. An American writer, stripping the thought of its veil, thinks that he finds an adequate solution when treating the good and the evil under the existing dispensation as matter of account, or by way of debtor and creditor; he finds that there is more to be set down on the credit side than on the side of debit. The insufficiency of these replies can hardly be doubted if they are intended to supply by their own force an explanation of the suggested difficulties and a vindication of the Divine methods in the government of the world. Hear rather the bold challenge of Dante:

> 'E tu chi se', che vuoi seder a scranna,
> Per giudicare tutto l' universo
> Con la veduta corta d' una spanna?'*

---

* Par. xix. 79.

Of this we have really the expansion in Bishop Butler. No full solution has yet been made accessible to us. But our faculties are of limited range, shallow depth, and feeble operation. That a solution does not meet the eye within this narrow precinct is neither a proof nor even a presumption against the possible existence of such a solution.

3. THE ATHANASIAN CREED.

(June 8, 1873.)

(1) The formularies of the Church content *me* for myself, with or without the Athanasian Creed.

(2) My chief reason for being thus content would be that in no other portion of the Church is the Athanasian Creed a document of popular worship. My second reason, which as far as it goes actually recommends a change, is that the clauses may mislead those who do not understand that an explanation which is technical, and appears to the uninformed oversubtle, may in reality be the rational, and the only rational, one.

(3) Also I am content with the Declaration of 1689, and think it an improvement in the rubrics.

(4) Also I have seen no other Declaration as yet that seemed to me free from objection.

(5) If, however, the Athanasian Creed were dropped out of the public service, or made optional, it seems to me that it ought to be introduced in ordinations and consecrations: where, perhaps, it would be more thoroughly in place.

(6) It seems to me that the scope of the 'damnatory' clauses is needlessly exaggerated: that their proper application is as follows:

(*a*) Of 1 and 2 to Clauses 3 and 4.

(*b*) Of Clause 28 to Clause 27.

(*c*) Of Clause 42 to the Clauses 3, 4, 27, 29, and possibly or probably to the following clauses down to 41.

(7) I do not believe that the clauses tend with the mass to disedification, for I think they are understood roughly as condemnations of unbelief; which, where wilful, is guilty.

(8) With these views, the question for me becomes one of

regard to others. There are very sincere believers both ways. But there is this to be observed: that the *bulk* of those who move against the Athanasian Creed are not firm in adhesion to dogmatic truth, desire and mean to go much farther, demand this as an initial change only, and chiefly desire the excision of the Creed as a practical negation of the title or duty of the Church to proclaim the 'damnatory' message (for of necessity there is a damnatory message) of the Gospel.

(9) The question whether an allowable concession shall be withheld, lest it should be followed up by an inadmissible demand, is one not to be answered by any unbending formula. In this case there is some reason to fear that a negative act would give an impetus to the widespread movement of the present day in favour of negation.

(10) The sum of the matter seems, then, to be, in a practical point of view, that a *certain* schism impends if the Creed be dropped, or even made optional. Individually I should be prepared to recommend the course described in No. 5, if acquiescence in it, so as to avert the danger I have described, could be had. But I am not prepared to face that danger which seems to me more formidable than any on the other side.

4. PRAYER AND THE DIVINE WILL.

(*December* 5, 1875.)

(1) There is One who foresees.

(2) *All* things are foreseen: both the acts of the free agents and of the unfree.

(3) The acts of the unfree (and lower or mechanical) agents are adapted and adjusted to the training of the free (and higher) agents.

(4) Prayer in all its parts, sorrowful, trustful, joyful, is, when normally offered according to its idea, healthy and improving for him who prays.

(5) Why should not such an exercise enter into the dispensations of God for the creatures whom He has to train?

(6) Why should we be told that God will not alter His modes of action because we wish and ask it?

(7) It is not a question of *impromptu* alteration, but of fore-ordered adaptation.

(8) If it be said this is 'unthinkable,' I admit it. But this is only saying that God is greater, and greatly greater, than we are. 'His ways are not as our ways, nor His thoughts as our thoughts.'

(9) To us, who are so little, much is 'unthinkable' or inconceivable that is also matter of daily experience. And the truly great, even of our own race, such as Homer and Shakespeare, are unthinkable — at least to me.

I submit these tentative propositions for examination.

VI. — CHILDREN

The following prayers and counsels were written for the use of his eldest son. The counsels are dated; the prayers were probably written in 1854, at the same time as the earliest counsels.

1. LITTLE PRAYERS.

(1) Upon entering a church, bow the head or close the eyes, think on God, and say, either aloud *or* to yourself:
'Oh how amiable are Thy dwellings, Thou Lord of Hosts!' (Ps. lxxxiv. 1).

(2) Before reading Holy Scripture, do in like manner, and say as above:
'Thy hands have made me and fashioned me: oh, give me understanding, that I may learn Thy commandments' (Ps. cix. 73).

(3) In church, before Divine service begins:
'O Lord Jesus Christ, Shepherd of the lambs, help me so to pray, and so to hear this day in Thy holy house on earth, that at the last I may join with holy children, to praise Thee for evermore, before Thy glorious throne in heaven.'

(4) After Divine service has ended, before leaving church:
'O God, hear me in that I have prayed to Thee, and pardon me in that my mind hath gone astray from Thee, and open Thou mine eyes that I may see Thee: through Jesus Christ our Lord.'

(5) In bed, before going to sleep, you may say:
'For He shall give His angels charge over thee, to keep thee in all thy ways.
'They shall bear thee in their hands: that thou hurt not thy foot against a stone' (Ps. xci. 11, 12).

2. MORNING AND EVENING PRAYERS.

Before morning or evening prayer, collect your thoughts: place yourself by reflection before God: and say:

'In the name of the Father, and of the Son, and of the Holy Ghost.'

Then go on as follows:

I. In the Morning.

Bless the Lord, O my soul, and all that is within me praise His holy name: for the mercies of the past night; for . . . all His goodness, and loving kindness, to me and to all men; but above all for our redemption in Jesus Christ.

Forgive me, O Lord, for His sake, all the sins of my past life. Make me grieve that I ever offended Thee, who hast so loved me. Grant that this day I may watch against sin, deny myself for the sake of the Lord Christ, and strive to avoid all temptation. [Here stop, and think of the kinds of temptation that you suffer most.]

Make me to live as a child of God, a member of Christ, and an heir of heaven. Make me gentle and loving to all men: lowly and obedient to my parents and elders, diligent and firm in all manner of duty, just and true and pure: that so living in this world, I may come to Thine everlasting kingdom in heaven.

Bless, O Lord, my father and mother, my grandpapa, my grandmama, my brother Stephen, my sisters Agnes and Jessy, all who are near and dear to me, all who are in need and sorrow, all the Bishops and clergy, and all Thy Holy Church throughout the world. All this I ask through Jesus Christ our only Saviour. Amen.

Our Father, which art, etc.

The grace of our Lord, etc.

II. In the Evening.

O almighty and tender Father, bless me before I lie down to rest. Forgive me through the precious blood of Christ whatever I have sinned this day [here stop: recollect, and confess distinctly whatever sins you have done or duties you have left undone] in thought, in word, or in deed. Enable me to serve Thee truly for the time to come, and to love Thee with all my heart.

Bless my father and mother, my brother Stephen, and sisters Agnes and Jessy, my grandpapa, my grandmama, those who teach me and attend me, and all for whom I ought to pray. And, oh, be Thou about my bed and about my path, and let Thine holy angels watch over me and keep me safe from evil in the watches of the night, through the merits of Jesus Christ our Lord. Amen.

Our Father, etc.

The grace of our Lord, etc.

3. COUNSELS, 1854–1857.

(1) On no consideration whatever omit your morning or evening prayers. If any obstacle prevent them at the proper time, say them at the first moment when you are free. If from illness or otherwise you cannot say them kneeling, say them in such place and posture as you can.

(2) Remember the Psalmist's words, 'I have set God always before me': which mean by taking care not only not to break His commands, but to cherish in the mind an abiding sense of His presence, of being near to Him, and even when in society or in bustle alone with Him.

(3) This sense of God's presence will both help and be helped by the practice of prayer by silent ejaculation, or inwardly addressing God in short sentences, though of but two or three words: although so short, their wings may be strong enough to carry upwards many a fervent desire and earnest seeking after God.

(4) So also it is good to form inwardly and to bear about with you upon the eye of your mind the image of Christ in whom we live: especially of Christ crucified, as He bled for us, and of Christ glorified, as at His Father's right hand He still offers the one everlasting sacrifice of Himself on our behalf.

(5) Let no day pass without reading some portion of the

Holy Scripture. If you can, let this course of reading follow the course of the Psalms, or of some of the Lessons, according to the Prayer-Book. It is good to acquire a habit of reading the New Testament for devotion in the Greek when you can do it with ease, by which much is learned that the English translation of necessity leaves in the shade.

(6) Sunday, the day of the Resurrection, is at once the emblem, the earnest, and the joy of the renewed life: cherish it accordingly: grudge, and as it were resent, any intrusion of worldly thoughts or conversation: except upon real necessity, strive to shut out rigorously any worldly business: always view the devotion of the day to God, not as a yoke, but as a privilege; and be assured that if and so far as this view of it shall seem overstrained, the soul is not in its health.

(7) Remember that the avoidance of sin, indispensable as it is, is the lower part of our religion: from which we should ever be striving onwards to the higher — namely, the life of Divine love, fed continually by the contemplation of God as He is revealed to us in Christ, nowhere better described in brief than by the Psalmist when he says: 'As for me, I will behold Thy presence in righteousness: and when I awake up after Thy likeness I shall be satisfied with it'—words which, like most words of Scripture, open deeper and more satisfying truths the more we humbly ponder them.

(8) Look to the Holy Communion as a great and wondrous key to unlock the things of God. In it our prayers are especially united with that sacrifice of Christ, and a new power seems to be given to them: whatever can at any time render them acceptable, there is a larger union with His people, the living and the departed — 'the whole family in heaven and earth,' as St. Paul says: a nearer identification with Him: and not a foretaste only, but, as it were, a taste of entry into His joy.

(9) The Christian should never forego any opportunity which may be offered him of access to that Heavenly Feast.

December 3, 1854.

Prayer, if understood as the mere repetition, with consciousness of their meaning, of words of petition addressed to

God, may be, as most men think it, a business requiring no great stretch or effort of mind. But, in truth, when it is such as it ought to be, it is the highest and most sustained energy of which the human mind is capable: and until we have come to know this each for ourselves, we may be assured that we have never yet prayed as we may and as we ought.

The precept, 'If any man will come after Me, let him deny himself, and take up his cross daily and follow Me,' is the perpetual and inseparable badge of a Christian. But so much are the contrivances of ease and of enjoyment multiplied nowadays, that many souls are utterly lost from want of occasions to remind them of this great precept and bring them into real contact with it. It is therefore an excellent rule to fix this, at least, that no day shall pass without some restraint put upon our natural inclination: not merely in the avoidance of sin, which is an absolute and uniform duty, but in our employments, recreations, or enjoyments — as, for example, in choosing the first according to duty and feeling, that they are not regulated by mere will and preference: in restricting the quantity of the latter: in doing some things for the pleasure or good of others, to our own inconvenience or distaste: or otherwise stinting the flesh, keeping the mind lowly, and strengthening the spirit.

Do not, because of the want of sensible fruit, grudge the time given to your prayers; and be liberal of it. As the keeping what is called good company leaves its mark on the manners of a man, so will it powerfully influence the tone of his spiritual life to have been much with God.

April 22, 1855.

I add first a few words upon what are called *relative* duties — *i.e.*, your duties to others. Do to them as you would they should do to you: and construe this precept liberally. Be strictly just to them: and not only so, but where there is a real doubt decide in their favour, not in your own. Always put upon their words and actions the best construction they will bear: you will find afterwards that it was the true one in many cases where at the time it seemed to you improbable. While avoiding all outward cringing and arts of currying favour, be most careful to cherish inwardly a habit of estimating yourself both as to intellectual and especially as to moral gifts meanly in comparison with others. No two things combine together better than meekness in asserting your rights and resolute resistance against all solicitations to do wrong, with a manifest determination to be governed in your conduct by your own judgment of right and wrong, and not by theirs. Of course this does not exclude deference to authority, age, experience, or superior means of forming a right judgment : but it is rather a rule for the common intercourse of companions. You have, I do not doubt, long known that kindness and a disposition to oblige are necessary parts of the Christian law of love. And that cheerfulness in bearing what is disagreeable, though it costs an effort at first, well and soon repays it by the goodwill which it honestly earns.

As to the duties of *self*-government, I add a few words on each of these three :

(1) Self-examination.
(2) Self-observation.
(3) Self-denial.

Give heed to self-examination ; use it from time to time : perhaps if used at fixed periodical times, with intervals not too long between them, it will thus be most profitable.

It will be of especial use in detecting, and after detection tracking, your besetting sin. When this is found, keep the eye close upon it, follow it up, drag it from its hiding-places, make no terms with it, never remit the pursuit ; and so by the grace of God's Holy Spirit may you cast it out.

When you have both found what was your besetting sin — that is, the sin *most easily* besetting you — and have by the same grace conquered it, then take the sin which besets you *next most easily*, and deal with it in like manner.

Besides self-examination, which is an act to be done from time to time, form a habit of self-observation. This will come to be a never-sleeping censor and corrector of your actions, always holding the rule of God's law against them and detecting them when they swerve.

The divisions of money necessary in order either to the use

or even the waste of it give us, without any trouble upon our own part, some sense of the relative quantities of it. But the more precious gift of our time is passing through our hands in a continuous and never-ending flow, and its parts are not separated from one another except by our own care. Without this division of it into parts we cannot tell what is little and what is much: above all, we cannot apply it in due proportion to our several duties, pursuits, and recreations. But we should deal with our *time* as we see in a shop a grocer deal with tea and sugar, or a haberdasher with stuffs and ribbons: weighing or measuring it out in proportions adjusted to that which we are to get for and by it. This is the express command of St. Paul, who bids us ἐξαγοράζεσθαι τὸν καιρον, imperfectly rendered by our version 'to redeem the time': for it means to make merchandise of it, and to deal strictly with it, as men deal with goods by which they mean to make a profit: to pursue the same means they pursue, energy, care, watchfulness, forethought, attention to small things, in order that we, too, may make that profit the greatest possible.

February 17, 1856.

When you reflect that your evil thoughts and dispositions, as well as acts, all lie naked and open before the eye of God, even though they may have escaped the view of man, is this a subject of satisfaction or of dissatisfaction? Would you have it otherwise if you could, and hide them from Him also?

The Christian hates sin, and, finding that neither his own nor any other human eye can effectually track it out in him, while he knows it to be the true and only curse and pest of the universe, must rejoice to think that there is one from whom it cannot lie hid: and who will weigh his own case, which he may feel to be to him unfathomable, in the scales of perfect justice and boundless mercy.

But if we are sensible of a lurking wish that we could hide the sad sight of our inner sins from God, this, while it abides, is a fatal sign.

Beware of taking kindnesses from others as matters of course.

The heart well purged by humility is so deeply conscious of its unworthiness, that to receive acts of kindness always excites some emotion of gratitude, of shame, of surprise, or all three together : of gratitude for the benefit, of shame upon thinking how ill it is deserved, of surprise that our brethren should bestow upon us what we so little merit.

March 12, 1856.

Try and reconcile your mind thoroughly to the idea that this world, if we would be well and do well in it, is a world of work, and not of idleness.

This idea will, when heartily embraced, become like a part of yourself, and you will feel that you would on no account have it torn from you.

February 8, 1857.

Try to found your religion, so far as any compendium of it is concerned, upon the Creeds : and remember always that the Catholic Faith is our religion — the Faith One, Divine, and Unchangeable ; which still, happily, is owned in a wonderful manner and degree by the great mass of Christians as it has been through eighteen hundred years, though in the minds of some it has been stinted and curtailed, or feebly and timidly owned, while by others it has been overlaid with dangerous usages, or associated with tenets that more or less mar its pure and perfect application. In one or other of these ways most religious systems have in time come to err, nor can we hope that our own is absolutely exempt from the common lot ; but let us remember the promise of God to His Church, that it shall be kept until the end of time in the possession of all that is needful for its life: and let us reflect with wondering thankfulness that the old Creeds are still repeated with one consent through every corner of the earth where the name of Christ is named ; nay, that even of those who have rashly ceased to use them a large part still cling to much of the precious truth enshrined in them.

April 25, 1857.

Vanity, unequivocal vanity, sometimes finds vent in self-depreciation. One mode of this is when we affectedly cry ourselves down with a hope — more or less concealed even from ourselves — that others will protest and set us up again. Another mode is when we cry ourselves down as to particular faculties of a secondary order, in order by implication to set up some faculty of higher rank.

He that has made a leap to-day can more easily make the same leap to-morrow ; and he will make a longer or higher leap soon, perhaps the day after. His muscles are stretched, and are also strengthened. This we call practice. From it comes a certain state of the body. So from practice in good or evil comes a certain state of the mind. This is called habit : and it tends to the doing again with more ease what we have already done with less. The thought of that mighty engine ! never slumbering, ever working : self-feeding, self-acting : powerful and awful servant of God who ordained it : powerful and restless, too, alike for the destruction and for the salvation of souls.

What we do without *habit* we do because it pleases at the time. But what we do by habit we do even though it pleases little or not at all at the time.

Place habit, then, on the side of religion. You cannot depend upon your tastes and feelings towards Divine things to be uniform : lay hold upon an instrument which will carry you over their inequalities, and keep you in the honest practice of your spiritual exercises, when but for this they would have been intermitted.

Again, observe the awful power of habit over the wicked. They forget, while they are taking pleasure in sin, that they are creating a power over themselves, which will make them practise it even when they have ceased to take pleasure in it. *Measure* that power by its effect upon them, and having measured, use it for the opposite effect, that it may help you to good as it is helping them to evil, and will presently constrain them.

But you will say, By the time habit is strong enough to constrain to good, a man will so love it that he will not want to be constrained.

Learn better : God has not one discipline for all. He now gives you easy lessons ; as your strength increases He will make them nobler, and therefore harder; and the power of habit, which you might not need for your present task, will be alike needful and useful for your future one; so that with it you will do what without it you would fail in.

Thus you see that, when God in the flesh bid us take a lesson from the banks where money is kept at interest, we are to read that lesson into the language of our spiritual life. And it is so with all the concerns of the worldly life: the children of this world have real wisdom in their generation: and all the lessons of worldly life when translated rightly are lessons of the Divine life.

Thus every day's good will enable you to do more good: the earnings of to-day are stock to work with to-morrow. Bread laid up will not produce bread to-morrow: but a good act done, strengthening the frame of mind that did it, will do — that is, you by it will do more good acts to-morrow. It is like money put out at usury one day, which makes more money the next; so does virtue beget daily more virtue, and grace more grace.

Photo, W. Bell Jones, Hawarden.

MEMORIAL TOMB AND CHAPEL IN HAWARDEN CHURCH.

ERECTED BY HENRY N. GLADSTONE.

Sculptured by Sir W. B. Richmond, K.C.B., R.A., D.C.L.

VII. — PERSONAL

THE contents of this part of the Appendix might be greatly extended. The examples chosen, with the exception of the first, have been taken almost at random. The Eucharistic Devotions have no date, and were probably brought together at various times. Of the three papers belonging to the Evangelical period, two have been already described. The second, the earliest in date, deals with the subject of separation from the world, which is handled at greater length in No. 7. The two next in order relate to Trinity College, Glenalmond, and the last to St. Deiniol's Library—the main interest of his latest, as Glenalmond had been of his earlier, years.

1. DEVOTIONS FOR INTERVALS OF THE EUCHARISTIC SERVICE.

BEFORE SERVICE.

Oh, how amiable are Thy dwellings : Thou Lord of hosts !
The hill of Sion is a fair place : and the joy of the whole earth.
The Lord hath chosen Sion to be an habitation for Himself : He hath longed for her.
Out of Sion hath God appeared : in perfect beauty.
Lord, I have loved the habitation of Thine house : and the place where Thine honour dwelleth.
Oh, worship the Lord in the beauty of holiness : let the whole earth stand in awe of Him.
O Lord, how glorious are Thy works : Thy thoughts are very deep.

O Lord, correct me, but with judgment: not in Thine anger, lest Thou bring me to nothing.

Oh, hold Thou up my goings in Thy paths: that my footsteps slip not.

O Lord, let it be Thy pleasure to deliver me: make haste, O Lord, to help me.

Oh, send out Thy light and Thy truth, that they may lead me: and bring me unto Thy holy hill, and to Thy dwelling.

First Act of Penitence and Humiliation.

Put me not to rebuke, O Lord, in Thine indignation: neither chasten me in Thy heavy displeasure.

For Thine arrows stick fast in me: and Thy hand presseth me sore.

There is no health in my flesh, because of Thy displeasure: neither is there any rest in my bones, by reason of my sin.

For my wickednesses are gone over my head: and are like a sore burden, too heavy for me to bear.

My wounds stink and are corrupt: through my foolishness.

I am brought into so great trouble and misery: that I go mourning all the day long.

For my loins are filled with a sore disease: and there is no whole part in my body.

I am feeble and sore smitten: I have roared for the very disquietness of my heart.

Lord, Thou knowest all my desire: and my groaning is not hid from Thee.

My heart panteth, my strength hath failed me: and the sight of mine eyes is gone from me.

Second Act of Penitence and Humiliation.

Coram Te, nec justus forem,
Quamvis totâ vi laborem,
Nec si fide nunquam cesso,
Fletu stillans indefesso.

Or in the English:

Nothing in my hand I bring,
Simply to Thy Cross I cling :
Naked, come to Thee for dress ;
Helpless, look to Thee for grace ;
Foul, I to the Fountain fly ;
Wash me, Saviour, or I die.

After the Sanctus.

(Hebrews xii.)

But ye are come
unto Mount Sion,
and unto the city of the living God,
the heavenly Jerusalem,
and to an innumerable company of angels,
to the general assembly and Church of the firstborn,
which are written in heaven,
and to God the Judge of all,
and to the spirits of just men made perfect,
and to Jesus the Mediator of the new covenant,
and to the blood of sprinkling, that speaketh better
 things than that of Abel.

Before the Prayer of Consecration.

Thou, that offerest by the eternal throne,
Suffer us by Thy footstool ;
Suffer us, albeit unworthy,
Yet, by Thine holy and perpetual ordinance,
Fellow-workers with Thee,
Suffer us with Thee to offer
The one everlasting Sacrifice.

Prayer preceding Access.

Tanquam, præ tremendo Tribunali Tuo, Domine, ubi nullus erit personarum respectus ; ita hodie, ante hoc sacrosanctum altare Tuum, coram Te et stupendis angelis Tuis, conscientiâ propriâ dejectus, profero improbas et iniquas cogitationes atque actiones meas.

Respice, oro, humilitatem meam, Domine, et remitte omnia peccata mea, quæ multiplicata sunt super capillos capitis mei. Quodnam enim est malum, quod non in animo commisi? Quin et multa et nefanda opera perpetravi. Reus sum invidiæ, iræ, luxuriæ, malitiæ, superbiæ, gulæ, desidiæ. Omnes sensus meos, omnia membra mea, pollui.

Sed infinita est multitudo misericordiarum Tuarum, incredibilis clementia bonitatis Tuæ. Quare, O Rex omni admiratione major, O Domine longanimis, clementissimæ propensionis Tuæ benignitatem manifestato: potentissimæ dexteræ Tuæ vim exercito: et me prodigum resipiscentem recipito, per Jesum Christum Dominum Nostrum. Amen.

NOTE. — I became acquainted with this remarkable prayer more, I think, than fifty years ago, when it had been published by Cardinal (then Mr.) Newman, in the 'Devotions of Archbishop Laud.' I have used it ever since in the altar service as the closing preliminary before personal access, as it appeared to be admirably suited for the occasion. It is here written out from memory, and may not be in precise verbal correspondence with the text given in the work from which I took it.

It was so taken, in the belief that it was an original composition of Archbishop Laud; and only from the 'Euchology,' printed in English at Kidderminster in the year 1891, and most kindly sent to me by the Chaplain to the Russian Embassy, I have found the true original in the devotions of St. Simon the Meditative, at pp. 240–243 of that manual.

The prayer as it stands in Archbishop Laud may be truly said to correspond with the first half of St. Simon's composition. There are changes in phraseology, but the spirit is maintained entire, and the structure of the sentences remains. It seems to me as if judgment was shown by the Archbishop (if the act were his) in the limitation. The latter part is indeed equally admirable in matter, but less pointedly adapted to the solemn purpose for which the Archbishop used it. Does it not express, with a depth and truthfulness rarely if ever exceeded, the intensity and virulence of sin, while it opens with boldness the new and living way? (Heb. x. 19, 20).

BEFORE RECEIVING THE SACRAMENT OF THE BODY.

O tremendum sacramentum Corporis Domini!
Deus meus, fac me capacem Corporis Domini!

After.

Incarnatus, Homo factus,
Passus tantos cruciatus,
Tractus et crucifixus,
Mortuus ac sepultus,
Redux ab inferis,
Sublatus in cœlum,
Regnans in gloriâ,
Venturus in judicium,
Per sacrosanctum Corpus Tuum,
Munditur Corpus immundum meum.

Before the Cup.

O suavissimum Sacramentum Sanguinis Domini!
Deus meus, fac me capacem Sanguinis Domini!

Agnus Dei, ante omnia et super omnia mihi dulcedo, accipe, propter immensum amorem Tuum, hoc quantulumcunque quod offero sacrificium : omne quod sum, quod habeo ; quod facio, quod sentio ; quod amo, quod spero.

After.

Agnus Dei, qui tollis peccata mundi
In Sanguine Tuo abluar,
Propter Te absolvar,
Pro Te vivam,
Cum Te patiar,
In Te moriar,
Sub alâ Tuâ requiescam
In valle umbraculi mortis :
Per Te inveniam misericordiam
In illo Die.

As Convenient at and about Reception.

Quod non vidimus
 Id tamen credimus :
Quod non tangimus
 Id comedimus.

Last among the last,
    Least among the least,
Can there be a place for me
    At the marriage feast?

Return from the Altar.

O vis magna Mortis atque Resurrectionis Domini, illabere in spiritum necnon in corpus meum, et fac me vivere vitam Domini, fac me in dies expectare Adventum Ejus gloriosissimum.

After Return.

Pater omnipotens,
Fili Unigenite,
Spiritus Sancte,
Da mihi jam depasto cœlestum cibum, et sic propius sito, orare

Pro omni creaturâ,
Pro genere humano,
Pro Ecclesiâ Catholicâ,
Pro parte ejus expectanti lucem, pacem, profectum versus Te.
Requiem æternam dona eis, Domine, et lux perpetua luceat eis.

> [And that it may please Thee to fill up the number of Thine elect, and to hasten the coming of Thy kingdom.]

Pro parte militanti
Ecclesiâ Orientali,
Occidentali,
Anglicanâ,
Universâ :
Pro Episcopis, Presbyteris et Diaconis :
Pro clero huic altari inservienti,
Pro politiis et imprimis pro nostrâ
Stabilitatem, pacem,
Pro populis et imprimis pro nostrati,
Ut in sanctâ simplicitate degens cibo ac potu Tuo pascatur.
Pro Regibus et imprimis pro Reginâ nostrâ,
Ut gregi Tuo fideliter intendat

Ut electis ordinibus ascribatur.

Pro Academis, Collegiis, et Scholis, et imprimis Etonensi Oxoniensi, Æde Christi.

Pro piis inceptis
[Nominatim Fasque, Glenalmond, Hawarden, Liverpool, Oxford, Ireland.]

Prayer for Conformity.

Fac ut ambulemus; sicut ambulavit Christus.

Fac ut qualis erat in Illo, talis et sit in nobis Spiritus.

Fac ut reformetur conversatio nostra, ad normam conversationis Ejus.

Fac ut ea faciamus, quæ fecisset Christus hodie in carne degens, et eo quo Christus modo.

Fac ut fiamus vasa gratiæ Ejus, organa voluntatis Ejus.

At the Close of Service.

Go forth with me, O Lord, from this Thy holy house; cast about me the fence which the Evil One cannot pass,

And clothe me in the armour which his darts cannot pierce;

And send down upon me Thy love, and light, and calm, wherein, as in a cloud, I may continually dwell, and worship Thee for evermore.

On Departure from the Church.

O blessed Peace, which hast here and now been ministered to us, leave us not, and let us leave thee not:

But descend upon us:

And be shed around us,

And go forth with us,

And abide in us, on every step of this world's upward way, until we come to dwell in thy bosom for ever.

O Semen immortalitatis, hodie in nos receptum, nullâ vi vel fraude pereas, vel carnis vel diaboli:

Sed vivas,

Sed vigeas,

Sed crescas,

Sed fructum feras,

Fructum centuplicem in vitam æternam.

2. SEPARATION FROM THE WORLD.
(*October* 14, 1832.)

'Our conversation is in heaven'; spirit, not persons; deadness to the worldly spirit as necessary now as ever.

Particular Rules.

(1) To cut off at once and unsparingly every act or intercourse which causes any known sin in self.

(2) To use the same measure with what affords natural encouragement to such in others.

(3) If progress in Christian truth be gradual, then, as the eye of the mind is quickened, new specks will be discerned, and the catalogue of forbidden things enlarged.

(4) But if a man shall have been suddenly converted, then he may under strong recoil have fled from many things allowable, and therefore for the sake of his fellow-men desirable.

(5) For whatever is allowable is desirable.

(6) But in approaching inquiry into lawfulness of any pleasure, we should reverse the judicial law (acting, in fact, upon the converse of its principle), and assume it guilty till it is found innocent.

(7) In whatever pleasures are retained and indulged, we must observe a *mean* as to quantity (from their dynamical nature).

(8) We must try to make all pleasures *considered as such* sit light upon us.

(9) We must keep constantly in view that they are good, not in themselves, but for ulterior ends, as —

> (*a*) Exciting thankfulness.
> (*b*) Repairing fatigue.
> (*c*) Expanding the lighter and more minute parts of character.
> (*d*) Attracting our fellow-men to substantial good—a good *secondary* principle, but a most pernicious *primary*.

(10) We must endeavour not only to keep in view their general ends and grounds, but to intermix all possible advantage in particular cases and times.

(11) Let a man thoroughly examine, to learn how he should mix with persons whom he deems too little sensible of God, the characters of Abraham, David, Daniel.

(12) But above all of Jesus Christ Himself, in His intercourse with the wealthy, and even with the less reputable classes of society.

3. MONEY.
(*September* 18, 1836.)

It is wrong to say we ought not to care about money. We ought to care about money. We might as well say we did not care about time ; or did not care about health and bodily strength ; or did not care about our mental faculties : for all these are referable to one and the same class, namely, the class of means and instruments which God has put into our hands (ourselves His primary instruments) to be employed for His glory. All may be made productive of or subsidiary [to] good, each in its several place and degree : which, on the other hand, all are alike open to perversion towards evil.

We ought, then, to care about money, as a means : to be utterly regardless of it, as an end. We ought to be careful (1) to spend it — always to have either (*a*) a present or (*b*) a prospective purpose for it ; (2) *so* to spend it that we may be the better able to open our books of pecuniary account, along with the rest of our proceedings, before God at the Day of Judgment : and to show that it has been given, where not to the necessary or decent expenses of our personal station, to those of our own improvement and that of our fellow-men, in all, but especially in those which are immediately spiritual respects.

There are what mathematicians would term different *orders* of means appointed by God in the world : whereof the inferior, ascending from the lowest of the scale, is in succession subordinate to *all* the higher. We ourselves, as spiritual agents, may be said to be in the first order of means towards the great end of God's glory. Our time, health, talents, and fortune, may again be said to be in the second order of means, towards the spiritual well-being of men, and so to God's glory. With this distinction among them : that the last is not essential beyond a very small quantity, nor, indeed, is bodily health altogether so.

But there are some men who boast that they do not care for money, while they avowedly are nice about meat and drink. They ought rather to blush; for meat and drink are in a third order of means, one subservient to that in which money stands. They are subsidiary to the preservation of health, and fortune, and time, and talents. They do not contribute to the glory of God, therefore, except at one remove farther than money : in the primary way, that is : for there is a secondary way in which all acts and functions contribute directly to the glory of God — that is, by the temper in which they are performed. Hence the Apostle, Whether ye eat or drink, or whatsoever ye do, do all to the glory of God.

4. THE WORLD AND THE FLESH.
(*September* 10, 1837.)

Another point in which it may appear that modern theology has departed from the mind and the analogy of Scripture is in the relative proportions which our preaching assigns to its operations against the flesh and the world respectively. We now hear very much of the world and of separation therefrom, but comparatively little of crucifying the flesh with the affections and lusts. And yet, surely, in the Apostolical teaching greater attention is paid to the flesh as the more formidable and subtle enemy of the two. If this be true, its principle applies with much greater force to our own days. For the demarcation between the Church and the world was then clear : and by the world was indicated the mass of men lying beyond the pale of the Gospel. Practically to us, in a land professing Christianity, the world in this sense has ceased to exist. The wickedness of Christians may be as great — may be far more guilty — but it is not denounced by St. Paul under the same term. The territory of the world is taken into the Church : and the life and practices condemned as worldly are in their truest and most primary sense much rather to be described as fleshly. The spirit that formerly worked in the children of disobedience still works in them against the influences of the Gospel : it is now, however, the working, not of heathen principles and practice in a mass unenlightened by the rays and unsaddled with the responsibilities of revelation, but simply of the evil principle of our nature with the malignant energies of Satan, a working intrinsic and not extrinsic to ourselves as a body : and only in part extrinsic to ourselves as individuals. The peril of a temptation is made up in part of the external allurement, in part of the internal prepossession, where the temptation is most external : and even in such cases there are those who can testify that the inward foe contributes by far the more formidable portion of the difficulty. While there are at least some men to whom the distinct class of temptations that are wholly within the individual, and therefore exclusively of the flesh (as contradistinguished from the world), entirely transcend in subtlety and force those which are in part extrinsic.

If this be so, and if experimental observation be here but collateral to the example and authority of Scripture, may we not rightly describe it as a defect of our modern theology that it spends more time and weapons against the term 'world,' which has wellnigh lost its proper signification, than against the term 'flesh,' which, alas ! retains all its awful power, and includes the springs and sources from whence proceeded those manifestations which, in a peculiar collective form, were denounced by the Apostles as characteristics of the world ?

It may, however, be demanded that we should point out practical disadvantage arising from an alteration which it may be contended is immaterial, since the same principle is attacked under either term.

It may suffice to notice the following mischievous results :

First, directing the attention mainly to the world instead of the flesh, does not the preacher run the risk of leading his hearers into spiritual pride ? For when the Apostles wrote the distinction was clear between the Church and the world : and when the inspired penman described a certain character as belonging to a certain community, it was obvious to the commonest understanding to whom the application was to be made. Is that the case now? No. Further, it is not possible, humanly speaking, certainly it is not consistent with the fact, that the character held up to reprobation under the term *world* should remain in a disembodied state, without application to individuals and bodies of individuals : and each person is thus tempted into the great peril of deciding for himself what others, partakers of the same Christian privileges with himself, he shall place in the condemned category. Wherein he must too probably set out with violating our Lord's idea of the Church as an enclosure containing both good and bad : and at every step he must as he proceeds judge his neighbour, with every risk of reflecting congratulations and complacent regards upon himself.

Next, the practice dilutes the strength of Christian doctrine and blunts the arrows of the preacher. When he reprobates the flesh, we know what he means, and we [need] not go abroad to look among our neighbours for the objects of his reproof; the evil and accursed thing is in ourselves, within our bosoms, and pervading all our life. The application, therefore, of threat, censure, remonstrance, exhortation, promise, comfort, encouragement, is immediate : it passes from the mouth of the speaker (by God's grace) to the heart of the hearer. Now, when he utters invectives only or chiefly against the world, it is true that he means us to beware of the spirit of evil within us, and would enable us to detect it at home by learning its lineaments from observation abroad; but is not this, as a general rule, an inversion of the Divinely constituted process and of the natural order of things? Shall we not in our corruption be too glad to let the denunciation rest upon the heads of those at whom it is primarily discharged? Will not our self-love have great facilities for evading any transmission of the reproach to our own heart and conduct? Is it not when the Voice of God is brought within one stage of ourselves that we most want aid from His servants to carry it onwards to its destination? When the flesh is assailed we know that means each one of us : but when the world, we fancy it a body from which we are separate — nay, in many cases we know it applies to persons practising a certain class of amusements, which we perhaps have foregone : at all events, the message of the preacher comes to us like a spent ball, and fails to break the obduracy of the heart.

5. DEPRESSION.

(June 5, 1838.)

When you are heavily depressed, take the Divine will as it comes to you in the stream of incidents of daily life, and do not seek to look out of it : for the farther you look the less certainly you can read it : and you are in a state to require near and immediate support : be content, then, with that which lies at your hand. Ask not in your dreamy mind, How shall I live through this year, and the next, and the next ? but think of the duties of the day, and gladly hide your head within its narrow fold. Even they may not be pleasant, but this is the right way in which you will be blessed : they will keep you out of a region of more pain. It is like the case of those in the 'Inferno' (c. xxi.) :

> 'Però, se tu non vuoi de' nostri graffi,
> Non far sovra la pegola soverchio.'

This seems a strange comparison : there is truth in it. But whatever be the pain, cling to the will of God : and in proportion as the atmosphere is dark, to the near will of God ; this alone will bear you through.

6. A 'THIRD ORDER.'

(March 9, 1838.)

(1) That great benefit might accrue to religion from the institution of societies within the Church, aiming at a greater yet a safer, less presuming and less egotistical separation from the world than can easily be attained where the ground of separation is in any notion adopted by merely individual judgment.

(2) That such institution would be in conformity with the principles of cathedral and collegiate institutions ; and with the longings of Archbishop Leighton, who lamented that the

Reformation generally had not made provision for those who were inclined to a stricter way of life.

(3) That, however, the beneficial objects would be by no means purely negative and consisting in the relinquishment of a more common for a more peculiar mode of life : they would have many positive uses besides those personal only or primarily to themselves, as for example :

(4) (*a*) The maintenance of daily worship.
   (*b*) The pursuit of divine learning.
   (*c*) The exemplification of Church rules and discipline.
   (*d*) The visitation of the sick, the aged, the poor.
   (*e*) Care of hospitals, prisons, workhouses.
   (*f*) The education of the young, whether charitable or otherwise.
   (*g*) The uses of society among those who have not close natural connections among whom to reside.

(5) All which in a more general view we may regard under the heads of devotion, study, society, charity, tuition.

(6) It would appear desirable that such institutions should, when practicable, be divided into two branches, each having a seat — the one in the country (where boarders might be educated), the other in one of our large towns, and among its densest districts.

(7) The members to pass by cycle from the one of these to the other, so as to equalize or distribute proportionably the pressure.

(8) That they should be partially eleemosynary in certain cases, offering pecuniary advantages, but never gratuitously.

(9) That they should embrace persons in different classes of temporal circumstances — not, however, on a footing of absolute equality.

(10) That they should consist of brethren, both clerical and lay.

(11) That personal duties should be assigned by fixed statute to all members in their several classes.

(12) That they should be bound to conformity with the injunctions of those statutes by solemn engagement.

(13) That such engagement, or vow, should in the first instance be for no more than twelve (?) months.

(14) That it should be renewable from year to year (or in the following scale) to be taken —

        1st time, for one year.
        2nd ,,   for two years.
        3rd ,,   for three.
        4th ,,   for seven.
        5th ,,   for life.

(15) No person under full age to be competent to enter into any such engagement, or vow.

(16) All members of such an institution to reside within its walls,

(17) And to attend daily worship:

(18) And in general to have common tables — at least for certain principal meals:

(19) And to have some distinguishing habit or symbol:

(20) And to divide among them the several departments of duty:

(21) And to act under the parochial clergy and the Bishop in every case:

(22) And within fixed and known limits:

(23) And to educate as follows:

    (*a*) The children of the poor — both in town and country, but many more, of course, in town — these in one day school or more.
    (*b*) The children of the lower middling class — in the country united probably with the foregoing — in town at a separate and entirely self-supporting school.
    (*c*) The children of classes higher than these, as boarders, in the country.

(24) All children of all the classes to attend public daily worship within the walls.

(25) And to be taught music among the elementary branches of education, in order to the use of it in the daily worship.

(26) Church within the walls, having departments for the clerical members, the lay members, the schools, and the public.

(27) Sermons to be delivered as frequently as may be, both on Sundays, festivals, fasts, and certain days of the week.

(28) Morning *and* evening service daily in the church, one at least of them with music.

(29) The Holy Communion to be administered weekly in the church, and on saints' days.

(30) Upon a certain number of saints' days, and of other days, lives of the saints and of other holy men not canonized to be commemorated.

(31) Adhesion to the three Creeds to be a religious test of all *members* upon admission, and a declaration that the motive is desire of the glory of God, and to be renewed in His image through the body of His blessed Son.

(32) All servants of the institution if practicable to be members.

(33) The entire Scriptures, and the Church Catechism, the Creed, and the Lord's Prayer, to be used and explained in all the schools.

(34) Such arrangements to be made that lessons may commence and end with prayer, whether in the church or in the school.

(35) The buildings to consist of church, hall, library, schools, bedchambers, sitting-rooms, apartments for the Superior and officers.

(36) No price to be fixed upon the benches in the chapel which shall be open to the public: but a collection to be made from man to man on Sundays, and at such other times as shall be ordered.

(37) The proceeds of such collections to be divided between local and general purposes of a nature either charitable or connected with the Church.

(38) But no portion of them to be applied for the pecuniary advantage of the institution, unless it be in establishing rewards or prizes for merit or eleemosynary funds, or in beautifying the House of God.

(39) Gates to be opened and closed at fixed hours.

(40) All members to attend at the funeral of any member.

(41) The inspection of schools out of the walls may be undertaken, with consent of the local clergy.

(42) Certain courses of lectures and sermons to be delivered (besides those of a more general nature):

   (*a*) In *continuous* exposition of the Scripture.
   (*b*) In explaining the harmony and order of the services of the Church.
   (*c*) In explaining her history from the time of our Redeemer and His Apostles until now.

(43) All clergy being members to have the licence of the Bishop.

(44) All persons desirous of becoming members to be subject to question by the Superior and his deputies, with a view to determining their class and functions.

(45) Trustees of the institution to be appointed, not being members: and the office of trustee avoidable on becoming a member.

(46) Private property may be retained or not by the members, subject to limitations in amount receivable within the walls, and in manner of expenditure.

(47) Where property is not retained, to be commutable for a fixed maintenance of a certain kind, as if in the nature of an annuity.

(48) Members to be bound to visitation of the sick as usual in time of pestilence or epidemic.

(49) To be restricted from certain amusements.

7. AMUSEMENTS.

(Good Friday, April 13, 1838.)

(1) Query whether the rule of the 'religious world' respecting amusements does not surrender either too little or too much: and whether it is based, as it professes to be, on a clear and palpable principle capable of uniform application?

(2) It is easy to understand such a rule as this: that one should not follow any practice of which the general and permanent effect is to deaden the sense and the desire of the presence of God, and the realization of spiritual life. It was

well said by Mrs. Wesley, 'Whatever such and such a practice may be to others, to you whom it thus affects it is sin.'

(3) It is easy to fix another rule of personal conduct, which is this : Wherever the practice involves a participation in sin, by literal or virtual necessity, on the part of those who are engaged in carrying it on, then it becomes undoubtedly wrong to be a contributor to its maintenance, even although there may be no sensibly evil effect on your own mind, and though you may be enabled to extract what is innocent or beneficial in the influences arising therefrom.

(4) But these rules do not reach the extent of that which is very commonly adopted by religious persons in our day, and made a sort of law among them, and almost a criterion of soundness in faith.

(5) The case before us is that of certain other amusements, enjoyments, indulgences, not essentially linked with sin, but opening up many channels of temptation : balls and assemblies, for example, would be taken as the most obvious exemplifications of what is meant.

(6) There is no reason that I am aware of, except want of faith and prayer, that should hinder a man from carrying his religion into his amusements where he is not acting nor encouraging sin.

(7) Nor am I aware that there is anything in the *essence* of balls and assemblies which, even in the case of our rebellious race, so connects sin with that essence as to render countenance of them in any form countenance given to sin.

(8) If the appeal be put in this way : Can you refuse to abandon these paltry and unsatisfying pleasures for the sake of the Lord who bought you ? the answer must undoubtedly be that we are ready to surrender them in a moment upon hearing the call of our duty and our love to Him.

(9) Some of us might add — and that not from superior spirituality — that to them these are not pleasures, but upon the whole a burden, borne like others in the hope of its being sanctified.

(10) But thus the question comes to be one of Christian expediency — and so it is generally regarded — we have to ask whether it is more expedient to join in this and that, or to

abstain from it : measuring expediency, of course, by religious results.

(11) Observe, however, that in this we assume that, if there be particular adjuncts of these amusements which are sinful or naturally conducive to sin, *those* we have already disposed of and cast away, and we are now arguing only about the practice as divested of these adjuncts.

(12) And if it be said, in going to a ball you may make a weak brother to stumble : I suspect the principle goes farther than is supposed by those who use it. Look at the state of *luxury* in which we live : the dress, the furniture, the equipages, the houses, the sumptuous fare. Are not these to the full as liable to be misunderstood as the particular amusements under the limitation already stated (11) which the religious world has branded?

(13) I do think they are : I feel quite as much scruple and doubt in their use. They jar as much at first sight with the idea of 'strangers and pilgrims.'

(14) It is not enough to answer, these are the requisitions of society which we must obey, unless the things required be essentially sinful : there is truth in this principle : but it is a counteractive to that stated in 12 : for in obeying these requisitions — in using luxuries which we feel to be dangerous, and the aspect of which we must know might well mislead one, at any rate, of hasty judgment — we are running the risk of making a brother stumble.

(15) But so, surely, was our Lord when He attended the marriage feast, and when He sat at meat in the house of a publican.

(16) We must come at the mind of Scripture by comparing St. Paul's practice respecting meats, and again his rebuke of St. Peter, with the cases just cited, and any others bearing upon the same issue.

(17) In point of fact, the inference in the case of the meat, against which St. Paul determined to guard, would have been a fair one — that is, so plausibly deduced from general practice, that none but a strong mind could be expected to detect the fallacy.

(18) The questions here are, whether the inference is equally

fair in the case of the (regulated) ball or assembly? and whether it is more fair than it would be in the other cases enumerated in 12?

(19) There is a point not yet touched upon. If any practice clash with the discharge of a religious duty, this constitutes a new and a fatal objection: and I am not prepared to say how far the head of a family, who must, one should think, desire his family to have daily worship, might be so circumstanced as to render this incompatible with evening amusements. This is, I think, an objection to be considered separately.

(20) As to the objection of the incongruity of religious conversation, or of conversation on religious principles, in the midst of these parties, it is undoubtedly possible to depict a case in which the apparent contrast shall be strong: but I think it is an apparent, not a real, incongruity: an incongruity of the same kind, for example, as that of praying to God in the middle of a debate in Parliament: or of saying grace at a London dinner-party between the dinner and the dessert.

(21) I would even ask whether evening amusements be not *capable* of having the sting taken out of them at least as effectually as dinner-parties?

(22) Both will undoubtedly remain dangerous: but our whole life is dangerous: and the question here is only about gratuitous and superfluous dangers which we are bound not to incur.

(23) Another rule of personal conduct undoubtedly is, to watch our native inclinations, and to be wary especially in that to which we have a propensity, and sometimes to deny it to ourselves for the mere benefit of the denial.

(24) All pleasure, we seem to have forgotten, which is sought as such, is evil and sinful. None of these amusements — and more, none of our most private relaxations — are good in themselves; they must all be sanctified by having an aim out of themselves, and higher than themselves. This applies chiefly to limitation in quantity: since it is when much limited in quantity that pleasure contributes to reinvigorate the mind.

(24A) But further: the *business* of the world is as unprofitable in itself as are its pleasures: and one's engaging in commerce, or politics, with earnestness, may be as liable to be mistaken as a participation, not engrossing, in common amusements. Both pleasure and business have the same need to be sanctified.

(25) Now suppose it be required of me that I should show cause why I do not give up these evening amusements, and the more so because professing to find little use or enjoyment in them:

(26) I should answer that it is because I cannot see a line to separate them from those other usages which I accept as a part of the constitution of society in which we are ordained to live, and as belonging to our juxtaposition with one another in the world.

(27) I can very easily imagine that, were I more free to choose respecting the whole subject of intercourse with men either in business or pleasure, than I am, it might seem needful or desirable for me to withdraw so feeble and so evil a nature from its temptations: but I think that the points enumerated in 12 are matters in which, with a view to real Christian mortification, the sacrifice of self-will, and the subjugation of our whole nature to God, it would seem needful to outstrip the religious world before so much as equalling it in its renunciation of certain amusements in which the generality partake.

(28) For I observe this peculiarity: the amusements are condemned in gross: and not so much for their essential qualities, as because they are practised by persons who are termed 'the world.'

(29) Now I very much doubt the Christian right of anyone to apply the appellation of 'the world' to any among the members of the visible Church except those who are hardened or avowed in the neglect of God. The tares in the field, the fish in the net, the unfruitful branches of the vine, and the practical conduct of St. Paul to his offending Christians, appear clearly to show the sense of Scripture in this matter.

(30) That against which we have to contend is the evil nature which is in as well as around us, and Satan working

through it; but much more are we concerned with the intrinsic than the extrinsic.

(31) I know not whether it be uncharitable—I cordially wish it were inaccurate—to say that there is now comparatively little preaching against the beam which is in our own eye, and much against the mote in our neighbour's.

(32) In the Apostolic times the world, being subject to no Christian influences, afforded a full and free development of the evil principle within us, namely, *rebellion* against God in the flesh and in the mind: and thus formed a ready and appropriate exemplification of the warfare which we have to carry on.

(33) But it is a very different thing for one portion (for example) of the Corinthian Church to condemn another — not, be it observed, *in respect of their acts*, but to condemn the acts in respect of them. To say, as is now commonly said, Such and such are the amusements of the *world* — avoid them.

(34) I have here an insuperable barrier. Show me an objection in the thing itself, and you are intelligible; but I know not how I can possibly separate myself from *persons* as such, or otherwise than on account of their acts. Well, then, I must judge by the acts, not by the persons.

(35) Who are these persons? Some, I am most firmly convinced, are earnestly desiring to govern themselves in all things by the grace of God. As to others, their fate is trembling in the balances. The question here becomes, How best can you lend them such assistance as is in your power?

(36) It is a solemn question: and one almost shudders at an argument, whose conclusion should seem to enlarge our scope for pleasure, when we reflect how we are already intoxicated.

(37) In truth this sentiment of the religious world is, I believe, a partial development of the old principle which led to asceticism: *a sense of the need of some systematic self-denial*, in order to give effect to the grace of God upon us and redress the evil constantly done upon us from the subtle action of self-will.

(38) This principle is entitled to all honour. Even in its excesses it is respectable: but in the religious world it is

surely not in excess, as it respects *quantity:* the licence to enjoyment there is sufficient, it may be thought.

(39) But it loses much of its efficacy because it stands upon a basis of private opinion only, and thus assumes an offensive aspect causing many to stumble. Let us by God's grace have a Church discipline : let us feel the Church a living power : and our own communion with the Head, and with one another. When we have realized in thought and practice the genuine force of this idea, we shall be better able to judge how to act than when acting upon a basis of opinion which does not support us by a sense of its legitimate authority.

8. PASTORAL LETTER OF THE SCOTTISH BISHOPS ON BEHALF OF TRINITY COLLEGE.

TO ALL FAITHFUL MEMBERS OF THE REFORMED CATHOLIC CHURCH, THE BISHOPS IN SCOTLAND, GREETING.

Grace be with you, mercy and peace, from God the Father and our Lord Jesus Christ.

Whereas certain lay members of the Church, moved by a pious desire to promote the glory of God and the welfare of the flock over which He hath made us overseers, have represented unto us that our Church, having been long depressed, hath suffered the total loss of temporal endowments ; that hence great difficulty hath been found in maintaining the decent administration of God's Word and Sacraments, more especially in so far as the same depends upon the due Education of Candidates for Holy Orders ; that the sense of this deficiency hath been frequently declared by various pious but inadequate bequests for this purpose, and more recently by the Church herself in her XL. Canon, and that the same still exists in almost undiminished magnitude :

And whereas they have represented unto us their desire, under God's blessing, to attempt a remedy for this want, and, in pursuance of such design, have proposed to us the foundation of a School and Theological Seminary, to be devoted to the training, under Collegiate discipline, of Candidates for Holy Orders, and at the same time of such other persons as may desire the benefit of a liberal, in conjunction with a religious, education :

And Whereas they have represented unto us that sufficient pecuniary support hath been secured to warrant their perseverance in their design, and that they are now desirous, under our sanction, to make a public appeal to the members of the Church in its behalf :

Now We, the Bishops of the Reformed Catholic Church in Scotland, in Synod assembled, desire to express our warmest gratitude to those with whom this proposal hath originated, and, above all, to God, who hath put it into their hearts to attempt the supply of wants, the reality and urgency of which we have long painfully experienced ; and having maturely considered the said design, we do hereby formally approve the same, and recommend it to you, our Brethren in Christ, as a fitting object for your prayers and alms.

We have, further, for the promotion of this good work, requested certain discreet persons to act in Committee, and, in concert with ourselves, to prepare a Scheme for its execution, to be submitted to the members of the Church.

In thus endeavouring to awaken your zeal and charity in behalf of that portion of the Church committed to our charge, we deem it fitting to state solemnly and explicitly that we are moved by no feelings of rivalry towards any religious community, but by a desire to supply the wants of our own communion, and thereby to fulfil a duty implied in the first principles of the Christian Church.

Brethren, the grace of our Lord Jesus Christ be with your spirits. Amen.

    W. SKINNER, D.D., Bishop of Aberdeen, and Primus.
    PATRICK TORRY, D.D., Bishop of Dunkeld, Dunblane, and Fife.
    DAVID LOW, LL.D., Bishop of Moray, Ross, and Argyll.
    MICHAEL RUSSELL, LL.D., Bishop of Glasgow.
    DAVID MOIR, D.D., Bishop of Brechin.
    C. H. TERROT, D.D., Bishop of Edinburgh.

EDINBURGH,
    September 2, 1841.

9. CONSECRATION OF ST. ANDREW'S CHAPEL, FASQUE, IN THE DIOCESE OF BRECHIN.

(August 28, 1847.)

The day was lovely throughout, and appropriate to its work. It is a solemn act to set apart anything for all time, particularly anything which will not end with time, but will live in its results after time is dead : and when the thing separated for ever is a temple of the living God, wherein souls are to be fashioned anew according to His image, a new Source opened from the fountain head of living waters, the waters that spring up out of almightiness and whose draughts give immortality, then the work is lovely too as well as very solemn — a work upon which angels surely look, and in which they minister with joy. Nor angels only, we may hope, but likewise the spirits of the faithful dead, and, if so, then that work of yesterday was contemplated with holy gladness by some of the departed from out of their peace ; by some of our own flesh and blood, though now after the flesh they know us no more ; by some spiritually akin to us — I mean in particular by our Bishop, whose mortal spoil we had only the day before laid, at the churchyard of Brechin, in its bed of earth.

I allow myself to put down with pleasure the proceedings of our happy day, the detail of the work ; not a great work, but done for the glory of God, and one in which I have been permitted to bear an auxiliary part.

At half-past ten the clergy and the guests had assembled in the house : the doors of the Chapel were then opened, and the bell rung, two persons being appointed with written directions to maintain order and keep clear certain parts of the Chapel. Written directions for the congregation were also posted up near the Chapel.

At a quarter to eleven the organ played in the Chapel, and the Bishops and Clergy assembled in their robes and walked to the Chapel. They were preceded by Sir John Gladstone, Bart., and his youngest son, the only one present, Sir John S. Forbes, Bart., who had accepted the office of churchwarden, and Mr. C. G. Reid, W. S., who prepared the deeds. Behind these walked the (five Presbyters present: the Warden of Trinity College, the Rev. Messrs. Henderson, Moir, Goalen, and Thorn), with Mr. Irvine, the licensed minister (in Deacon's orders) and intended presentee, and last came the Bishop of Aberdeen (the consecrator) and the Bishop of Oxford, who had been appointed to preach. Sir John Gladstone and the other conductors carried wands with bands of black crape in memory of Bishop Moir.

On their arrival at the Chapel some minutes before eleven, they passed through the persons collected outside and advanced up the aisle to the altar-rails, where the Right Rev. the Bishop of Aberdeen, Primus, stood upon the step, the remainder of the procession arranging themselves on either hand, and delivered an address to the congregation, stating the occasion of his appearing as consecrator in this diocese, and his authority under the canons for the purpose.

Sir John Gladstone then presented to the Primus the petition for consecration, which the Primus handed to Mr. W. E. Gladstone to be read aloud. After it had been read, the Primus received it back, and expressed before the assembled people the gratification which he would have in complying with it. His Reverence then passed down the aisle followed by the Clergy, and beyond the west door of the Chapel; he then re-entered, and led them eastwards, repeating Ps. xxiv. in alternate verses with them and the congregation.

The Primus then went within the rails, as did the other Clergy, except the warden of Trinity College, who took his place within the reading-desk to officiate there.

The Bishop of Oxford had, in the meantime, been compelled by severe indisposition to quit the Chapel.

The altar was covered as usual with a white cloth, and on it were hangings of crape in memory of the late Bishop of the diocese.

The Primus then received the instruments of endowment, handed to him by the Rev. Mr. Henderson from Mr. W. E. Gladstone, and laid them on the Lord's Table. He next proceeded with the service until the place for the sentence of consecration,* which was read by the Rev. Mr. Henderson, and then signed by the Primus.

His Reverence then handed back the document to Mr. W. E. Gladstone, who stood immediately below the altar-rails, and desired that it should be duly registered.

The middle aisle was now filled with benches for the accommodation of a portion of the people, and a portion stood : but some were unable to find entrance into the Chapel, and sat or stood within view and hearing outside the west door. The entire number present was about 180, of whom much the greater part belonged to the middle and lower class. The Chapel is calculated ordinarily to accommodate with seats less than 120.

The Morning Service then proceeded according to the usual form, except that Ps. lxxxiv. was sung after the Third Collect,† with the sanction of the Primus, and the Sanctus‡ was sung before the commencement of the Communion Service.§ The responses to the Commandments were chanted to the organ, and Ps. c.|| was sung before the sermon.

The Canticles had been chanted as usual.¶

The Bishop of Aberdeen performed the Communion Service, assisted, in the absence of the Bishop of Oxford, by the Warden of Trinity College : and his Reverence's chaplains reading the Epistle and Gospel respectively.

After the Creed his Reverence gave notice of the Holy Communion for the following day, and of the destination of the offerings — viz., those of the consecration for the Episcopal Church Society.

Those of Sunday for the ordinary purposes of the Chapel, as defined by the Constitution.

His Reverence then preached from Ps. cxxxii., 14, 15. Before the sermon his Reverence used the bidding prayer. After the doxology at the close he descended forthwith, and took his place at the altar.

While the Offertory Sentences were read, the alms were

---

*P. 7.   †Bedford.   ‡Tonelli.
          §Humfreys. ||Savoy.
¶ *Venite*, 5th Greg. ; *Te Deum*, 6th Greg. ; *Benedictus*, Farrant.

collected by the Rev. Mr. Irvine from the Clergy, by Mr. W. E. Gladstone from the rest of the congregation. The amount was £14 18s. 3d., viz.,

	£	s.	d.
Gold and notes	9	10	0
Silver	5	6	5
Copper		1	10
	£14	18	3

When they had been presented, the elements were brought by Mr. W. E. Gladstone from the Vestry and were presented by the Primus.

The Prayer for the Church Militant was then read, and the non-communicants quitted the Chapel.

After the Consecration, the Primus administered to all the Clergy, and the Primus with the Warden to the laity.

There were thirty-six communicants. The remaining elements were consumed in part by the Clergy, in part by some of the lay communicants, kneeling.

The holy office of the morning closed shortly after two.

The Clergy and the guests met for luncheon at Fasque immediately afterwards. The Chapel was duly arranged in the interval, the Communion plate remaining on the altar.

At three o'clock a congregation of from sixty to seventy persons were in attendance, when the Bishop of Aberdeen, with the Warden of Trinity College, the Rev. Mr. Goalen, and the Rev. Mr. Irvine, preceded by Sir John Gladstone and others in the same manner as in the morning, walked from the house by the south side of the Chapel to the vault. The Bishop descended into and went round it, and then took his place on the steps, the stone covering having been removed: and the service of consecration proceeded according to the authorized form. The Psalm was sung, as allowed in it (Ps. xxxix., 5, 8)* by the congregation standing round. They then again took their seats inside the Chapel, and the

* Abridge.

afternoon service commenced. The Primus was on the north side of the altar and delivered the Absolution and the Blessing. The prayers were read by the Rev. Mr. Goalen. The Psalms were, Ps. xxiv. 1, 2, and four last, before sermon;*
Ps. cxxxii. 6–9 and four last, after sermon.†

The Canticles‡ were sung in the usual manner.

The sermon was preached by the Warden of Trinity College, from 1 Cor. xiv. 26.

Both in the morning and afternoon sermons honourable mention was made of the pious work of the Founder; and while the grace of God which had moved him to it was magnified, the example was commended and the blessing of the Most High implored upon him. The Rev. the Warden also expressed the anticipation that the day of the Consecration would be annually celebrated in the Chapel.

The afternoon service closed at five o'clock.

D. O. M. Gloria.

W. E. G.

Fasque,
August 31, 1847.

. . . Let it not be an offence that I have thus minutely described the particulars of these blessed offices, in which we went up with one heart before God to set apart another temple of peace amidst the strife of tongues, of light amidst the darkness of the world. For the very skirts of the Lord's garments are glorious, and full of virtue if they be touched and seen in faith. To see the parts alone is trifling; and to see the whole alone is vague, and is like the memory of a pleasant song that has passed away, or like the beholding of a man's self in the glass, after which he goes, and he forgets what manner of man he was. But the Psalmist, the type of all true and holy worship, who so loved the habitation of the Lord's house, and the place where His honour dwelleth, *he* said, 'Walk about Sion, and go round about her: and *tell* the towers thereof: mark well her bulwarks, consider her palaces: that ye may tell them that come after.' §

May this record then of my father's work be a holy and a happy record. May the work be blessed, and in the

---

* Peterborough.
† Margaret.
‡ *Magnificat*, Wesley; *Nunc Dimittis*, 8th Greg. (second ending).
§ Ps. xlviii. 11, 12.

days and years to come, by the gathering up, and the building up of many souls to Christ, and may the gifts they shall receive by means of this Church ascend upwards in glory to God who prompted the work, and descend again in blessings on the venerable head of him who did it. May his vigorous old age be gladdened with the thoughts and with the fruits of it, and when he goes down to lay his head in the grave which he has there solemnly prepared for the wife of his bosom, and for all his flesh and blood, may his deeds done for God's honour follow him; as he passes into rest and felicity may they survive him and work after him and help to hasten the coming of the Lord Jesus. To whom be glory for ever and ever. Amen.

W. E. G.

FASQUE
August 31, 1847.

Photo, W. Bell Jones, Hawarden.

ST. DEINIOL'S LIBRARY AND RESIDENCE, AND PARISH CHURCH, HAWARDEN.

VIII.—ST. DEINIOL'S LIBRARY

IN 1903 the following report was presented to the trustees of the St. Deiniol's Library by the Warden, Canon Joyce. I reprint it here as the best statement of the objects and possibilities of the foundation.

The purpose of the institution was defined by the founder to be the 'promotion of Divine learning.' I desire to point out what is being done at present, and what I hope may be done in the future to further that object.

Taking into account the conditions of Church life at the present day, I believe that the chief object of our efforts at St. Deiniol's should be the encouragement of theological study among the parochial clergy. Each year there is a considerable output of theological writing, and a high degree of learning is maintained by the distinguished theologians of the Church. But it is commonly admitted that there is room for improvement in lifting the general level of intellectual attainment. During the period when the English Church was deservedly famous for her learning, some of the most noteworthy books on which her reputation rested were produced by country clergy like Bull and Bingham. In this respect there is perhaps a somewhat painful contrast between then and now. Various tendencies have combined to turn the energies of the clergy in other directions. Parochial activity has increased, but theological study has suffered in amount and quality. In the endeavour to provide a remedy for this diminished attention to study, St. Deiniol's may take a part which is not filled by any other institution. I hope that an increasing number of clergy will be attracted by the opportunity of residence at the hostel, admission to which is made explicitly conditional upon the intention to make use of the library. In this way we endeavour to secure that a certain number of clergy should devote a few spare weeks to theological study. It may not seem a very ambitious programme, nor can the results obtained be easily estimated by statistics. But even a few weeks so spent will give a tone to the rest of the year, and will prevent the habit of study from falling into abeyance. There is no lack of evidence to show that the visitors to St. Deiniol's make good use of, and warmly appreciate, the opportunities provided for them by the founder's benefaction.

The theological studies of the parochial clergy may be further assisted from St. Deiniol's, if the Warden, Subwarden, and any other officials connected with the institution, will hold themselves ready to render any aid in their power to clerical reading societies by means of lectures and addresses. Such work has been carried on in connection with the Central Society of Sacred Study, and may be further developed.

Secondly, there is an opportunity before St. Deiniol's in the preparation of clergy for special work other than parochial. There is a marked and probably an increasing tendency on the part of our ecclesiastical authorities to set apart some men in each diocese for special service, whether as lecturers at the Diocesan Theological College, or as special preachers, or in other capacities. For work of this kind a few years' further theological study is surely a most valuable equipment. For example, during the four years which our late Subwarden spent at St. Deiniol's he was enabled to qualify himself for the work which has now been assigned to him in relation to the students at the University College of Bangor. We hear much of the value of a course of post-graduate study; as much and more may be said in favour of a post-ordination course. We shall therefore be doing good work if, carefully selecting from among the younger clergy men with some special aptitude for study, we give them the opportunity of developing their natural gift. They may pass from us to take up some special work — tutorial or otherwise — they may return to parochial work, but not without an increased power to deal with the intellectual difficulties of religious belief; or finding their vocation in literary work for the Church, they may become permanent members of the institution.

It is not intended that St. Deiniol's should come into competition with the ordinary theological colleges. Its objects and methods are different. But there are occasions, especially in the case of men taking Holy Orders somewhat late in life, when the usual course at a theological college would prove unsuitable. Some men of this kind, with the approbation of the Bishops by whom they had been accepted as ordination candidates, have spent their time of preparation at St. Deiniol's. We are in a position to take in one or two such with mutual advantage to them and to ourselves.

In conclusion, the life at St. Deiniol's should be so arranged as to combine with the pursuit of theological study the regular practice of devotion. And as the lecture should be the expression of the former, so the devotional address should be the outcome of the latter. There are good reasons against the indiscriminate acceptance of invitations to preach sermons, but the conduct of retreats and 'quiet days' may well be considered as coming within the scope of our duties, provided that such work is not permitted to interfere with the primary object of the institution as defined by the founder. Something of this kind has been already attempted, and it is probable that further opportunities will offer themselves.

GILBERT C. JOYCE,
Warden.

The numbers of visitors to St. Deiniol's for the years 1908, 1909, are as follows (the new buildings were opened in 1907):

1908.

Clergy (Church of England)	69
Ministers of other denominations	6
Theological students	45
Laymen (various professions)	14
Total	134

1909.

Clergy (Church of England)	88
Ministers of other denominations	4
Theological students	49
Laymen	25
Total	166

INDEX

ABERDEEN, Bishop of. See Suther
Aberdeen, Earl of: Gladstone's letter on the Holy Eucharist to, i. 372; alteration of the Canons, ii. 172; on the temptations of the mind, ii. 179
Abolition Bill, Gladstone on the, ii. 171
Accuracy in work, necessity for, ii. 161
Acland, Sir Thomas, on Gladstone and the Gorham case, i. 83; Gladstone's letter on the Bradlaugh case, i. 178; on the Bishop of Worcester's charge, ii. 294 *et seq.*
Acton, Lord: Gladstone's letters to, i. 404; on Ultramontanism, ii. 49–52; on Döllinger and Trent, ii. 69; on *Robert Elsmere*, ii. 109; on miracles and will, ii. 111; on the researches of scientists, ii. 112; on the Mosaic books, ii. 116; on Homeric critics, ii. 119; and Dr. Liddon, ii. 187, 188; Gladstone's duty to, ii. 311; the Old Testament, ii. 329; Gladstone's Oxford lecture, ii. 331
Africa, South, and the English Church, i. 143 *et seq.*
Agnostic ethics, i. 76
Alderson, Baron, ii. 339
Alexander, Mr., difficulties as to his consecration, i. 230
Allies, Mr., on State aid for schools, ii. 140
Altkatholicismus, ii. 61
Amusements, Gladstone on, ii. 437
Andrewes, Bishop, i. 365
Anglican settlements, the three, ii. 350 *et seq.*
Anson, Canon, illness of Dean Wellesley, i. 207

Anstice, Professor of Classics at King's College, London, death of, i. 408
Argyll, Bishop of. See Ewing
Argyll, Duke of: Gladstone's letters to, on the religious question in Scotland and England, i. 172; on the idea of sin, ii. 87; on the fossil man, ii. 90
Aristophanes, *The Clouds*, ii. 97
Aristotle, *Politics*, Gladstone's opinion of, ii. 163; compared with Plato's *Republic*, ii. 164
Arnold, Dr., and Gladstone, i. 168, 274
Arnold, M., Gladstone's letter on Disestablishment to, i. 167
Arundel, Lord, and the Education Bill, i. 132
Ashley, Lord, and the Bishopric of Jerusalem, i. 245; on education, ii. 125; on Gladstone's Church and State speech, ii. 344 *et seq.*
Athanasian Creed, Gladstone on, ii. 91, 408
Athenæum, The, on Tupper's Life, ii. 189
Auckland, Lord, Bishop of Bath and Wells, and the Denison case, i. 364
Augsburg Confession, the, i. 240, 250
Authority, Sir George Lewis on, ii. 101, 102
Awdry, Sir John, i. 433

Badeley, Mr., *Considerations on Divorce a Vinculo in Connection with Holy Scripture*, i. 133, 296 n.
Bagot, Bishop of Bath and Wells, and the Denison case, i. 363
Baptism, decision in the Gorham case on, i. 85 *et seq.*

456 INDEX

Barrett, Dr., Chairman of the Congregational Union: Gladstone's letter on Apostolic Succession to, i. 401, 409; sketch of Cardinal Newman, ii. 335

Barry, Dr., Principal of King's College, i. 202

Bath and Wells, Bishop of. See Hervey

Beaconsfield, Earl of. See Disraeli

Beard, Rev. C., his Hibbert Lectures, ii. 325

Bennett, 'Shepherd V.,' i. 366, 379

Benson, E. W., Archbishop of Canterbury: 'Establishmentarian fanaticism of,' ii. 212

Bentley, Mr., on the *Epistles of Phalaris*, ii. 119

Bernard, Rev. J. H., Dean of St. Patrick's, ii. 337

Bishops, and Parliamentary Churchmen, i. 41; Gladstone on the responsibility of, i. 175 *et seq.*, 107 *et seq.*; on power of Prime Minister to appoint, i. 180 *et seq.*; inaction in the Gorham case of, i. 88; and Papal aggression, i. 119; action in Convocation of, i. 160; and the House of Lords, i. 181; Gladstone's appointments of, ii. 363

Blackburn on clerical subscription, i. 139

Blomfield, C. J., Bishop of London: Gladstone's letter on the Hampden case to, i. 66, 80; and the Gorham case, i. 91, 105 *et seq.*; and Gladstone, i. 122, 139, 369, 404; and the Jerusalem Bishopric, i. 228 *et seq.*, 236, 249 *et seq.*; Gladstone on, i. 272, 304; and Oakeley, i. 334

Blyth, Bishop, and the Jerusalem Bishopric, i. 352

Bolingbroke, Viscount, and Pitt, ii. 167

Bonn, Old Catholics at, ii. 57, 64

Books, three recommended to W. H. Gladstone, ii. 163

Bradlaugh, Charles, Gladstone's attitude towards, i. 175 *et seq.*

Brewer, Dr., Gladstone on, ii. 92

Bright, Dr., ii. 69

Bright, John: Gladstone and the Irish Church, i. 154; and the Burial Bill, i. 173, 174; Gladstone and the Education Bill, i. 142, 145, 146

British Critic, i. 289, 303, 304

British Magazine, i. 289

Brodie, Sir B., i. 361

Broughton, Bishop, ii. 136

Brown, Rev. Baldwin, on religious education in the Universities, i. 213, 219

Browne, Harold, Bishop of Ely, afterwards of Winchester, i. 162; Gladstone on his sermon, i. 180; the vacant Archbishopric of Canterbury, i. 209, 394

Brutus, Gladstone's opinion of, ii. 159

Buccleuch, Duke of, ii. 205

Buchanan, Rev. R., the Scottish veto law, i. 44

Bunsen, Baron, and the Jerusalem Bishopric, i. 227 *et seq.*; his character, i. 228; and Gladstone, i. 237; his views, i. 238; *Kirche der Zukunft*, i. 352

Burdett-Coutts, Miss (afterwards Baroness), i. 143

Burke, Edmund, Gladstone on, ii. 168, 326

Burnet, Bishop, *Exposition of the Thirty-nine Articles*, i. 139

Buss, Rev. Septimus, ii. 148

Butler, Bishop: Gladstone's opinion of, i. 407, ii. 30, 101, 117, 192, 219; *Analogy* and *Sermons*, ii. 163, 301; and Theism, ii. 337

Cairns, Lord Chancellor, i. 388

Canterbury, Archbishops of. See Benson, Davidson, Howley, Sumner, Tait

Capes, Mr., i. 328

Carnarvon, Earl of, opinion on accuracy in Eton Examinations, ii. 160

Cathedrals and the Church Commission, i. 40

Catholics, duty of, i. 277

Cavendish, Lord R., ii. 309

Chalmers, Dr.: on Church Establishments, i. 12; his financial skill, i. 189

Chamberlain, Right Hon. Joseph, and Gladstone, i. 179

Cheyne, Patrick, an Aberdeen incumbent, deprived of his cure, i. 413, 423 *et seq.*, 445

Chichester, Dean of. See Hook

Children, Gladstone's prayers and counsels for, ii. 411 *et seq.*

Christ Church, Oxford, W. H. Gladstone a student of, ii. 162

Church of England: and the State,

i. 1 et seq., ii. 343 et seq.; changes in the air, i. 9, 10; Chalmers on, i. 12; two views of Church Establishments, i. 23 et seq.; possibility of reforms, i. 28; objections to concurrent endowment i. 30; limits of compromise, i. 33; individual and collective obligations, i. 36; and the Presbyterian Church, i. 38; discipline in and extension of, i. 53; effect of the Gorham case, i. 83 et seq., 333; two views of Royal Supremacy, i. 94, 98, 100; Maskell's view of, i. 99; Gladstone's faith in, i. 104; duty of the Bishops, i. 107 et seq.; and the constitutional position of the King, i. 111; in fractions, i. 114 et seq.; shameful hesitation of, i. 117; and the Ecclesiastical Titles Bill, i. 122, 123; and the Colonial Church Bill, i. 125; tendencies towards Disestablishment, i. 126 et seq., 165, 178 et seq., 184 et seq.; and the Divorce Bill, i. 129 et seq., ii. 358 et seq.; in South Africa, i. 132, 133, 143 et seq.; and Church Rates, i. 142; Disestablishment in Ireland, i. 148 et seq.; and Convocation, i. 160, 170; no longer helpless, i. 169; alteration of her constitution, i. 171; Disestablishment in Scotland, i. 186; ecclesiastical patronage and University reform, i. 190 et seq.; service at St. Paul's, i. 193; her duty to the State, i. 197; preferments, i. 199 et seq.; University reform, i. 211 et seq.; the Oxford Movement, i. 226 et seq.; and the Jerusalem Bishopric, ii. 364 et seq.; Tract 90, i. 256, 321; *Tracts for the Times*, i. 270; Newman's difficulties, i. 281 et seq.; her debt to Newman, i. 318; Article XIII., i. 324; the Oxford Convocation, i. 327; opposing systems, i. 329; the Anglican claim, i. 330; Margaret Chapel, services at, i. 335, 375; Gladstone's views on, i. 335 et seq.; the bane of, i. 347; reverence and ceremonial, i. 350; destiny of, i. 352; opposite lines of teaching, i. 353; change in Manning, i. 357; the Denison case, i. 363 et seq.; Gladstone on the Bishop of Oxford's Charge, i. 369; ritualism, i. 377 et seq.; the Bennett case, i. 379; prayers for the dead, i. 382; and legislation, i. 383; Public Worship Regulation Act, i. 386 et seq., ii. 371; Gladstone on, ii. 3, 6 et seq.; controversy with Rome, ii. 23 et seq.; The *Filioque*, ii. 63; the Eastern position, ii. 64; the Thirty-nine Articles, ii. 66, 367 et seq.; definition of a Protestant, ii. 70; the Athanasian Creed, ii. 91, 408; and the Education Bill, ii. 125 et seq.; waiver of claims, ii. 169; Church rates, ii. 170, 171; temporal sacrifices, ii. 172; the Ridsdale Judgment, ii. 182; and the Waldenses, ii. 197; alienation of Church property, ii. 236; office or benefice, ii. 296; a brighter picture, ii. 329; factors in the English Reformation, ii. 348 et seq.; the three Anglican settlements, ii. 350 et seq.; government of, ii. 364 et seq.

Church, Rev. R. W., Dean of St. Paul's, i. 190; *Life and Letters of*, i. 192 n., ii. 80 n.; his appointment, i. 193, 206; and Gladstone, i. 210, 401; *The Oxford Movement*, i. 260 n., 261 n., 262 n., 296 n., 297 n., 300 n., ii. 330; Public Worship Act, i. 394; Gladstone's opinion of, ii. 79, 107, 335

Church Discipline Act, i. 364-366

Church Principles considered in their Results, by W. E. Gladstone, i. 48

Church Rates, ii. 170, 171

Claughton, Mr., and the Professorship of Poetry, i. 266

Clerical Fellowships, i. 224

Cleveland, Duke of, Irish Church Bill, i. 162

Clifford, Bishop, ii. 260

Cole, O. B., on the will of God, ii. 229

Colenso, Bishop, deposed, i. 132, 144 et seq.

Coleridge, Derwent, i. 202

Coleridge, Sir John, Solicitor-General, afterwards Lord Chief Justice: University reform, i. 221; and the Vice-Chancellor of Oxford, i. 296; Gladstone on, i. 433

Collegiate and Professorial Teaching and Discipline, by Dr. Pusey, i. 211

Colonial Church Bill, i. 124 et seq.

INDEX

Common Prayer Book. See Prayer-Book
Confession, the Augsburg, i. 240, 250
Confirmation, Gladstone on, ii. 151, 185
Conscience Clause, the, ii. 137
Contemporary Review, The, ii. 316 n.
Convocation, meeting of Irish demanded by Irish Episcopate, i. 159; a moral influence, i. 170
Cosin, Bishop, i. 134
Cowper-Temple clause, the, ii. 127, 141
Creeds, the, i. 241, ii. 91, 408
Crown and Church preferments, i. 195
Curtis, Mr., of Lichfield Theological College, i. 202

Dale, Mr., on religious instruction, ii. 144
Dalmatia, by Wilkinson, ii. 109
Davidson, R. (Archbishop of Canterbury), his Life of Archbishop Tait, i. 386
Deerbrook, by Miss Martineau, ii. 75
Delane, J. T., editor of *The Times*, i. 160; refuses to insert Gladstone's letter on the meeting of the Bishops, i. 279
Denison, George Anthony, Archdeacon of Taunton: threatened deprivation for his sermons on the Holy Eucharist, i. 363 *et seq.*, 382; Education Bill, ii. 213; his character, ii. 215, 302
Denison, Edward, Bishop of Salisbury: Education Bill, ii. 134; his death, ii. 181
Depression, Gladstone on, ii. 433
Derby, Earl of, his episcopal appointments, ii. 363
Discipline, Gladstone on Church, i. 52 *et seq.*
Disraeli, Benjamin and Ritualism, i. 375; and the Public Worship Act, i. 388, 395; his episcopal appointments, ii. 363
Dissenters, and the Church, i. 49; rights of, i. 55; and the Universities, i. 218; Chapels Bill, ii. 4, 379; and the Education Act, ii. 125, 143, 145
Ditcher *v.* Denison, i. 363 *et seq.*
Divorce Act, i. 129, 374; Gladstone on, ii. 358
Dodsworth, Rev. W., at Margaret Chapel, i. 408

Döllinger, Dr., Roman Catholic theologian: Gladstone on the helpless condition of the Church, i. 169, 395; Disestablishment, i. 183; his opinion of the Church of England, i. 384; on Palmer's work, i. 407; on the Papal Government, ii. 33, 45; the Bonn meeting, ii. 57, 62, 312; Gladstone's paper on Ritualism, ii. 59, 60; meaning of persecution, ii. 68; and Council of Trent, ii. 69; the Holy Eucharist, ii. 180, 212; Gladstone's opinion of, ii. 69, 264, 340; Père Hyacinthe, ii. 314; Bishop Hamilton's Catechism, ii. 320; *Madame de Maintenon*, ii. 327; on Consubstantiation, ii. 336; Gladstone's conversation with, ii. 383 *et seq.*
Doubt and scepticism, ii. 77
Drew, Mrs. See Gladstone, Mary
Duchesne, Abbé, ii. 73
'Durham letter,' by Lord John Russell, i. 118, 122

Eastern position, the, ii. 64
Ecce Homo, ii. 88, 216
Ecclesiastical Commission, i. 19
Ecclesiastical Courts Bill, i. 53 *et seq.*
Ecclesiastical Judgments of the Privy Council, by Fremantle, i. 139, 203
Ecclesiastical patronage, i. 190, 191
Ecclesiastical Titles Act, ii. 5
Eden, Bishop of Moray and Ross, i. 435
Edinburgh, Bishop of. See Terrot
Edinburgh Review, The, i. 139
Education, ii. 125 *et seq.;* religious, ii. 143, 145, 213
Elizabeth, Queen, and persecution of the Papal party, ii. 68, 69
Ellicott, Bishop of Gloucester: Irish Church Bill, i. 162; his appointment, ii. 363
Elwin, Mr., editor of the *Quarterly Review*, i. 202
Ely, Bishop of. See Browne
Encyclical of Leo XIII, ii. 73
Endowment, objections to concurrent, i. 30
English Review, The, i. 303
Episcopal appointments, ii. 363
Episcopal Church. See Scotland
Erastianism, i. 143, 167
Essays and Reviews, 199 *et seq.*
Establishment and Church Rate, i. 142

INDEX

Eucharist, the Holy, i. 363 et seq., 373, ii. 180, 212; Gladstone's devotions for, ii. 421.
Evangelicalism, and education, i. 2; Gladstone on, i. 6, 7; incompleteness of, i. 8; German Church, i. 252; position of, i. 334, 365, 408
Evil, origin of, ii. 117
Ewing, Bishop of Argyll, i. 415, 430, 437
Exeter, Bishop of. See Phillpotts

Factory Bill of 1843 (Education Clauses), ii. 125
Fairbairn, Rev. Dr., ii. 333
Farquhar, Sir W., i. 139, 177, 182
Farrar, Dr., ii. 120
Fasque, church at, ii. 203; consecration of, ii. 445 et seq.
Fawcett, Mr., ii. 46
Fellowships, non-resident, i. 214 et seq.
Filioque, ii. 62, 64
Finch, George, i. 108
Fleming, Rev. V. R., Irish Church Bill, i. 164
Forbes, Alexander, Bishop of Brechin: Gladstone on, i. 412, 434; his Charge, i. 413; Scottish Episcopal Communion, i. 440, 443
Forbes, William, Bishop of Edinburgh: his *Considerations*, i. 355, 416
Forster, W. E., Education Bill, ii. 127 et seq., 137, 147
Fox, Charles, compared with Pitt, ii. 166, 167
Fremantle, Mr., *Ecclesiastical Judgments of the Privy Council*, i. 139, 203
Furlong, Bishop, his letter on the Irish Land Bill (1870), ii. 53
Future retribution, Gladstone on, ii. 403

Garbett, Mr., and the Poetry Professorship at Oxford, i. 256, 266, 279; Pusey's sermon, i. 287
Genesis, the Book of, Gladstone on, ii. 80, 108
Gilly, Mr., and the Waldenses, ii. 223
Gladstone, Agnes (afterwards Mrs. Wickham), letters from W. E. Gladstone, ii. 185, 186
Gladstone, H. N., letters from W. E. Gladstone, ii. 184, 185

Gladstone, Helen, letters from W. E. Gladstone on her birthday, ii. 190, 191; how to read Butler, ii. 192; on capacity and duty, ii. 193; offer of the principalship of Holloway College, ii. 194, 195
Gladstone, John, father of W. E. Gladstone: son's admiration for, ii. 197; chooses his son's profession, ii. 198, 199; dignity of Orders, ii. 223 et seq.; his son's views as to work, ii. 228; a rule of marriage, ii. 231 et seq.; a church at Fasque, ii. 237 et seq.; death, ii. 287
Gladstone, John, brother of W. E. Gladstone: his character, ii. 197; the Waldenses, ii. 222; man and his Maker, ii. 226, 227
Gladstone, Mary (afterwards Mrs. Drew): letters from W. E. Gladstone, ii. 186 et seq.; her article on the founding of St. Deiniol's, ii. 219 et seq.
Gladstone, Rev. Stephen: letters from W. E. Gladstone on Divorce Bill, i. 137; Disestablishment, i. 189; terrors of the Lord, ii. 123; school compulsion, ii. 147; advice to, ii. 173 et seq.; the time and training for Orders, ii. 176 et seq.; being understood, ii. 181; the Ridsdale Judgment, ii. 182, 183
Gladstone, W. E.: early religious training, i. 1 et seq.; first visit to Italy, i. 7; friendship with Manning, i. 8; the Oxford Movement, i. 10, 226 et seq., 364 et seq.; *The State in its Relation to the Church*, i. 12 et seq., 45 et seq., 62, 148, ii. 205; his friendship with Hope, i. 12, 83, 84; Disestablishment of the Irish Church, i. 14, 148 et seq.; *A Chapter of Autobiography*, i. 14; the Ecclesiastical Commission, i. 19; patronage question in Scotland, i. 20, 44, 51; reform of the Ecclesiastical Courts, i. 22, 53–60; on Church Establishments, i. 23 et seq.; Parliament and Church temporalities, i. 40 et seq.; the Scottish veto law, i. 44; *Church Principles Considered in their Results*, i. 48; Church and Dissenters, i. 49, 55; his attitude towards controversies, i. 51;

grant to Maynooth College, i. 51, 52, 62 *et seq.;* Church discipline, i. 52 *et seq.;* purpose of his Parliamentary life, i. 61; two questions, i. 62, 63; his diplomatic relations and conversation with the Pope, i. 65, ii. 395; votes for removal of Jewish disabilities, i. 66, 122 *et seq.;* on the unfairness of Hampden's censure, i. 67; resignation of his seat, i. 68–71; on the relation of the State to religion, i. 71 *et seq.,* 135, ii. 209 *et seq.;* and Wordsworth, i. 74; and Sir J. Graham on the responsibilities of Bishops, i. 75 *et seq.;* on the Prime Minister's power to appoint Bishops, i. 80–82; and the Gorham case, i. 83 *et seq.,* 95 *et seq.,* 330, 333; on Royal Supremacy, i. 94, 98, 101, 110 *et seq.,* 145, 146, 169; justification of his Parliamentary action, i. 99; on continuance in political life, i. 101; agony of an ancient Church, i. 103; denial of rumours about Manning, i. 105; on the duty of Bishops, i. 107 *et seq;* constitutional position of the King, i. 110 *et seq;* Church in fractions, i. 113 *et seq;* the Bishops and Papal aggression, i. 119; the 'Durham letter,' i. 120, 122; his speech on Ecclesiastical Titles Bill, i. 120 *et seq.;* Colonial Church Bill, i. 124, 125, 132; tendencies towards Disestablishment, i. 126–128; on divorce, i. 129 *et seq.,* 374, ii. 358; authorities on clerical subscription, i. 139; Establishment and Church Rate, i. 142; South African Church, i. 143–147; Scottish Patronage Bill, i. 166, 167; his attitude towards Scottish Presbyterianism, i. 168, 172; Convocation and moral influence, i. 170; alteration of Church's constitution, i. 171; reunion and exchange of pulpits, i. 172; recital to Burial Bill, i. 173; and the Bradlaugh case, i. 175 *et seq.;* his resignation, i. 178; question of Disestablishment, i. 178 *et seq.;* on Bishop Blomfield's sermon, i. 180; a Denominationalist, i. 188; ecclesiastical patronage, i. 190 *et seq.,* 342–347, 384; on *Essays and Reviews,* i. 201–210; Dean Wellesley's death, i. 207, 208; on University reform, i. 211–225; Tract 90, i. 234, 256 *et seq.,* 314–316, 318–325, 405, 406; the Augsburg Confession, i. 240, 250; and the Thirty-nine Articles, i. 242, 243, 300, 323, 324, ii. 66, 367 *et seq.;* and the Poetry Professorship at Oxford, i. 254, 255, 266–269; his power of work, i. 259; his letter on the *Tracts for the Times* refused by *The Times*, i. 270–279; changes in Newman, i. 281 *et seq.;* his changed attitude towards the Oxford Movement, i. 293 *et seq.;* and the *British Critic,* i. 302–305; his article on Ward in *Quarterly Review,* i. 305-314; and the opposing systems in the Church, i. 327 *et seq.;* and Oakeley, i. 334, 335; explains his views to Hope, i. 335–342; Have we the right men? i. 348–350; the Jerusalem Bishopric, and Mr. Gobat, i. 351; the destiny of the Church, i. 352; the analogy of Jansenism, i. 354; his replies to Manning, i. 355–359; F. D. Maurice and King's College, i. 360, 404; the Denison case, i. 363 *et seq.;* and Wilberforce, i. 367–369; on the Bishop of London's charge, i. 369; and ritualism, i. 375 *et seq.,* ii. 59; his letter to the Queen on Church and legislation, i. 383–386; the Public Worship Act, i. 386 *et seq.;* the road to peace, i. 371, 396; no deprivations, i. 400, 402; on contempt of court, i. 403; Newman, i. 404, 405; and Dr. Barrett, i. 409; the Scottish Episcopal Church, i. 411 *et seq.;* Bishop Forbes, i. 412; Cheyne, i. 413, 422 *et seq.,* 445; and the proposal to abolish the Scottish Office, i. 413–446; and the Oxford elections, ii. 1 *et seq.,* 373 *et seq.;* on different kinds of Protestantism, ii. 3; *The Functions of Laymen in the Church,* ii. 6; his relation to the parties in the Church, ii. 10 *et seq.;* explains his vote on the Jew Bill, ii. 16–18; his farewell address to the Oxford electors, ii. 20, 381; the controversy with Rome, ii. 23 *et seq.,* 383 *et seq.;* exchange of views with Manning, ii. 26, 35–44, 52–54; his letters to

Miss Stanley, ii. 27-31; the Pontifical States, ii. 33; *The Vatican Decrees in their Bearing on Civil Allegiance,* ii. 46, 47, 59; Ultramontanism, ii. 49-51; the Bonn meeting, ii. 57, 62, 312; the Papal Church, ii. 60; Bishop Reinkens, ii. 61, 62; the *Filioque,* ii. 63; the Eastern position, ii. 64; and the Prayer-Book, ii. 66, 67; persecution defined, ii. 68; Döllinger and Trent, ii. 69; meaning of the term 'Protestant,' ii. 70, 71; the controversy with unbelief, ii. 75 *et seq.*, 403 *et seq.;* his opinion of *Deerbrook,* and of *Robert Elsmere,* ii. 75, 76, 109, 110; on doubt and scepticism, ii. 77; on future punishment, ii. 78, 106, 120, 403; his opinion of Dean Church, ii. 79-81, 107, 330, 335; on the Book of Genesis, ii. 80, 108; on Bishop Tait's sermons, ii. 82-84; on Mill's works, ii. 85, 97, 101, 193; idea of sin, ii. 87; *Ecce Homo,* ii. 88, 216, 300; on the fossil man, ii. 90; on Strauss's book, ii. 90; Church and Parliament, ii. 91; *Dean Stanley and St. Socrates,* ii. 96; on science and opinion, ii. 98, 112; on Christianity and man, ii. 99; on Professor Jevons' book, ii. 100; on Christ and authority, ii. 101, 102; on universalism, ii. 103; on natural immortality, ii. 104; on miracles, ii. 111; on belief, ii. 113-116; the Mosaic books, ii. 116, 119; origin of evil, ii. 117-119; on God's foreknowledge, ii. 121; the seen and the unseen, ii. 122; paper on 'Eternal Hope,' etc., ii. 123, 124; education, ii. 125 *et seq.;* his position and views as to religious education in schools, ii. 125 *et seq.*, 213, 297, 310; the Church's means, ii. 133; Queen's Colleges in Ireland, ii. 135, 136; on secular teaching and unsectarian schools, ii. 138, 139; and the Roman Catholics, ii. 140; Oxford opinion, ii. 146; on compulsion, ii. 147, 148; letters to his children, ii. 149 *et seq.;* to W. H. Gladstone, ii. 149-173; to S. E. Gladstone, ii. 173-183; to H. N. Gladstone, ii. 184, 185; to Agnes Gladstone, ii. 185, 186; to Mary Gladstone, ii. 186-190; to Helen Gladstone, ii. 190-196; to his grandson, Edward Wickham, ii. 196; his affection for his father and brother, ii. 197; Evangelicalism, ii. 198, 200, 333; his choice of a profession, ii. 198; and Unitarianism, ii. 199; *A Third Order,* ii. 200, 400; the Episcopal chapel at Fasque, ii. 201 *et seq.*, 238-241, 445; his close association with Hope and Trinity College, Glenalmond, ii. 203 *et seq.*, 242 *et seq.;* his difficulty in fighting the Church's battle in Parliament, ii. 209 *et seq.; The Vatican Council and the Old Catholics,* ii. 212, 400; his friendship with Döllinger, ii. 212, 383; the secessions of Hope and Manning, ii. 214; his praise of Bishop Wilberforce, ii. 215; and George Denison, ii. 215, 302; and the Duke of Newcastle, ii. 216; on Scott and Lockhart, ii. 217; his edition of Butler, ii. 219; foundation and object of St. Deiniol's, ii. 219-222; letters to his father and brother, ii. 222-241; dignity of Orders, ii. 224; on his father's wishes for his future, ii. 226, 228; on the will of God, ii. 229; on marriage, ii. 231-233; on the House of Commons as a calling, ii. 234; on Church property, ii. 236; and Ward, ii. 250; to his wife on discipline, ii. 252, 259; on increase of grant to Episcopal Communion of Scotland, ii. 255; description of Calais, ii. 260; visits the South German churches, ii. 261; visits Munich, ii. 262; interviews with Döllinger, ii. 263; at Baden, ii. 265; on the religious crisis, ii. 265, 270; letters to Manning on prayer, fasting, and the state of the Church, ii. 266 *et seq.;* on suicide, ii. 282; letters to Hope on their separation, ii. 283-286, 290-292; and to Manning, ii. 287; his father's death, ii. 287; on Robert Wilberforce's book on the Eucharist, ii. 288; and the death of the Duke of Newcastle, ii. 292; on truth and party, ii. 293, 294; on Bishop Philpott's Charge, ii. 294-297; on Scripture teaching, ii. 297; advice to Lady Herbert,

ii. 298; on Newman and Butler, ii. 300, 301; on Scotland's first son, ii. 303; the Bulgarian schism, ii. 304; reconciliation with Pusey, ii. 306; on *Kenelm Chillingly,* ii. 306; his letter to the Queen on Bishop Wilberforce's death, ii. 308; death of Lord R. Cavendish, ii. 309; brink of a crisis, ii. 310; a duty to Lord Acton, ii. 311; on Père Hyacinthe, ii. 314; on spiritualism, ii. 315; *The Sixteenth Century arraigned before the Nineteenth,* ii. 316 n.; the *Civitas Dei,* ii. 318; on *Hymns Ancient and Modern,* ii. 319; on Wordsworth's Platonism, ii. 319; on Hamilton's Catechism, ii. 320; on Hope's fascination, religion, and belief, ii. 322, 323; Luther in England, ii. 324; and Spurgeon, ii. 324; on St. Augustine and Bishop Butler, ii. 325; faith and *fiducia,* ii. 326; on Madame de Maintenon, ii. 327-329; his lecture at Oxford, ii. 331, 332; and Lord Northbourne, ii. 332; on Archbishop Benson, ii. 333; on Bishop Guest and Consubstantiation, ii. 336; Butler and Theism, ii. 337; on Purcell's biography of Manning, ii. 338-341; his conversation on Church and State with Lord Ashley, ii. 344-347; factors in the English Reformation, ii. 348-350; the three Anglican settlements, ii. 350-354; on Queen Elizabeth, ii. 354-357; on the Restoration settlement, ii. 357, 358; his episcopal appointments, ii. 363; on Church government, ii. 364-367; Wordsworth on, ii. 373-376; his vote on Ward's case, ii. 376-378; his Oxford election circular and farewell address, ii. 378-382; his controversy with Döllinger on religion, ii. 383-390; on the Roman question, ii. 391-395; his conversation with Pius IX., ii. 395-400; on future retribution, ii. 403-406; on Theism, ii. 406-408; on the Athanasian Creed, ii. 408; on prayer and the Divine will, ii. 409; prayers and counsels for children, ii. 411-420; his Eucharistic Devotions, ii. 421; on separation from the world, ii. 428; on money, ii. 429; on the world and the flesh, ii. 430; on depression, ii. 433; on amusements, ii. 438; pastoral letter of Scottish Bishops, ii. 443

Gladstone, Mrs., wife of W. E. Gladstone: letters from her husband on the hesitation of the Church, i. 117; on the black political outlook, i. 135; on the Divorce Bill, i. 136; on the Public Worship Act, i. 393-395; on labour troubles, ii. 250; on resignation and submission, ii. 252-254; on discipline, ii. 259; description of his visit to Calais, Augsburg, and Munich, ii. 260-262; on his conversations with Dr. Döllinger and other Roman Catholics, ii. 264-266; on clergymen and cases of suicide, ii. 282; on Trinity College, Glenalmond, ii. 282; on the death of the Duke of Newcastle, ii. 292, 293

Gladstone, W. H.: letters from W. E. Gladstone on prayer, ii. 149; on labour and duty, ii. 151; on Confirmation and self-examination, ii. 151, 152; on the meaning of life, ii. 153-156; on duties to others, ii. 156; on self-observation and self-denial, ii. 157; on ancient history, ii. 158; the eye of God, ii. 159; a world of work, ii. 160; the need for accuracy, ii. 161; books and discipline, ii. 163, 164; on the eve of an examination, ii. 165; on Pitt, Fox, and Bolingbroke, ii. 166-168; on Church Rates and concessions, ii. 169-173; prayers and counsels for, ii. 411-420

Glenalmond, Trinity College, foundation of, ii. 203 *et seq.*, ii. 242 *et seq.;* pastoral letter on behalf of, ii. 443, 444

Gloucester, Bishop of. See Ellicott

Glyn, Rev. C. J., Gladstone explains his position to the Church of England to, ii. 293.

Gobat, Mr., i. 352

Gorham case, the, i. 83 *et seq.*, 95-97, 330; results of, i. 332 *et seq.*

Graham, Sir James: the General Assembly and the Government, i. 21; Manchester Bishopric Bill, i. 75; and the Marriage Bill, i. 136; on Gladstone's power of work, i. 259; Factory Bill (1843), ii. 125, 131

INDEX

Grane, Mrs., i. 236, 237
Grant, Sir A., *Ethics*, ii. 176
Granville, Earl: Gladstone on Dean Wellesley's death, i. 206; religious education in schools, ii. 297, 310; death of Bishop Wilberforce, ii. 308
Gray, Bishop, i. 144
Grey, Earl de, Gladstone and secular teaching, ii. 137
Guillemard, Mr., Senior Proctor, i. 301
Gurney, Russell, his speech on Ecclesiastical Titles Bill, i. 395
Guthrie, Dr., Gladstone on the Pope's claims, ii. 54

Haddan, Rev. A. W.: Dissenters and the University, i. 217; Gladstone's vote on the Jew Bill, ii. 17
Halifax, first Viscount, letter to, on the repression of ritualism, i. 397–399
Hallam, Henry, i. 48, 110
Hamilton, Archbishop, Primate of Scotland, his Catechism, ii. 320
Hamilton, J., letter to, on Established Church of Scotland, i. 50
Hamilton, Walter Kerr, Bishop of Salisbury, i. 199; ii. 81, 181
Hampden, Professor of Divinity, censure on, i. 67; and Macmullen, i. 294
Hannah, Dr., Trinity College, Glenalmond, i. 202
Harcourt, Sir William, i. 395, 402
Hardy, Mr. Gathorne, succeeds Gladstone as University member, ii. 22; the foundations of religion, ii. 101
Harrowby, Earl of, and Gladstone, i. 395–397
Hartington, Marquis of: Disestablishment, i. 179; Bishops and the House of Lords, i. 181
Hatherley, Lord Chancellor, and Deceased Wife's Sister Bill, i. 132; cathedral preferments, i. 202
Hawkins, Dr., Provost of Oriel, i. 314–325; ii. 91
Heathcote, Sir William: Colonial Churches, i. 124; the Marriage Bill, i. 135; Gladstone's defeat at Oxford, ii. 20
Henderson, Mr., i. 416, 420
Herbert, Lady Mary (Baroness von Hügel), ii. 298
Herbert, Lord, and the Abolition Bill, ii. 171

Herschell, Lord Chancellor, ii. 70
Hervey, Lord Arthur Charles, Bishop of Bath and Wells, and ritualism, i. 381, 382
Hessey, Dr., Merchant Taylors', i. 202
Heywood, Mr., his clause in the Oxford Reform Bill, i. 217, 218
Highton, Mr., his pamphlet, ii. 96
Hodges, Rev. G. F., treatise on Bishop Guest, ii. 336
Holland, Canon Scott, ii. 335
Holt, Mr., Public Worship Act, i. 392, 393
Homer, ii. 109; criticisms, ii. 119
Hook, Rev. W. F., Dean of Chichester: Ecclesiastical Titles Bill, i. 122; the Irish Church, i. 161; Gladstone's opinion of, i. 202, ii. 17; offered the Deanery of St. Paul's, i. 205; his doctrines, i. 271; religious education in schools, ii. 133
Hooker, Richard, *Ecclesiastical Polity*, i. 2
Hope, James R. (afterwards Hope-Scott): revises Gladstone's *The State in its Relation with the Church*, i. 12, 13, 45, 46, 61, 335; his secession from the Church of England, i. 84, 85; and the Bishopric of Jerusalem, i. 98, 99, 232, 242, 247; origin of his friendship with Gladstone, i. 226; Ornsby's Life of, i. 227 n., ii. 204 n., 218 n., 323; his influence on Gladstone, i. 263, 265; and the Poetry Professorship at Oxford, i. 269; Gladstone explains his views, i. 335–342; and the Jewish Bill, ii. 5; and Trinity College, Glenalmond, ii. 203 *et seq.*, 242, 247; on Gladstone's engagement to be married, i. 208, ii. 242; his conditions as a godfather, i. 208; Gladstone's attitude after secession of, ii. 214, 283–286, 290–292; his abridgment of Lockhart's *Life of Scott*, ii. 217, 218, 301; the Oxford elections, ii. 373
Howley, W., Archbishop of Canterbury: and the Jerusalem Bishopric, i. 228; and Glenalmond, ii. 248
Hubbard, Right Hon. J. G., Gladstone and Bradlaugh, i. 176
Hutton, R. H., and Cardinal Newman, i. 400, 405
Hymns Ancient and Modern, Gladstone on, ii. 319

INDEX

Ideal of a Christian Church, The, by Rev. W. G. Ward, i. 296 *et seq.*
Ignatius, St., ii. 154
Immaculate Conception of the Blessed Virgin Mary, the, ii. 57
Immortality, natural, ii. 104
Infallibility, the doctrine of, ii. 57, 61
Inglis, Sir Robert, i. 7, 233
Innes, A. Taylor, i. 188
Ireland, the Church in, i. 14, 16, 39; Disestablishment, i. 148 *et seq.;* Convocation, i. 159; and Gladstone, ii. 210
Irons, Dr., i. 202
Italy, Gladstone's first visit to, i. 7
Italy, King of, and the power of the Pope, ii. 31 *et seq.*

James, Sir Walter H.: the 'Durham letter,' i. 122; Oxford Fellowships, i. 221
Jansenism, analogy of, i. 353, 354
Jerusalem, Bishopric of, i. 226 *et seq.*, 351; proposed changes in scheme, i. 243
Jevons, Professor Stanley, Gladstone's opinion of his book, ii. 100
Jewish Emancipation Bill, i. 66, 122–124; Gladstone votes for, ii. 5; and Dr. Pusey, ii. 18
Johnston, the Rev. J. O., *Life and Letters of H. P. Liddon*, i. 196 n.
Jowett, Benjamin, and Ward, i. 299
Judicial Committee, and the Gorham case, i. 90; a secular tribunal, i. 122; and South African Bishops, i. 144

Keats, John, and *The Quarterly*, ii. 189
Keble, Rev. John: criticism of *The Church in its Relation with the State*, i. 17; Canada Clergy Bill and Colonial Church Bill, i. 124; the Divorce Bill, i. 136; his Professorship of Poetry at Oxford ends, i. 254
Kenelm Chillingly, Gladstone on, ii. 306
King, Rev. Edward, appointed Bishop of Lincoln, i. 210
Knox, Alexander, on Church Establishment, i. 17, 28
Kynaston, Dr., of St. Paul's, i. 202

Lacey, Rev. T. A., ii. 73
Laing, S., ii. 113
Lambeth Declaration, the, i. 143
Laud, Archbishop, i. 378
Lavington and Manning, i. 358
Law, Rev. T. G., and Gladstone, ii. 68, 326
Lewis, Sir George, *On the Influence of Authority in Matters of Opinion*, ii. 101
Lichfield, Bishop of. See Selwyn
Liddon, H. P., Canon of St. Paul's, i. 194; and the eastward position, i. 195; Johnston's *Life and Letters of*, i. 196 n.; refuses a bishopric, i. 210; University reform, i. 213; ritual judgments, i. 380; and the Archbishops' Bill, i. 394; and Lord Acton, ii. 187, 188
Lightfoot, J. B., Bishop of Durham, i. 194
Llandaff, Bishop of, i. 204
Lockhart, J. G., editor of the *Quarterly Review*, i. 305; and Newman, i. 405; *Life of Walter Scott*, ii. 217, 301
London, Bishop of. See Blomfield
Lord, James, i. 51
Lowe, Rev. H., i. 170
Lushington, Dr., and the Denison case, i. 364; on the rubric of 1662, i. 380
Lycurgus, Archbishop of Syra and Tenos, ii. 63, 64
Lyndhurst, Lord, and Gladstone, ii. 166
Lyttelton, Arthur, (afterwards) Bishop of Southampton, and H. N. Gladstone, ii. 184
Lyttelton, fourth Baron: Gladstone's letters to, on Church and Dissenters, i. 48–50; on Jewish emancipation of the Church, i. 79, 80; on the Divorce Bill, i. 133, 134; on *Tracts for the Times*, i. 233, 234; on religious education, i. 130, 141; on expurgating the classics, ii. 243, 244
Lytton, Lord, ii. 306

Macaulay, Lord: his criticism of *The State in its Relation with the Church*, i. 15, 16; and Robert Montgomery, ii. 189
MacColl, Rev. Malcolm, and the Bonn meeting, ii. 62; *Civitas Dei*, ii. 318
Mackey, Rev. Donald J., *Memoir of Bishop Forbes*, i. 412
Macmillan, G. A., i. 404, ii. 319

INDEX

Macmullen, R. G., Fellow of Corpus, and the Oxford authorities, i. 293, 294, 302
Magee, Bishop, and Disestablishment of Irish Church, i. 191
Maintenon, Madame de, ii. 327
Malabari, B. M., letter to, ii. 117
Manning, H. E., Archdeacon (afterwards Cardinal): Gladstone's friendship for, i. 8; Gladstone's letters to, on Church Establishments, i. 23-28; Catholic Christianity and public affairs, i. 29-33; the Scotch Church, i. 33-39; Parliament and Church temporalities, i. 40-43; Church discipline, i. 52, 60; Gladstone's resignation, i. 67; on Royal Supremacy, i. 100, 101, 104, 105, 111-117; agony of an ancient Church, i. 102-104; rumours about, i. 105; the Judicial Committee and the Church, i. 117, 118; supports the Irish Church Bill, i. 149, 163; Gladstone's private fears, i. 235, 236; the Oxford address, i. 269, 279; changes in Newman, i. 281-293; Gladstone's article in the *Quarterly*, i. 307-309; his partiality to the Church of Rome, i. 329-333, 347; Newman's secession, i. 348-351; the Church of England conflict, i. 352-354; change in, i. 355-359; and the controversy between the Roman and Anglican Churches, ii. 23, 26, 27, 32, 35-44, 52-54, 60; the Life of, ii. 73; and the Roman Catholic University in Dublin, ii. 140, 145; Gladstone's changed attitude towards, ii. 214, 287, 288; the House of Commons 'a most blessed calling,' ii. 234; on prayer and fasting, ii. 266-270, 274 278; Gladstone explains his ideas, ii. 270-274, 277-280; religious education, ii. 281, 282; Purcell's biography of, ii. 338
Margaret Chapel, services at, i. 335, 375, 408
Marriage (see also Divorce): the test of Christian civilization, i. 138; a rule of, ii. 232
Marriott, Rev. C.: the Oxford Bill, i. 216; Gladstone and the Oxford elections, ii. 18
Martineau, Miss, *Deerbrook*, ii. 75
Maskell, Rev. W.: Gladstone's criticism of his pamphlet on the Church of England, i. 97 *et seq.*; the opportunity of Churchmen, i. 355
Matheson, Mr., ii. 54
Maurice, Rev. F. D., his dismissal from Professorship at King's College, i. 360, 404
Maynooth College, Gladstone on the grant to, i. 51, 52, 62 *et seq.*, ii. 4
Mayor, Professor, ii. 60
McAll, Dr., i. 245
Medwyn, Lord, ii. 254
Meyrick, Rev. F.: the Marriage Bill, i. 135; University reform, i. 215
Miall, Mr., ii. 91
Mildert, Bishop Van, ii. 26
Mill, Dr., and the Jerusalem Bishopric, i. 247, 248
Mill, James, and Butler, ii. 101
Mill, John Stuart, and Westminster, ii. 85; the autobiography of, ii. 97; and Butler, ii. 101; his textbook, ii. 193
Miller, Dr., of Greenwich, i. 203
Miracles and will, ii. 111
Mivart, Mr. S. G., *Happiness in Hell*, ii. 123
Moberly, Rev. George, succeeds Dr. Hamilton as Bishop of Salisbury, i. 199
Moir, Bishop of Brechin, death of, i. 412
Money, Gladstone on the care of, ii. 429
Montalembert, M., ii. 41
Moore, Rev. D., i. 203
Moray and Ross, Bishop of. See Eden
Morier, Sir R., i. 184, ii. 90
Morley, John (afterwards Viscount), *Life of W. E. Gladstone*, i. 1, 64, 65, 120, 130, 179, ii. 317
Morning Herald, The, on Gladstone's article in the *Quarterly*, i. 113
Mozley, Rev. J. B.: his appointment, i. 190, 198; reform at Oxford, i. 214; on the Vice-Chancellor's reply to the address, i. 295, 296; Stanley and Socrates, ii. 96
Murray, John, publisher, and Gladstone's article in the *Quarterly*, i. 305, 306; Beckett's book, ii. 319

Natal, Church matters in, i. 132, 133
National Review, The, ii. 189

VOL. II — 30

Nelson, Robert, i. 8
Newcastle, Duke of, Gladstone's resignation, i. 68
Newdegate, Mr., inspection of convents, ii. 46, 53
Newman, Rev. J. H. (afterwards Cardinal) : his influence on Hope, i. 13, ii. 14; and the reasons for Gladstone's resignation, i. 69-74; result of his secession to Rome, i. 95, 96, 232, 282, 328, 348, 349; and the Jerusalem Bishopric, i. 229, 231; Tract 90, i. 233-235, 256, 257, 264, 297, 300, 301, 317, 321, 323, 406; his influence at Oxford, i. 260, 261, 262, 327; his position in 1839, i. 263; changes in, i. 281; his difficulties, i. 282, 283, 286-288; and the Bishops, i. 291; his defence, i. 292; Gladstone's article in the *Quarterly*, i. 312-314; the Church's debt to, i. 318; Hutton's essay on, i. 400 n., 405-408; Gladstone's opinion of, i. 404 *et seq.*, ii. 72; Gladstone's letter to, ii. 88
Nicholl, Right Hon. J., the Queen's Advocate, Ecclesiastical Courts Reform Bill, i. 21, 53, 57
Nineteenth Century, The, article on Undenominationalism in, ii. 148; Mrs. Drew's article on St. Deiniol's in, ii. 219
Nonconformists and the House of Commons, i. 11, 12; and religious education in schools, ii. 125, 143 *et seq.*
North, Lord, and Fox, ii. 166
Northbourne, Lord, ii. 332
Northcote, Sir Stafford, Gladstone's letters to, i. 141, ii. 21
Nottingham, the Archdeacon of, ii. 137

Oakeley, Rev. F., and the *British Critic*, i. 289; and Ward, i. 309-312, 326; resigns Margaret Chapel, i. 328; Gladstone's opinion of, i. 334, 335, 408
Oaths Bill, Parliamentary, i. 175
Oriel College, Provost of (Hawkins), Gladstone's letters to, on Tract 90, i. 314-325
Ornsby, R., *Memoirs of J. R. Hope-Scott*, i. 227 n., ii. 203, 204, 207 n., 218 n., 321-323
Ossory, Bishop of, his Charge, i. 287
Owen, Sir Richard, ii. 107
Oxford, Bishop of. See Wilberforce

Oxford (see also Universities) : state of religion at, i. 2 *et seq.;* University reform, i. 211-225; theology at, i. 222-225; contest for the Poetry Professorship at, i. 254, 255; life in, i. 260; Gladstone and the elections at, ii. 1-22, 373-382; Self-Government Act, ii. 172; changes at, ii. 196
Oxford Movement, the, i. 10, 226 *et seq.;* the Jerusalem Bishopric, i. 227 *et seq.*, 243, 351; object of, i. 229; effect of scheme on Hope, i. 232; Tract 90, i. 234-256, 257, 321; Gladstone refuses the trusteeship, i. 234; Bunsen's and Gladstone's views, i. 238-242, 244-247; proposed changes in scheme, i. 243; Dr. Mill's view, i. 247, 248; the Augsburg Confession, i. 250; rival Churches in the East, i. 252; its two distinctive features, i. 259; Dean Church's history of, i. 260 n., 261 n., 296 n., 297 n.; influence of Newman, i. 261; Gladstone's relation to, i. 263-266, 293; Gladstone's letter to *The Times*, i. 270-278; address to the Vice-Chancellor, i. 279; changes in Newman, i. 281-288; Newman's defence, i. 292; action of the Heads of Houses, i. 293 *et seq.;* publication of *The Ideal*, i. 297; the new test, i. 298, 300; feeling in Oxford, i. 299; the three proposals, i. 301; Gladstone's article on Ward, i. 306-309, 313; the Heads' proposal, i. 322; the crisis, i. 328 *et seq.;* results of the Gorham case, i. 333; Maurice and King's College, i. 360; the Denison case, i. 363 *et seq.;* Archbishop Sumner, i. 373; Margaret Chapel services, i. 375; the Bennett case, i. 379; Public Worship Regulation Act, i. 386 *et seq.*, ii. 371; Gladstone on Church Government, ii. 364-367; the Thirty-nine Articles, ii. 367, 370

Pall Mall Gazette, The, ii. 317
Palmer, Rev. W., editor of *The British Critic:* his *History of the Church*, i. 271, 406, 407, 410, ii. 23, 174; and the *Tracts for the Times*, i. 280; Gladstone on *The British Critic*, i. 302-305

INDEX

Palmer, Sir Roundell: (afterwards Earl of Selborne; see also Selborne); Deceased Wife's Sister Bill, i. 132; Irish Church Bill, i. 155, 156; religious education, ii. 141

Palmerston, Viscount: the Divorce Bill, i. 136; and Gladstone, i. 196; his episcopal appointments, ii. 363

Panizzi, Sir A., Gladstone on Christianity and man, ii. 99

Parker, Rev. Joseph, Gladstone on reunion and exchange of pulpits, i. 172

Parliament and Church temporalities, i. 41

Parliamentary Churchmen and Bishops, i. 40

Parliamentary Oaths Bill, i. 175

Pascendi Gregis, Encyclical, and Vatican degree, ii. 48

Patronage, ecclesiastical, i. 190 *et seq.*, 342-347

Patteson, Sir J.: Maurice and King's College, i. 361; Cheyne case, i. 433

Peel, Sir Robert, and Germany, i. 228; Gladstone on Church preferments, i. 342-347; influence on Gladstone, ii. 4; education, ii. 125, 135

Pembroke, Earl of, Letter to, ii. 92

Penal proceedings in Ecclesia, mischief of, i. 140

Perrone, Father, on Palmer, i. 407

Persecution, Gladstone's definition of, ii. 68

Peyrani, Father, ii. 223

Phillimore, Sir R. J.: Gladstone's letters to, on the Gorham case, i. 95; justification of Parliamentary action, i. 99; clerical subscription, i. 138; Irish Church, i. 153, ii. 9; the Denison case, i. 372; Cheyne's case, i. 432; Oxford elections, ii. 7-9, 12; on the death of John Gladstone, ii. 286

Phillimore, Sir Walter G. F.: Divorce Court proceedings, i. 137; Papal action, ii. 74

Phillips, James, ii. 315

Phillpotts, Henry, Bishop of Exeter, and the Gorham case, i. 85; his surrender, i. 93; Gladstone on, i. 116; on Tract 90, i. 321

Philpott, H., Bishop of Worcester, Gladstone on, ii. 294

Pitt, William, compared with Fox and Bolingbroke, ii. 166, 167

Pius V., ii. 67

Pius IX.: diplomatic relations with, i. 65; Gladstone's view of the power of, i. 359, ii. 31 *et seq.*; England and the Vatican, ii. 44; and the laity, ii. 48; his reasonable claims, ii. 55; Papal Infallibility, ii. 57, 61; and Gladstone, ii. 73, 395-400

Pius X., ii. 49

Plato's *Republic*, ii. 164

Poetry Professorship, contest at Oxford, i. 254 *et seq.*

Ponsonby, Sir H., Luther in England, i. 324

Pontifical States, the, ii. 33

Pope, the. See Pius

Potter, Rev. G. W., ii. 105

Prayer and the Divine will, Gladstone on, ii. 409

Prayer-Book, the: ratification of, i. 165, 169; proposal to revise, i. 430 *et seq.*; what it represents, ii. 66, 67

Preaching, Gladstone on the power of, i. 203

Presbyterian Church, the, i. 33 *et seq.*, 49, 188; and the young, ii. 202

Prevost, Sir George, i. 187, ii. 306

Protestantism: Gladstone on, ii. 3; meaning of, ii. 70

Prussia, King of: the Jerusalem Bishopric, i. 237; his proclamation, i. 252

Public Worship Regulation Act, i. 386 *et seq.*; Gladstone's resolutions, ii. 371

Puller, Father, ii. 73

Punishment, future, ii. 105, 120

Purcell, E. S., his biography of Manning, ii. 338

Purchas case, i. 376, 381

Pusey, Rev. E. B.: the Divorce Bill, i. 136; and Gladstone, i. 199, 228, 264, 288, 325, 348, ii. 188; *Collegiate and Professorial Teaching and Discipline*, i. 211; and the Jerusalem Bishopric, i. 228, 230, 351; and the Poetry Professorship, i. 248, 267; Puseyism, i. 270; Tract 90, i. 275; on the crisis in the Church and his own position, i. 288-290; condemned for heresy, i. 294, 344; the Bennett case, i. 379; Scottish Communion Office, i.

434, 435; on errors in the Gospel, ii. 108; on eternal punishment, ii. 120

Quarterly Review, The: Gladstone's article on Ward, i. 131, 306 *et seq.*, ii. 377; the eastward position, i. 398; on Tupper, ii. 189; the Waldenses, ii. 222
Queen's Colleges, ii. 136

Radclyffe, Rev. C. E., i. 123
Radstock, Lord, ii. 85
Rainy, Dr., Disestablishment in Scotland, i. 186
Ramsay, Dean, and Gladstone, i. 414, 429, 439, ii. 303, 304
Rawlinson, Professor, i. 202
Reformatio Legum, i. 118
Reformation, factors in the English, ii. 348-350
Reinkens, Bishop, ii. 60, 62
Religious education in schools, ii. 125 *et seq.*
Restoration settlement, fragment on the, ii. 357
Retribution, future, Gladstone on, ii. 403
Richmond, George, R. A., i. 409
Ridsdale Judgment, ii. 182
Ripon, Marquis of, ii. 72
Robert Elsmere, Gladstone on, ii. 75, 109
Rochester, Bishop of, i. 384
Rogers, Sir F., ii. 300
Roman Catholics (see also Pius IX.), in Ireland, i. 65; Papal aggression, i. 119; errors of, i. 323; controversy with, ii. 23 *et seq.;* the Pontifical States, ii. 33; their increase in England, ii. 50; reasonable claims of, ii. 55; the Bonn meeting, ii. 57, 62, 64; civil loyalty, ii. 59; their claims, ii. 60, 61; Dublin University, ii. 140, 145; Gladstone's conversation with Döllinger, ii. 383-391; Gladstone on the Roman question, ii. 391-395; the Vatican Council and the Old Catholics, ii. 400-402
Romilly, Lord, and Bishop Colenso, i. 133
Rorison, Dr., the Scottish Office, i. 443-445
Round, Mr., Gladstone's unsuccessful opponent at Oxford elections, ii. 4
Royal Supremacy, i. 100, 110, 145

Russell, Dr., President of Maynooth, ii. 144
Russell, Lady, ii. 327
Russell, Right Hon. G. W. E., ii. 326
Russell, Lord John, afterwards Earl: his 'Durham letter,' i. 118, 122; University reform, i. 211; and religious education, ii. 134, 138
Russell, Odo, ii. 45, 46
Russian Church, i. 113

St. Andrews, Bishop of. See Wordsworth
St. Davids, Bishop of. See Thirlwall
St. Deiniol's, foundation and object of, ii. 219, 451
St. Paul's Cathedral, service at about 1850, i. 193
St. Paul's, Dean of. See Church
Salisbury, Bishop of. See Hamilton
Science and opinion, ii. 98
Scotland: patronage question in, i. 20 *et seq.*, 166; Established Church in, i. 34 *et seq.*, 50, 166, 182 *et seq.;* veto law, i. 44; Presbyterianism, i. 168, 172; Episcopal Church in, i. 411 *et seq.*, ii. 201; Communion Office, i. 413, 414; pastoral letter of the Bishops in, ii. 443
Scott, Dr., Master of Balliol, i. 202
Scott, T., ii. 97
Scott, Sir Walter, Gladstone's opinion of, ii. 217
Selborne, Earl of (see also Palmer, Sir Roundell): Burials Bill, i. 173; and Disestablishment, i. 179, 187, 210; and law of contempt of court, i. 403
Self-denial, self-examination, and self-observation, Gladstone on, ii. 152, 157
Selwyn, Bishop of Lichfield, i. 191; and Gladstone, i. 201
Sewell, Rev. W., his outrageous paradox, i. 102
Shaftesbury, Earl of: Gladstone on Convocation, i. 170; Public Worship Act, i. 387
Sheil, Mr., his speech on Maynooth grant, i. 52
Shepherd *v.* Bennett, i. 366
Shirley, Rev. W. W., *Undogmatic Christianity*, ii. 175
Shorthouse, J. H., ii. 319
Sibthorp, Rev. R. W., i. 276
Sin, the idea of, ii. 87
Skinner, Bishop, Primus of the Scottish Episcopal College, ii. 248

INDEX

Smith, Adam, ii. 193
Smith, Bosworth, i. 179
Socrates, controversy about, ii. 96
Somerset, Duke of, Gladstone on his book, ii. 110
South Africa. See Africa
Spectator, The, and the Bonn meeting, ii. 57
Spencer, Herbert, ii. 98
Spurgeon, Rev. C. H., Gladstone's letter to, ii. 324
Stanley, Lord, Gladstone's conversation with, i. 64
Stanley (Dean) and St. Socrates, ii. 96
Stanley, Hon. Maud, Gladstone's advice on religion to, ii. 27-31
State and Church, i. 1 *et seq.*, 69 *et seq.*, 197
State in its Relation with the Church, by W. E. Gladstone, i. 12 *et seq.*, 45 *et seq.*, 62, 148, ii. 205
Stephen, Sir James, ii. 319
Stokes, Rev. E., i. 126
Stopford, Archdeacon, i. 163
Strahan, A., i. 168
Strauss, Herr, Gladstone on, ii. 90
Stundists, their belief, ii. 71
Suffield, Rev. R. R., ii. 68
Sumner, Dr., Archbishop of Canterbury, and the Denison case, i. 363 *et seq.*, 373
Suther, Bishop of Aberdeen, i. 432
Syra, Archbishop of, ii. 304

Tait, Dr. A. C., Archbishop of Canterbury, and Burial Bill, i. 174; his illness, i. 190; and the Jerusalem Bishropric, ii. 229; and Ward, i. 299; and ritualism, i. 375; the Public Worship Act, i. 386 *et seq.*; his sermons, ii. 82
Temple, Dr., Bishop of Exeter, i. 191; *Essays and Reviews,* i. 199
Tenos, Bishop of, ii. 71
Terrot, Bishop of Edinburgh, i. 421
Theism, Gladstone on, ii. 406
Theology at the Universities, i. 222 *et seq.*
'Third Order,' Gladstone on a, ii. 433
Thirlwall, Bishop of St. Davids: *Remains, Literary and Theological,* of, i. 151 n.; and Gladstone, i. 161, 192, 201, 202, ii. 86
Thirty-nine Articles, the, i. 242, 243, 300, 323, 324; rules of construction for, ii. 367; Gladstone on, ii. 367 *et seq.*

Thomson, W., Archbishop of York: Gladstone and the Welsh Episcopate, i. 203; and Puseyism, i. 272
Times, The: Dr. Liddon's letter, i. 183; Bosworth Smith's letters, i. 184; King of Prussia's proclamation, i. 252; Gladstone's letter to, i. 270-279; comments on Gladstone's article, i. 313
Tracts for the Times, i. 11, 254, 270; Tract 90, i. 233, 255, 256, 275, 281, 297, 300, 320, 405, 406
Transubstantiation, ii. 26
Trench, R. C., Archbishop of Dublin, and the Irish Prayer-Book, i. 153; Gladstone on the Irish Established Church, i. 157-160
Trent, Council of, and Dr. Döllinger, ii. 69
Trinity College. See Glenalmond
Tupper, Martin, and the *National Review,* ii. 189

Ultramontanism, ii. 49, 50
Uniformity, Act of, i. 218
Unitarianism, Gladstone on, ii. 199
Universalism, ii. 103
Universities, the (see also Oxford): position in the House of Commons of members of, i. 174; reform at, i. 211 *et seq.*; theology at, i. 222, 223

Vatican, the. See Roman Catholics
Vaudois, the. See Waldenses
Vaughan, Dr., Master of the Temple, i. 202
Veto law in Scotland, i. 44
Victoria, Queen, Gladstone's letters to, on Church and legislation, i. 383-386; on Bishop Wilberforce's death, ii. 308
Voysey, Rev. C., ii. 102

Wackerbarth, Mr., Tracts of, i. 276
Waldenses, the, ii. 197, 222, 223
Walpole, Right Hon. S. H., and Convocation, i. 171, ii. 172
Ward, Mrs. Humphry, *Robert Elsmere,* ii. 75, 109
Ward, Rev. W. G.: *The Ideal of a Christian Church,* i. 296 *et seq.*; Newman's influence over, i. 296, 297; Oxford's treatment of, i. 297 *et seq.*, 326; Gladstone's article on, i. 307-314; leaves Oxford,

INDEX

i. 328; Gladstone's letter to, ii. 250; Gladstone explains his vote for, ii. 376-378
Warter, Rev. J. W., ii. 14
Waterland, Mr., and Arian subscription, i. 139
Watson, Life of Ellen, ii. 188
Wellesley, Dean of Windsor, i. 190; his death, i. 206 *et seq.*
Wellesley, Hon. and Rev. G., i. 360
Wellesley, Hon. Mrs., i. 208
Wellington, Duchess of, i. 208
Wellington, Duke of, Gladstone on, ii. 150
Welsh Episcopate, i. 203
Whewell, Mr., ii. 109
Whiston, Mr., i. 139
Whitworth, Rev. W. A., i. 408
Whyte, Rev., ii. 238
Wickham, Mrs. See Gladstone, Agnes
Wickham, Edward, ii. 196
Wilberforce, Robert, the Ven. Archdeacon, i. 367; on the Eucharist, ii. 212
Wilberforce, Samuel, Bishop of Oxford and, Winchester: Gladstone on result of Gorham case, i. 88-90; ecclesiastical patronage, i. 191; Gladstone's complaint of, i. 196; and the Poetry Professorship, i. 269; the Bishop of London's Charge, i. 369-371; Gladstone on the *status quo*, i. 377; Purchas Judgment, i. 381; the Scottish Office, i. 438; Gladstone's opinion of, i. 215, 308; his tragic death, ii. 215, 308; an address to, ii. 302
Wilkinson, Mr., *Dalmatia*, ii. 109
Williams, Rev. Isaac: *Reserve in communicating Religious Knowledge*, i. 254; candidate for Oxford Poetry Professorship, i. 254, 255, 266-268; his withdrawal, i. 256
Williams, Rev. G., ii. 309
Winchester, Bishop of. See Browne
Windsor, Dean of. See Wellesley
Wolff, Rev. Joseph, i. 371
Woolley, Rev. J., University College, Sydney, ii. 135
Worcester, Bishop of. See Philpott
Wordsworth, Rev. Charles, first Warden of Glenalmond (afterwards Bishop of St. Andrews), and Gladstone, ii. 4; his gifts to Glenalmond, ii. 206; explains his vote at the Oxford elections, ii. 373-367
Wordsworth, Rev. Christopher, Master of Trinity (afterwards Bishop of Lincoln), and Gladstone, i. 60, 74
World and the flesh, the, Gladstone on, ii. 430-433
Wortley, Right Hon. J. Stuart, ii. 10

York, Archbishop of. See Thomson

Zola, *Lourdes*, ii. 190